AUTO PACT:
CREATING A BORDERLESS NORTH AMERICAN
AUTO INDUSTRY, 1960–1971

The 1965 Canada–U.S. Automotive Products Trade Agreement fundamentally reshaped relations between the automotive business and the state in both countries and represented a significant step towards the creation of an integrated North American economy. Breaking from previous conceptions of the agreement as solely a product of intergovernmental negotiation, Dimitry Anastakis's *Auto Pact* argues that the 'big three' auto companies played a pivotal role in – and benefited immensely from – the creation and implementation of this new automotive regime, which effectively erased the Canada–U.S. border.

Drawing from newly released archival sources, Anastakis demonstrates that, for Canada's automotive policymakers, continentalism was a form of economic nationalism. Although the auto pact represented the end of any notion of an indigenous Canadian automotive industry, significant economic gains were achieved for Canadians under the agreement. Anastakis provides a fresh and alternative view of the auto pact that places it firmly within contemporary debates about the nature of free trade as well as North American – and, indeed, global – integration. Far from being a mere artefact of history, the deal was a forebear of what is now known as globalization.

DIMITRY ANASTAKIS is an assistant professor in the Department of History at Trent University.

Auto Pact

Creating a Borderless North American Auto Industry, 1960–1971

DIMITRY ANASTAKIS

UNIVERSITY OF TORONTO PRESS
Toronto Buffalo London

© University of Toronto Press Incorporated 2005
Toronto Buffalo London
Printed in Canada

ISBN 0-8020-3903-0 (cloth)
ISBN 0-8020-3821-2 (paper)

∞

Printed on acid-free paper

Library and Archives Canada Cataloguing in Publication

Anastakis, Dimitry, 1970–
    Auto pact : creating a borderless North American auto industry,
    1960–1971 / Dimitry Anastakis.

    Includes bibliographical references and index.
    ISBN 0-8020-3903-0 (bound)   ISBN 0-8020-3821-2 (pbk.)

    1. Canada. Treaties, etc. United States, 1965 Jan. 16.   2. Duty-free
    importation of automobiles – Canada.   3. Duty-free importation of
    automobiles – United States.   4. Automobile industry and trade – Canada.
    5. Automobile industry and trade – United States.   I. Title.

    HD9710.N672A53 2005   382′.456292′097109046   C2005-901501-2

University of Toronto Press acknowledges the financial assistance to
its publishing program of the Canada Council for the Arts and the
Ontario Arts Council.

University of Toronto Press acknowledges the financial support for
its publishing activities of the Government of Canada through the
Book Publishing Industry Development Program (BPIDP).

This book has been published with help from the AUTO21 Network of
Centres of Excellence.

For Victoria

Contents

Illustrations follow page 114

Tables

Acknowledgments

This book began as a doctoral dissertation in the Department of History at York University. At York, John Saywell, Chris Armstrong, Viv Nelles, and Robert Cuff all deserve thanks for helping to shape it. I could not have asked for a better group of mentors and teachers. Chris Armstrong was an excellent supervisor for the project, and has remained extremely supportive and helpful. As a mentor and friend, John Saywell is in a class by himself. I simply cannot imagine where I would be today if I had not had the good fortune of being his student and research assistant. My professional and personal debt to him is great.

I also appreciate the many comments I received from people over the years as this project was completed: Dianne Labrosse, Penny Bryden, Steve Penfold, and Dennis DesRosiers all read earlier versions of the book or papers derived from it. Archivists in Ottawa, Toronto, Oakville, Washington, DC, Detroit, Boston, and Austin all deserve thanks for their help.

I would also like to thank everyone at the University of Toronto Press. Len Husband has been an excellent editor and a kind friend. I want to thank him for his support, patience, and encouragement. I would also like to thank the three anonymous reviewers, Frances Mundy, and Kate Baltais, whose excellent work improved the writing considerably.

A few other individuals and institutions also deserve thanks. Maureen Appel Molot of Carleton University was an excellent postdoctoral supervisor, and has been incredibly helpful to me in finishing this book and providing feedback and comments on much of my work. The AUTO21 Network of Centres of Excellence provided funding and support towards the completion of the book. Peter Friese, Bill Woodward, and the rest of the staff at AUTO21 are to be commended for their continuing support of the social science investigations into the automobile and its impact on Canadian society. I would like to thank the Canada-U.S. Fulbright Foundation, and everyone at Michigan State University, where I enjoyed a wonderful academic visit in 2003. I also spent a productive term at the University of Toronto's Munk Centre as a Social Sciences and Humanities Research Council of Canada postdoctoral fellow. Other grants towards the completion of the project were provided by the Ramsay Cook Fellowship at York University, an Alfred D. Chandler, Jr, Traveling Fellowship from the Harvard Business School, a John F. Kennedy Foundation Research Grant, and a Moody Grant from the Lyndon B. Johnson Foundation. I thank all these institutions for their support.

Simon Reisman, W.W. Rostow, Philip Trezise, Jake Warren, Tom Kent, C.D. Arthur, Dennis DesRosiers, and J.F. Grandy all agreed to be interviewed for the project, and I thank them. Dennis DesRosiers kindly allowed me to reprint his company's statistical tables in the appendices.

More personally, I would also like to thank my parents Angela and Ernie Anastakis, and my friends and colleagues Matthew Evenden, Magda Fahrni, Chris Frank, Sarah Elvins, Steve Penfold, Joseph Tohill, James Muir, Jeet Heer, Janet Miron, and Stephen Henderson.

Finally, I would like to express my greatest thanks and appreciation to my best friend and wife, Victoria Yankou. Without her patience, understanding, and help, this book would be much less than it is today, as would its author.

Abbreviations

AMC	American Motors Corporation
APTA	Automotive Products Trade Agreement
APMA	Automotive Parts Manufacturers Association (Canada)
ASIA	Automotive Service Industries Association (U.S.)
CACC	Canadian Automobile Chamber of Commerce
CUSFTA	Canada–U.S. Free Trade Agreement
CVA	Canadian value added
DEA	Department of External Affairs
DFAIT	Department of Foreign Affairs and International Trade
DISC	Domestic International Sales Corporation
DPSA	Defence Production Sharing Agreement
FTA	Free Trade Agreement
FMC	Ford Motor Company
GATT	General Agreement on Tariffs and Trade
GM	General Motors Corporation
IET	interest equalization tax
ITC	Industry, Trade and Commerce, Department of
JDTC	job development tax credit
MFN	most favoured nation
MVMA	Motor Vehicle Manufacturers Association
MVTO	Motor Vehicle Tariff Order
NAFTA	North American Free Trade Agreement
NSC	National Security Council (U.S.)
NTBs	non-tariff barriers
SUB	supplemental assistance benefits
TAB	transitional assistance benefits

TEA	Trade Expansion Act, 1962 (U.S.)
UAW	United Auto Workers
USTR	U.S. trade representative
WTO	World Trade Organization

AUTO PACT

Introduction

As conditions unfolded after the Second World War, nothing defined a nation's industrial maturity or its international economic standing like the success of its automotive industry. In the 1950s and 1960s, the cars coming off the assembly lines in Detroit represented the ultimate in terms of the American dream and the post-1945 ascendancy of U.S. industry, technology, culture, and economic might. For the war-torn countries of Western Europe, the slow rebuilding of their auto industries marked a return to economic prosperity and what they considered to be their rightful place among the nations of the 'developed' world. For a devastated Japan, the stunning emergence of its auto industry in the 1960s and 1970s was nothing less than a 'miracle': The ubiquitous 'Japanese import' became the unmistakeable sign that Japan had joined the modern world and had become a leading industrial nation.[1]

For Canada, the auto industry also symbolized a coming of age. After the war, Canada had one of the most successful auto industries in the world, even if this was largely by default, as the country had escaped the destruction of the war and shared in the benefits of a wider North American boom in population and consumer demand. A successful auto industry meant that Canada was perhaps free of the limitations of its economic past, with its dependence on the seasonal extraction of staple goods. For a time, it seemed as if the growing and prosperous auto sector would finally break Canada out of its resource-based economy and lead it into a securely industrial economic age.

Yet by the early 1960s, this most important sector of Canada's industrial economy faced a deepening crisis. High tariffs on automobiles and the early penetration and domination of the Canadian market by U.S.-owned companies had created a classic branch plant economy that was not able to cope with the new realities of the fast-changing industry. The protected Canadian sector was hampered by a small market, inefficient plants dating from the war or earlier, production techniques that could barely keep up with the latest technological changes and consumers demanding the same wide range of models as was available to their American friends and relatives just across the border. Worse yet, the rusting Canadian industry depended heavily on imported American parts. This helped generate a massive trade deficit with the United States, approaching half a billion dollars by 1963. Auto parts from the United States accounted for more than 90 per cent of Canada's total trade shortfall and this situation was becoming a threat to Canada's finances.

The realities of the auto industry limited Canadian possibilities for taking action in the sector, however. The governments of Conservative Prime Minister John Diefenbaker (1957–63) and Liberal Prime Minister Lester Pearson (1963–8) knew that dramatic measures were needed and that any of their available choices involved immense danger. Greater protectionism in the industry was a costly political and economic choice, one that could lead to fewer American-designed cars in Canada, perhaps some production of 'all-Canadian cars,' and certainly a greater number of unhappy Canadian citizens. Free trade in automobiles with the overwhelmingly U.S.-dominated industry, the other logical choice, and the solution for the Canadian sector's difficulties that the Americans were forcefully pressing, could result in the end of production in Canada and the ensuing loss of thousands of jobs and economic devastation for the country as a whole. Studies, royal commissions, and two different tariff manipulation programs to help the auto industry by encouraging exports to the United States had only made the choice more stark. By 1964 Canadian auto tariff measures had so infuriated the administration of President Lyndon B. Johnson in the United States that Canada's automotive dilemma threatened to turn into a continental trade war, worsening by far an already difficult period in Canada–U.S. relations.

Greater protectionism or freer trade, the two choices for the auto industry with which Canadian policymakers grappled, reflected the larger currents that were shaping discussions of Canada's economic future. The 1960s were a decade during which ideas of free trade and of protection coexisted uneasily and jockeyed for attention. Many Canadians had begun to think of working towards an economically integrated North America, as they observed the slow integration of the European continent on a free trade basis and participated with enthusiasm in the growing and influential General Agreement on Tariffs and Trade.[2] At the same time, a new nationalism was emerging in Canada, led by the mercurial Walter Gordon – Pearson's finance minister – that was calling on Ottawa to protect Canadian industry and resist the creeping continental integration with the colossus to the south.[3]

Faced with these two extremes, Canadian policymakers negotiated an ingenious third way that resolved the difficulties of the industry, provided the benefits of both protectionism and freer trade, and pointed to a new direction for the North American economy. The Canada–U.S. Automotive Products Trade Agreement – or auto pact – was signed by Prime Minister Pearson and President Johnson at the latter's Texas ranch in January 1965. The agreement would create a borderless North American auto industry. It would allow continental duty-free trade in auto products, if with certain specific limiting provisions governing each country. Imports to the United States could only come from Canada and had to have 50 per cent North American content to be duty-free. In Canada, specified manufacturers who maintained regulated Canadian-content levels and continued to produce as many vehicles in Canada as they sold in Canada could import duty-free from any country, although the United States was the most likely source. On the face of it, the auto pact provided for selected free trade in the automotive sector, advanced American goals for trade liberalization in North America, and avoided a difficult trade dispute between Canada and the United States. It was a tightly managed agreement: For their part, Canadians could take comfort in the production guarantees that ensured them what they considered to be a 'fair share' of the North American automotive market and reflected the nationalistic goals of the policymakers who had negotiated the agreement.

The auto pact was heralded as a success and evidence of close ties and cooperation between Canada and the United States. But the two governments were not the only parties responsible for solving the problems of the North American auto industry. General Motors, Ford, and Chrysler – the Big Three multinational automotive corporations – proved key to resolving an impasse that the two governments by themselves could not, namely, the gap between U.S. expectations for free trade and Canadian demands for a fair share of the North American automotive industry. The structure of the North American auto industry, particularly the cross-border U.S. ownership and similarities in markets and tastes, enabled the Big Three to work together with both Ottawa and

Washington towards the creation of a new, managed trade regime. In addition to production guarantees outlined in the agreement itself, the auto companies promised to increase their Canadian content and investments in Canada, in the short term, in 'letters of undertaking.' The letters of undertaking made assurances that Canada would receive its fair share of automotive investment and production and were crucial to the consummation of the agreement. Without the letters of undertaking, the Canadian government would not have agreed to the new arrangement. These state-directed investment and production measures provided a further element of protectionism that the Canadian negotiators sought in securing the future of the Canadian auto industry. The automakers agreed to them as the price of rationalizing their operations on a continental scale.[4]

In return, the conditional nature of the agreement ensured that the U.S. multinationals remained the predominant manufacturers of motor vehicles in North America. Conditional free trade for producers – not consumers – was to govern the new borderless continental auto trade. The auto companies' operations could now range freely across the whole continent, unimpeded by national borders or national tariff constraints. The Canadian auto industry was irreversibly integrated into a larger North American auto sector, and the auto agreement tied the fate of the Canadian economy even more securely to the fortunes of the United States. The auto pact remained in effect in the United States until the 1989 Canada–U.S. Free Trade Agreement (CUSFTA) and in Canada until February 2001, when the World Trade Organization (WTO) ruled that it violated international trade rules.[5]

By the time that the pact passed out of existence, it was clear that the Canadian auto industry had benefited immensely from the conditional trade regime that had been in place for thirty-six years. After 1965, as the Big Three fulfilled their requirements under the program, Canadian production and employment increased immensely. The Canadian trade deficit in automotive products disappeared, and by the 1990s, Canada had a massive trade surplus in the overall North American automotive sector. The share of Canadian production in the continent's auto industry grew impressively. Canadians produced fewer than one in twenty of the cars manufactured in North America in 1964. By 1999 Canadian factories were turning out nearly one of every five vehicles produced in North America, while Canadians were exporting nearly $100 billion dollars worth of automotive goods annually. One in seven Canadians could trace their employment either directly or indirectly to the auto industry. This impressive growth was reflected in the motor vehicle parts industry, as well. Initially, some Canadian parts companies withered under the auto pact; however, others flourished in the new borderless competitive environment and became giant industrial entities, such as Magna International, Wescast, and the ABC group.[6] Although physically centred in southern Ontario, by the end of the twentieth century the automotive industry dominated the entire Canadian economic landscape.

The creation, implementation, and consolidation of the auto pact regime in North America between 1960 and 1971 was one of the most significant events in the recent political and economic evolution of North America, and a major step towards the creation of a continental economic community.[7] It is therefore an excellent case through which to examine a number of questions fundamental to the development of Canada within a North American context in the 1960s. To begin with, how did the Canadian state manage to achieve such an outcome, what was the nature of this state intervention, and to what extent was this state intervention limited by domestic and international constraints in the auto industry? How does Canada's auto pact experiment fit within the context of other international experiences during this period, wherein a number of other countries also engaged the multinational automotive firms in their midst? How does the evolving relationship between big business and the state (particularly between multinational firms and host countries) help to explain the outcome of the auto pact regime? Finally, what can the auto pact, which became a foundation stone for an emerging North American economic community, tell us about the changing nature of relations between Canada and the United States in this period?

First, we must consider the question of how the state creates public policy in the context of domestic and international constraints, in this case, in the auto industry. Canadian policymakers had long experience in utilizing various governmental means to foster Canadian industrial 'defensive expansionism,' as is reflected in the automotive duty-remission programs created by Ottawa in 1962–4. Canadian civil servants used the tools available to them to shape outcomes in Canada's auto industry. This state intervention to further national economic development took the form of innovative incentive programs designed to spur exports, a goal that butted up against the interests of the United States. When the Canadian measures provoked U.S. resistance, state actors in both governments competitively and aggressively negotiated in efforts to achieve the best possible outcome for their side.

To understand this process requires an examination of state actors, those 'rational planners' who are either restricted to an inevitable fate by the proponents of rigid political and economic models or are given, by whiggish historians and biographers, too much influence in shaping outcomes. Such interpretations often seem insensitive to the realities of both international relations and history. Simply put, it was not just faceless bureaucrats who created the auto pact, and the agreement was not inevitable given circumstances within the North American and global auto industries.[8] Yet, it is impossible to imagine the creation of the 1965 auto pact without Simon Reisman and, therefore, consideration must be given to the motivations of this determined Canadian negotiator and his dedicated team of civil servants. Their experiences helped guide government responses to the automotive industry's difficulties, and their innovative solutions resulted in an unprecedented departure for what was, and remains, Canada's most important economic sector. Other actors, too, such as the unions or the automakers – constituent structural parts of the industry – had a role in determining the responses of the state. These factors all affected each other: The planners (and their personalities) shaped the agreement to fit the contours of the industry's structure. These factors were, in turn, all shaped by the historical and contemporary specifics of Canada–U.S. relations and the dynamics of the U.S., Canadian, and North American auto industries.

People learn from their past. The auto pact emerged as it did, in part, because the Canadian civil servants who negotiated it remembered their unhappy experience in an earlier case: the farm implement case. In 1941, Canada entered into a continental agreement that resulted in a significant decline in the Canadian share of North American production of farm implements. Ottawa policymakers were still well aware of that experience.[9] Certainly, civil servants such as Reisman had learned (the hard way) that this was an outcome they wanted to avoid. They also understood that the legacy of Canada's automotive branch plants was going to be difficult to overcome, but it might also hold the key to a new departure that would take advantage of the Canadian auto sector's proximity and close ties to the U.S. industry. Thus, the agreement integrated the auto industry on a continental basis, and for Canadian policymakers, paradoxically, this continentalism was a form of economic nationalism. Far from exposing the Canadian auto sector to the harsh realities of an unrestricted continental market, the auto pact ensured that it benefited through the fair share production and investment guarantees that Reisman and his team achieved as terms of the agreement.

Planners and politicians both are constrained by the internal dynamics that shape a state's responses to any situation. On questions of policy, governments are often portrayed in a simplified, onedimensional manner, acting as singular interests. But this certainly cannot be said of the United States in this case. Enactment of the auto pact was complicated greatly by the separation of powers that exists between the U.S. Congress and the president, and long-standing conflicts over which of the two was ultimately responsible for determining U.S. trade policy threatened passage of the agreement. Furthermore, conflict erupted within the administration among the State, Treasury, and Commerce departments over how to shape the U.S. response to the 'Canadian auto problem.' Although the dynamics of interbranch and interjurisdictional competition have been well documented for other important trade issues in recent American history, the auto pact has not been a focus of these efforts.[10] The Canadian response to the auto problem was far less conflicted. It was shaped by a number of factors including the fused nature of the executive and legislative branches in the structure of Canada's government, the smaller civil service in Ottawa, and the basic fact that the auto issue and relations with the United States were at the top of the federal government's agenda. Nonetheless, within the government different approaches to the auto negotiations were favoured, as protectionist politicians like Walter Gordon and civil servants more favourable to freer trade solutions like Simon Reisman worked together to formulate the Canadian strategy.

Second, the creation of the Canada–U.S. auto pact needs to be understood within the postwar context of the automotive sector elsewhere in the world. As in Canada, during the 1960s, governments in Brazil, Mexico, and Australia took a far more active role with regard to their automotive industries. These countries had some things in common with Canada, for example, widespread penetration by U.S. multinational auto companies, little or weak indigenous vehicle assembly and parts production, and, hence, difficulties with their international trade balances. In response to these conditions, the range of intervention by these host countries included increased local content rules, wholesale nationalization (or the threat thereof), and innovative approaches to import substitution. These efforts achieved varying levels of success, and civil servants in 'auto-dependent' countries everywhere were work-ing the range of interventionist policies that would yield the best out-comes of automotive investment to the host country.[11]

Brazil used infant-industry and import-substitution methods to im-prove its production, but encouraged foreign capital to help build its domestic industry. Brazil's state-directed goals for the domestic auto industry were limited to some degree by the vagaries of market-driven transnational corporations. Nonetheless, the Brazilian automotive in-dustry, which was virtually non-existent in the 1950s, flourished in the 1960s even with its very high requirements for local content.[12] Mexico – after threatening to nationalize the industry outright – forced the multi-nationals, in its 1962 and 1969 automotive decrees, to increase their local content and focus on export production. This intervention strategy was only partially successful because of both internal and external factors, namely, the resistance of the multinationals, the realities of productivity and efficiency levels in Mexico, and the pressures of inter-national competition.[13]

These examples help to explain the Canadian government's interven-tion in the auto industry in the period 1960 to 1971. Most of all, Cana-dian policymakers in the 1960s effectively used the models of state intervention that these other countries had implemented to contrast their own position with that of American officials and representatives of the Big Three, as they searched for a way to resolve the difficulties faced by Canada's auto sector. In the words of one U.S. negotiator, the Canadians kept 'the sombrero under the table' and continually re-minded the United States that if the negotiations failed to achieve their preferred outcomes, they had recourse to measures such as the harsh decrees that Mexico had imposed on the U.S. multinationals.[14] With economic arch-nationalist Walter Gordon as the Canadian finance min-ister, the U.S. government, and the U.S.-based multinationals took quite seriously the possibility that Canada might follow the Brazilian and Mexican examples.

The models employed in Brazil and Mexico themselves help to ex-plain the approach taken by Ottawa. The case of Brazil showed that unrestrained market forces or direct state intervention were not the only possibilities for state planners to consider when developing poli-cies for the auto industry. Mexico City's interaction with the automotive industry has strong similarities with the Canadian experience. In shap-ing the Canada–U.S. auto pact, the Canadian state was not a mere functionary of capital, nor was it without any agency of its own. The

Canadian state did make choices, and these choices were tempered by international, national, and historical experiences that Ottawa and its representatives understood, as did the other actors within the Canadian environment. They had numerous constraints, yet they did have some choice.[15]

The Canadian case also departs from those of Brazil and Mexico in a number of important ways. Most obviously, Canada was not as dependent on the United States as were industrially underdeveloped Brazil and Mexico.[16] After the Second World War, Canadian economic fortunes came increasingly under the influence of the United States, yet Canada demonstrated a large degree of independence in the period, as evidenced by its willingness to embark on aggressive export incentive programs typified by the automotive measures it instituted in 1962 and 1963. Even 'dependent' Canadian companies, such as Ford of Canada, had an independent streak that broke from traditional notions of subservience. Until the 1960s, Ford of Canada maintained its own overseas empire in Australia and New Zealand, quite independently of the U.S. parent corporation. Differences also hinged on the issue of commonality. Although for political and economic reasons the Mexican government could never have tolerated wholesale integration into the U.S. auto industry in the 1960s, Canada could and did because of its close relationship with the United States, the long-standing presence of the Big Three in Canada, and the similarity of both markets and consumer tastes in the two countries.

Canada's case departs from the Latin American and Australian experiences for another fundamental reason. Whereas other countries sought greater *direct* and *national* control over their auto industries, Canadian policymakers sought to tie their industry's fate to that of another nation on a *continental* basis, one that would be managed by the industry itself. Obviously, this alternative had long-term implications for Canada that differed dramatically from these other international examples. In Brazil, Mexico, Australia, and other countries, the emphasis was on import substitution, local content, nationalization (or the threat of nationalization) in the name of greater domestic control that was to be powerfully directed by the state. In the case of Canada, state actors sought to improve Canadian production, but within the context of a continentally integrated industry, a context that reflected the economic and political realities facing Canadian policymakers. The goals directed by the Canadian state were to be achieved through working in cooperation with the manufacturers in ways that were unique to the Canadian and

North American situation. The Canada–U.S. auto pact came into being because of the particular difficulties presented by the immediate circumstances surrounding the pre-1965 shape of the automotive industry.

In a very real sense, the auto pact was a milestone in the evolution of Canada's economic history. It marks a transition from the old protectionist National Policy of John A. Macdonald to the new national policy of free trade that was embraced by Canadian policymakers in the 1980s and 1990s. The Canada–U.S. auto pact represents a shift in Canadian policy, from the defensive expansionism of tariff protection through the post-1945 efforts to liberalize trade, with an eye towards further national development, to the market-driven ethos espoused by Canadian policymakers after 1982.[17] The auto pact emerged from the unilateral tariff-manipulating remission programs that were developed by civil servants in the years 1962 to 1964, and contained elements of state-directed investment, while providing for duty-free trade in the automotive sector. The auto pact's unique production and investment guarantees ensured Canadians their fair share of the automotive market. The auto pact was a product of its time, and it represents the confluence of the free trade and protectionist ideas that prevailed in Canada in the 1960s. In the context of international trade regimes, the Canada–U.S. auto pact marks a clear step towards both freer trade and the creation of a regional trade bloc in North America.

Third, we must appreciate that the role of non-state actors in the creation of this international trade treaty is the auto pact's most important characteristic. Although many interpretations of the pact's evolution focus almost solely on the role of the two governments, without the agreement of the U.S.-based multinationals the auto pact could not have been consummated, and its structure clearly reflects the involvement of the Big Three.[18] An analysis of the interaction of the multinational auto companies and governments on both sides of the Canada–U.S. border allows us to examine the complicated relationship between business and the state and how companies and states can play each other off to achieve their desired outcomes. Furthermore, it allows us to examine the differing positions in response to the state initiatives taken within particular industries in the automotive sector. Various actors among the manufacturers as well as among the parts makers, on both sides of the border, reacted differently, reflecting the wide range of interests within the industry.

The auto pact shows that Canadian governments could influence multinationals to achieve their own goals. The complex relationship between the Canadian government, the U.S. government, the Canadian subsidiaries of the Big Three, and the parent corporations of the Big Three together gave Canadian policymakers opportunities to further their goals – opportunities not usually present in business-government interactions. The agreement illustrates, too, the influence that foreign companies can have with the Canadian government and in playing governments off each other to attain their desired outcomes.[19] This 'triangular diplomacy' resulted in winners and losers in the bargaining process between states and firms and demonstrates the complex relationship in the 1960s between nations and multinational firms.[20]

At no time were the wishes of the Big Three the sole factor in determining the final shape of the agreement. Nevertheless, the motives and actions of these giant U.S. multinationals were essential in facilitating a solution to the troubles of the Canada–U.S. automotive sector. The structure of the automotive sector in North America was unique, and the auto pact could not have been duplicated in any other sector of the economy or between any other two countries in the world. With 90 per cent of the 'Canadian industry' owned and operated by three major U.S. multinationals, concentrated and located but a stone's throw from Detroit, and servicing market tastes virtually identical to those of the United States, the automobile industry afforded opportunities not present in any other sector. Moreover, negotiation of the Canada–U.S. auto pact took place by calling on, quite literally, only a handful of people. Implementation was just as simple, and required little state action. The auto industry was a very exclusive club, and industry associations such as the Motor Vehicle Manufacturers Association (the Big Three plus American Motors, International Harvester, and Studebaker) could count on regular access to government officials. This intimacy greatly eased interactions between government and business in shaping the new regime.

The importance of the auto companies in the creation and implementation of the agreement was matched by their role in keeping the agreement safe from those in the United States who wanted to destroy it. After 1968, when elements of the U.S. government wished to abrogate the pact because of its adverse effects on the U.S. balance of payments, the Big Three were pivotal in ensuring the agreement's survival. Indeed, the divergence of interests between the U.S. government and the U.S.-based multinationals is an essential component to a proper understanding of the agreement and its role in shaping the relationship between states and multinationals. This divergence of interests was especially stark during the administration of President Richard Nixon, when American pressure to change or end the auto pact was greatest.[21] Ironically, given its fair trade elements, the auto pact marks a fundamental step towards corporate globalization. The severing of national corporations from national interests created supranational entities which were no longer burdened by international borders – a significant step in making transnational companies truly global enterprises. By 1970 the Canada–U.S. auto pact had brought home the brutal reality to U.S. policymakers that what was good for General Motors was no longer necessarily good for the United States.

Finally, fourth, the auto pact provides a touchstone against which to examine an especially sensitive moment in the evolution of the relationship between Canada and the United States. In the mid-1960s, relations between the two countries were at a particularly low ebb. Conflicts over a wide array of trade and foreign policy issues ranging from magazines to selling wheat to recognition of China to seafarers' unions throughout the Kennedy and Johnson administrations, and the Diefenbaker and Pearson years, were at times almost debilitating. Relations were considered so poor by President Kennedy that he initiated a cross-border study that might clarify for him why things were so bad with America's northern neighbour and supposedly closest friend and ally; the result was the controversial Heeney-Merchant report entitled *Principles for Partnership*.[22] It should perhaps be remembered that the auto pact was signed in January 1965, just four months before, in a speech he made at Temple University in Philadelphia, Pearson famously infuriated Johnson by calling for a temporary halt to American bombing of the North Vietnamese.[23] Yet for all of the not inconsiderable fallout from that incident, Johnson never once wavered in his determination to see the auto pact passed by the U.S. Congress.

An examination of the auto agreement must account for how such a divisive issue was resolved so quickly and – or so it seemed at the time – successfully. The Canada–U.S. auto pact only makes sense within the larger context of this cross-border relationship if one considers the various models that have been advanced as explanations of the course of relations between the two countries. The auto pact is not evidence of the mythical 'special relationship' between Canada and the United States.[24] Nor does it illustrate any particular strain of Canada's 'dependency' on the United States.[25] Instead, the auto pact shows that the relationship between Canada and the United States has been based on cooperation, punctuated by short bursts of conflict over specific issues, although the particulars of the auto agreement require a more complex reading.[26]

The notion of a Canada–U.S. relationship based upon cooperation and some conflict suggests a basic interdependence between the two countries that necessitates their working together to resolve conflicts. The case of the Canada–U.S. auto pact bears this out. The auto pact shows that realist approaches to international political economy are insufficient for understanding the multitude of political, cultural, industrial, trade, and military factors that make up relations between states. Instead, complex interdependence, in which countries and their governments exercise power beyond the usual military and diplomatic arenas, approximates more closely the interactions between and among nations. Differing international regimes play key roles in shaping the complex interdependence. Relationships such as that between Canada and the United States, for example, need to be viewed in global terms rather than seen simply as bilateral. The United States acceded to Canada's demands in the automotive field to advance the cause of trade liberalization and to avoid what may have developed into a destructive and embarrassing trade war with its closest ally – not because it felt some special feeling towards Canada. This helps explain why Canada apparently won many of its postwar conflicts with the United States, including achieving its fair share of a North American auto industry that was almost entirely owned by Americans. This was not an insignificant accomplishment, given the constraints Canada faced.[27]

All of these factors – the role of the state, the international context, the part played by the U.S. multinationals, and the nature of Canada–U.S. relations at the time – in combination explain how the auto pact was consummated and why it took the shape that it did. Yet, the story of the auto pact is also much more than this. It is an ironic tale of how Canadians, through their nationalistic determination to secure for themselves a greater share of the immense North American automotive industry, embarked on a new and innovative path that ultimately turned Canada's economic (and, to a lesser extent, political) organization towards a continental destiny. In seeking to secure forever a vibrant auto industry, Canada's negotiators of the auto pact were undoubtedly successful, but possibly they also got more than they and Canadians had bargained for.

This book divides the story of the Canada–U.S. auto pact into six chapters. Chapter 1, as background, traces the development of the

Canadian auto industry from its very beginnings under the National Policy to the creation of innovative tariff manipulation schemes designed to solve the structural crisis that the industry faced by the late 1950s and early 1960s. Chapter 2 examines the adverse reaction of U.S. policymakers in response to these unilaterally taken Canadian initiatives, and the failure of intergovernmental negotiations to resolve the cross-border trade problems. It goes on to explain why the Canadians rejected the free trade plan that the United States offered and instead held so strongly to their fair share demands for the Canadian automotive industry. Chapter 3 shows how the Big Three and the auto industry itself provided a unique solution that was both protectionist and for free trade to the impasse between Canadian fair share demands and the Americans' desire to see the sector operate on an unrestricted free trade basis. Chapter 4 analyses how during its implementation opposition to the auto pact failed in Ottawa, Washington, and at the General Agreement on Tariffs and Trade (GATT) in Geneva. Chapter 5 examines the auto pact's impact on the Canadian sector as the automotive industry rationalized its operations on a North American basis and the problems that emerged as the two governments and the industry learned to manage the new continental regime. Chapter 6 details how the auto pact survived attempts to end or modify it in the face of renewed trade difficulties and cross-border differences over the meaning and operation of the agreement. The transformation of the agreement following the 1989 Canada–U.S. Free Trade Agreement and its eventual demise at the hands of the World Trade Organization in 2001 are briefly explained in the Conclusion.

This monograph does not purport to be a political or economic history of Canada in the 1960s or a complete examination of Canada–U.S. relations of that era. Essentially, this is a history of the creation of a borderless North American automotive industry which had a significant influence on the politics and economics of the period. Thus, not every incident that may have in someway influenced the outcome of the auto issue is examined here in detail, and some significant issues of the period receive but cursory treatment. The many stories of firms, communities, and individual workers who were all so deeply affected by the pact and by how the auto industry operated were left out, not because these stories are unimportant, but because the focus here is on the policy decisions critical to the origins and implementation of the Automotive Products Trade Agreement of 1965.

1

The Canadian Auto Industry, 1900–1963

The issue of protectionism versus free trade, which has bedevilled Canadian leaders since Confederation, was central to discussions on the automotive industry. The National Policy, the main plank of Canada's economic strategy for most of the country's history – and the most significant factor in shaping the Canadian auto sector – emerged from the failure of Canada's first prime minister, Conservative John A. Macdonald, to establish a free trade regime with the United States.[1] In 1879, therefore, the Macdonald government put in place a tariff structure that, for example, made finished goods entering Canada dutiable at a rate of 35 per cent. The framework survived for decades, as over the next half-century Macdonald's party transformed itself into the party of protection. Meanwhile, the Liberal party had advocated free trade since before Confederation, but disastrous defeat in the elections of 1891 and 1911 convinced them that free trade could be pursued only in the most prudent manner. Thus, protection, albeit in a less stringent form than that advocated by the Tories, became part of Liberal policy as well.[2]

By the 1920s the Canadian auto sector was among the protected industries, having grown up as a 'creature of the tariff.'[3] The tariff rate of 35 per cent set in 1879 applied to carriages and established the rate for automobiles, which at the end of the nineteenth century were called 'horseless carriages.' Some of the carriage makers converted their facilities in an effort to take advantage of the protection afforded by the tariff wall (particularly in southern Ontario), resulting in numerous indigenous attempts to create a viable Canadian motor car company, but virtually all of them failed. More often the Canadian firms lacked technological capabilities and were short on capital, or they were simply unable to sell enough of their product in such a small, scattered, and poorly linked market.[4] Even with the high protective tariff, the Canadian companies were hard-pressed. A few attempted to survive by importing cheaper American parts (at 30 per cent, the duty was lower than that for completed autos). In 1921 the last one, Gray-Dort, went out of business after its American parts maker closed its doors, and soon no strictly Canadian-owned concerns were left in the auto industry.[5]

South of the border, in the late nineteenth century the U.S. auto industry flourished, as hundreds of new companies and firms took off from the Midwestern carriage industry, much of which was centred in Michigan. Led by Henry Ford and his company in Detroit, the American auto industry grew impressively, as American manufacturers developed new and innovative production and sales techniques. By the end of the First World War, the U.S. auto industry required massive economies of scale to make production profitable, because of its intense capital requirements, and its need for engineering ingenuity and extensive sales and dealership networks. As in Canada, many companies could not compete in an industry that required such large-scale production. By the 1930s, after a period of intense consolidation, the General Motors, Ford, and Chrysler corporations stood as the undisputed Big Three of the automotive industry.[6]

The large American automakers that remained had penetrated the Canadian market as well, using Canadian labour and raw materials, but importing American capital, management, technology, and parts. Ford was first in Canada, with its plant at Windsor, Ontario, built in 1904 – directly across the river from Detroit. Canadian Gordon McGregor, whose own firm, the Walkerville Wagon Works, was seeing its last days, managed to convince Henry Ford to partner with him to produce Ford's products at McGregor's converted wagon factory. Although the early Canadian automotive market was tiny (McGregor personally delivered each vehicle during the first few years), with the introduction of the Model T in 1908, the Canadian Ford firm grew spectacularly.[7]

The largest indigenous Canadian car manufacturer had been Oshawa's McLaughlin Motor Works. It became part of General Motors after Sam McLaughlin decided to join the company founded by William Durant. McLaughlin's decision in 1918 gave GM a beachhead in Canada from which GM would secure its position as Canada's leading auto manufacturer. It also established Oshawa, Ontario – along with Windsor – as a centre of the Canadian automotive industry. Chrysler was the last of the Big Three to arrive in Canada, when in 1921 it built its plant in Windsor. From then on, 90 per cent of the Canadian auto industry was based in southern Ontario, either in Windsor or around Toronto, where the Canadian companies were close to their American parents. Because of these branch plant operations, between 1918 and 1923 Canada was the second-largest motor vehicle producer in the world. By 1926 the Canadian industry was building more than 200,000 vehicles a year, while it employed some 12,000 people.[8] A small Canadian parts industry developed alongside the American-owned manufacturers, supplying assemblers with various parts and thereby contributing to increasing the proportion of Canadian content in the U.S.-designed vehicles. In 1913, for example, Ford of Canada began building a significant portion of its own engines and transmissions, using parts supplied by dozens of small Canadian producers that had sprung up in Windsor, Ontario. By the beginning of the next decade, nearly three-quarters of Canadian Ford's parts were being made in Canada.[9]

Much of the Canadian vehicle production was intended for the domestic market, but a significant proportion was exported to other areas in the British Commonwealth. Canada was within the imperial preferential system and so maintained a lower import tariff of 22.5 per cent for the mother country and its fellow dominions. The imperial system added another dimension to the Canadian branch plants, as it encouraged U.S. companies to assemble their products in Canada and then export them from Canada to gain the benefit of the lower duties. The Ford Motor Company of Canada, thus, held exclusive rights to market Fords in Australia, New Zealand, South Africa, India, and a host of other Commonwealth destinations.[10]

This was a lucrative business. Canadian exports of autos and auto products to the United Kingdom and other Commonwealth countries were valued at more than $33 million in 1924, while in 1925 nearly half of all passenger cars built in Canada were exported.[11] Ford of Canada took the most advantage of the imperial preferential system, but the other American-owned companies (and they were usually wholly owned subsidiaries) made hefty profits from building cars in Canada and selling them in Canada and overseas.[12] Canadians benefited from this economic boom through increased employment and production. In this sense, the tariff was a success, at least in Ontario.

With Ontarians receiving the full benefits of the new industry, other regions of Canada complained, claiming that they were unfairly subsidizing the operations of U.S.-owned companies in Ontario. The import tariff was at the heart of such criticism, and by the late 1920s the issue was being intensely debated as a question of regional inequality. Dependent for his survival on the largely western-based pro-free trade Progressive party, Liberal Prime Minister William Lyon Mackenzie King took the precarious position of lowering tariffs in order to stay in office after the 1926 federal election. Instead of a general 35 per cent rate, the auto tariff would be tied to the price of cars: those priced at $1,200 and under were to be taxed at 20 per cent, while those over $1,200 would have a tariff of 27.5 per cent. Thus, the average weighted general rate became 26 per cent when added excise taxes were factored in. King also established a non-partisan Tariff Board which he hoped would de-politicize the issue.[13]

The lower rates, however, helped little when the Great Depression took hold of the industry. After 1930, the Canadian sector, which had been such a force in the 1920s, slipped badly as world trade ground to a halt. Commonwealth export markets dried up, and so did consumer demand in Canada. In 1929 Canada produced 203,000 cars, almost 65,000 of them for export. But in 1931 Canadian factories built only 61,000 vehicles, and not even 10,000 of them were exported. The Con-servative government of R.B. Bennett (1930–5) agreed to duty-free en-try for autos coming from the United Kingdom, which was a curious departure from his pledge to 'blast' a way to markets with more tariffs. However, the duty-free treatment for British vehicles was of little conse-quence at the time, although it proved crucial in the future.[14] King and the Liberals were returned to power in 1935, but they were no more effective in solving the problems caused for Canadians by the economic downturn.

In 1936, following an examination by the Tariff Board, the Tariff Act was significantly altered. The new most-favoured-nation (MFN) tariff (which stipulated that the rate given to a country's most favoured trading partner should be extended to all of the country's other trading partners) was 17.5 per cent for all autos and most auto parts. The most important change to the act was a new sliding scale for duty-free entry based on the proportion of a car's Commonwealth (essentially Cana-dian) content. To gain duty-free designation for a selection of imported parts, a company's cars had to have 40 per cent Commonwealth content if it was annually producing 10,000 units, 50 per cent if it was producing between 10,000 and 20,000 units, and 60 per cent if producing more than 20,000 (see Table 1.1).[15] The new tariff schedule had the effect of facilitating significant Canadian production, although the auto parts made in Canada were usually much more expensive than their U.S.

Table 1.1 Evolution of Canada's auto tarifs, 1879–1936

A   Early tariffs (%)

	General tariff	Intermediate tarriff	British preference
Finished autos, 1879–1925	35	30	22.5
Parts, 1879–1936	35	30	22.5

B   Finished autos, 1926–1930 (%)

Autos valued at	General tariff	Intermediate tariff	British preference
$1,200 and under	20	17.5	12.5
Over $1,200	27.5	25	15

C   Finished autos, 1931–1935 (%)

Autos valued at	General tariff	Intermediate tariff	British preference
$1,200 and under	20	17.5	0
Over $1,200	27.5	25	0
Over $2,200	40		0

D   Tariff revision of 1936 (%)

Item	Most-favoured-nation tariff	General tariff	British preference
Finished autos	17.5	27.5	0
Products of parts makers	17.5	30	0
Products of automakers	17.5 if made in Canada; duty-free if not made in Canada and car makers production is: 40% Commonwealth content if fewer than 10,000 cars; 50% Commonwealth content if 10,000–20,000 cars; 60% Commonwealth content if over 20,000 cars	25	0

Table 1.1 (*Concluded*)

D Tariff revision of 1936 (%)			
Item	Most-favoured-nation tariff	General tariff	British preference
Parts of commercial vehicles	17.5 if made in Canada; duty-free if not made in Canada and commercial vehicle makers production is 40% Commonwealth content (no scale)	27.5	0
Parts not included in above	25	35	0

Note: Parts of a class or kind not made in Canada were duty-free, while those of a kind made in Canada were subject to a 25% duty. If certain parts contained 50% Commonwealth content, the duty was remitted.
Source: Compiled from Vincent Bladen, *Royal Commission on the Automotive Industry* (Ottawa, 1961) and Tom Traves, *The State and Enterprise: Canadian Manufacturers and the Federal Government, 1917–1931* (Toronto, 1979).

equivalents. The duty-free status granted to any parts of a 'class or kind' not made in Canada allowed the major auto manufacturers to import substantial quantities of expensive parts, particularly main body stampings and complex transmissions, that could only have been built in Canada at a prohibitive cost. Thus, for example, headlights were built in Canada by the Canadian Lamp Company, and therefore any import of such parts was dutiable, while automatic transmissions, which were not built at all in Canada, entered the country duty-free.

The Second World War boosted vehicle production to an all-time high, although consumer products were restricted. Canadian auto factories converted to wartime production, and if Detroit was America's 'arsenal of democracy,' surely the Canadian auto industry was just as important in the Allied war effort. By the mid-point of the war, Canadian Big Three factories in Windsor and Oshawa were producing more than 4,000 mechanized vehicles per week, and in 1943 Canada's 'Minister of Everything,' Munitions and Supply Minister C.D. Howe, celebrated the completion of the 500,000th Canadian-built vehicle.[16] Canadian automotive workers at Ford and Chrysler used the war effort to achieve union recognition, which had been accomplished at General Motors in 1937.[17]

After the plants were returned to civilian production, in 1945, consumer demand pent up through years of government imposed wartime austerity measures and unleashed also with the return home of hundreds of thousands of veterans led to a massive post-war economic boom. By the late 1940s the Canadian auto industry was again firing on all cylinders. Annual production increased from 92,000 to 375,000 units between 1946 and 1954, and employment in the auto industry went from 22,000 to 29,000.[18] The number of auto plants increased in Canada, and the country's parts industry blossomed. The Automotive Parts Manufacturers Association (APMA) was founded in Toronto, in 1952, demonstrating the new strength of the parts sector. To keep up with consumer demand, two years later, Ford built a new plant and head office in Oakville, Ontario. Labour problems had wracked the auto sector since the 1930s. In the early postwar years they were much less prominent as auto workers gained the benefits of the well-functioning industry. But the postwar boom in auto production was fuelled by more than just Canadian postwar consumer demand and returning veterans, as the market for Canadian exports rebounded (although to nowhere near the prewar level). In the decade between 1946 and 1955, Canadian automakers exported almost 175,000 autos to Europe and countries of the British Commonwealth.[19]

By the mid-1950s the automobile had become the epitome of the postwar ascendancy of American industrial and cultural hegemony. Detroit's new cars became the outward signs of Canadian prosperity, too, as families moved into the new suburbs that were growing up around Canada's cities. In embracing the automobile, Canadians followed their American neighbours closely. Canadians purchased many of the same vehicles as Americans did. Like the Americans, Canadians, too, designed their homes and communities around the automobile. And like in the United States, in Canada, too, millions of dollars were allocated to highway and road construction.[20] In the glow of the postwar overall consumer boom, the auto industry became the cornerstone of the Canadian economy – and the automobile, the undisputed symbol of 'modern' Canada.

In the midst of this boom period for the Canadian automotive sector, the industry had problems which lurked just below the surface but could very quickly become overwhelming should the industry be faced with any significant downturn. American trends, which Canadians seemingly inevitably followed, were moving towards an ever-proliferating range of choices for car buyers and to a level of selection that

Canadian producers were soon going to be hard-pressed to match. When Canadian automakers could not build all the models in their parent firms' full and growing lineups, models not produced in Canada would have to be imported to satisfy Canadian consumers. So, too, would the increasingly complex technologies that were needed to produce these fancy new vehicles. Canadian branch plants lacked the technological capabilities to build many of the advanced components, for example, increasingly popular automatic transmissions. Nor did the Canadian offshoots of the Big Three have the marketing, sales, or organizational wherewithal to withstand a prolonged slump in Canadian demand. This was the situation apparent to industry leaders such as Henry Ford II, who reorganized his Canadian company so that it could better cope with these postwar automotive realities.[21]

The boom could not last forever. When the inevitable economic downswing began, it coincided in Canada with the surprising outcome of the 1957 federal election. John Diefenbaker's Progressive Conservative party ousted the Liberals in 1957 and then routed them thoroughly with their landslide victory at the polls in 1958. Few had anticipated this turn of events. During the years of the postwar boom the Liberals, led by Louis St Laurent, were seen to be effective if staid managers of a Canadian economy fed largely by American investment. But by the mid-1950s the Liberals were tired and devoid of ideas, as the economy crept towards the downturn that was sure to come. The Royal Commission on Canada's Economic Prospects (1955–7), chaired by Liberal insider Walter Gordon, it had been hoped, would re-energize the party, but proved to be too little and too late. Diefenbaker was in as prime minister on a mix of prairie populism and the promise of new faces after twenty-two consecutive years of Liberal government.[22]

Although the Tories were traditionally the party of protectionism, during his march to power Diefenbaker had advocated new economic ideas. His 'Roads to Resources' plans and vision of Canada's north as a spark to ignite economic growth were both romantic and inspirational concoctions. There was little real planning behind the rhetoric of Diefenbaker's vision. Diefenbaker also advocated loosening America's ever-expanding grip on Canada's trade, and in his first weeks as prime minister, he proposed to divert 15 per cent of Canada's trade to the United Kingdom. Artificial redirection of trade would be costly and politically dangerous, however, and the idea quickly disappeared from sight.[23] Instead of being able to act on his northern vision or diversifying Canadian trade patterns, Diefenbaker was beset by very real and pressing economic problems. Unemployment grew after 1958 to a post-war high of 7 per cent, while the national debt and Canada's trade deficit also increased. The Tories were further hurt by controversy over the activities of Bank of Canada Governor James Coyne, who clashed with the government over the direction of economic policy. Coyne's tight money policies exacerbated problems in an already troubled economy.[24]

Predictably, the end-of-decade slowdown in the Canadian economy was devastating for the auto industry which already was beset by deep structural problems. Created as branch plants at the beginning of the twentieth century, the U.S.-owned Canadian manufacturers produced along American lines. The result was a 'miniature replica' of the U.S. market, where every automaker offered all available models and options. This degree of choice became unsustainable in Canada during the consumer-driven 1950s. To offer the same array of car models as their parent companies, Canadian automakers had to resort to very short production runs, with costly downtimes while plants retooled. In the late 1950s and early 1960s, for example, Ford's engine plant in Windsor was producing seven different engine blocks for 186 different varieties of engine! Just across the Detroit River, the Ford plant produced only one engine, while turning out four times as many assembled units.[25] This wide range of vehicle models forced Canadian branch plants to import the many parts and vehicles not produced in Canada yet necessary to fill out their product lineups. By the end of the 1950s, these imports represented a structural deficit for the Canadian auto industry of more than $300 million a year. In the early 1960s, the annual trade deficit topped the $400 million mark. Both the industry and the federal government recognized the seriousness of what was quickly becoming a chronic, structural deficit in Canada's auto sector (see Tables 1.2, 1.3, and 1.4).

Adding to the sector's woes, when the economy took a downswing, offshore imports began to flood the Canadian market. European and Japanese automakers, having recovered from the effects of the war, offered smaller and less expensive models which Canadians preferred when the economic climate was uncertain. The United Kingdom, in particular, could export duty-free to Canada because of the tariff policies established in the 1930s, and by 1960 imports of British cars to Canada had increased dramatically. This deluge of imports was further encouraged by a strong Canadian dollar (in 1962 Ottawa devalued and pegged the Canadian dollar at U.S. 92.5 cents). Nearly one-third of the

Table 1.2 Canada's auto industry, 1950–1960

Year	Employees	Vehicles produced	Vehicles exported	Vehicles imported	Balance
1950	29,355	390,102	34,334	88,528	−54,194
1955	33,428	453,597	18,431	57,949	−39,518
1960	27,683	396,943	20,620	180,029	−159,409

Source: Dominion Bureau of Statistics, and Motor Vehicle Manufacturers Association (1971).

Table 1.3 Canada's automobile parts and accessories industry, 1950–1960

Year	Employees	Plants	Produced in canada ($)	Exports ($)	Imports ($)	Balance ($)
1950	19,719	151	226,539,000	12,036,000	162,298,000	−161,262,000
1955	19,996	188	285,071,000	20,333,000	278,366,000	−258,033,000
1960	15,531	114	288,080,000	34,173,000	325,850,000	−291,677,000

Source: Dominion Bureau of Statistics, and Motor Vehicle Manufacturers Association (1971).

300,000 cars sold in Canada in 1960 were imports.[26] Meanwhile, Canadian exports declined and now represented only a tiny slice of production. The impact on the auto industry and on employment was devastating. Membership in the Canadian arm of the United Auto Workers union dropped from 33,000 to 27,000 between 1956 and 1960 (See Table 1.2)

Faced with such a threat to the industry and its membership, the union took action. Canadian UAW director George Burt led a delegation to Ottawa in July 1960 to press the government to consider the union's views on how to save the industry. A no-nonsense mechanic from Oshawa, Burt had been a member of this union since its founding in 1937 and was voted its Canadian director in 1939. Burt understood the challenges facing the industry very well. The UAW's presentation to the government, entitled 'How Canadians Can Get a Made-in-Canada Car They Want and Can Afford,' called for a radical approach to the auto industry's problems. It placed blame for the industry's woes squarely on the shoulders of the manufacturers themselves. Nationalistic in tone, the brief declared that the time had come for the Canadian government to 'protect the Canadian people.' The union argued that

Table 1.4 Canada's trade with the United States, automotive products, 1955–1963 (Can$ millions)

Year	Imports	Exports	Total	Balance
1955	361	4	365	–357
1956	439	4	443	–435
1957	356	6	362	–350
1958	324	9	333	–315
1959	369	17	386	–352
1960	407	4	411	–403
1961	398	9	407	–389
1962	519	16	535	–503
1963	555	40	598	–515

Source: *DesRosiers Automotive Yearbook 2000* (Richmond Hill, 2000), 190, and Statistics Canada cat. nos. 65-202 and 65-203, as cited in John Holmes, 'From Three Industries to One: Towards an Integrated North American Automobile Industry,' in Maureen Appel Molot, ed., *Driving Continentally: National Policies and the North American Auto Industry* (Ottawa: Carleton University Press, 1993), 27.

this could be accomplished by encouraging small car builders to set up plants in Canada, by boosting Canadian content requirements from 60 per cent to 75 per cent for those companies producing more than 20,000 units, and eliminating the 7.5 per cent excise tax on Canadian-built cars that had been in place since the 1930s.[27]

The UAW also argued that the feasibility of closer integration with the U.S. industry should be explored. More specifically, it suggested a model that did not impose tariffs on products used by any company that 'allocated an appropriate proportion, relative to sales in Canada, of its total production in Canadian plants.' The UAW's idea of a 'restricted free trade area' did not contradict plans to boost content or eliminate excise taxes, but it did seem to clash with the otherwise nationalistic tenor of the document. Undoubtedly, Burt had hoped that the document's patriotic tone would appease the more nationalistic elements in his union, which had grown increasingly vocal since the onset of the sector's problems. Integration and the UAW's other ideas, suggested the union, could be looked at more closely if a Royal Commission were created to investigate the entire industry.[28]

Other segments of the auto industry had also begun pressuring the Tories to do something. Both the Canadian Automobile Chamber of Commerce (CACC, which in 1962 became the Motor Vehicle Manufacturers Association) and the parts makers' association (APMA) had long-standing relations with Ottawa and had often made suggestions on tariff and industry matters during budget time.[29] Led by their proactive president James Dykes, the CACC was an exclusive club that comprised the presidents of the major automakers in Canada, that is, GM, Ford, Chrysler, AMC, and International Harvester. The APMA was a larger and more diffuse group of Canadian parts makers, both large and small. Their leader, D.S. Wood, was also a keen lobbyist, although at times many members of the APMA were not in agreement with the direction pursued by the association's leadership. Diefenbaker met with CACC members in June 1960 to discuss problems in the industry.

Confronted with public demands from the UAW and private pleadings by the major manufacturers that something be done to save the auto industry, the Diefenbaker government moved swiftly. Discussions with Finance Minister Donald Fleming and opposition member Paul Martin, Sr, whose Windsor riding was in the heart of Canada's auto industry, led to the decision to appoint Vincent Bladen, who was dean of arts at the University of Toronto, as a one-man Royal Commission.[30] English-born and an economist, Bladen was known as fair-minded by members of the industry and government representatives alike. Although smaller by far than most government inquiries, the Bladen Commission was extremely thorough, and Bladen was granted wide scope to conduct his investigation. Bladen held five days of public hearings in Ottawa, received nearly two hundred public and private submissions, and personally visited vehicle manufacturers and parts companies in Canada, the United Kingdom, France, West Germany, and Sweden, as well as in the United States. Presentations and submissions ranged from those by the Canadian Big Three to the eclectic advice of Bladen's colleague at the University of Toronto, Marshall McLuhan, and Queen's University historian A.R.M. Lower.[31]

Most of the submissions came from the industry itself. The major manufacturers were unanimous in recommending lifting the 7.5 per cent excise tax on cars built in Canada. In place in some form since Mackenzie King's tariff changes of the 1920s and 1930s, the excise tax made Canadian cars more expensive than duty-free models imported from Britain. Generally, the automakers favoured reducing tariffs rather than increasing Commonwealth or Canadian content which, they argued, would serve to raise costs and lower sales. Three of the five automakers (GM, Ford, and International Harvester) recommended some kind of closer integration with their U.S. parent companies. The APMA took a far more protectionist view. The parts makers' association called for a tariff increase to 17.5 per cent for those within the imperial preference sphere and 25 per cent for most-favoured nations, an end to duty-free entry for British autos, and extricating the auto tariff schedules from the General Agreement on Tariffs and Trade. Submissions from the UAW's leadership recommended some sort of closer integration with the United States (which, they expected, would result in wage parity), while submissions from the nationalist locals demanded higher Canadian content and more protection, if not outright government ownership of the auto industry.[32] Bladen considered most of the protectionist demands to be untenable, but he was curious about the idea of continental integration, which had appeared often in submissions to his commission. The idea had also been in the foreground during Bladen's discussions with Big Three executives in Detroit and in New York.[33] In November 1960, Bladen asked a few key witnesses to submit further thoughts on the issue of continental integration of the auto industry.

The responses illustrated the various positions within the industry. The automakers were keen on the idea, as long as more onerous content levels were not a requirement. But, as Ford's answer indicated, the U.S. parents were not interested in any concept that cut back on U.S. parts and auto exports to Canada, which by then were valued at more than $300 million a year. Substituting Canadian parts, or forcing automakers to build the whole range of cars that Canadians desired, promised to be tremendously expensive for the automakers. Parts manufacturers, represented by the APMA, staunchly opposed the idea of integration, which they perceived would cause them hardship and create chaotic conditions in the industry. The 'cure,' argued the APMA, 'would be much worse than the ailment.' Instead, the association reiterated what it said in its original submission to Bladen, which called for greater protection and increased Canadian content.[34]

Bladen was definitely influenced by the idea of somehow expanding production, which underlay the proposed integration plan. As an economist he understood that Canada could benefit immensely from the economies of scale that could be achieved under integration. But the submissions showed that integration would be extremely difficult to implement and could not be realized without serious dislocations in the Canadian auto industry. Moreover, continental integration was a highly charged issue that struck at the heart of Canada's survival as an independent nation, as Bladen himself admitted. He knew, for example, that the idea of continental integration had torn the Canadian UAW into pro-integration and nationalist factions.[35]

When Bladen presented his report to the government, however, there was little mention of the difficulties that the idea of integration was fostering within the industry. Instead, he emphasized two points. First, Bladen expressed his disagreement with most of the pro-integrationist submissions that any such arrangement required a bilateral Canada-U.S. agreement. He was convinced that 'an advantageous scheme of integration could be implemented by unilateral action.' Second, Bladen did not believe that there should be guarantees, as called for by some advocates of integration, based on employment objectives. An increasing share of production in an expanding market was more important for Bladen, than assuring jobs.[36]

Bladen made seven principal recommendations, and they centred around two main policies that, he argued, should be implemented as a single plan. The first six recommendations suggested that various automobile excise and tax changes be considered, as most representatives had suggested.[37] Bladen's seventh recommendation introduced a novel concept: an 'extended content' plan. Aware that the only way to boost Canadian productivity and efficiency would be through improving Canada's exports dramatically, Bladen suggested that Ottawa allow companies to import cars and parts duty-free as long as a stated percentage of Canadian content was achieved. This would eliminate the 'class or kind' distinctions that riddled the tariff. Canadian-made original equipment parts would qualify as content whether used in Canada or exported to another country. Instead of focusing on particular parts, then, the percentage of duty-free parts and vehicles could be used anywhere in the product lines, while parts produced in Canada would be considered as Canadian content if put in vehicles produced in any country for sale anywhere, thus giving the manufacturer a certain measure of flexibility. The plan also would have the benefit, Bladen argued, of keeping auto prices within 'politically acceptable limits.'[38]

The extended content plan may have made it easier for smaller producers to take advantage of the more flexible content rules, but the bigger manufacturers would now have to include much more Canadian content then they were accustomed to in order to achieve duty-free status. General Motors, for example, was only required to have 60 per cent Commonwealth content (it built more than 20,000 vehicles) under the 1936 Tariff Act. Under the Bladen plan, GM would be required to include 70 per cent Canadian content, since by 1959 it produced more than 150,000 passenger vehicles per year in Canada. Bladen's plan also would put Canadian parts makers at risk. For the first time, they would be forced to compete with American parts makers without 'class or kind' protection. For example, lamps built at Canadian Lamp Company received 17.5 per cent protection against similar U.S.-made lamps. Under the extended content plan, Canadian Lamp would have to compete without any protection. Some parts makers could flourish under the proposal, but many of them would be put out of business. The extended content plan, if enacted, would represent a dramatic change in the functioning of the Canadian automotive industry.

Diefenbaker's response to Bladen's scheme was tepid. Because the plan advocated tariff and excise tax changes, Finance Department officials thought it best to hold off publishing the commission's report until the next budget, which was to come out in June 1961. But even before Bladen completed his study, the Conservative government (and Finance Minister Donald Fleming in particular) was being pressured to change the structure of the auto tariff. GM Canada's president E.H. Walker had visited Assistant Deputy Minister of Finance A.F.W. Plumptre in June 1961 to tell him that should certain conditions be met, GM would start producing automatic transmissions in Canada, which, because of the costs and high technological demands involved, had so far not been produced in Canada at all. Bladen estimated that a company must build 400,000 vehicle transmissions a year to be economical, a figure larger than that of the total number of units annually built in Canada. That was why Ottawa, in 1950, had suspended the 25 per cent duty on increasingly popular automatic transmissions, ensuring Canadian automakers were not left behind without models having automatic transmissions. The terms as outlined by Walker, however, would put GM in a much more advantageous position relative to its competitors – once GM was exempted from paying duty on the parts and special components that had to be imported to build automatic transmissions. The 25 per cent duty on automatic transmissions would have to be reimposed on the other automakers to make GM's plan profitable. Walker acknowledged that his competitors would no doubt complain if GM were granted these concessions, but pointed out that the government's difficulties in this area would be offset by the increased employment and production at GM. To make the plan work, Walker explained, 'certain arbitrary decisions would have to be taken.'[39]

Walker pressed the government further by stating that an immediate response was needed for his plan to be successfully launched. Canadian officials understood this to be a pre-emptive strike on the part of Canada's largest automaker. GM could not know exactly what Bladen was planning, but it did have the most to lose if any significant changes were made to the tariff structure, especially with regard to Canadian content. The giant company, which already controlled more than 50 per cent of the Canadian market, was taking the initiative in hopes of getting even more distance between itself and the competition.[40]

The GM initiative put the government in a difficult situation. In the past, manufacturers and parts makers had produced joint submissions whenever they made suggestions to the government on tariff issues; generally, whenever changes in the industry were contemplated, all segments were consulted. Walker's plan was entirely his own. Were it to present the industry with the GM plan, the government would be seen as playing favourites. Moreover, the plan could scuttle the Bladen Commission's recommendations. The reimposition of the 25 per cent duty on automatic transmissions was inconsistent with Bladen's extended content plan. Not willing to be swayed by Walker's claims of urgency, Finance Department officials recommended to Fleming that he delay any decision until after the Bladen Commission proposals had been fully assessed.[41]

Finance officials analysed Bladen's report between April and June 1961 and concluded that it would be extremely difficult to implement its recommendations in a single plan. Fleming admitted to Diefenbaker that Bladen's proposals were 'the most imaginative and ingenious' that he had seen in a long time. But Fleming also had serious reservations, and he went as far as to say that he was sceptical or perhaps simply did not understand some of the recommendations. The excise and sales tax changes proposed by Bladen were easy enough to implement. Changing 'Commonwealth content' to 'Canadian content' could also be achieved easily. Since virtually all parts in Canadian cars were either made in Canada or imported from the United States, there would be little impact regarding those very few parts that were imported from other Commonwealth countries.[42]

The difficulties had to do with the tariff recommendations. Fleming found the extended content plan 'so radical that, on short notice, one cannot grasp all the implications.' Granting duty-free treatment under the new and untried criteria listed in Bladen's recommendations would be to 'take a real leap in the dark.' Furthermore, the plan would entail difficult negotiations with MFN countries to gain concessions in return for duty-free treatment. These concessions, thought Finance officials, might offset the problems stemming from the recommended 10 per cent tariff rate for British autos and parts (which previously had been zero) that was sure to cause 'bitter resentment' in the United Kingdom and have profound effects on the attitude of British ministers towards Canada. The British were doing well exporting smaller cars such as the Austin Mini to Canada. With the United Kingdom thought to be on the verge of joining the European Common Market (precursor to today's European Union) and with the Dillon Round of tariff negotiations at the GATT (named for then U.S. Undersecretary of Economic Affairs Douglas Dillon), a 10 per cent tariff would create serious problems between Canada and the United Kingdom. The British might use such a tariff to demand more concessions from Canada at the negotiations taking place in Geneva.[43]

Ottawa balked at implementing the far-reaching Bladen proposals. When he delivered his budget and tabled the Bladen report in June 1961, Fleming included only two of the commissioner's more minor recommendations relating to the excise tax and pricing. Rather than go the whole hog with Bladen's recommendations, the Tories went only with those proposals that were easiest to enact. In his budget speech, Fleming announced that additional study of Bladen's more complex recommendations would be required, and he called upon interested parties to comment upon when, how, and if the tariff suggestions made in the Bladen Report were to be implemented.[44]

Industry response to Fleming's announcement varied. Days after the budget speech, GM president Walker met again with Finance Department officials. Walker made the case that he had been led to believe that the Bladen recommendations supported his plan for automatic transmission production in Canada. Furthermore, he intimated that Finance officials had promised him a decision on his plan as soon as the Bladen Commission's findings were released. Walker suggested that without an answer from the government within days, GM's plans would be irreparably harmed and that this would lead to massive layoffs at GM's Windsor and St Catharines (Ontario) transmission plants. However, Walker also made clear that if GM were to be given some assurances, namely, that GM would get duty-free treatment for certain machinery and components, the company would go ahead with producing automatic transmissions even if the extended content plan were not implemented. With the prospect of more jobs and the production of automatic transmissions, Finance officials felt that Ottawa could promise Walker that the 25 per cent duty on transmissions would be reimposed. Such a situation would not embarrass the government even if the Bladen plan were implemented, since all products faced duties if companies did not meet content requirements. If the Bladen plan were not implemented, however, the government could find itself in a compromising situation, as GM would be seen to have been given preferential treatment. In that case, Finance officials advised Fleming, Ottawa would have no choice but to allow the duty on transmissions to lapse.[45]

Of the other Big Three manufacturers, Ford remained relatively muted in its comments on Bladen's proposals, although it congratulated the government for removing the excise taxes and changing the sales taxes. Chrysler, however, was enthusiastic about the extended content plan and said that it hoped that the Canadian government would implement it promptly. APMA's D.S. Wood visited Ottawa to relay his association's views. Most parts makers, reported Wood, were apprehensive about the loss of protection that the extended content plan would entail.[46] Meanwhile, UAW officials on both sides of the Canada–U.S. border said they were wary of any plan that did not provide adjustment assistance to dislocated automotive workers.[47]

Fleming's call for further examination of the practicality of the Bladen recommendations brought little response from the automotive industry. Only the APMA submitted an alternative plan. Wood, the activist manager of the association, kept in close contact with government officials following the budget speech, and by November 1961 produced the APMA's own detailed strategy for the auto industry. The APMA's plan reflected the more cautious approach of the parts makers, who worried about being suddenly exposed to cut-throat U.S. competition should Bladen's extended content plan be implemented. Instead, the APMA proposed a 'derivation' of the Bladen scheme, described by Wood as an 'export credit' plan. Under the APMA's proposed system, auto companies would be able to deduct from the value of imported goods on which they paid duty the dollar value of goods exported in a given year, *if* they increased exports from Canada beyond the level of the previous year's exports. Non-manufacturing companies that imported autos (such as European assembly operations) could deduct duties based on the amount of Canadian content that such companies exported in a given year. This would mean that foreign companies could gain import credits if they increased their purchases of Canadian parts and sent them to their home countries for inclusion in the cars they would then send back to Canada. The idea was to ensure that both automakers and parts makers gained the benefit of duty-free treatment for increased exports. The plan would be operated through duty draw-backs, wherein the government would 'pay back' the duty paid on imported items if the manufacturer or company achieved the required export targets. Wood argued that the plan also had the advantage of not requiring a reopening of international trade obligations under the GATT, as it could be initiated unilaterally.[48]

Finance Department officials were intrigued. When Wood visited Ottawa in late 1961, he discussed the plan in detail with Wayne Plumptre, Simon Reisman, Arthur Annis, and C.D. Arthur. The latter three would form a significant contingent of Ottawa's auto team in the years to come. Reisman, who would before long have the leading role in shaping Ottawa's automotive policy, was typical of the group. When the Second World War broke out he was studying economics at McGill University, from which he received a Master's degree in 1941. Reisman served as a gunner during the war, and after that went to work for the federal government. He was well established in the Finance Department by 1958, when he was chosen to head a research project with Irving Brecher on Canada–U.S. economic relations for Walter Gordon's Royal Commission on Canada's Economic Prospects.[49] In 1961 Reisman was appointed assistant deputy minister of finance. Eventually, he became deputy minister of industry and deputy minister of finance.[50] Another Second World War veteran, Annis was appointed director of economic affairs, industry tariffs, and trade tariffs in the Department of Finance in 1960. Arthur had worked for Vincent Bladen during the Royal Commission on the Automotive Industry before he went to the Finance Department.

The other senior civil servants who had key roles in shaping policy regarding Canada's auto industry had similar backgrounds. D.A. (David) Golden joined the civil service in 1945 following his discharge from the army. Golden had survived four brutal years as a Japanese prisoner of war after the fall of Hong Kong. Deputy minister of defence production since 1954, Golden became the first deputy minister of the new Department of Industry in 1963.[51] J.H. (Jake) Warren was made deputy minister of trade and commerce in 1964. He, too, had served in the Second World War and had joined the civil service shortly thereafter. By the 1960s, like Reisman and his other colleagues, Warren had accumulated considerable experience as a trade negotiator.[52]

Finance officials were taken by the APMA's plan. Plumptre thought of it as 'something less' than the Bladen plan, yet he found it attractive on the ground that it could be implemented without any changes to Canada's tariff structure. Moreover, the plan would assist parts manufacturers, who represented a substantial segment of the auto industry in

Canada.[53] The APMA's plan had the potential to provide a new departure for the Canadian auto industry – while not as radical as the Bladen proposals, it held out the possibility of noticeably increasing Canada's exports. This went to the heart of the difficulties facing the industry, which were responsible for an enormous proportion of the shortfall in Canada's balance-of-payments account. But the APMA's plan was put on hold, as was all further consideration of the auto industry's problems.

Instead, between June 1961 and August 1962, especially, the Diefenbaker government was preoccupied with a number of other difficult issues. Following release of the budget in June, and the conclusion of the Coyne affair, foreign affairs took centre stage, as the Cold War came to a crisis that summer with the erection of the Berlin Wall. In the spring, Ottawa had to scramble to avert a potential fiscal catastrophe brought on by an overvalued dollar and falling gold reserves. This difficult situation led to the May 1962 decision to peg the Canadian dollar at U.S. 92.5 cents. Throughout these months, the Diefenbaker government was also wrestling with the thorny question of whether to make nuclear weapons available to the Canadian armed forces. Parliament was dissolved, and an election was called.[54]

On election night, 18 June 1962, Canadians voters dealt the Conservatives a serious setback and sent them back to Ottawa with only a minority government. After a lacklustre campaign showing that the fire of Diefenbaker's prairie populism had dulled, the government lost nearly 100 seats. Taking only 116 seats to the Liberals' 98, the Tories needed the support of the Social Credit party to survive.[55] The great Conservative majority had been squandered, and Diefenbaker was personally profoundly wounded by the result.

The minority government was immediately confronted by new difficulties, as Canada's trade balance declined further. In an effort to protect the badly slipping trade surplus, right after the election the Conservatives imposed a 10 per cent surcharge on all imports. The additional taxes, coupled with the repeal of the excise tax on Canadian-made cars, had a devastating impact on imports of cars from Europe. Prices on German and British cars were discounted, but with little effect. In 1960 imported cars held 28 per cent of the Canadian market, but by the end of 1962 their share was only 14 per cent.[56]

Notwithstanding the 10 per cent surcharge, however, imports of parts and vehicles from the United States continued to flood into Canada. The surcharge boosted sales of Canadian-assembled U.S. models which, ironically, had the effect of far greater imports of American parts being required for automotive assembly in Canada. Thus, even while the Canadian automotive industry experienced a small recovery, Canada's balance-of-payments surplus continued to decline precariously. Consecutive trade deficits in the automotive sector totalled $460 million by 1962, and this accounted for more than 90 per cent of Canada's overall trade shortfall (see Table 1.3).[57] The overwhelming majority of this deficit had accumulated because cars and parts made in the United States entered Canada duty-free. The Canadian industry was in a Catch-22: the better the Canadian economy performed, the more Canadians demanded the more expensive American models that had to be imported, and the worse the trade deficit became. Alternatively, if the economy took a downswing, the demand for cheaper European imports grew.

By then it was clear that the government could no longer postpone action, and that something had to be done for the auto industry. The Bladen proposals had been tabled for more than a year, and pressure was mounting for the Tories to take steps to solve the difficulties of the auto industry and balance of payments.[58] Finally, the government convened an interdepartmental Committee to Study the Bladen Plan. Chaired by Simon Reisman, representatives from the departments of Finance, Trade and Commerce, National Revenue, and the Bank of Canada – the core of Canada's auto team, and the backbone of the future Department of Industry – met in August 1962 to tackle the issue.

Over the next two months, the committee analysed the state of the Canadian automotive industry. Canada faced a unique situation. Few countries as industrially developed depended so much on imports in their auto industry. The Canadian automotive market was large, but Canadians were not producing enough vehicles. Reisman and his colleagues estimated that Canadian production accounted for only 55 per cent of the value of the market. The committee was slowly coming to the conclusion that, with the right type of plan, Canada could improve her balance-of-payments deficit and significantly increase production in this important secondary manufacturing sector.[59]

The committee considered a number of different approaches. Its members conducted hypothetical studies of the impact of the original extended content plan and variations of it, which boosted Bladen's suggested Canadian content levels by 5 and 10 per cent. But the problems inherent in Bladen's plan, namely, the need to renegotiate tariff rates under the GATT and the expected difficulties with increasing tariffs on goods from the United Kingdom, were deemed too difficult to overcome. The feasibility of a plan whereby content levels were increased, but without any corresponding duty-free entry based on exports, was also considered. Such a plan, which would certainly promote import substitution and thus increase 'exchange savings,' was judged to be too costly to implement, as well as too protectionist. It would have the effect of raising automobile prices beyond what, the committee thought, the Canadian consumer would bear. Another plan, which offered a drawback provision on the basis of one dollar in duty for every two dollars exported, was also looked at. This one had similarities to the APMA's plan of November 1961. It had the benefits of providing incentives for increasing exports without changing Canada's tariff structure and of ensuring that Canadian parts makers retained nearly all of their present levels of protection. The automakers might also have found such a plan to be satisfactory, since it did not force them to increase their Canadian content commitments.

The program eventually decided on in September 1962 was something of an amalgam of the various schemes that the committee had considered. As an interim measure, the committee recommended that the government test the waters by creating a much modified and scaled-down version of an export incentive plan, along the lines suggested by the APMA. Duty-free entry of imported automatic transmissions would be contingent; the importing company could earn a credit equivalent to the value of goods by exporting Canadian parts to the country from which it was importing the automatic transmissions. In 1961 Canadian companies brought $32 million worth of automatic transmissions into Canada duty-free. This amount represented a significant part of Canada's trade deficit. Under the new program, only companies that increased their export levels over and above a base year (say, 1961) could import automatic transmissions duty-free. Significantly, the plan would allow U.S. automakers credits to their Canadian subsidiaries for parts purchased and shipped directly from independent Canadian parts producers to the parent companies. Thus, if American Ford purchased more springs from the Canadian Spring Company than it had in the base year (say, 1961), Ford of Canada gained credits for those additional Canadian exports and could then import a corresponding value amount in transmissions from its American parent duty-free.

The committee calculated that exports would increase by as much as $20 million a year, and thus believed that this arrangement could mark a first step towards redressing Canada's trade deficit and helping its auto industry. The plan had much to commend it: Canada's tariff schedule would not need to be altered, and the plan would not impinge on Canada's international trade obligations. Although unilateral, the plan provided incentives for foreign companies, specifically the U.S. Big Three, to purchase more from Canada. Timing was also a consideration, as the current Order-in-Council suspending payment of the 25 per cent duty on transmissions, which had been renewed yearly since 1950, was nearing its annual 31 October termination date. The imminent expiration of the current order provoked much speculation from the industry and the Liberal opposition about what the Conservatives were intending to do.[60] The committee suggested that the new plan should run for one year as a pilot project, during which period each company would be allowed to import as many transmissions as its credits permitted. A drawback of 99 per cent of the duties paid would be remitted to the importing company if its exports were at a level over and above the 1961–2 base year. Significantly, in the event that the plan did not provoke a backlash from the automotive industry, the U.S. government, or American producers, the committee suggested that it might be possible to extend the program. The transmission plan would be a dramatic departure in tariff making: instead of imposing duties to force import substitution, the incentive of duty-drawbacks would encourage increased levels of targeted exports.

In October 1962, at the height of the Cuban missile crisis, the Diefenbaker government approved the Bladen Plan committee's recommendations. They came to be known as the automatic transmission duty-remission plan.[61] This innovative plan certainly showed the willingness of Reisman's auto team to break the mould when it came to trade policy, while at the same time it was a relatively cautious approach to the auto problem, since it did not require tariff changes and could be implemented unilaterally. The duty-drawbacks would apply only to transmissions, and therefore the plan might pre-empt attacks from countries as a subsidy. Because the plan enabled the major manufacturers to avoid import duties, it might escape criticism from the Big Three, whose opinions mattered the most in the auto industry. The Canadian government had also managed to keep its promise to GM, which had sought the reimposition of duties on automatic transmissions in support of its planned undertaking to build transmissions in Canada. The parts makers, too, could not complain. They would retain their protection and also gain many of the benefits of the export credit plan that they themselves had proposed in late 1961. The Canadian UAW could look forward to the increased employment in the industry that was expected to occur as a result of increased export levels. Finally, Canadian consumers would have the benefit of lower car prices resulting from the longer production runs in Canada for parts and from the duty-free import of automatic transmissions. By taking a less ambitious route in their attempts to solve Canada's auto industry and balance-of-payments problems, the Tories had addressed many of the industry's own concerns.

Finance Minister George Nowlan announced the new plan in the House of Commons on 29 October 1962. As an added wrinkle, the government decided to also apply the new program to engines, which faced a duty of 25 per cent. This benefited smaller companies, such as Studebaker and American Motors, which did not produce engines in Canada. Each automaker was allowed to import up to 10,000 engines duty-free, depending on the increase in goods that it exported. Ottawa believed that the engine provision softened the blow for the two smaller manufacturers, which were most dependent on the duty-free importation of transmissions and which would face the greatest adjustments because of the new program. The aim of the transmission and engine provisions, Nowlan explained, was to provide 'substantial inducement' for the automakers to achieve a better balance between exports and imports. The program was to be considered, Nowlan concluded, to be one step towards improving Canada's international balance of payments and increasing production in Canadian industry.[62]

Reaction to Nowlan's announcement of the program was swift. In the House of Commons Paul Martin, Liberal MP for Windsor, attacked the government for ignoring the Bladen Plan committee's report for two years and for not fully implementing its recommendations. The press saw the plan as a 'carrot and a stick' regime to offset imports by boosting exports.[63] The Big Three remained relatively quiet. Earl K. Brownridge, president of American Motors of Canada, said the new plan was going to be a hardship on his company, although he liked the idea of moving towards freer trade in auto products. Ford officials warned that if they were forced to build automatic transmissions in Canada, consumers would see a drastic increase in the price of their cars.[64]

The Canadian subsidiaries moved quickly to take advantage of the new program. In December 1962, Studebaker Canada announced the export of $350,000 worth of hubcaps from its affiliate, Canadian Lamp, to its parent in the United States for credit. Shortly after, Chrysler hired 170 new workers at its Windsor plant, a result of the export of several thousand engines to its subsidiaries in Switzerland, the Philippines,

Australia, and New Zealand. In February 1963, American Motors Corporation purchased $4 million in goods from a number of Canadian companies, creating over 400 jobs in Canada. AMC stated that the purchases had been negotiated by its Canadian subsidiary, and credit gained from the sales was used towards the importation of automatic transmissions into Canada. The same week, GM finally announced the production of automatic transmissions at its St Catharines plant, resulting in 600 new jobs. Walker stated that after many years of study, the company could produce the transmissions at a slightly higher cost than in the United States, and sell them for less than imported transmissions on which duty would now be paid.[65]

By the spring of 1963, Ottawa's policies were having an impact on the auto sector. Production had increased dramatically in Canada, in part because of the tariff policies the government had initiated, but also because of a general recovery in the economy. In 1962 Canadian automakers produced 383,000 passenger vehicles, the highest total ever in the industry. Imports of finished cars had dropped so much that, in April 1963, the Diefenbaker government decided to end the 10 per cent import surcharge on automobiles. The trade balance, while still massively tilted towards the United States, was beginning to show the first signs of improvement, as Canadian automotive export levels began to rise (see Table 1.4).[66]

Reisman and his colleagues were pleased with the results, as was the Tory government. However, there were a number of problems associated with the new plan. Many Canadian companies with no previous relationship with any of the Big Three (either as a wholly owned parts supplier or a company that had had contracts with one of the three) found it difficult to get orders from them.[67] Some manufacturers were not gaining any benefit from the program. Willys-Jeep, for example, built its own engines in Canada and did not use or require automatic transmissions; although it purchased more than $3 million annually in Canadian parts, Willys-Jeep could not receive any credits under the new program. Also, many companies complained that the short-term nature of the agreement was problematic, given the long lead times required in the industry.[68]

In further meetings of the Bladen Plan committee, which had been renamed the Industry Committee, Reisman directed his colleagues to examine other sectors where the export incentive plan might be introduced, including business machines and parts and tractors and all automotive parts, which could bring the independent parts manufacturers under the program's umbrella. Along with further expanding the scope of the automatic transmission duty-remission program, Reisman probed the possibility of extending its term so that the auto companies could formulate longer-term plans for the industry.[69]

The Diefenbaker government did not get the chance to consider the Industry Committee's findings. Already barely hanging on with a parliamentary minority, early in the new year, the Diefenbaker government foundered on the nuclear question. The cabinet itself was torn over accepting nuclear warheads for Royal Canadian Air Force Bomarc missiles, while pressure mounted for the government to make a decision. When Diefenbaker vacillated on the question, comments from U.S. Air Force General Lauris Norstad, retiring chief of NATO, and a 'timely' press release from Washington that contradicted the prime minister's position pushed the minority government over the brink.[70] On 5 February 1963 Pearson's Liberals moved a motion of non-confidence and brought the government down.

Although auto policy was put on hold as Canadians went back to the polls, for the second time in less than a year, the issue had clearly become a central aspect in Ottawa's approach to both economic development and Canada's fiscal health. The downturn in the industry and the increasing automotive trade deficit had forced the federal government to respond. This led to the appointment of the Bladen Commission which, in turn, provoked a flood of new ideas about the operation of the industry. A dedicated core of Ottawa civil servants led by Simon Reisman was able to shape these disparate approaches into an innovative, if cautious, pilot program that yielded undeniable results. Questions remained, however, about the long-term health of the automotive industry and the country's financial situation. These questions would be tackled by a new government and a new prime minister. But they would face the same challenges and utilize many of the same approaches as did the Diefenbaker government before them. Even so the direction of Canadian automotive policy still had many unexpected turns to take.

2

Canadian State Intervention in the Auto Industry and the Failure of Automotive Free Trade, 1963–1964

The election of 8 April 1963 resulted in a minority Liberal government led by Lester Pearson. With the same constraints in the automotive sector that prevailed under Diefenbaker and the Conservative regime, and following the same advice offered by the same automotive team in the federal civil service, the Liberals were able to aggressively expand the Tories' auto policies as part of their own economic agenda. Yet the overall strategy of the Liberals emerged only with difficulty, as the government's determined interventionism in the auto industry brought it into conflict with the United States, and for a time it seemed that there was sure to be an open trade war between the two countries. Underlying this interventionist strategy were two differing visions of Canada's future clashing against one another within the party. One promoted the economic nationalism of Walter Gordon, while the other was the traditional Liberal view favouring good continental relations with the United States and freer trade. Both would shape Ottawa's economic policy in the mid-1960s as the search for a solution to the difficulties in the auto sector continued.

Before entering electoral politics in 1948, Lester Pearson had enjoyed a very successful career as a civil servant and diplomat, representing Canada as its ambassador in Washington and at the United Nations. In 1956, as minister of external affairs, he brokered a peace deal during the Suez crisis that won him worldwide fame and the Nobel Peace Prize. Pearson captured the Liberal leadership in 1957, but suffered a humiliating loss at the polls in 1958. As a rookie opposition leader Pearson was ineffective, although his performance improved considerably. If the 1963 victory was not resounding, for a party that had come to see itself as the natural governing party of Canada, the return to power certainly was gratifying.[1]

This resurrection of the Liberals was largely the work of one man, Walter Gordon. A close Pearson adviser and friend, Gordon was a successful accountant before becoming heavily involved with government work after the Second World War. His close ties to the Liberal party secured his appointment as head of the Royal Commission on Canada's Economic Prospects. With the commission's 1958 report Gordon established his place as an economic nationalist. By then the Liberals were out of office, and Gordon took it upon himself to revive their fortunes. He reorganized the party's apparatus and finances and even personally paid Pearson's expenses. Gordon's influence in the party became so pervasive that many long-time Liberals came to resent his close ties to Pearson. Nonetheless, in the 1962 election Gordon successfully ran in Toronto, and when the Liberals were returned to power in the 1963 election he was made minister of finance.[2]

Gordon's views on the American economic influence in Canada were not informed only by his work as head of the Royal Commission. He had a deep-seated resentment towards Americans which stemmed from unsuccessful dealings with them when he was a younger man. As a scion of Bay Street, Gordon favoured protectionism, a stance that led to the charge that he was a Tory interloper in the Liberal party. But Gordon also had more practical motives for his economic views. He owned Cancorp, a major Canadian company with significant industrial and financial concerns, and so he was well positioned to benefit personally should government policy privilege Canadian-owned and -operated companies over those that were foreign owned. Gordon's ideological stance was not one of pure self-interest; still, there can be no denying that on the issue of foreign ownership and protectionism it was one shaped by both his position and class.[3]

Prime Minister Pearson wanted to reward Gordon with the key economic portfolio, but Gordon's brand of economic nationalism had not captured the entire party. Other influential Liberals such as Mitchell Sharp were more comfortable with traditional party policies such as freer trade and close economic ties with the United States. Like Pearson, Sharp had been a high-ranking civil servant before he was elected to Parliament.[4] As the new minister of trade and commerce, Sharp was the main counterpoint to Gordon's economic nationalism in cabinet and within the party. Paul Martin, Sr, was no great fan of rampant capitalism, and he remained wary of any extreme position, especially one that might upset the giant to the south. Pearson chose Martin to head the Department of External Affairs.[5] A lawyer with a military background,

Charles 'Bud' Drury (Gordon's brother-in-law and an MP from Montreal) became minister of defence production. This was a crucial post in an era when Canada's military budget was still significant. Not an economic nationalist, especially, Drury could nevertheless be expected to support Gordon.[6] Along with Pearson, then, Drury, Gordon, and Martin were the key individuals who shaped the Liberal government's economic policies.[7]

During the election campaign, Pearson and his team had promised 'Sixty Days of Decision' in which they would act on their interventionist ideas. The government's maiden budget was scheduled for June 1963, and would be the first test of the Liberals' new policies. Gordon had made no secret of his views, yet few people outside the government could have anticipated the extent of the measures contained in that first budget. In keeping with the Liberal's campaign promises and the May Speech from the Throne, the government showed its determination to improve Canada's balance-of-payments account, its export trade, and ultimately, its employment numbers.[8] Gordon announced the creation of the Department of Industry and the Economic Council of Canada.[9] The government would be taking measures to stem the rising levels of American ownership in the Canadian economy. After noting the very extensive degree of foreign ownership in particular sectors of the economy – 57 per cent in manufacturing, 75 per cent in oil and gas, and 61 per cent in mining and smelting – Gordon announced a number of changes regarding the taxation of corporations. Withholding taxes on dividends paid to non-residents were to be reduced if a company was 25 per cent Canadian-owned. Conversely, taxes would be raised where the proportion of domestic ownership was lower. But Gordon's most radical proposal was the introduction of a 30 per cent takeover tax on shares of companies purchased by non-Canadians. He also suggested that the government would work towards achieving a target of 25 per cent of Canadian ownership for companies operating in Canada.[10]

Reaction to these measures was devastating. Once considered Bay Street's darling, Gordon was now branded a pariah by the financial community. His policies prompted a run on Canadian markets and the Canadian dollar. Fearful that the new measures would cut off the flow of U.S. dollars into Canada, the financial community began to sell off Canadian securities at a discount. Gordon was soon forced to abandon the takeover tax plan, and stocks on the exchanges in Toronto and Montreal immediately soared upwards. The markets had spoken. They had punished the finance minister and damaged the credibility of the new government. Pearson's 'Sixty Days of Decision' were a bust.[11]

Lost in the furor over the takeover taxes were Gordon's provisions for the manufacturing sector, the most important being the new Department of Industry, which was to be made responsible for the automotive sector. As 'minister-designate,' Drury was to seek ways to expand Canada's manufacturing capacity. This would help to improve Canada's foreign trade and its balance-of-payments account, while raising employment numbers. In his budget speech, Gordon specifically referred to the auto industry when pointing to Canada's $400 million annual trade deficit. The government had decided that something had to be done about the automotive deficit.[12] An interventionist approach would intersect nicely with innovative measures such as the engine transmission duty-remission plan that Simon Reisman and his colleagues had developed (see Chapter 1). With Reisman's team still in place, and eager to further develop its export-incentive concept, the Liberals took action.

When the dust stirred up by the budget debacle had finally settled, the Liberals moved on setting up the new Industry Department, which was to be the base for Reisman's interdepartmental automotive group. In the House of Commons on 27 June, Drury explained the rationale for the additional department, which he would run in addition to the Department of Defence Production. While Canada's prosperity had traditionally depended on its abundant natural resources, the government now had to commit itself to improving opportunities for the manufacturing sector, especially since the structural and technological requirements of secondary industry were changing so rapidly. The new department would gather information from various sources and promote the growth of manufacturing industries, in particular through departmental programs to help them cope with the changing conditions in both the domestic and export markets. The Industry Department would work closely with the departments of Defence Production and Trade and Commerce. Opposition members were somewhat sceptical as to the need for an entirely new department, but there was little criticism concerning this initiative.[13]

One main goal of the new department would be to promote possibilities for more manufacturing in Canada. This would require 'the closest working relationship between government and industry' possible.[14] Along with a deputy minister (Simon Reisman), the department would have two assistant deputies, each responsible for a number of sectors of the industrial economy, among them aircraft, shipbuilding, machinery, and the mechanical transport branch – which would devote itself to the automotive industry.[15] Although they had been interrupted by the election and further delayed in their work by the creation of a new department, by July 1963 the Canadian civil servants responsible for auto policy had been settled into their new home.

In planning strategy for the automotive sector, the Liberal government's first step was to gauge the feelings of the automakers, whose support – or resistance – would be pivotal for the success of any new measures to help the industry and redress the automotive deficit. The automakers had been relatively supportive of the automatic transmission duty-remission scheme. But the Liberals had plans far more ambitious than the Conservatives' pilot project. These could engender serious reservations, particularly from the Canadian Big Three. Having been briefed by Reisman, Drury and Gordon met with the major automobile manufacturers in May 1963, and spoke plainly about the need for cooperation in solving the auto industry's and Canada's balance-of-payments problems. Drury told them that the government aimed to lower the automotive deficit by $200 million by the next model year, starting in July 1964, and warned that without the cooperation of the Canadian subsidiaries, the alternative would be a much greater degree of government interference in the industry. He recommended that the auto companies begin considering ways to help Ottawa lower its trade deficit, because the government was determined to improve its automotive balance of payments, with or without their cooperation.[16]

In response to this ultimatum, the major manufacturers directed their industry association, the Motor Vehicle Manufacturers Association (MVMA), to formulate a plan that would meet the government's expectations. The MVMA made it clear that it understood the necessity for bringing the auto deficit into balance. But, it argued, there were few products that automakers or their affiliates could make in Canada economically. Instead, the companies could individually try to increase Canadian content and exports. The MVMA envisioned a plan that would allow manufacturers to export *any* product for credits to offset duties, and this would spur exports, it claimed. Furthermore, the companies proposed that all machinery and other means of production be allowed into Canada duty-free and that these purchases be written off for tax purposes.[17] Government officials went to work analysing the automakers' suggestions.

The government's senior civil servants took stock of the relationship between the automotive sector and the balance-of-payments situation.

Table 2.1 Canada's trade with the United States, automotive parts, 1960–1964
(Can$ millions)

Year	Exports	Imports	Total	Balance
1960	4	407	411	−403
1961	8	398	406	−389
1962	16	519	535	−503
1963	40	555	595	−515
1964	105	723	828	−618

Source: *DesRosiers Automotive Yearbook 2000* (Richmond Hill, 2000), 190, and
Statistics Canada, cat. nos. 65-202 and 65-203, and Statistical Review of the Canadian
Automotive Industry (Ottawa, 1990).

The transmission/engine export incentive program was certainly having a positive impact on Canada's trade balance; however, results were
uneven. Automobile production in Canada was at an all-time high. To
date, GM and Ford had not yet taken full advantage of the plan, while
Chrysler and American Motors were exporting more vehicles than
before in order to gain credits against their transmission and engine
imports.[18] Canadian auto exports to the United States were increasing,
although imports from the United States continued to be very high and
reached half a billion dollars for 1963 (see Table 2.1). The auto group in
the civil service was determined to reduce that figure by weaning the
Canadian auto industry off its unhealthy structural dependence on
expensive automotive imports from the United States.

As part of their consultations with the industry, government officials
met with Chrysler representatives in July regarding the location of a
new stamping plant that the company was considering. Stamping is the
process of pressing steel into the vehicle's basic body parts, and it is a
significant (and expensive) part of the automobile production process.
A stamping plant, even one operated by Chrysler, the smallest of the
Canadian Big Three, would go a considerable way in reducing the $200
million in stampings imported annually from the United States. It was
obvious that Chrysler's U.S. officials and their Canadian counterparts
(virtually all of whom lived in Detroit and commuted to Windsor every
day) were reluctant to locate the new plant in Canada. Chrysler Canada
representatives claimed that they had been doing their best to persuade
the parent company of the necessity to address the issue of Chrysler's
enormous volume of imports to Canada and reported that the labour
difficulties in Windsor were cited as the reason for the company's

unwillingness to build a plant in Canada. Reisman was not convinced. He believed that American Chrysler officials remained ignorant about Canada and the scope of its problems in the automotive sector, and Gordon's and Drury's warnings that something had to be done about Canada's $400 million deficit in automotive products – or else – had made no impression on them whatsoever. The July meetings left government officials convinced that, while the Canadian subordinates of the Big Three might espouse a willingness to solve the industry's problems, and that they might indeed make some efforts to redress Canada's trade deficit, their Detroit bosses were unwilling to move beyond the status quo. The auto parts deficit would shrink only if the Canadian subsidiaries were provided some obvious incentives to increase the level of their exports, incentives that would gain the attention of their parent companies. Failing that, the automakers might be aroused by the implementation of trade measures far more stringent than those already in place. Either way, a more radical approach was needed.[19]

After the Chrysler meeting, Drury informed the MVMA that its plan was unacceptable, explaining that it would only perpetuate the classic Canadian problem. Allowing companies to export any product for credits would open the door to manufacturers to claim these credits by exporting easily procurable raw materials such as wood or iron ore to their parent companies. Imports of labour-intensive manufactured goods from the United States would then actually increase. Instead of solving the problems in the auto industry, the MVMA's plan would exacerbated them. Because of the urgency of the situation, Drury told the automakers, Ottawa was giving priority to the preparation of alternative plans. It would be willing to consider further suggestions from the association, but it was now committed to forging ahead with a unilateral plan that included little direct input from the auto companies.[20]

Reaction was swift, and within a week after the government rejected the MVMA's proposed plan, GM Canada president E.H. Walker told news reporters that if Ottawa intended to restrict the import of parts, car prices would go up. He admitted that GM and the other automakers had been in meetings with government officials, but insisted that he was unsure of the direction the government wished to take. Further meetings in late August resulted in little change. The current auto imbalance, Walker told government officials, was 'one of the facts of our economic life.' The major automakers were against any measure that might reduce their imports, while the Canadian government was determined to correct Canada's trade imbalance.[21]

In solving the problems in the auto industry, which had such an enormous impact on the balance of payments, Ottawa's options were limited. Bladen had emphatically recommended that the government adopt a program that would encourage producers to specialize for export (see Chapter 1). But the unwillingness of U.S. automakers to source production in Canada remained a serious obstacle, as was illustrated by the attitudes of Chrysler U.S. officials. Parts makers, too, were very sensitive to any changes in the structure of the industry. Many of them were Canadian-owned companies, and this gave them added political weight. Should a new policy in Ottawa discriminate against these companies or cause them to fail, there was sure to be political fall-out.[22]

By September Industry Department officials, working closely with Finance Department officers, had developed three possible plans. The first proposed the reimposition of duties on all automotive parts, including those designated as a 'class or kind not made in Canada.' This would force automakers to produce them in Canada, thereby increasing the proportion of Canadian content, while lowering imports – and raising the price of automobiles. The second proposal was to merely continue the current transmission/engine remission plan for the immediate future, with little change. The third proposal endorsed the former Industry Committee's conclusions formulated in the period before the 1962 election: Reisman and his colleagues judged that an extension of the transmission/engine remission plan so that it would include all auto parts was the best option.

The new program would maintain current content requirements, but provide incentives for increasing exports levels by remitting duties on one dollar of imports for every additional dollar of exports above the level in the base year 1962–3. Industry Department officials reasoned that, because the program would not penalize companies that did not take advantage of it, the automakers would have no objection to it, although they admitted that GM and Ford would be less enthusiastic towards the proposal than the smaller manufacturers would be. They also believed that most parts makers would agree to such a plan because it did not lower the content requirement, and did provide incentives for U.S. parent companies to place parts orders in Canada. To avoid disruption and allow the industry long lead times to gain the maximum benefits of planning their production, the program would run for no less than three years (ending in 1966) and come into effect with the expiration of the current transmission/engine plan. It was anticipated that the new arrangements would increase production and exports from Canada by between $150 and $250 million per year, representing a considerable proportion of the balance-of-payments shortfall. Furthermore, the new plan would not require renegotiation under the General Agreement on Tariffs and Trade, since no tariff rates were being altered.

But the new program also posed some serious problems. For one, Finance Department officials were sure it would upset the British, who already enjoyed duty-free access to the Canadian market and so would lose their competitive advantage. For another, more worrisome problem, as R.B. Bryce of Finance admitted to Gordon, the United States 'would obviously not like the proposed plan.' Under U.S. trade law, countervailing duties could be slapped on Canadian imports should it be found that the new Canadian plan amounted to a 'subsidy' or 'bounty,' as defined under U.S. rules.[23] Such a finding could effectively block all Canadian auto exports to the United States and interrupt the annual $500 million cross-border trade in auto products. While unsure whether the United States would actually go to such lengths, Bryce noted that the Americans had not yet said that the engine/transmission duty-remission scheme contravened U.S. law. Nonetheless, Bryce cautioned that the safest course would be to consult with U.S. authorities before implementing the new program.

The reasoning behind the plan was simple. In the American-dominated Canadian auto industry, imports from the United States would be duty-free, but only if Canadian production levels increased dramatically. If U.S. manufacturers purchased large quantities of auto parts from Canadian sources (whether independent companies or their own affiliates), their Canadian subsidiaries could import the parts they were already bringing into the country duty-free, even those parts that were previously dutiable. Thus, if Detroit-based Ford purchased an *additional* $2 million in parts from Canadian Spring Company, say, Ford's Canadian subsidiary could import $2 million in parts from the United States *duty-free*, and this would include parts on which duties had been applied until then. Trade across the border would increase in both directions, hopefully narrowing Canada's enormous import-export gap. The program would also create specialization and longer production runs for Canadian manufacturers and parts producers, as recommended in the Bladen Report. Therefore, although the federal government might lose the tariff revenues on imported vehicles and parts, the national economy would gain the benefits of increased production and higher employment levels.

The plan facilitated the rationalization of the Canadian auto sector into the larger North American auto industry. Although patently continental in structure, the solution was not come out of any particular ideological stance. The auto experts in Ottawa were not attempting to foist some particular type of free trade or protectionism on the industry. They were simply suggesting an ingenious form of tariff manipulation that would help solve Canada's difficult balance-of-payments position and also help its poorly structured automotive industry. This was a pragmatic and practical approach to the very real problems facing the Canadian auto industry and the Canadian government. In designing a plan that turned the tariff protection of the National Policy on its head, Reisman's auto team showed a willingness to move beyond the straitjacket of long-standing policies. Notwithstanding Walter Gordon's protectionist bent, the plan also meshed well with the Liberal party's ingrained predilection towards continentalism. While cabinet had not yet considered the scheme, the expanded remission plan was seen as the best and most likely solution.[24]

What Washington's opinion of the new Canadian plan would be was less obvious. News of the proposed plan might reignite the difficulties experienced during Diefenbaker's rocky relationship with charismatic U.S. President John F. Kennedy.[25] Relations had improved with Diefenbaker's ouster, but still, it was not clear how the Americans would react to a plan that unilaterally encouraged exports to the United States and that could be labelled an export subsidization scheme. By the time Pearson became prime minister, he had known Kennedy for years, and the two men were far better personally and politically suited to each other than were Diefenbaker and Kennedy. Observers felt that relations were sure to improve. In May 1963, the newly elected prime minister visited Kennedy at his compound in Massachusetts.

At the time of this meeting, Ottawa's auto policy was barely an issue in Canada–U.S. relations.[26] The new Canadian government had taken steps to reassure the administration in Washington that its auto initiatives would not complicate economic relations between the two countries. In June Drury had personally paid a visit to the U.S. embassy in Ottawa to discuss the new Department of Industry. He told Griffith Johnson, the State Department's assistant secretary for economic affairs, that the Canadian government was merely trying to streamline industrial activities and that he anticipated that no radical measures would emanate from the new department; if anything, said Drury, it would be looking for ways to specialize productivity, in the hopes that these might lead to free cross-border trade in certain sectors.[27]

Then things began to sour. In June Gordon had to retreat from his protectionist foreign investment measures which were clearly upsetting the Kennedy administration.[28] The tax measures were rescinded, but not before significant damage had been done to the relationship between Ottawa and Washington. Differences were exarcerbated further when in July President Kennedy announced that an interest equalization tax (IET) would be imposed on all foreign borrowing in the United States to help stabilize the U.S. dollar and America's trade balance, which had come under pressure because of the tremendous outflow of American funds. Foreign shares were taxed at 15 per cent and bonds at from between 2.75 and 15 per cent, depending on their maturity. Already heavily dependent on U.S. investment to redress its trade deficit, the Canadian economy went into free-fall after Kennedy's announcement. The Canadian dollar dropped precipitously, and the value of shares listed on the Toronto Stock Exchange plunged.[29]

Desperate to avoid an economic meltdown, Canadian officials flew to Washington right away to plead for an exemption. Bank of Canada Governor Louis Rasminsky was able to convince American officials that, if anything, Canada actually supported the U.S. balance of payments because it imported so many American goods and services, far in excess of its capital borrowings. On 22 July, four days after the IET was made public, Canada was granted an exemption from the U.S. measures, and eventually, this exemption was made permanent.[30] But Gordon's tense discussions with Treasury Secretary Douglas Dillon in August during his visit to Washington indicated that Canada–U.S. relations were much cooler than many observers had imagined.[31]

American objections to the proposed expansion of the transmission/ engine remission program only added to these woes. U.S. officials were kept well informed of Canada's plans for its automotive industry. Both Ford and GM stayed in close contact with the administration and kept the State Department aware of progress with the Canadian plans, which they learned about through their subsidiaries. GM chairman Frederic Donner met with Dillon and State Department officials in September to discuss balance-of-payments issues, including the proposed Canadian auto program.[32] In response to the automakers' warnings, State developed a position paper expressing concern about the direction that the

Canadian plan seemed to be taking and indicated that such a scheme might be vulnerable under American countervailing duty trade law.[33]

Alerted to the possibility that Ottawa was about to expand the duty-remission plan, U.S. officials demanded that the auto industry be included on the agenda of the upcoming meeting of the Joint Canada–United States Committee on Trade and Economic Affairs, scheduled for that September.[34] Held approximately once a year since the mid-1950s, these meetings brought together ministers and secretaries from each country for discussions of issues and problems that arose from the bilateral relationship.[35] The 1963 meeting was the eighth such summit, and in accordance with the custom that the venue alternate between the capitals, it was held in Washington.

The new Canadian automotive policy immediately became a flashpoint of the discussions. Led by Gordon and Drury, the Canadians would not divulge the extent of their plans and admitted only that the new program would most likely be an extension of the current transmission/engine remission regime. When Commerce Secretary Luther Hodges asked Drury whether the plan constituted a subsidy, Drury was evasive. Instead, Drury emphasized that the plan would lead to rationalization of the North American auto industry and, perhaps, eventually to freer trade between the two countries. Unaffected by obviously negative American reaction concerning the direction that Canadian industrial policy would apparently be taking, Drury and Gordon refused to budge on the automotive measures.[36]

The Americans were deeply disappointed by the Canadians' position, as they made obvious during the private meetings and in public afterwards. Undersecretary of State George Ball and Hodges were both unhappy with the Canadian proposal. While conceding that U.S. reaction to the Canadian automotive duty measures had been slow in developing, Ball left no doubt that the administration now felt 'outrage and alarm' that such a strategy would be implemented by Canada. These export incentives, they contended, artificially manipulated markets, discriminated against U.S. producers, and might be copied by other nations. Hodges told the press that the Canadian plan was unacceptable and that Washington would be considering countermeasures. The commerce secretary also wondered about whether the Canadian plan might not contravene international trade rules under the GATT. Editorial writers south of the border sided with Hodges and screamed that the rumoured plan smacked of protectionism.[37]

To quell American criticism, Drury flew to Washington again in

October to further explain his government's proposed auto policies. In consultations with the relevant secretaries prior to the meeting, President Kennedy's National Security Advisor McGeorge Bundy and Secretary Ball hammered out the U.S. position. For now, they took the line that U.S. trade laws forced them to immediately impose countervailing duties and that government lawyers had indicated that the Canadian plan could be subject to such laws. This would give the administration maximum leeway in dealing with the Canadian plan. In discussions with Ball and Hodges, Drury refuted the Americans' claims that the plan was an artificial manipulation of the automotive industry, could hurt the U.S. balance-of-payments position, or shift U.S. production to Canada. He argued that the plan was really a tariff-removing device and, 'if carried far enough, would result in free trade,' especially if the expected Kennedy Round of tariff reductions at the GATT were successful. Moreover, Drury let it be known that the Canadian subsidiaries were in favour of any plan that did not require raising Canadian content or other restrictive measures. Unbowed by their criticisms, Drury told the Americans that Ottawa would officially announce at the end of October, and it would go into operation after 1 November.[38]

With such clear evidence that their protests could not persuade the Canadians to consider alternatives to their program, American officials pondered their options. They recognized that the proposed plan was the least objectionable of the alternatives to both administration and the automotive companies since it did not impose higher content requirements or tariffs. But early legal opinions from the Treasury Department indicated that should the plan be put before U.S. trade law, a subsidy would be found, requiring the imposition of countervailing duties.[39] When State Department officials met with representatives of American Ford, Assistant Secretary Griffith Johnson admitted to them that although the United States would protest the scheme, 'Canada would not listen.' At a press conference Secretary Hodges suggested that since the Canadians were determined to proceed with it, the U.S. auto industry should 'get up on its hind legs' and fight the plan. U.S. automakers, however, feared that Ottawa would impose even more restrictive measures on them than the remission plan. They had already felt the sting of such measures in a number of other ncountries in which they operated and hoped that Canada was not headed along a similar path.[40]

American concerns about the new program and the Canadian government's unilateral approach were justified. When the U.S. embassy in Ottawa reported that Gordon had made a speech in Hamilton stating his government's determination to go ahead with the auto plan, and that similar programs might be tried in other sectors of the economy, Washington officials went to work drafting an official protest. The resulting memorandum elaborated the difficulties that the U.S. government had with the current duty-remission scheme and the expected expansion of that program. It emphasized the long tradition of cooperation between the two countries and the hope that some efforts were being made to 'explore this problem, particularly in the context of alternative solutions.' This was not the time, it warned, for aggressive new measures that might provoke a heavy American response.[41]

The Canadians, however, were not to be denied. By the time of Gordon's Hamilton speech, in late October 1963, the Pearson government had already decided to go ahead with the expanded remission plan. In cabinet, there was little debate over the issue. The expanded duty-remission plan was by then a poorly kept secret. Throughout October news reports from the United States and well-rehearsed friendly questions from Liberal party members had prepared the House of Commons for the announcement of the duty-remission plan. Drury finally introduced the program on 25 October 1963, authorizing the remission of duties on one dollar of imports for every extra dollar of parts exports above their 1962–3 base amounts. The program would come into effect on 1 November, at the conclusion of the current remission program. If an automotive company such as GM exported or purchased parts for export (from a Canadian company or from one of its own Canadian subsidiaries) in an amount over and above that in the base year, GM could import products corresponding to the value of the additional amounts duty-free. The objectives of the plan were threefold: (1) to increase production and employment, (2) to improve Canada's balance of payments, and (3) to give parts producers and auto manufacturers incentives to achieve longer production runs and a greater degree of specialization.

Reaction from the other parties in the House of Commons was muted. The Conservatives could only criticize the Liberals for delaying implementation of the plan, preferring to take credit for the idea of the program itself. George Nowlan, who had introduced the transmission/engine plan in the previous government, remarked that he was very glad to see that Drury and the Liberals were 'following the path and the program' that the Conservatives had established. The other political parties were generally supportive of the initiative. Créditiste leader Réal Caouette even congratulated the government.[42]

Reaction outside of the Commons was favourable as well. Among the Canadian Big Three, support for the plan was diplomatically and carefully positive. GM Canada's Walker announced that his company would continue its efforts to increase exports and decrease imports by whatever practical means. Karl Scott, president of Ford of Canada, said his company would give all possible assistance to help Ottawa achieve its aims. Privately, Scott admitted to U.S. consulate officials in Toronto that he was 'rather pleased' with the plan, and that GM felt 'substantially' the same way.[43] Chrysler, Studebaker, and AMC officials reserved judgment until further study. George Burt, director of the Canadian UAW announced that his union was in favour of the new program, as did D.S. Wood for the APMA.[44] Editorial writers and columnists also found the plan useful, and even called for the idea to be applied to other industries.[45]

Predictably, American reaction to the announcement of the new program was far less positive. Although Canadian officials had explained to U.S. embassy staff in Ottawa that their government had considered and rejected far more restrictive schemes, the Americans were unimpressed. Such Canadian unilateralism towards what was so obviously a continental problem challenged the very basis of Canada–U.S. cooperation on economic issues, they said. Clearly, the program required some sort of official response from Washington. Assistant Secretary of Commerce Richard Holten declared that the plan coloured the American position on other trade matters with Canada; 'We will have to temper our sympathy because in a sense we are being kicked in the shins.'[46] In the American press, reaction was similar. Ottawa's new program was portrayed more as an attempt to steal U.S. production than an effort to rationalize the industry.[47]

In the wake of the announcement, relevant U.S. departments and agencies assessed the impact of the program. Most analysis centred on whether the plan was a subsidy under U.S. trade law, thereby requiring the immediate imposition of countervailing duties by the Treasury Department. The Treasury and State departments, along with the recently created office of the U.S. Trade Representative (USTR), headed by former Secretary of State Christian Herter, all concluded that the plan was indeed a form of subsidy and required some response. However, caution was also stressed. All departments felt that hasty retaliation might only lead to more difficulties. As one USTR official argued, because of the close economic and political ties to Canada it seemed unwise 'to precipitate a crisis by retaliating in some way on the matter.'

The U.S. government was concerned that retaliation could lead to Canadian countermeasures that might further damage the American surplus with Canada or result in restrictive measures aimed at U.S. companies operating in Canada. The political fallout might be disastrous, leading to 'a sharp deteriorating in political relations between the two Governments and a rise in anti-American sentiment in Canada.'[48]

For now, the administration would move slowly on the plan and try to engage the Canadians in discussions before making any hasty decisions on retaliation. If no petition for action against the Canadian plan was brought by a private company, Washington had some discretion in the timing of the imposition of countervailing duties. There had been a few complaints, but no company had as yet officially petitioned the Treasury Department for action against the Canadian program.[49] There was no certainty, however, that an American company claiming that it had been adversely affected by the Canadian remission plan would not demand that the administration retaliate, forcing Washington to impose countervailing duties. While the administration wished to avoid direct confrontation on the issue, it was clear that the unilateral Canadian action in the automotive sector could lead to conflict.

With tensions over the program rising on both sides of the border, the strained diplomatic parlance continued. In early November, Ottawa responded to the U.S. memorandum of protest against the duty-remission program. The response was firm in tone and showed that the Canadian government was unwilling to alter or end its plan. While Ottawa did not respond directly to the suggestion that the two sides continue further talks on resolving the problem, Canadian embassy officials in Washington indicated that they were willing to engage in further discussions. A few days later, Undersecretary of State George Ball telephoned Finance Minister Gordon to tell him that the Treasury Department had received a rash of complaints from U.S. components manufacturers, all of them asking that Washington take action on the Canadian plan. The complaints could turn into a demand for countervailing duties. With that in mind, Ball suggested that the two countries have representatives at the official level discuss the matter. Gordon agreed and made arrangements to send Canadian officials to Washington within the week. These discussions settled little, however.[50]

The shocking assassination of President Kennedy a few weeks later delayed matters only temporarily. Kennedy's successor, Vice-President Lyndon B. Johnson, chose to keep the Kennedy team in the administration largely intact. Johnson had had a long and distinguished career in

Congress before becoming Kennedy's running mate in the 1960 election. Although less familiar with Canadian issues than Kennedy, he was a keen student of politics and understood the importance of Canada–U.S. relations for his government. Johnson also was aware of the immense size of the Canada–U.S. auto trade and sensitive to the needs of what was undeniably America's most important, most visible, and most successful industry. Prime Minister Pearson was soon invited to Washington to get to know the new president and to discuss a number of cross-border issues, including the Canadian automotive trade programs.[51]

In preparation for Pearson's January 1964 visit to Washington, Johnson was briefed on the Canadian auto problems. Johnson's advisers suggested that he follow Kennedy's strategy on the auto issue. Instead of threatening the immediate imposition of countervailing duties in response to the scheme, and exacerbating an already difficult situation, Johnson took a more conciliatory tack with Pearson. He asked the prime minister to consider creating a joint committee to examine the Canadian program and consider possible alternatives to it, including new approaches to the operation of the entire North American automotive industry. But Johnson also struck a cautious note and voiced his concern about the December announcement by Studebaker that it would be closing down all auto assembly operations in Indiana but boosting production at its Hamilton, Ontario, plant. The president wondered whether the announcement was a direct response to the Canadian program and whether Studebaker's plan would result in a flood of cheaper Canadian cars into the American market. The Studebaker announcement had sparked congressional concerns which the president was eager to assuage. Pearson assured Johnson that the decision taken by Studebaker had nothing to do with his government's new program. As for the discussions on alternatives, Pearson was interested in talks but would not commit himself to any idea that might jeopardize the Drury plan. The meeting showed that there might be a sliver of hope for further talks on the issue, but neither man had forfeited his position.[52]

Although Pearson had done his best to convince Johnson that the new program was relatively innocuous, by spring 1964, the remission program was clearly having an effect on the auto industries in both countries and on cross-border trade. In February Reisman reported that the major manufacturers had begun to take advantage of the plan. Although GM and Ford had not yet made any major purchases, Chrysler and American Motors were participating actively in the scheme. Chrysler had purchased Walker Metal Products in Windsor and was planning to export enough engines to the United States within the year 1964 to gain free entry for all of its imported parts. American Motors was increasing the export of engine block castings produced at its foundry in Sarnia.[53] When trade numbers were tabulated in late March, it was obvious that the remission scheme was working. Even though imports from the United States had jumped considerably since 1962, exports had also improved markedly. Sales of Canadian vehicles and parts to the United States had leapt from less than $10 million in 1962 to nearly $30 million in 1963, and 1964 promised to be even better.[54]

The booming Canadian auto industry was making headlines, which threatened to cause the remission program problems. In February 1964 the *Globe and Mail* reported that Canadian exports to the United States had risen 'embarrassingly.'[55] A month later, the *Financial Post* stated that the program was 'ticking' and that the Canadian auto industry was poised to take off. The newspaper listed a host of companies that were benefiting from the plan, and noted that 'official Washington' had 'started to yell' about it.[56] Then in May industry newspaper *Ward's Automotive* reported that shipments of $13 million to the United States in the first quarter of 1964 were triple those of the previous year and six times those of 1962. With such a dramatic increase in Canadian exports, Industry Department officials cautioned Drury that it was 'advisable that no public relationship should be acknowledged between the specific plant construction plans announced recently by the automotive companies and the export incentive program,' because of the effect such an announcement might have on U.S. sensitivities and the ongoing threat of countervailing duties.[57]

In the United States. increasing Canadian imports had indeed caught the attention of American civil servants. David Baker, counsel for the Senate Labor Committee, bitterly complained to the Canadian desk officer in the State Department that he understood that Chrysler planned to move its entire foundry operation to Windsor, the exact type of U.S. investment that Canadians supposedly deplored, since it represented further 'foreign domination.'[58] The Commerce Department was also becoming increasingly sensitive to the northward shift in production. In March, Commerce officials asked the major auto manufacturers to meet with them in Washington to obtain responses to a questionnaire developed by the Automotive Service Industries Association (ASIA), a lobby group representing non–Big Three parts makers. These officials believed that an 'appreciable increase in Canadian exports was in process,' and they had aligned themselves with ASIA and the American parts industry to fight the plan. If answers to the questionnaire pointed to further moves by the major manufacturers to source parts in Canada, ASIA planned to submit the questionnaire to the Treasury Department in an effort to demonstrate injury and to help expedite the investigation of what they termed 'pending' countervailing duties.[59]

The shift in production was also noticed by American politicians. When Indiana Democratic Senator Vance Hartke learned that 700 workers at the Borg-Warner parts plant in Muncie, Indiana, were to be laid off, he demanded that Washington target the Canadian auto program. In mid-March, Hartke sent a scathing letter to President Johnson on behalf of the unemployed workers and began to agitate in Congress over the issue.[60] Democratic Senator Stuart Symington attacked the plan and presented evidence that claimed auto workers were being hurt by the Canadian program in all regions of the United States, including his own state of Missouri. When on 26 March the *Wall Street Journal* carried a front-page story on the Canadian program and its impact, State Department officials feared that even more difficulties would emanate from Capitol Hill. Although they considered the article 'wildly over-alarmist' and inaccurate, they also felt the need to warn Secretary Dean Rusk of the problems that the story might create for the executive.[61]

The real difficulties for the administration appeared in early April, in the form of a 'most interesting communication' addressed to the Treasury Department from the Modine Manufacturing Company of Racine, Wisconsin. Specializing in automotive radiators and commercial heating and air conditioning, Modine was one of the largest independent parts manufacturers in the United States, with annual sales of U.S. $35 million and 2,000 employees at plants in Wisconsin and Virginia.[62] According to Commerce officials, this was the first indication that a company 'appeared to be heading towards legal action' over the remission plan. Modine retained Washington-based Alfred McCauley, a lawyer who had previously served on the Tariff Commission and the House Ways and Means Committee. In its letter, Modine claimed that it had lost $9 million in sales of radiators to American Motors, Ford, and International Harvester. Modine blamed the Canadian plan, arguing that the company's orders were now being filled by Canadian parts makers and Big Three–owned companies north of the border. The seriousness of Modine's complaint was underlined by the company's notice that it was preparing a brief for the Treasury Department requesting that countervailing duties be invoked.

Under section 303 of the 1930 U.S. Tariff Act, the secretary of the treasury was obliged to impose countervailing duties whenever a foreign entity provided any subsidies, 'directly or indirectly, [to] the manufacture, production or export of a product imported into the USA.' Since passage of the act, this provision had been used only sparingly, owing to the severity of the response. Duties had been slapped on Canadian cheese in the early 1950s, and other countries had been targeted since then. Although the Tariff Act intimated that the U.S. government must immediately impose countervailing duties if a petition were brought, the administration did have some leeway before taking any action. The treasury secretary could call for arguments for and against countervailing duties and determine the timing and scope of the investigation. As always, political pressure could also influence the course and tempo of any investigation.[63]

On 15 April the Modine petition was formally submitted to the commissioner of customs in the Department of the Treasury. It was brutal in its assessment of the impact of the remission plan: 'Hundreds of companies, mostly small businesses, and thousands of workers stand to be severely hurt unless the Canadian Scheme is checked. The Canadian raid on the U.S. market, now going on in ever-increasing intensity, is the single most important threat that now faces the continued existence of these companies and the welfare of their employees.' Modine claimed that it was being severely hurt by the new plan, and that three of the company's plants could close, with a loss of over 1,000 employees. Modine demanded that countervailing duties be applied to Canadian imports as a response to the losses it had incurred. State Department officials confided to the Canadian embassy in Washington that the petition was a 'fairly serious move' and that more than Modine was behind it. In early April ASIA had launched a very public campaign against the Canadian program on Capitol Hill. The duty remission plan now faced a frontal attack in the United States.[64]

Reaction to the Modine petition was swift. The pro-ASIA *New York Journal of Commerce* heralded the move as a 'bold and long-awaited challenge' to the Canadian program. The journal called the remission program an export subsidy and announced that UAW locals in Indiana and Michigan were mobilizing to fight the plan in response to reports that the Big Three were considering buying even more products from Canadian sources.[65] In Congress, Senator Symington demanded that the Treasury Department impose countervailing duties on Canadian goods in retaliation for the Canadian 'tariff trick.' Symington claimed that 60,000 American jobs would be lost because of the remission plan and threatened to request an open hearing of the Senate Foreign Relations Committee if the administration did nothing.[66]

In Washington and Ottawa both sides realized the seriousness of the Modine petition. If countervailing duties were imposed on Canadian imports to the United States, the results could be devastating for Canadian industry and lead to further reprisals. A cross-border trade war seemed a distinct possibility. New talks would give Americans the chance to pursue the idea that they had been considering since the remission plan was first announced: continental free trade in autos and parts and a rationalization of the North American auto industry. Automotive free trade would not only mesh with the larger U.S. goals when it came to Canada, but it would be a handy solution that would benefit producers and consumers in both Canada and the United States. The State Department's position, usually the most influential in matters dealing with Canada, was to avoid any application of countervailing duties. The U.S. embassy in Ottawa also suggested tariff reduction in the auto sector and, at the very least, a joint committee to study the North American auto industry.[67]

The Treasury Department, however, felt an obligation to pursue the Modine application. Secretary Dillon saw the issue as a legal question as opposed to a political one. The Tariff Act was clear. If there was the question of a bounty or grant on an item that unduly helped foreign imports and hurt American producers, the U.S. Customs Bureau had to launch an investigation, and were it to find that there was indeed a bounty or grant, the bureau was to impose countervailing duties of a like nature on the imports. As such, Dillon decided to issue a *Federal Register* announcement that the U.S. Customs Bureau would accept arguments from interested parties regarding the Modine petition for thirty days before coming to a decision. The implication was that the investigation would go ahead, introducing time constraints on any negotiations.[68] The Department of Commerce also agitated for countervailing duties.[69]

In response, William Brubeck, who covered Canadian issues at the White House, suggested to President Johnson that, during the upcoming joint cabinet meetings in Ottawa, the U.S. side should make it clear that there was serious pressure on Washington to apply countervailing measures. The U.S. position was that the two sides should create a joint task force to look at ways to immediately alleviate the problems and explore a long-term plan to rationalize the auto industry on a continent-wide basis. While Johnson agreed that countervailing duties should be mentioned to the Canadians during the meetings, he was emphatic in his instructions to the secretaries of State, Treasury, and Commerce that he wanted a solution that did not include countervailing duties. Instead of a potential trade war, the administration sought to 'develop a plan for rationalization (that is, free trade) in the North American auto industry.'[70] Johnson notified the secretaries of his decision on 28 April, the day before the two sides met in Ottawa: 'I think it is essential that we do everything possible to find an agreed solution that does not require countervailing duties.'[71] For the time being, the White House had quelled the interagency wrangling over the issue.

In Ottawa senior civil servants began preparing their ministers for the inevitable American pressure on the auto issue. By late April the Canadian strategy was almost in place. With Drury in the lead and Gordon playing the supporting role, the Canadians would argue that the remission plan was in no way a bounty or grant under U.S. law, that it was of 'far too fundamental importance to be set aside or frustrated by United States Government action,' and that there would be serious implications for Canada–U.S. relations if the plan was frustrated by U.S. action. Should the Americans suggest studying the possibility of some sort of continent-wide rationalization of the auto industry, the Canadians felt that they had little option but to agree. But they were to be firm in conveying that this would in no way sway the Canadian government from the current scheme and that any plan that achieved anything less than the remission program would be unacceptable.[72]

As part of his last-minute preparations, Gordon asked Reisman to formulate a response should the U.S. side suggest outright free trade in the auto industry between Canada and the United States. Reisman considered it highly unlikely that the United States would make such a proposal, given the inequities between the two industries and the domination of the Canadian sector by the U.S. makers: 'Such a proposition is so obviously unbalanced in favour of the U.S. that we doubt whether the U.S. side would seriously put up a proposition as crude and obvious as this.' The only reason that the Americans would ever suggest such a plan, speculated Reisman, was to threaten Canada on lumber in retaliation for its automobile program. He suggested that Gordon should avoid reacting quickly and sharply and 'at least appear to be treating their proposition on its merits.' As the Canadian ministers headed to the meeting, the notion of free trade – the centrepiece of the U.S. proposal on the 'auto problem' – was being dismissed by Canadian policymakers as too 'crude and obvious' to be taken seriously. Instead, cabinet had decided that the Canadian representatives at the meeting should stick to the remission program, no matter what suggestions or threats U.S. representatives might make.[73]

The wide gulf between Canadian and U.S. cabinet members became apparent as soon as the auto issue was raised by the U.S. side. Speaking for the administration, Dillon stated that, while he was sympathetic to the Canadian aims of the auto program, the United States had serious reservations about it. His government's legal counsel had concluded that the remission plan constituted a subsidy, and that the best solution was for the Canadians to end it. Failing that, the two sides could work towards some sort of rationalization of the industry on a continent-wide basis. But, Dillon admonished, the two sides had little time to come to any agreement before a decision to impose countervailing duties would surely be rendered.[74] Commerce Secretary Luther Hodges continued the attack. Until now, said Hodges, the United States had been generous to a fault in its dealings with Canada, but it could no longer afford to be so generous. He told the Canadians that Congress was becoming impatient with the scheme and that he was bound under the law to take action. Hodges also told them that, ideally, he would like to see a free trade plan worked out, which was something the auto producers and parts makers were in favour of.[75] Rusk summed up the U.S. position in his usually succinct manner: The governments needed to find a solution, he argued, before they found themselves in a destructive 'eyeball-to-eyeball confrontation.'

But the Canadians were not moved. Initially, Drury expressed delight that all were agreed on the objective of rationalizing the North American auto industry. This was, after all, the main objective of the program, he pointed out. However, the auto industry had for so long been skewed in the Americans' favour that it was only natural that Ottawa had to do something to redress the imbalance. According to Canadian government lawyers, Drury continued, the auto plan was not a subsidy. Moreover, the Canadian public was overwhelmingly in favour of the program. Gordon was emphatic in making the argument that unrestricted free trade in the North American auto industry was not the solution. 'The government,' Gordon stated, 'is committed to the program and would be in serious trouble if it withdrew or seriously watered it down.' Gordon agreed that it might be practical to start some talks to see if, at the last moment, 'a rabbit could be pulled out of the hat,' while stressing that this was not to be taken to mean that Canada was retreating from the program. With no movement on the issue, the Canadians gave their consent to further talks on the problem just before the meeting broke off. The Canadians had played hardball. In Dillon's opinion they very simply 'wouldn't give an inch.' In the belief that no other recourse was available, in May the State Department's general counsel submitted the proposed announcement of countervailing duties to both the State and Treasury departments and then awaited clearance from the White House.[76]

Ottawa received notification that the forthcoming *Federal Register* would contain announcement of the legal investigation. A flurry of phone calls to the American capital ensued. Martin protested to Ball that the notice went well beyond the situation and would cause serious trouble for the government, while Gordon loudly took up the challenge with Dillon. Like Martin, Gordon was upset at both the wording and the timing of the release. Dillon reminded Gordon that the Treasury Department had been 'holding up, for four or five months' the reference to the Customs Bureau and could delay no longer. If the Canadians wished to discuss the issue further, as the investigation proceeded, the Americans were willing to talk.[77]

Washington triggered the Customs investigation in order to force Ottawa back to the table, and the ploy was working. Gordon now understood that the Canadian hard line may have backfired and that the Americans were taking the initiative. He grudgingly admitted that the U.S. administration 'concluded that we would not amend our automobile policy unless we were forced to do so. Having proceeded with this display of strength, they probably feel they have us at a disadvantage. And this is true.' The minister of finance knew that Canada had to act quickly to salvage its position. He immediately asked senior Ottawa officials to prepare a full memorandum detailing all of the courses open to the Canadians.[78]

An ad hoc committee chaired by Reisman developed a position paper which painted a dismal picture of the situation and evaluated four possible courses of action. First, the Canadian government could maintain the remission program and fight the Modine petition. The committee did not consider this to be a practical option, as the threat of countervailing duties would still hang over the program even if there was a decision against Modine. Second, Ottawa could negotiate with the United States on the basis of the proposals put forth by Hodges at the joint cabinet meeting. However, Canada might get little in return, other than assurances that countervailing duties would not be initiated.

Third, the government could develop a substitute program based on capturing a larger share of the Canadian market for Canadian producers. This would be a difficult path to take, because any such move required higher tariffs or quantitative controls, most certainly leading to higher costs for consumers. Taking this direction was further constrained by Canada's commitments under GATT and would require renegotiation of tariff rates and compensation for the United States. The potential for retaliation would be enormous. Canadianization could be achieved, but at a high cost to the consumer and to the Canadian economy as a whole. Fourth, Canada could seek a negotiated settlement based on the concept of rationalization within the North American market. Reisman's committee saw this as 'the only practical course open at the present time.'[79]

Any such settlement, argued the committee, must include certain elements. At the very least, the new agreement would have to satisfy the objectives of the current remission program. Reisman was convinced that there were special institutional factors, such as the overwhelmingly American ownership and control of the auto industry, which made it imperative that the United States guarantee definite minimum production levels of automobiles and parts in Canada. These levels should be based on what the remission scheme would eventually be expected to yield and its projected growth in the near future. Should the Canadian industry not achieve such a minimum production guarantee, Ottawa would be entitled to apply import controls. As part of the agreement, both the United States and Canada would reduce its tariff rates during the Kennedy Round at GATT, while at the same time Canada would redefine its content requirements.[80] Reisman and his colleagues did acknowledge that such an agreement would be difficult to negotiate. There was, it could be said, a certain amount of gall to the Canadian proposal. Canada would be asking the United States to decrease its own output and exports so that Canadians would receive a 'fair share' of the benefits of increased production and employment. As for the Americans' proposal for free trade based solely on tariff reductions, the Canadians considered it a non-starter.

Achieving an agreement along the lines proposed by Reisman's committee did, indeed, prove exceedingly difficult. Negotiations in July and August on proposals for a reordering of the auto industry on a continental basis resulted in an impasse. The U.S. side held strongly to the notion of unrestricted free trade as the only solution to the problems in the industry. The Canadian side remained steadfastly committed to a proposal that, while lowering tariffs, would achieve a 'fair share' of the North American auto industry for Canada. The meeting in August began in an atmosphere described as 'friendly and constructive,' but as soon as discussion turned to the American outline and the Canadian plan it became apparent that the two sides differed fundamentally in their approach to the problem. Lead U.S. negotiator Phillip Trezise, the State Department's deputy assistant for economic affairs, argued that a straight free trade regime would result in a substantial increase in investment in Canada. He told the Canadians that it was impossible for the U.S. government to accept the quantitative commitment that they were proposing, particularly because it required that a percentage of the North American auto industry's production had to be located in Canada. Reisman opened his reply to Trezise by emphatically asserting that the Canadian automotive industry was not being allowed to fulfil its potential. Were Canada to participate in a rationalization process, it would need new investment and plant facilities. The process of rationalization would be irreversible. It was therefore not enough to depend on tariff reduction to spread the benefits of rationalization continent-wide. The changes in Canada resulting from rationalization would be fundamental, while those in the United States would be of relatively little consequence.[81] Tariff removal alone, Reisman told the delegates, was not enough; the United States needed to recognize this. Tariff removal had been utilized in the case of the farm implements industry, with disastrous results for Canada. They 'could not just remove tariffs and let the ball roll where it would,' because although the Canadians 'did not think the ball would roll badly, they could not be sure and could not therefore fail to take precautions.' Such a plan would be 'a colossal gamble for Canada.' Safeguards must be built into any agreement, although Reisman admitted that this would be a difficult drafting problem. Trezise quipped that it was more than just a drafting problem and that the Canadians were suggesting that Washington acquiesce in officially directed investment. This, he said, was unacceptable.

The Canadians were not moved. Simply put, Canada needed to expand its auto production so that it would be more in line with the country's consumption of auto products. If these objectives were not achieved, Canada would be required to take alternative measures. All the United States had to do was to agree to not oppose the Canadian countermeasures. In Reisman's estimation, the U.S. government would not have to intervene in any way: 'Detroit would be more worried about Canada moving in the direction of Australia or Mexico than about Canadian intervention in the industry.' In other words, the United States needed to be aware of the possiblity that Canada could and would impose higher content provisions if the current plan did not work.

The thinly veiled threat regarding Canadian content was supplemented by another comment intended to alert the Americans to how the outcome of the auto negotiations could negatively influence Canada's position during the upcoming Kennedy Round at GATT. Trezise promptly reminded the Canadians that the U.S. auto industry was 'not a wing of the Democratic Party and that if the administration presented an agreement that would be criticized, it would be unfortunate in an election year.' As a parting shot, Trezise suggested that statisticians for both sides should meet, since each had forecast very optimistic figures regarding the growth of the Canadian industry. Reisman was equal to the challenge and to this replied that 'management didn't operate on the basis of statisticians' estimates.' With that, Trezise declared that the two sides were so far apart that there was no point in meeting again any time soon. Reisman agreed. Negotiations had broken down completely.

The dismal outcome of the August discussions was greeted by a sense of foreboding in both capitals. Bryce and Gordon were informed that the two sides had reached a complete impasse.[82] In Washington, State Department Deputy Director of International Trade Julius Katz circulated a 'rather gloomy report' that revealed just how far apart the two sides were.[83] In a telephone conversation with Brubeck on 26 August, Ball admitted that the United States was in 'lousy shape so far as the talks' were concerned.[84] The American effort to create automotive free trade in North America had failed. With the threat posed by the Customs Bureau investigation now under way, time became a primary concern.

Canada's aggressive stance, and its unwillingness to yield to the threat of countervailing duties, can be explained by examining the nature of the negotiations and the weapons that each side had at its disposal. The United States threatened to use a specific and powerful weapon: countervailing duties, which would effectively cause a trade war. Canadian counter-threats were more subtle and existed more in the realm of potential outcomes. The greatest of these was the potential Canadianization of the domestic auto industry in the form of increased Canadian content requirements for the Big Three or, more damaging yet less likely, outright Canadian control of the industry through a crown corporation. Trezise recalled that, in an early Saturday morning phone call from Gordon, during the height of negotiations in the summer of 1964, Gordon 'went on to threaten that Canada would opt for legislating a Canadian "people's car" if we were to impose retaliatory duties on Canadian exports.'[85] A State Department position paper in June 1964 had also concluded that Ottawa was undoubtedly thinking of higher Canadian content requirements as a solution to the industry's problems. With the failure of talks in August, Treasury Department officials were convinced that there was 'little reason to doubt [the] seriousness' of the Canadian threat to boost content requirements.[86] Whether or not this Canadianization was a realistic threat in terms of practical implementation, Washington took it seriously.

The threat of Canadianization was also taken very seriously by the U.S. parent companies. After all, Canada was really not much different from countries such as Mexico, Australia, or Brazil. All of these countries had developed early dependent relationships with the American automotive transnationals, yet by the early 1960s were looking at ways to acquire more of the benefits of the auto industry for themselves. In 1962 the Mexican government launched a 'Mexicanization' drive that threatened the expulsion of the U.S. producers, and their replacement by a state-owned auto company, unless the Americans raised their levels of content produced in Mexico considerably. Only after Washington applied serious pressure were Ford and General Motors allowed to maintain control of their factories in Mexico, at a cost of accepting much higher Mexican content.[87] A 1957 Australian Tariff Board plan called for greater local content; this eventually led to the government-imposed '95 per cent' plan announced in May 1964.[88] In 1956 the Brazilian government banned all car imports and imposed punishing local content restrictions which, in some cases, required manufacturers to use 99 per cent local content in assembling their products.[89] In both the July and August negotiations the Canadians had prominently featured references to the Mexican and Australian examples.

U.S. automakers saw little difference between Canada and these other countries in which they had operations. S.L. Terry, a top Chrysler executive, made this abundantly clear in March 1964 when he compared the 'more moderate' provisions of the Canadian duty-remission scheme with some of the high content requirements in other countries: The Canadian 'long-standing 60% local content requirement for cars of over 20,000 annual production is relatively easy to attain and has been moderate indeed compared to the three year 90% local content program in Argentina and the five year 100% local content program in Brazil.

Both of these latter countries were and still are far less developed industrially than Canada and have far less volume potential; their local content programs have become an accomplished fact.'[90] In offering its support for the 'more moderate' Canadian remission program, Chrysler was hoping to avoid the much harsher alternative of higher content requirements, an alternative other Big Three executives, too, feared was becoming more likely given the uncertainty in the Canadian industry in the first half of 1964. With the aggressive nationalist Walter Gordon at the helm of the team that was shaping Ottawa's auto policy, punishing content measures were not an impossible outcome.

In May Ford representatives in Washington spelled out to State Department officials the estimated cost of increased protection in the Canadian market if the remission plan were thwarted. The numbers were astronomical. If content commitments were raised from 60 to 75 per cent, U.S. companies would have to invest a further $200 to $300 million in Canada, and exports to Canada would decrease by $200 million annually. If content were increased to 90 per cent, which seemed to be a strong possibility from the perspective of the auto companies – given their experience in other countries – American manufacturers would have to invest at least $400 to $600 million in Canada, and their exports to Canada would decrease by $400 million annually. Ford representatives understood that increased content requirements, a not unlikely outcome in the wake of the unsuccessful talks, could cost them as much as $1 billion dollars. GM had also determined that the current course of events could result in higher Canadian content requirements, with damaging consequences for the company.[91]

Another major factor in accounting for Ottawa's unwillingness to back down was that the U.S. government was likely to find itself in difficult circumstances should it not accept Canada's remission plan and the result be a trade war between the two countries. White House officials informed President Johnson that the damage caused by a full-blown trade dispute would be enormous: 'This is a substantial economic issue (could involve several hundred millions) and a hot political issue in Canada. Retaliation back and forth with the Canadians could hurt both sides, political and economically.' More importantly, Canada's apparent willingness to enter into a long, debilitating trade war was enough to give Washington officials pause. As Canadian officials pointed out time and time again, this was clearly the case in the auto dispute. The Pearson government had staked a lot on this industrial policy and would not easily be denied its benefits.[92]

Domestic political concerns played a role, too. The November presidential election was fast approaching, and while Canada normally mattered little in U.S. domestic concerns, a very public trade war with America's closest ally and largest trading partner might damage the administration's credibility. This factor was raised on numerous occasions during the negotiations, and following the impasse in August 1964, Brubeck was certain that President Johnson did not want the breakdown made public before November. These difficulties could be compounded by congressional pressures, as well. Michigan Senator Philip Hart advised that disruption in the auto trade between the two countries would produce 'a degree of indignation' which would not be tolerated and emphasized that a solution should be found as soon as possible.[93]

Washington was also concerned about the possible effects on the domestic political situation in Canada. As Walter Gordon had stated during the joint Canada–U.S. cabinet meeting in April, the remission plan had become a political issue on which his government had staked its reputation. Given a minority government's shaky hold on power, if the plan was stymied and a trade war resulted, the political consequences would be disastrous not only for the Liberals. They would be damaging to the Americans, as well. Canadians claimed that they could not withdraw the duty-remission scheme 'without the most serious results [and] even indicated that the matter [was] sufficiently sensitive so that failure of the plan could bring about the downfall of the Pearson government' and the consequent return of Diefenbaker and the Tories.[94] Both sides were well aware that in such an event there could be a quick relapse to the anti-Americanism and the terrible Canada–U.S. relations of the Diefenbaker-Kennedy period. This was an outcome that neither side desired, and although possibility of it certainly was not pivotal in the conflict, it helps to explain why the Canadians were so determined.

International pressures were at stake, as well. The Canadians had continually brandished the threat that Canada would not support American goals at the Kennedy Round of the GATT negotiations should its remission plan be frustrated. This was a plank of the Canadian strategy that had been agreed to by cabinet, announced to Dillon by Gordon, and prominently mentioned during the July and August Canada–U.S. negotiations in 1964. While it is not clear what impact this threat had on the administration in Washington, the Canadians were convinced that they could use the Kennedy Round as leverage for getting agreement on the remission plan.

Canadian negotiators refused to accept any plans for free trade in the automotive industry. The unique institutional structure of the auto industry, previous experience with the farm implements sector, and the uncertainty that free trade would inject in the automotive sector all contributed to the rejection of the idea of free trade. The Canadians were determined to achieve all of the goals of the remission plan in a new deal that included tariff reductions, yet provided Canada a 'fair share' of the North American auto industry. The Canadian proposal was the closest thing to free trade that the Canadians could agree to given the circumstances. Nevertheless, it was not enough for the United States. So far, the search for a bilateral solution to what had become a fundamental problem in the North American auto industry had failed. With discussions at an impasse, the two sides braced for coming conflict.

3

The Big Three and the Creation of a Borderless Auto Industry, 1965

By late 1964 negotiations to resolve the North American auto problem were at an impasse. Unrestricted free trade, the solution suggested by the American negotiators, was unacceptable to the Canadians. With no new ideas, the two sides had parted, and officials in both capitals were pessimistic, believing that no answer could be found before the Modine petition (see Chapter 2) forced the U.S. government to impose countervailing duties on Canadian products entering the United States. Although the negotiations had been secret, word leaked out that the talks did not go well and there was the perception that the two countries were on the brink of a dangerous trade conflict. In Canada and in the United States, newspaper headlines warned with foreboding that a debilitating trade war in the most important sector of the North American economy loomed if the two governments failed to find a solution to their differences.[1]

Long before Canadian and American negotiators reached this stalemate, a number of different ideas had been suggested for the operation of the North American auto industry. The idea of a continental auto industry had been debated publicly by academics for decades. In 1943 a short study appeared under the title, *The Midcontinent and the Peace: The Interests of Western Canada and Central Northwest United States in the Peace Settlements*. Commissioned by the governments of Manitoba and Minnesota, the study anticipated new continental challenges that awaited the mid-western region in the coming postwar world.[2] It argued that the two countries' virtually identical automotive industries had already been 'badly scrambled up' by the Second World War and should be integrated for good. The proposal made in *The Midcontinent and the Peace* was two decades later echoed by Vincent Bladen. Canada should produce only auto products that it could make profitably, concentrating its production on only a few items or auto lines, and importing the rest. All of these products would 'flow with equal freedom' into Canada or the United States, raising efficiency in the industry and lowering prices. Significantly, however, the Manitoba-Minnesota study did not call for outright free trade, which the study's authors realized would be impossible, given the vast inequalities between the auto industry in Canada and the auto Industry in the United States. Any such plan should only be pursued, they recommended, on the condition that 'joint managers' from the industry in both countries would, for a given period of years, maintain employment levels in Canada.[3]

By the early 1960s the structural problems in the Canadian auto sector had generated a host of new ideas about the industry. A proposal by former civil servant and diplomat Hugh Keenleyside was published in May 1960 in the *Financial Post* in response to the Canadian UAW's pleas for action to save the industry. Keenleyside suggested a system of free trade in selected items, whereby each country allocated only specific models for production in Canada; he did not, however, elaborate on any details of his plan.[4] The 1961 Bladen Commission stimulated discussion of various concepts of integration (see Chapter 1). Chief among these was the plan submitted by Canadian UAW leaders calling for a 'restricted free trade area' in which any company that allocated a share of its production to Canadian plants (based on Canadian sales) should not have to pay duties on imports of its own products.[5] The auto companies also considered the possibility of a new arrangement for the North American auto industry. Chrysler suggested they look at the Keenleyside proposals, but warned against the difficulty of expanding Canadian facilities or increasing exports.[6] GM and Ford made guarded endorsements favouring trade liberalization, but were wary of any proposal for increased Canadian content requirements.

Ford of Canada toyed with the idea of using Drury's remission program to integrate its production continentally. The idea foundered, however, because Ford executives and dealers in the United States insisted that Americans would never buy cars made in Canada. Under the direction of its president, K.E. Scott, Ford of Canada began an extensive study on the possibility of using Ottawa's remission plan as an opportunity to rationalize all of Ford's North American production into an integrated system. In January and February 1964, Ford of Canada presented a plan to its parent company proposing that Canada export 75,000 vehicles to Ford in the United States by taking full advantage of the remission scheme. The Canadian company would simplify its product mix (that is, make fewer types of cars), many of which would now be built for export to the United States. The remaining Ford models sold in Canada would be imported from the United States.[7]

Detroit's reaction to the plan was not promising. Chief of the Ford Division, Lee Iacocca, was convinced that Americans simply would not buy 'American' Ford products made in Canada. A survey of Ford owners and dealers in the Great Lakes region corroborated Iacocca's concerns: nearly 60 per cent of Ford owners and 80 per cent of Ford dealers interviewed were generally against the idea. Iacocca estimated that the Ford Division's sales would be reduced by 43,000 units if the cars were made in Canada. Ford's Washington office also panned the idea; such a move might be seen in the future to mean that Ford had caved into the demands of other countries, and to expose the company to attacks from protectionists in Congress. The failure of the Ford of Canada plan proved that the 'institutional barriers,' which Industry Deputy Minister Simon Reisman had pointed to during the earlier negotiations as being an impediment to an even playing field for Canadian products, were very real.[8]

Like the Ford of Canada plan, the numerous proposals for continental integration were all sunk by the same fundamental problems. First and foremost, Canadians were not willing to agree to unrestricted free trade in the auto industry. Behind any and all proposals for integration of the North American auto industry lurked the only previous example of a sectoral free trade between Canada and the United States, namely, the removal in 1944 of tariffs on farm implements. In Canadian eyes, the experience with farm implements put any plans for a continental auto industry under a cloud, as became evident during the failed negotiations with the Americans in July and August 1964. Reisman had argued that because the farm implement treaty was based on unrestricted free trade, production had shifted southward in the two decades since that agreement had been struck.[9] Given that Canada could boast being home to one of the world's great implement producers, the Massey-Ferguson Company, what would happen if it had no indigenous manufacturers, as in the auto industry? Unrestricted free trade such as that practised in the farm implements sector was unacceptable to Canadians. The two sides needed to agree on some arrangement that would provide Canada guarantees that its production and employment levels would be maintained. Should there be anything approaching free trade in the automotive field, it would have to be tightly restricted to ensure that Canada was not overwhelmed by the preponderance of the U.S. multinational auto industry. The Canadians simply would not back away from their demand for a 'fair share' of the North American auto industry. This hardened stance was based not only on the pragmatism of Reisman and his fellow civil servants. It was also fuelled by the emerging nationalist sentiment in Canada, as evidenced by the popularity of Walter Gordon and the many other Canadian nationalists of the period who saw the United States as a threat to Canada's survival, and this included many members of the Canadian UAW.[10]

On the other side of the table, the United States faced difficulties in agreeing to any proposal that was not based on unrestricted free trade. An American government could not countenance any proposal that required the visible hand of Canadian state intervention or specifically guaranteed Canadian production targets. Many of the previous proposals for a North American auto industry had suggested just such terms. *Midcontinent and the Peace* called for 'joint managers,' while the UAW called for production guarantees based on sales, as did the final proposal put forth by Reisman and his colleagues in August 1964. For the United States, this was the worst kind of industrial intervention. It not only offended the precepts of the free market economy, but also potentially damaged the U.S. trade balance and hurt employment and production in the American industrial heartland. Chief U.S. negotiator Phillip Trezise argued that it was simply out of the question that Ottawa should expect to be able to punish U.S. corporations for not meeting production levels in Canada.

The U.S. side was committed to the free trade option. It fit well within the context of greater trade liberalization, as pursued by the United States especially since the end of the Second World War. Successive postwar administrations had promoted a policy of lowering tariffs through instruments both domestic and international, with varying degrees of success. The GATT was first and foremost a creature of American design. The Trade Expansion Act of 1962 authorized the president to make sweeping tariff cuts without having to withstand Congressional scrutiny. The Special Representative for Trade Negotiations (STR), established that same year, created a powerful office to promote the trade liberalization agenda, and during the Kennedy Round of GATT negotiations, the Americans looked to be the most active players in the international trade scene.[11]

From the American perspective, Canada was a necessary partner if this long-term project of trade liberalization were to succeed, and the automotive field was fertile ground in which to plant the seed of free trade. The failure of the comprehensive free trade proposals made in 1948 and 1953 had not dissuaded dedicated free traders in the State Department, such as George Ball, from continuing their pursuit of the free trade arrangements. The election of the Liberals in April 1963 had rekindled American hopes for free trade. William Brubeck, the White House official in charge of Canadian issues, alerted U.S. National Security Advisor McGeorge Bundy to that possibility, telling him that 'a Liberal government might eventually approach the U.S. and request bilateral talks, aimed at selected free trade between the U.S. and Canada. They would undoubtedly be dismayed should they be refused out of hand.'[12]

Just how serious U.S. officials were about free trade became apparent in April 1964. A few days before the joint cabinet meeting in Ottawa, Undersecretary of State Ball addressed a meeting of the American Assembly in New York. His speech was entitled 'Interdependence: The Basis of U.S.–Canada Relations,' and in it he outlined the general thrust of American's economic intentions with regard to its northern neighbour: 'There is no doubt that Canada and the United States could employ the resources of North America most efficiently by developing the North American continent as a single great market.' Ball did not mention the Drury remission plan specifically, but it was obvious that he was challenging the Canadian scheme and calling for a new approach to the auto industry in North America. Widely reported in the Canadian press, Ball's speech triggered a flurry of questions in Ottawa, particularly on the eve of the joint cabinet meeting, at which the touchy debate over Canadian–U.S. economic relations would be reopened. Ball's comments raised the tension in Ottawa over the remission plan and what the Americans might have in mind and served to remind the Canadians of the free trade option.[13]

Between the choices of unrestricted free trade and tightly managed trade, efforts to find new methods for the governments of Canada and the United States to operate the North American auto industry had not yielded results. Some other approach was needed that would allow each government to achieve its particular primary goal: for Canada, the goal was to ensure the continued existence of a viable and productive automotive sector and in doing so improve prospects for the country's balance-of-payments position; for the United States, the goal was to avoid a difficult and potentially destructive trade war through the creation of a continental industry that furthered freer trade. The auto companies needed assurances about what would be their role in any new arrangement. Indeed, the cooperation of the major automakers proved key to solving the problems of the North American auto industry.

The idea for the new regime came out during a round of drinks. In early September 1964, Simon Reisman met with Francis Linville, who at the time was the U.S. economic affairs specialist at the American embassy in Ottawa. Over cocktails, the two mused about ways to solve the quandary in which their countries were finding themselves. Linville suggested that perhaps the Canadian requirement for production guarantees could be agreed to if the industry itself were to be brought more fully into the picture. In Washington, Trezise followed up by making the same suggestion to Canadian embassy officials. Trezise speculated that, while Washington could not guarantee Canadians production levels north of the border as stipulated in any agreement that Ottawa might submit to it, perhaps the auto companies themselves might better be able to do so. Intrigued, Reisman and his committee went to work converting the general idea of increased involvement by the Big Three into concrete proposals that could be presented if and when negotiations resumed.[14]

The Johnson administration was eager to see agreement on a reasonable solution before countervailing duties might have to be applied to Canadian imports. With the date of the election approaching fast, the last thing the U.S. government wished to see was a trade war with America's closest ally. While there was intermittent pressure from Congress for an agreement, even greater pressure was coming from the auto industry. The Big Three were anxious to avoid any outcome that would disrupt the industry. Because of the long lead times required for production and for original equipment orders, the automotive industry could not afford any delay or uncertainty in the enormous cross-border trade in parts and autos. President Johnson was well aware of the industry's concerns, particularly because they were put to him by Henry Ford II personally. Grandson of the automotive legend, and a giant in his own right, having saved his company from collapse at the end of the Second World War, Henry Ford II had followed the Canada–U.S. negotiations through his subordinates. In mid-September he told Johnson that, while he was aware of the deadlock, he did not consider the problem to be insoluble. He advised that Washington should give every opportunity the chance to succeed, and that countervailing duties should be seen was the least desirable of the possible outcomes.[15]

Johnson had been warned that the countervail decision would be made following Secretary Dillon's return from talks at a summit of finance ministers in Tokyo in September.[16] Accordingly, Dillon informed the president that the Treasury Department would probably impose countervailing duties on Canadian auto imports by 1 October 1964. Dillon was convinced that the Canadians 'had given every indication that they do not believe, when the chips are down, that we will go ahead with a countervailing duty order. The conclusion seems justified that if there is any hope for a negotiation with them, it will be following notice that we definitely are going to issue the order.'[17] Bundy, Rusk, and Ball all counselled the president to instruct Dillon to hold off on the countervail decision until further talks could be held with the Canadians.[18] When it was agreed that there would be new talks – at the official level – before the end of September, the countervail hawks in the Treasury Department were temporarily restrained.[19]

Reisman and his committee had meanwhile completed three new proposals based on the idea of bringing the auto industry closer into the fold. The first proposal involved two agreements, one with the U.S. government and the other with the auto industry. Putting the new arrangement into two parts could perhaps solve the problems that had stalled the earlier talks. Ottawa and Washington would sign an agreement on general principles committing their countries to limited duty-free trade in automotive products. This would not be completely free trade because the program would not apply to a range of original equipment parts such as tires and tubes, or replacement parts, which had a large market in both countries. In addition, Ottawa would obtain commitments from the autmakers regarding precise levels of production in Canada, in return for which the automakers would enjoy the benefits of this duty-free trade. Collectively, the automakers would need to meet particular objectives within a three-year period (the length of the remission program). Reisman emphasized that the proposal's success would depend on the companies' performance in realizing the agreed-on objectives. Should a company not meet its objectives, the government would point out that such a failure would result in termination of the agreement and 'introduction of alternative policies designed to achieve Canada's objectives for the industry.'[20] Implementation of the proposal would result in a duty-free automotive trade regime, conditional on the willingness of the manufacturers to produce a guaranteed proportion of their North American output in Canada.

The second proposal continued roughly along the lines of the duty-remission plan, although there was to be no direct tie between exports and remissions. Instead, automakers would make applications for re-mission of duties on certain imported products to a government-appointed board. The board would determine whether a company were to receive rebates on duties that would be based on growth and production objectives as determined by the board and the company. Although parts companies would suffer under this plan, the major automakers would benefit greatly, even more than under the current remission scheme. But there would be no production guarantees. Companies would not be obligated to achieve certain objectives.

The third proposal was much more restrictive and was to be considered only if the United States did not accept the export-oriented Canadian proposals. The government, under this system, would effectively force manufacturers to produce only certain models and with higher Canadian content. This would be accomplished through changes to the current content, valuation, and tariff schedules. This would result in a far more domestically oriented industry focused on fewer models of less-expensive cars. Reisman did realize that such a plan would 'bring forth strong representations' from the auto manufacturers and from countries other than the United States that exported to Canada. Furthermore, the plan could not ensure the Canadian automotive industry a larger part of the growing North American market.

Convinced that the first plan was the most promising of the three, Industry Minister Drury recommended that the dual government/auto industry proposal be brought before cabinet for consideration, and that arrangements for negotiations with U.S. government representatives and with representatives of the Canadian auto industry be initiated.[21] Reisman's team set to work putting the two sets of agreements into more precise form.[22] At the cabinet meeting on 17 September, Drury laid out the three proposals, recommending that the government pursue the first one, the dual agreement plan. Gordon concurred and suggested that the third proposal be 'held in reserve' in the event that negotiations with the United States on the first proposal failed. Sharp urged caution. The third proposal should be considered only as a last resort, he urged, and needed to be examined very carefully before any decisions were made. The cabinet agreed and authorized Canadian officials to begin talks with the U.S. government and with the Canadian auto industry. Significantly, it was decided that government officials should meet with auto industry representatives as soon as possible, before any new talks with the American government officials.[23] A meeting with the heads of the major automakers was quickly arranged for 21

September, while U.S. officials would travel to Ottawa for meetings on 24 and 25 September.[24]

Led by Drury, Canadian government officials met with the six auto manufacturers (the Big Three plus American Motors, Studebaker, and International Harvester) and James Dykes, general manager of the Motor Vehicle Manufacturers Association. Drury began by alluding to the precarious position that Ottawa was finding itself in, a position that might result in dramatic measures for the auto industry. It looked as though the U.S. Treasury Department would find against the Canadian program, said Drury, and for this reason, his government had been examining alternatives. He warned that Canadian officials were to meet the following week to consider an alternative to the duty-remission plan, implementation of which would significantly affect operations in the auto sector. Should the Americans not accept the proposal, the Canadian auto industry would 'find its own role.' Then, Drury presented the government's plan. He explained that the proposal called for the removal of duties but, because of the historic disadvantages of the Canadian economy, Ottawa would need assurances that the Canadian auto industry would be able to participate fairly in the growth of the Canadian automotive market. To that end, Ottawa required 'something in the way of insurance.' The companies would have to give some specific undertakings as to levels of Canadian production. Drury admitted that the only way the proposal would work would be with the full cooperation of the automakers. But, he warned, if the government did not secure an agreement, it would use the devices that were 'available to the Canadian government alone.'[25]

Reisman expanded on Drury's cryptic warnings when the automakers began to ask for details. How permanent would the new arrangement be? Reisman was confident: 'The U.S. Administration could upset the scheme if they wanted to be foolish. They are not dull. They know what the Australians and the Mexicans did. They know it would not be in keeping with their objectives for international trade to force us into an inward looking policy.' What of the present remission plan? Would it end before the countervailing duty investigation? Reisman promised that there would be no gap between the two programs so that the companies could be confident that their purchasing plans would not be upset. What would happen if a company did not fulfil its obligations? The government would shy away from tight administrative control, Reisman stated. If the companies made a promise, that should be enough. Beyond that, Reisman did not believe that a company would risk the more onerous measures that might be brought to bear by non-compliance. 'The thought of the alternative,' warned Reisman, 'should be all that is needed. We can always terminate the agreement or we can take other measures.' The auto men were generally amenable to the plan. They said they would confer with their U.S. parent companies and agreed to reconvene with Canadian government officials after their meeting with U.S. representatives. For Reisman and his team, industry reaction was reassuring: so far, the plan seemed to be working.

Having launched talks with the auto industry, Canadian officials started on the second plank of their proposed plan and began discussions with U.S. officials in late September. When the Canadians proposed a general outline of the dual agreement plan, the Americans showed what the Canadians felt was 'a lively interest' in the idea. The Canadians made it plain that they expected the results from the duty-remission plan to constitute the objectives to be met by the new arrangement. Although in the intergovernmental agreement the United States could not accept an explicit statement that the two countries' automotive trade accounts should be brought into better balance, its negotiators did admit that if such a small shift were to occur, the administration would not be against it. By conceding that the U.S. industry could withstand a 'shake-up' along the lines desired by Ottawa, the United States had agreed to sacrifice some production for the well-being of the North American industry.[26] U.S. consent on this point marked a fundamental turning point in the creation of a continental auto industry.

Nonetheless, the American negotiators did express some reservations. They voiced concerns regarding the exact definition of a manufacturer under the plan (they were anxious to not have foreign firms simply set up in Canada to take advantage of the plan and export duty-free into the United States). Reisman assured them that such companies (for example, Volkswagen) would not qualify under the plan. Because Ottawa determined who was a manufacturer under the agreement, only those companies that produced in Canada in the base year 1963–4 were to be granted duty-free status. Any late-arriving companies would be left outside the agreement. The Americans were also curious about the duration of what they called the 'transitional' arrangements between the Canadian government and the automakers. Although the Canadians had not actually spelled out the exact duration or nature of these transitional arrangements, the U.S. negotiators assumed that these measures would no doubt be temporary – in keeping with the inherently free trade nature of the agreement. Although they expressed some concern, at the time, the Americans did not pursue the issue.

All in all, the U.S. side was optimistic. While the negotiators could not guarantee that Secretary Dillon would not impose countervailing duties, they indicated that the suggested plan might convince him to postpone such action. At the end of the talks, Canadian officials informed the Americans that the government of Canada had passed an Order-in-Council on 24 September specifically excluding exports of auto products under the defence production sharing program, thereby easing a long-standing complaint of the Americans.[27] Both sides agreed that this concession might also help persuade Dillon to hold off. Furthermore, the Canadians told the Americans that they would be again meeting with the Canadian manufacturers within the week. The two teams agreed to meet in mid-October to discuss the progress of industry-government negotiations and report on their own intergovernmental talks.

In briefing Washington, Phillip Trezise and Robert McNeill emphasized the progress that had been made. The new Canadian proposal offered 'realistic possibilities for a resolution to the problem, and which, indeed, might point U.S.–Canadian commercial and economic relations in a new and promising direction.' Although the possibility of countervailing duties remained a sticking point, the dual agreement proposal would allow Canadian subsidiaries of the Big Three to achieve the production levels that Ottawa desired, without involving the direct consent of the U.S. government. In the tentative agreements with the automakers, Ottawa agreed not to include any explicit punishment mechanism if the companies did not reach their goals. The intergovernmental agreement committed the two countries to the development of a rationalized and efficient North American automotive industry through the reduction of tariffs. On the U.S. side, tariffs would be reduced immediately under the Trade Expansion Act, although an act of Congress would be required to go to zero duties. The two U.S. negotiators recommended that the United States pursue the agreement as outlined. While such an endeavour might be difficult to achieve because of the many outstanding problems – such as the role of replacement parts, the GATT, and the duration of the 'transitional' period embodied in the side agreements with the Canadian companies – Trezise and McNeill concluded that it would be a 'great mistake if [the United States] did not pursue the U.S.–Canada free trade possibility energetically and affirmatively.' In the meantime, U.S. officials continued their talks with the Canadians.[28]

With the Americans apparently onside, the ball now bounced back to the manufacturers' court, and negotiations with the automakers were resumed. Before the Canada–U.S. meeting, however, State Department officials had learned of the Canadian proposal to be made by the Canadian subsidiaries of the Big Three.[29] On the eve of those negotiations, Henry Ford II contacted William Brubeck in the White House by telephone to tell him that he had heard that the Canadians were making a new effort towards a 'liberal solution of the auto parts problem' which the administration should not take lightly.[30] With the weight of captains of industry such as Henry Ford pressing down upon the administration, it was clear to Washington that the automotive company parents and siblings were closely working together to achieve the best possible outcome. As Canadian negotiator J.F. Grandy remarked following the meetings of 24 and 25 September, 'our outline of the kind of intergovernmental agreement and undertakings by the Canadian industry we envisaged came as no surprise to them. They had already had discussions with the head offices of the three largest auto companies. The latter had been informed by their Canadian companies of the discussion with Mr Drury last Saturday [21 September].'[31] U.S. officials informed their Canadian counterparts that of the Big Three, Ford and Chrysler would go along readily, although industry leader GM was somewhat less forthcoming about its position.[32]

Armed with this knowledge, Canadian officials met with auto industry executives in Ottawa, on 29 September, and presented a draft form letter outlining the commitment to increase production and making specific mention of the agreement that each company was to sign. The letters confirmed that each manufacturer was expected to contribute its share of $260 million, which would have been the total amount of increased production projected over the next three years had the Drury duty-remission program continued in force. During the meeting, the Canadian officials made it clear that, although the plan outlined goals for the next three years, the program would not be limited to that initial period and the industry 'would be expected to continue to work toward a better balance' at the end of the three years. The industry was also expected to report their progress under the program, although the government presentation indicated that no punitive actions would be taken if the companies did not achieve their specified goals. Informed of the general details of the proposal, the auto companies withdrew to ponder the plan and consult with their parent companies again. Reisman judged the automakers' initial reactions to the details of the plan to have been favourable.[33]

Word of the new agreement leaked out, and Canadian parts makers expressed their concerns about it to government officials. In an effort to quiet their fears, Canadian officials met with the parts makers in Ottawa and Windsor in late 1964. Reisman and his colleagues emphasized the benefits that would accrue to parts makers under the plan. The official explained that with a hugely expanded market, continuity between the duty-remission plan and the new agreement, and most importantly, because of the Canadian content requirements included in the manufacturers' commitments, the parts makers had little to worry about. Should the parts makers have any further doubts, government officials indicated that adjustment measures in the form of financial assistance for their companies could be made available. Some parts manufacturers remained wary of the new provisions and hoped that Ottawa would raise Canadian content requirements to protect their position. But others had already gained considerably under the duty-remission plan and could see the benefits that would come under the new program. As more of the proposal was slowly revealed to the parts makers, their principle industry association, the APMA, became more enthusiastic. The association's chief reservation was that the automakers 'transitional' safeguards – the ratio and Canadian value added (see below) – should not be reduced too quickly, if they should be reduced at all. Although government officials were not completely certain that all Canadian parts makers would come out in favour of the plan, they were confident that the measures designed to ease Canadian companies into the competitive North American market would be sufficient to convince most of them of the benefits of the new arrangement.[34]

With tentative approval for the new agreements from the U.S. government and from the auto industry, Drury took the revised dual agreement plan to cabinet, where reaction was generally favourable. Cabinet members foresaw some difficulties as the Canadian industry adjusted to the new competitive market, but they believed that rationalization would be beneficial to the Canadian economy, even though it might result in greater vertical integration and U.S. ownership in the industry. Cabinet undertook to authorize government officials to negotiate a draft treaty with the United States, while simultaneously conducting negotiations with the auto companies to secure the commitments that had been outlined in the Reisman proposals. Finally, and not insignificantly, cabinet approved a recommendation that 'nothing in the intergovernmental agreement [should] preclude further production commitments from the companies after the initial period of three years.'[35] This specific recommendation was in direct conflict with Washington's understanding that the 'transitional' measures were to operate only for three years and expire once the Canadian auto industry had adjusted to the new 'free trade' realities under the agreement. The exact nature and meaning of the 'transitional' elements of the agreement would prove to be a source of enormous contention between the two countries.

In Washington, Trezise and McNeill reported that the basis for a Canada–U.S. automotive agreement that would be in the interests of the United States and that also had widespread industry support had been reached. However, they remained concerned about the safeguards, which they considered to be transitional. In stark contrast to the endorsement from the Canadian cabinet, Trezise and McNeill pointed out that in further talks Washington ought to 'insist on a provision in the agreement expressing the desire of the two governments to leave to the industry the maximum freedom of economic choice.' The American negotiators were determined to ensure that the safeguards were for a maximum of three years. Having voiced this concern, Trezise and McNeill asked for authorization to negotiate a draft agreement with the Canadians, after which they would consult with key countries about the possibility of a waiver under the GATT (because the pact would bestow preferential treatment). White House officials went to work to secure congressional allies in anticipation of the unavoidable legislative contest that passage of the automotive agreement would entail.[36]

Canadian and U.S. representatives met again in Ottawa in December to continue negotiations. Reisman's team presented a draft intergovernmental agreement on automotive trade to the Americans.[37] Although the American's reaction to the draft agreement was generally favourable, problems persisted. Foremost was the question of further company requirements (the safeguards) beyond the initial three-year plan. American negotiators were determined to ensure that any such plans would be expressly prohibited and proposed a confidential side-agreement that would check the Canadian government from exacting additional production requirements from the Big Three. The Canadians were able to successfully resist these American demands. Indeed, they reported to the government that nothing in the agreement precluded such further agreements. They did caution, however, that any new production demands on the major manufacturers would be vigorously resisted by the U.S. government. The Canadians were determined to obtain language that explicitly recognized the non-tariff factors that could impede trade between the two countries. By the end of the December talks, the Canadian team felt that the automotive agreement effectively satisfied their concerns. However, the Canadians had not been able to obtain a clause that specified the exact breakdown in the North American market that each of the two countries was expected to have under that new agreement. Such a clause was seen as anathema by the U.S. negotiators, who were loath to include any specific market targets in the automotive trade agreement.[38] Both sides sacrificed specific clauses. The United States did not get a clause that specified the termination date of the safeguards; Canada did not get a clause on the percentage share it would have of the North American market. These sacrifices were made in order to successfully and quickly conclude the agreement.

Satisfied that they had achieved all of the principle Canadian goals for the draft agreement, Reisman and his team forwarded it to cabinet. In his accompanying submission, Reisman reiterated that 'nothing in the agreement precludes further direct intervention by the Government of Canada in the production decisions of the companies.' Although most outstanding issues had been resolved, the final approval of the automakers had not yet been obtained, nor had the details of the agreement's signing been determined. The question of GATT approval remained unclear, as well.[39] At the 21 December cabinet meeting, Drury outlined the status of the negotiations, including the revised version of the intergovernmental agreement and the tentative acceptance by the auto companies of the letters of undertaking in which their specific commitments under the new agreement were spelled out (although GM's position still remained unknown). Drury pointed out that the agreement pertained only to new parts and vehicles for original assembly and that replacement parts had been excluded from the agreement in an effort to protect the Canadian replacement parts industry.[40]

Cabinet response to the proposal was surprisingly undivided. Both Walter Gordon and Mitchell Sharp were in support of the agreement, as was Pearson. For Gordon, the proposal achieved the nationalist goals aimed for in the original Drury plan: The automotive industry would get an element of protection in the form of the content and production guarantees built into the agreement, and the plan also promised to redress the balance-of-payments difficulties, still paramount in the government's thinking. Sharp and the other cabinet members who favoured closer economic ties with the United States appreciated the duty-free nature of the plan. Martin suggested that some measures to ease dislocation might be necessary in order to win the widest possible support for the agreement, especially among the automotive unions. That said, cabinet agreed to give Reisman's team the go ahead to conclude the agreement as quickly as possible, as the countervailing duty petition had not yet been neutralized. Care would be taken, however, to ensure that no public statements were made that could imply that some segments of the Canadian or American auto industry might be adversely effected by dislocation. Furthermore, cabinet decided that parliamentary approval of the agreement should be delayed until it had been passed by the U.S. Congress.[41]

One major obstacle remained. Most of the manufacturers had indicated their agreement on the safeguards as specified in the letters of undertaking between the government and the companies. But by mid-December General Motors still had not done so. As the industry leader, the participation of GM was crucial to the operation of the entire agreement. GM officials were concerned that the company was being unfairly penalized for having made a greater effort in recent years to increase its Canadian content. Furthermore, they were claiming that their plan to produce transmissions in Canada was the reason that they were at a disadvantage compared with the other automakers. They pointed out that under the new automotive agreement, the tremendous expense of building the new transmission plant would be unnecessary, since the company could simply import transmissions duty-free. Although GM could include the Canadian-built transmissions towards their Canadian content targets, the new Canadian transmission plant made no economic sense under the agreement. Moreover, as the largest manufacturer, GM would be required to make the greatest commitment to increasing Canadian production. Without General Motors, the agreement would not fly, since Ford and Chrysler alone would have no reason to agree to any safeguards. GM was also concerned about political ramifications. The company 'didn't want to take sides with either one of the governments and push against the other. As a consequence it didn't offer too much help to either one of the government's sides in negotiation.'[42]

By the end of the year, negotiations between the auto companies and the government had resulted in detailed draft letters, and all the companies – except GM – had agreed to the plan.[43] Knowing that the alternatives to the new arrangement could be much less palatable, and knowing that the United States was willing to 'foster the Canadian interest' through the agreement, GM finally agreed to the provisions laid out in the letters and to the plan. On 8 January 1965, Trezise was able to report to Undersecretary Ball that he had spoken to officials at GM in Detroit and that 'they would have no trouble' with the giant automaker.[44] That same day, the U.S. embassy in Ottawa reported to the State Department that Drury had met with GM Canada president E.H. Walker in Ottawa to hammer out the details of an agreement between the Canadian government and the company.[45] After being vetted by GM lawyers, the final version of the letter of undertaking was delivered to the Department of Industry on 13 January.[46]

With the acceptance of GM, auto industry participation in the program was secure. In the first weeks of January, letters of undertaking from the participating companies poured into the Department of Industry in Ottawa. Ford and Chrysler officials met with Industry representatives on 11 January to finalize the wording of their letters of undertaking. The Big Three letters were nearly identical and illustrated the effectiveness of Ottawa's negotiations with the companies. Each company made two key promises: First, the company assured the government that it would increase the Canadian content in their vehicles by 60 per cent of any increases in production beyond the 1963–4 base year levels. Effectively, this meant holding to the 60 per cent Canadian content level that the companies were to achieve under the terms of the agreement. Thus, in a given year, if a company in Canada experienced a production increase valued at $50 million, then $30 million in Canadian added value was required in its production in Canada.

Second, the letters of undertaking stated the amount above and beyond its normal expenditure that each company was expected to invest in the Canadian industry during the next three years. Of the $260 million expected by Ottawa (Reisman's estimated amount of additional investment that would have been generated under the Drury remission program), GM's share was to be $121 million, while Ford and Chrysler were to make new investments of $74.2 million and $33 million respectively. American Motors was expected to invest an additional $11.2 million in its production facilities. Various other manufacturers, including Studebaker, Mack Trucks, and Freightliner, also signed letters of undertaking with the Canadian government, although their investment targets were but small fractions of those required of the Big Three and AMC, and together amounted to only about $20 million. Originally it was intended that the letters were to remain private, but pressure from elected officials on both sides of the border resulted eventually in their release to the public. (See Appendix B.)

The final wording of the intergovernmental automotive products trade agreement was worked out by mid-January 1965. Final-hour concerns over the date of a comprehensive review of the agreement and of its progress at the end of the three-year term, which coincided with the life span of the letters of undertaking, and the definition of what constituted a bona fide manufacturer under the agreement, as well as over the exact wording of the French and English versions of the agreement had all been resolved.[47] The official Automotive Trade Products Agreement was a brief and simplified version of what had originally been proposed by Reisman and his team the previous September.

On the face of it, the document sang a paean to free trade. It emphasized the gains that were to be achieved by further integrating the two auto industries on a basis of specialization and liberalized trade, that would enable 'the development of conditions in which market forces may operate effectively to attain the most economic pattern of investment and trade.' This was to be achieved 'within the framework of the established policy of both countries of promoting multilateral trade.' The agreement was to be of unlimited duration, but could be terminated by either government upon twelve months' notice. The agreement also stated that other countries could join it on similar terms.

The only hints that the auto industry was to be regulated or managed in any way were found in the two annexes. In Annex A the Canadian definition of a manufacturer was given. The definition would remain key to limiting what companies (and therefore countries) could become party to it. To be considered a Canadian manufacturer, a company had to have been producing passenger vehicles in Canada in the 1963–4 base year, maintain a ratio of net production to sales that was equal to that of the base year, and maintain a Canadian value added of no less than that of the base year. In real terms, the official definition meant that only already established manufacturers would be able to import duty-free. Furthermore, companies had to continue to produce as much as they sold in Canada based on a ratio of their production in 1963–4. Since the base year production-to-sales ratios for the Big Three were all approximately 1:1, the measure was meant to ensure that the Canadian manufacturers continued to produce as much as they sold in Canada, a principal Canadian concern. Finally, companies were required to maintain a base year dollar amount floor of production in order to have the right to duty-free importation.[48] While the agreement allowed that any other company might join if it fulfilled these terms, it seemed unlikely that Japanese or European companies would build plants in Canada. Furthermore, they could not fulfil the requirement for production in the base year, a point that was hotly discussed at the GATT later in 1965. This limitation appeared to clash with the provision that other countries could join under similar terms, a contradiction that became pivotal to the agreement's evolution in the future.[49]

Annex B also supported the restrictive nature of the agreement. To further protect U.S. manufacturers from possible offshore competitors, it stipulated that 50 per cent of the content of components or completed cars that entered the United States (60 per cent until 1 January 1969) had to be produced in Canada or the United States. These rules of origin prevented non-U.S. companies from setting up a sales enterprise in Canada for the purpose of importing cars from their home countries and then re-exporting them to the United States. In conjunction with the Canadian manufacturer provisions, the agreement – far from being a wide-open free trade environment – reflected a desire by the two governments and the major auto manufacturers to tightly control the auto industry (see Appendix A). By January 1965, the essentials of a basic reorganization of the North American auto industry had been agreed upon by Canada and the United States. With GM on side, the automotive industry had also signalled its acceptance.

Where and when the automotive trade agreement was signed remained undecided. Initial White House and State Department reaction to the idea of President Johnson himself signing the agreement was not enthusiastic. U.S. government officials were wary of the president putting his own prestige on the line, given that the agreement required congressional approval. If, for example, opposition was effectively mobilized and the agreement ran into trouble in Congress, the president could be hurt politically. For their part, the Canadians felt that Johnson's signature on the agreement would hasten the process of acceptance and provide a measure of insurance for legislative passage. After all, the agreement was, in Undersecretary of State for External Affairs Norman Robertson's view, 'probably the most important tariff agreement in history between Canada and the U.S.'[50] The question depended on whether, as Ball put it, 'the President wanted to make a big thing of a new relationship with Canada.'[51] While many in the State Department and the White House were against the president signing the agreement, Ball recommended that Johnson should sign it.[52] Defense Secretary Robert McNamara also felt that the president should go ahead and sign it, but that his should not be the only American signature. Dean Rusk agreed with this and suggested that either he or Ball should also sign the document and that Martin should countersign with Prime Minister Pearson.[53] Chester Cooper, a White House protocol official agreed: 'I don't think the Republic will collapse if the President did sign; he and Pearson signed the Columbia River Agreement and the Canadians feel the present agreements are of that order of significance. Perhaps all four could sign.'[54] On 13 January 1965, Julius Katz informed State Department officials that Johnson might wish to sign the agreement himself.[55] In the end, it was agreed that Johnson, Pearson, Rusk, and Martin would sign at a ceremony in Texas at the LBJ Ranch. Pearson, who had been on vacation in Florida since 3 January, would stop off there on his way home.

The meeting between the two heads of state began awkwardly. Pearson arrived on 14 January and, expecting cold weather, wore a diplomat's attire of a formal black suit with a matching homburg. Texas in January was warm and dusty, and Pearson's clothing made him feel rather uncomfortable and look out of place. Johnson was dressed in ranch-gear: a cowboy hat, boots, and dungarees. Their press conference made the situation even more uncomfortable, when Johnson misstated the prime minister's name. In his memoirs, Pearson wrote that Johnson called him 'Prime Minister Wilson' and that in quick response he had quipped, 'think nothing of it, Senator Goldwater.' Paul Martin was sure, however, that Johnson had actually called Pearson 'Drew Pearson,' the influential *Washington Post* reporter and Johnson intimate. The latter version is more likely accurate. The prime minister was then treated to a bumpy and raucous jeep tour of the Texas countryside. Over an informal dinner that night, while not gossiping and trading tales with Texas governor John Connolly, Johnson tried to make amends by explaining to his wife Lady Bird Johnson that he had made 'a big boner' earlier by calling Pearson by the wrong name. Pearson accepted the apology, although he was unimpressed by the informality of the setting and by the president's actions.[56]

The next morning, Pearson and Johnson sat down to sign the automotive trade agreement. Martin and Rusk countersigned. Following the outdoor ceremony, the prime minister and the president read prepared statements, after which they answered questions about the agreement and its implications. Johnson began by stating that 'two years ago it appeared that our two countries might have grave differences in this great field of trade. We faced a choice between the road of stroke and counterstroke and the road of understanding and cooperation. We have taken the road of understanding.' In his remarks, Pearson stated that he considered the agreement 'one of the most important accords ever reached by us in the trade field.' Although the negotiations had at times been difficult, Pearson held up the agreement as another example of the 'mutual good understanding, goodwill, and confidence which has been built up between our two countries.' When asked whether the auto agreement provided the basis for further such arrangements, Pearson was optimistic, saying, 'we should like to explore that possibility.' The prime minister said that he was pleased about the agreement and by what he called the 'short but very, very happy visit' to the ranch.[57]

In the days immediately following the signing, political reaction to the auto agreement was generally muted on either side of the border. Diefenbaker and the Tories had initially questioned the agreement, but now their criticisms were more reserved.[58] Since the Conservative government had set in motion the chain of events that had led to the auto pact, they could not outwardly challenge it. Furthermore, with most Canadian observers agreeing that the pact would be a boon to the Canadian auto industry, the Opposition could scarcely attack a deal that seemed so advantageous to Canada. Nevertheless, Conservative and New Democratic Party (NDP) opponents of the agreement energetically challenged aspects of it during its implementation phase. The same was true in the United States, where criticism by opponents to the agreement was heard loudly and clearly during the nearly year-long process of passing it through Congress.[59]

The UAW's official response to the 1965 automotive pact came from Solidarity House in Detroit. International President Walter Reuther stated that the union concurred with the principles of the deal, but continued support for it would depend on whether adequate worker protection legislation was implemented – on both sides of the border.[60] Some senior American UAW officials were more wary of the agreement and made their adverse opinions known to the UAW president. But Reuther was determined to wait to see what legislation the government tabled and how the agreement affected the auto industry over the short term.[61] Canadian UAW director George Burt had no choice but to wait. Once the agreement was signed, Ottawa officials were in no hurry to consult Burt, and when he finally met with Labour Minister Allan MacEachen in March, little had been done to assuage his concerns about adequate worker protection.[62] The Canadian union had no choice but to cool its heels while government officials on both sides of the border contemplated possible adjustment provisions for assistance to workers and parts makers alike.

Although Canadian parts makers had been briefed on the broad outlines of the new arrangement, segments of the American parts industry had heard but vague rumours about it. The Modine Company and the American association of parts makers, the Automotive Service Industries Association (ASIA), which had led the battle against the Drury remission plan, were determined to fight any agreement between the two countries that might discriminate against U.S. parts makers. On 12 January 1965, ASIA and four parts makers (not including Modine) filed a suit in U.S. district court for the District of Columbia seeking a writ of mandamus to oblige the Treasury Department to apply countervailing duties against imports of Canadian parts. State Department officials believed that the tactic was initiated to cause the new agreement difficulties in Congress. In its press release, ASIA argued that the reported new agreement only benefited the vehicle manufacturers and the Canadian government and that Congress should take a 'searching look' at the new arrangement.[63] *Motor Age*, the parts makers' industry newsmagazine, reported the industry's criticism of the new arrangement and noted that the Johnson administration could expect a fight over the agreement's passage in Congress.[64]

Press reaction in both Canada and the United States was generally favourable. Major Canadian newspapers such the *Globe and Mail*, *Financial Post*, *Toronto Star*, and *Montreal Gazette* all praised it. In the United States, the *New York Times*, *Business Week*, *U.S. News and World Report*, and the *Detroit News* were all agreed that the new pact would foster rationalization, reduce costs, and build better Canada–U.S. relations.[65] Some American press reaction, was less enthusiastic. The *Washington Post* led with a very critical editorial on 18 January intimating that the automotive trade agreement was 'treacherously misleading,' contained a number of 'unpleasant surprises,' and fell far from the ideal of free trade.[66] The *Philadelphia Bulletin* agreed that the matter had been solved, 'within the family,' but grumbled that 'Canadians particularly ought to welcome it, for it seems to portend further expansion of the automobile "family's" activities north of the border.'

Thus, while initial reaction to the auto pact from industry players and editorialists ran the gamut, most were generally in favour, seeing it as a positive step towards better use of the continent's industrial resources. Framed by the context of multilateralism and trade liberalization, which characterized international relations in the 1960s, most commentators welcomed the direction taken by the Canada–U.S. auto agreement, if not the precise mechanisms employed to achieve its ends. Many saw the auto pact as a potential first step towards a larger free trade agreement between the two countries.[67] Critics of the obviously continental aspects of it remained few. Even Walter Gordon, the most outspoken economic nationalist of the period, and as finance minister in a key position to influence the course of negotiations, believed that the 1965 agreement was the best possible outcome for the Canadian auto industry. Indeed, even though by the 1960s fears of U.S. domination were gaining ground in debates about Canadian political economy, few attacked the agreement itself.[68] However, even as many observers hailed the agreement, explanations of its evolution and its meaning for the future remained vague. It was still too early to accurately assess the reasons behind the creation of the auto pact.

The Canadians achieved their goals for the agreement because of a number of significant factors. First, they were determined to unilaterally bring about changes to the auto industry because in the late 1950s and early 1960s the Canadian auto sector was problematic as an industry and because it was having a devastating effect on Canada's current account. Demands to retool the Canadian auto industry and the urgency created by a deteriorating balance-of-payments position forced Canadians to think creatively and daringly about the functioning of their auto industry and their tariff structure. New thinking led to the Diefenbaker automatic transmission/engine plan and the Drury duty-remission plan, which Canadian politicians were determined to defend. Essentially, they had nothing to lose. The United States either had to accept the Drury plan (a possibility, since it had voiced little concern over the limited Diefenbaker plan) or face a trade war forced on it by its own parts corporations and trade legislation. A trade war would have been very destructive to both sides, and Canadian policymakers believed that the United States would try to avoid such an outcome. Although a trade war would have hurt Canadian interests more than theirs, the threat of such a war made the Americans realize how serious the Canadians were on the auto issue. The alternative, therefore, was that the two countries work together on a new bilateral scheme, one in which the Canadians were determined to include all of the benefits that would have been expected under the Drury scheme. This explains the negotiators' steadfastness in resisting the unrestricted free trade scheme and in ensuring that most of their objectives were met. The Canadians did not achieve everything that they had hoped for (for example, in the agreement there was no specific percentage stated for the North American market to be allotted to Canadian producers), but generally, the agreement met all the Canadian aims.

Second, the Canadians' determination was fortified by the personalities of the individuals on their team which turned out to be ideally suited to the situation. Led by Simon Reisman, the Canadian negotiators were creative and independent. The duty-remission plan was an ingenious incentive program, and the auto pact itself was a creative mix of freer trade and protection. There was more at stake for the Canadian bargainers than there was for the Americans, and the Canadians took more care in their planning and execution. The Canadian team drafted all the initial proposals and did most of the legwork on the issue.[69]

When it came to the negotiating sessions, Reisman displayed all the tenacity of a pitbull and refused to be cowed on any issue. By the mid-1960s, American negotiators were familiar with Reisman's tactics, and they considered the Canadians to be hard-nosed negotiators.[70] On one of the most fundamental issues surrounding the agreement, that is, the nature of the letters of undertaking signed by the automakers, the Canadians especially proved their canniness. The Americans had argued that these measures should be considered transitional, but the Canadians had refused to agree with that position. In a conversation with Canadian official C.D. Arthur, following the agreement's signing, U.S. embassy officer Maynard Glitman was surprised to hear him say that the letters of undertaking were to run for only three years. But, Glitman admitted, he did not believe that this had actually been agreed on during the negotiations: 'I do not believe that the Canadians had in fact specifically said during the negotiations that they considered the definitions were transitional in nature, although Mr Reisman had spoken of eventually moving to complete free trade as Canadian industry become more competitive.'[71] The personalities and skills of the negotiators played a key role in the outcome of the auto pact agreement.

The Canadians also had the determination of Walter Gordon hanging over the negotiations. By autumn 1964, Gordon was considered a loose cannon by the Americans, and they wondered how far the finance minister would go in his economic nationalism. The United States had already dealt with Gordon's poorly received plans for Canadianization in the mergers and acquisitions field, and they considered that outright nationalization in the auto field was not an unrealistic possibility. During the Canada–U.S. joint cabinet meetings in 1963 and 1964, Gordon had hinted that more protectionist measures could be in the future for the Canadian auto industry should the remission plan be frustrated. Although the final shape of the auto pact pointed to continentalism and the utter domination of the Canadian auto industry by American producers, Gordon was not greatly upset by this prospect. Like the determined Canadian civil servants who negotiated the agreement, Gordon found that in its final form the agreement achieved the goals that they had set for themselves. For Canadian policymakers dealing with the auto sector in the 1960s, continentalism, such as embodied in the auto pact, was a form of economic nationalism.

Third, Washington was generally happy with the outcome, at least initially. Although some segments of the administration were disturbed by the process by which the agreement had been achieved (the Treasury Department, for example, had been thwarted in its attempt to impose countervailing duties and saw the Canadian tactics as underhanded), the Johnson administration found the auto pact to be a practical solution to a North American problem, a real advance in Canada–U.S. relations, and a step forward on the issue of trade liberalization. The president's briefing notes made on the eve of signing the agreement show 'U.S. Views' to be unequivocal:

1 We welcome this important agreement, thereby avoiding serious trading problems which would have resulted from U.S. countervailing duties on Canadian auto exports.
2 We believe this agreement is an important positive contribution to the liberalization of trade.
3 We believe the industry in both countries will be strengthened as a result.[72]

Senior U.S. officials shared the view that the auto pact was a practical step towards free trade with Canada. When Philip Trezise, the chief American negotiator, reported to White House official Henry Wilson about the agreement's progress, he wrote, 'We have been considering a free trade approach as a way out of the problem ... The free trade approach is constructive and sensible.'[73] George Ball, in a speech in Toronto a few months after the agreement was signed, also saw this resolution of the auto problem as a practical response to a complex situation which advanced American interests. The agreement marked an example of how closer economic interdependence was mutually beneficial: 'The handling of the automotive problem is a good example of how two nations can live together rationally on a single continent.' Moreover, the negotiations succeeded because 'we did not let ourselves get bogged down in political theory but acted in the tradition of pragmatism that is the heritage of both our countries. We knew good business when we saw it and were not deflected by doctrinal speculations as to the far-out implications of what we were doing.'[74]

The American multinationals also knew good business when they saw it, and their role in creating the Canada–U.S. Automotive Products Trade Agreement of 1965 was perhaps the most important factor in determining its success and ultimate form. Whatever the outcome, the Big Three certainly did not wish to see the Canadian auto industry nationalized or higher Canadian content regulations imposed on them. In this sense, the outcome was beneficial for the automakers, if only because they did not have to face alternatives far worse than the auto agreement. Time and again during the negotiations, the Canadians warned both the Americans and the automakers that frustration of the duty-remission plan would result in more protectionist measures. In the context of changes in the world auto industry, namely, protectionist measures implemented in Australia and Mexico, the auto companies thought it not improbable that similar moves would be taken by Canada. During congressional hearings on the auto pact later in 1965, Fred G. Secrest, vice-president and controller of the Ford Motor Company succinctly explained to representatives the effects of alternatives to the agreement:

Australia, Mexico, Britain, the Common Market bloc – all, as well as Brazil and Argentina, have restricted automotive imports through content provisions, high external tariffs or import licenses. We see no basis for assuming that Canada, in its own self-interest, would not take similar action if the pending agreement is not implemented. It should be pointed out that Canada would be under no obligation to work out an 'agreement' with the U.S. government in order to raise its local content requirements.

Ford naturally prefers the limited-free-trade solution worked out by the two governments ... The terms, although not perfect from our standpoint, are fully acceptable to us as reasonable products of negotiation.

Parenthetically, it should be noted that neither the United States nor the Canadian government forced us to make the assurances described earlier in this statement. We think the Agreement, and the associated assurances given by Ford of Canada, are in the best interests of both Ford-U.S. and Ford of Canada. If the agreement should not be implemented we think

Canada would eventually take actions that would reduce the already unsatisfactory profitability of our Canadian operations, by forcing even greater inefficiencies.[75]

The sentiment that the auto agreement was in Ford's 'best interests' was also expressed by General Motors and Chrysler officials, who also were convinced that Canada was quite willing to institute harsh new rules to govern its auto trade if it did not achieve its goals under the Drury remission plan. All of the Big Three had analysed the potential cost of higher content requirements, and the resulting figures were enormous.[76] By avoiding these alternative outcomes, the Big Three realized that they had gained a lot with the creation of the agreement. Thus, they willingly accepted it.

Finally, the unique structure of the North American automotive industry also facilitated the speed and relative ease with which the agreement was consummated. Simply stated, the auto pact could not have been created in any other industry of equal size or scope because of the domination on both sides of the Canada–U.S. border by a few huge companies. Essentially, the agreement was implemented by the automakers, acting as private corporations, and this meant that they determined the best manner by which to achieve the rationalization and economies of scale that would result in benefits for them and for consumers in both Canada and the United States. This approach allowed both governments to pre-empt criticism. The United States could avoid the charge that it was allowing another government to manipulate the market economy, while the Canadian government could avoid the accusation that it was becoming more protectionist or that its actions were directly responsible for a loss of jobs or production (although later on the government nevertheless was blamed when there was dislocation in the auto industry).

The unique nature of the auto industry in North America as a factor in facilitating the Canada–U.S. auto pact has been mentioned often. Philip Trezise admitted twenty years after the agreement was signed, 'There were rather unique conditions surrounding the 1964 negotiations ... We were dealing with a major industry, dominated by a few large companies which operated in both countries and produced virtually identical products in each ... The auto talks succeeded in 1964 for reasons peculiar to that time.'[77] Walter Gordon, perhaps the most outspoken economic nationalist of his period, also acknowledged the unique position of the industry within the North American economic firmament. In his memoirs, Gordon noted that the Canada–U.S. auto agreement 'accepted the rationalization of the automobile industry on a continental basis.' Although Gordon did not like this in principle, the new regime 'merely acknowledged the existing fact.'[78] Without question the auto pact was to meld together two identical and closely connected, yet separate, industries into one seamless North American automotive industry.

The uniqueness of the auto industry explains, too, why similar agreements could not be extended to other sectors of the economy. On his return from President Johnson's Texas ranch, having just signed the auto pact into being, Prime Minister Pearson was (again) asked whether the auto pact could be applied to other industries. In responding that such new ventures were possible, the prime minister was being more hopeful than realistic. Later, government officials were hard-pressed to dispel the notion that Pearson's remarks at that time were anything more than a 'generalized declaration of principle.'[79] In the years after the auto pact was signed, further auto pact-like agreements proved ephemeral. Only the auto industry was dominated by so few and such powerful players, who could be called on to significantly change their industry within a short space of time. Only in the auto industry was the Canadian sector owned almost entirely by a few American companies. And only in the auto industry, where production and investment decisions could affect the fates of entire cities, did the governments care so greatly about the operation of the industry.

It is not entirely surprising, then, that the auto problem was resolved in the manner that it was. The interdependence of the two nations provided much leeway in accommodating each country's demands, even if it seemed as though Canada was in the subservient position. In relationships such as those between Canada and the United States, the dominant power will often concede on some issues to improve its position in negotiating for its larger goals. In this case, the United States sacrificed some production and investment in the auto industry to achieve the larger goals of continental rationalization and a significant move towards further trade liberalization. The Canadian position was fortified by the support of the U.S. multinationals, who favoured the Canadian solution. This was a significant factor in favour of the Canadian position. When multinationals align with the less dominant of two nations, the wishes of the stronger nation often go unanswered.[80]

The principals were initially satisfied with the outcome. But clouds loomed on the horizon before long. Immediate problems had been solved, but the auto agreement itself pointed to the potential for further difficulties between the governments in Ottawa and Washington and the auto industry. The structure of the agreement was confusing – was it free trade or managed trade? If managed trade (because of the Canadian 'safeguards'), when was there to be unrestricted free trade in North America? What would occur during the pact-mandated governmental review, set for 1968? These questions, and others, would still require answers.

4

The Implementation of the Auto Pact, 1965–1966

In January 1965, Prime Minister Lester Pearson and President Lyndon Johnson signed the Canada–U.S. auto pact. Immediately afterwards the pact would come under attack from determined opposition on both sides of the border, as a wide range of individuals, associations, and other interests attempted to have the auto pact changed, suspended, or terminated. They opposed the agreement, because of its practical implications, for ideological reasons, and on procedural grounds. Some were against it for all of those reasons, others because of a specific impact it would have on their part of the auto industry or on the national interest. The attacks came on three major fronts: the American and Canadian legislatures, significant automotive industry players such as parts makers and the UAW, and the General Agreement on Tariffs and Trade (GATT).

In the U.S. Congress and in Canada's Parliament opposition coalesced around particular individuals. In the United States, division between the legislature and executive branches of government allowed elected representatives to attack administration initiatives with little fear of punishment. Critics from both the Republican and the Democratic parties challenged the pact. In contrast, the rigid party discipline inherent to the parliamentary system, ensured that in Canada the auto pact debate would be a partisan affair. Yet, even though at the time Canada had a minority government, passage of the agreement was in much less doubt in Ottawa than in the U.S. Congress. With effective management of the House of Commons timetable, the Liberals made sure that the auto pact was easily passed, albeit nearly two years after it was signed.

In Washington, opposition centred on one individual, Albert Gore of

Tennessee. A senator since 1952, Gore was a defender of the New Deal, a populist, and a progressive. He had helped to create America's interstate highway system in the 1950s and had voted for civil rights and medicare in the 1960s. Gore was willing to defy his fellow Democrats: He had refused to sign the pro-segregation Southern Manifesto in 1956 and was an outspoken opponent of the Vietnam War, a stance that many would blame for his defeat in 1970.[1]

Between January 1965 and his final attempt to have the auto pact repealed, in 1969, Gore was its most outspoken opponent in Congress. Together with a few other senators who had been voicing concerns about Canada's auto policies since the duty-remission plan was instituted in 1963, notably Stuart Symington of Missouri, Vance Hartke of Indiana, and Abraham Ribicoff of Connecticut, Gore led a campaign to block the ratification of the agreement. Gore's opposition was not on ideological grounds. He was neither a protectionist, nor a free trader, nor an isolationist. He was, after all, a Tennessean, a southerner, and a Democrat. The agreement was signed by a progressive, Democratic, president from the south and it would be debated by a Congress dominated by Democrats.

Gore saw himself as a defender of America's interests and institutions.[2] The Canada–U.S. auto pact, thought Gore, did nothing to increase either his country's economic power or the prestige of its government. From the unsatisfactory way in which the negotiations had been initiated (to discuss unilateral Canadian measures) to the manner of its final negotiations and passage (disregarding normal constitutional procedure) to its impact on American auto workers and auto parts firms and the U.S. balance-of-payments account, Gore was firmly convinced that the pact did not advance the interests of the United States. As time wore on, he also became increasingly incensed at what he saw to be the government's cavalier treatment of the legislated terms of the agreement itself, including its mandated review. All these factors contributed to Gore's doggedness to subvert the agreement. Furthermore, Gore's anti-auto pact campaign helps to explain many of the reasons for opposition to the agreement more generally in the United States – as well as why this opposition ultimately failed.

Gore took a keen and early interest in the Canada–U.S. auto pact. It was not usual for a legislator of his stature to attend the tiny Subcommittee on Canadian Affairs of the Senate Foreign Relations Committee. Yet he appeared before the subcommittee in early 1965, and proceeded to badger administration witnesses as to why the agreement had been passed so quickly, with so little consultation. Most importantly, Gore demanded to know why the auto pact was being passed as an executive agreement, and not as a treaty, which would allow the Senate to properly vet it. Why was the Senate being presented with already completed legislation, with a fait accompli?[3]

Government witnesses claimed that the administration did not want to bother Congress with two legislative burdens, wasting its time over the agreement once as a treaty and again as enabling legislation. They argued that, by taking an executive agreement and asking that enabling legislation be passed, Congress would be deciding on the agreement and on the legislation enabling it at the same time.[4] In an era when presidential heavy-handedness was beginning to irritate Congress (the Gulf of Tonkin Resolution had been pushed through less than a year before the auto pact was signed), many senators resented such a manoeuvre by the executive branch. Gore believed that President Johnson was twisting the Constitution to the detriment of Congress. The auto agreement had 'short circuited' the Constitution, he argued, and clearly exemplified a loss of congressional power at the hands of the executive.[5]

But Gore's protestations did little to stir his congressional colleagues, and by the fall of 1965 the agreement had gone from the House of Representatives to the Senate.[6] However, the senator from Tennessee was not easily dissuaded. When the auto agreement came before the Senate Committee on Finance, Gore was ready with new questions. In his detailed interrogation of the various government, industry, and labour witnesses who appeared to defend the pact, Gore showed his populist colours by hammering away at the two themes that he would constantly return to: Why was the auto pact so tilted in favour of big business (in this case the Big Three), and what benefits did the 'little guy,' especially the American auto worker, stand to gain? After all, from Gore's perspective, it seemed that the major automakers (along with the Canadian government) were really the chief beneficiaries of this agreement. They would now be able to transport their goods across the border duty-free, while the average American could not; they could determine the most efficient ways to produce their goods, wherever they wished, independent of American employment or investment concerns; they could also take advantage of lower Canadian wage rates, with little concern about the impact of this on American workers. The Detroit automobile giants, who owned the Canadian companies, were the 'real gainers' in this agreement. Gore could understand why Henry

Ford II wanted the agreement, but he could not understand why President Johnson would.[7]

The average American auto worker, claimed Gore, was getting the short end of the stick, as dislocation would certainly threaten American jobs. Independent parts makers would be threatened, too, as they would be faced with unfair competition from similar Canadian outfits.[8] In the Senate Finance Committee hearings, Gore called the agreement a sell-out of these relatively powerless interests. Even after UAW president Walter Reuther voiced support for the agreement, and after evidence was presented to demonstrate that American workers and parts companies were not suffering as he had expected, Gore persisted in identifying instances which, he asserted, proved that the agreement was a bad one for auto workers and parts makers in the United States. In 1967, for example, Gore and his allies pointed out that in his home state workers had been laid off by American Motors, and they claimed, this was because of the Canada–U.S. auto agreement.[9]

Nevertheless, the agreement passed through Congress relatively unscathed. Last-minute filibustering attempts by both Gore and Hartke failed, and the auto pact was ratified by the U.S. Senate on 30 September 1965, by a vote of 53 to 18.[10] Opponents did, however, exact amendments to the bill that made congressional approval a requirement for similar agreements with other countries and for the re-imposition of duties if any additional undertakings such as the ones signed by the auto companies and the Canadian government were introduced after 1968.[11] The latter amendment was intended as a warning to the Johnson administration, to Canada, and to the auto companies: There were to be no more 'unnatural' letters of undertaking or side agreements between Ottawa and the Big Three, which skewed investment and production because of government interference. Additional legislation established an Adjustment Assistance Board with a mandate to alleviate any dislocation for workers, but this did little to console the opponents of the pact.

As in the House of Representatives, Senate support for the bill was bipartisan, and the lopsidedness of the legislation's passage was a result of the confluence of a number of factors. Significantly, Johnson's enormous political capital, built up over decades of leadership on Capitol Hill, had not yet been exhausted, and the president could count on a Democratic Congress to support an agreement that fell, however murkily, within the general ambit of the U.S. government's policy of trade liberalization. Chairman of the House Ways and Means Committee

Wilbur Mills was recruited to shepherd the pact though the House, with the promise that there would be worker-friendly adjustment assistance legislation in the Trade Expansion Act in the following session.[12] A spirited defence by government, industry, and labour witnesses in both the House and Senate also helped to convince a generally uninterested Congress that the only alternative to the agreement was what would be a disastrous trade war with America's closest economic, political, and military ally. Finally, presidential prestige was on the line: Lyndon Johnson himself had signed the auto pact, giving it the status of an international agreement. The White House was determined to avoid any embarrassment over it and threw its full weight into ensuring that the auto pact legislation was passed.[13]

Significantly, Gore and his allies failed to articulate a coherent alternative vision of the North American auto industry beyond pressing a critique of the auto agreement, stressing that it would hurt the 'little guy.' Representatives and senators from those states with heavy concentration of the auto industry generally took their cue, instead, from the automakers and threw their support behind the agreement. In particular, the Michigan senators and representatives, whose opinions on automotive-related issues mattered so much, sided emphatically with the agreement.[14] On 22 October 1965 President Johnson signed the auto pact into law, and at the same time established the Adjustment Assistance Board to ease any dislocation that might be caused be the new regime.[15]

This did not close the issue for Gore and his allies. The legislation itself provided another opportunity for attack. The terms of the agreement required the president to submit an annual report to Congress on the progress of the agreement and the state of the auto industry. Indiana Democratic Senator Vance Hartke rose in February 1967 to complain that the Johnson administration had not yet submitted such a report to Congress. This 'credibility gap,' as Hartke put it, provided a new opening for the auto pact's opponents. What was the government hiding, demanded Hartke? Why the delay? Was the president's own study so damaging? A month later, when Hartke again demanded that the president produce his report, Senator Gore chimed in by wondering if the mass unemployment in the auto industry caused by the agreement would be noted in the president's submission.[16]

Then Gore took the offensive, by reminding his fellow senators that the process by which the auto agreement had been negotiated and implemented was, in his view, illegitimate, and yet it had been approved by Congress 'with barely a ripple.' Now, the 'full fruits of folly were being harvested.' Gore was convinced that matters were far worse than the government could admit, and since the White House had chosen to bottle up the facts by delaying the report, things might well be worse than anyone in the Congress knew. Gore introduced S-1265, entitled An Act to Repeal the 1965 Canada–U.S. Automobile Parts and Trade Agreement. It was time for action, he declared, and unless action were taken, thousands more Americans would be thrown out of work. Reaction was quick. Within a week, the administration presented the president's first annual report on the Canada–U.S. auto pact.[17] Johnson had avoided a major embarrassment. With the report in hand, the Finance Committee to which Gore had referred his repeal was under no pressure to submit it to the Senate for consideration. Bill S-1265 died in committee.[18] The administration had deflected Gore's attacks, and the auto pact survived.

The Canada–U.S. auto agreement faced far less criticism or obstructionism in Canada's House of Commons. This was because of careful management by the Liberals and because the agreement stemmed, however tenuously, from the Bladen Commission and the Diefenbaker automatic transmission duty-remission plan. Since both of these earlier initiatives that formed the origins of the pact were Tory measures, it was difficult for the Conservatives to attack an agreement based on their own work. The civil servants such as Reisman and Grandy who had designed the automatic transmission remission plan for the Tories had also put together the auto pact. Moreover, on the face of it, it was hard to criticize a plan that seemed to offer so much for Canada and for its automotive industry.[19] To many parliamentary observers, it was clear even from the outset that the auto pact had achieved all of the Bladen goals, and perhaps more.

Nonetheless, the agreement did face minor challenges in Parliament. Most outspoken of the opponents were old-line protectionist Tories such as Alfred Hales, the member of Parliament for Wellington South (a riding in southwestern Ontario). Hales led a guerrilla campaign against the agreement from the time it was signed in January 1965 until the early 1970s.[20] Hales and some of his Conservative colleagues saw the pact as a direct challenge to the very bedrock on which Canada had been built, the National Policy. At the heart of his criticisms was the fear that the Liberals had sold Canada out to the Americans, forever abandoning the great national project of the country's first prime minister, Conservative Sir John A. Macdonald. During the 1950s, Conservatives had been highly critical of the Liberals willingness to embrace American capital. Now, Hales argued, it was obvious that with the auto pact, the Liberals had finally managed to sell Canada's economic birthright, which would lead inevitably to the loss of the country's political birthright. By stripping the auto industry of a national tariff, Canada was abandoning the last vestiges of national control.[21]

Fellow Conservative Mac McCutcheon was part of the prime minister's entourage in Texas for the agreement's signing. Like Hales, he, too, was concerned that the Americans had outsmarted Ottawa. McCutcheon reported a conversation with a resident of Johnson City, Texas, who

> had a word of advice which I am going to pass on to the Prime Minister of Canada. We ... got into discussion about this automobile agreement. I said to him 'What do you think of this deal between the President and our Prime Minister?' ... 'Well,' said this man from Johnson City with his Texas drawl, 'I reckon your Prime Minister better have his shirt well buttoned down, 'cos if'n he ain't, I can tell you who is going to have that shirt pretty soon; it's going to be our Lyndon.' He went on, 'You know, our Lyndon is one of the biggest wheeler-dealers in Texas, and if'n your Prime Minister don't have his underwear on tight, he may lose that, too.' Well, I guess he could see that I, as a Canadian, did not like the idea of our Prime Minister losing his shirt and underwear to LBJ even in the cause of cementing the long friendship between Canada and the United States, so he added these words, 'Of course, our Lyndon is a real Texas gentleman, and he will lend your Prime Minister his shirt so he can get back home safe.'[22]

Certainly there was a partisan tone to the Conservatives' attacks, but there was also little doubt that Hales and McCutcheon did believe that the Liberals were selling out the country and the national interest for short-term gain. They remained steadfast in their conviction that traditional protectionist measures provided the best solutions for the problems with Canada's auto industry.

When not challenging the principles behind the agreement, critics in the House of Commons berated the government for the consequences of the pact. They pointed out that the agreement would allow the Big Three to avoid paying over $50 million in duties every year. Where would the treasury make up such a shortfall, demanded Hales? Along with the Conservatives, New Democratic politicians objected to the 'free ride' the major automakers were receiving. NDP members also attacked the agreement for what they believed was its cavalier treatment of the average Canadian consumer. Although the car companies were being forgiven more than $50 million in duties, they had not yet pledged to lower car prices. Indeed, in the first full model year following introduction of the pact, car prices in Canada increased. It seemed that the average car buyer was subsidizing the Big Three. To make matters worse, the initial rationalization in the industry fuelled further criticism: Both opposition parties questioned the wisdom of the auto pact regime when it was learned that Ford and Chrysler would be laying off workers as they readjusted their workforces along continental lines.[23]

Like Gore and his allies in the U.S. Congress, the Progressive Conservative opposition in Ottawa attacked the agreement on procedural grounds. The Canadian parliamentary system, with its fusion of the legislative and executive branches, enabled the Liberal government to dictate the terms and timing of the debate and, thus, passage of the agreement. Liberal ministers were able to evade direct questioning, and through their use of procedure, managed to push debate on official passage of the pact forward to May 1966, which was almost a year and a half after the agreement was signed – in the meantime the agreement was in operation by Order in Council. To Hales and his Conservative colleagues, this was an abuse of the democratic system. Even worse, bringing the agreement about by an Order in Council, denied Parliament any debate on the matter whatsoever. Fifteen months after the agreement was signed, the Liberals sought its quick passage in the House. But the Conservatives were unwilling to oblige: 'The agreement was signed, sealed and delivered, without the elected members of Parliament having an opportunity to voice their opinion one way or another ... We object to the way in which this matter was introduced.'[24] The government, however, was able to ignore objections from Hales and anyone else, and the legislation easily passed the House of Commons on a voice vote, and by the end of 1966 it was law.[25] The small band of Canadian parliamentarians opposed to the Canada–U.S. auto pact could do little to stop its the passage.

The pact also faced opposition from within the auto industry itself. With the signing of the agreement, the implications of the virtual disappearance of the international border for the automakers struck terror into the hearts of the parts makers, who were most dependent on the manufacturing strategies of the auto companies. In both Canada and the United States, the parts industries were deeply divided over the agreement. Parts makers and their associations launched spirited attacks in the United States, and north of the border the smaller, Canadian-owned independent parts makers were extremely concerned with the operation of the pact.

The Automotive Parts Manufacturers Association (APMA), although committed to the agreement, worried that the Liberals would not provide adequate support for their industry to cope with the increased competition that would ensue. The APMA lobbied government officials, presented petitions, and organized letter-writing campaigns in protest of what it saw as the auto parts industry's sudden exposure to cutthroat American competitiveness. Within weeks after the agreement was signed, D.S. Wood, the APMA's tenacious president, pleaded with Ottawa officials for additional help to meet the challenges the agreement would impose. 'We are already feeling,' complained Wood, 'the shock of abruptly removed protective tariffs and are quickly grasping the cold reality of competitive pricing.'[26] Nonetheless, the APMA maintained its support for the agreement, judging that the long-term viability of the industry would be assured by the pact. Only a few independent Canadian parts makers continued to oppose the deal, but with little success.[27]

In the United States, the opposition of parts makers was more strident and reflected their ongoing battle against Canadian auto policies. Although challenges to the remission plan, such as the Modine Company's demand for countervailing duties, had been effectively defeated with the signing of the agreement, other U.S. parts makers were determined to oppose the pact as well.[28] They saw the new regime as further discrimination against their industry. Unbowed by the pact's signing on 16 January, parts makers attacked it on a number of fronts and launched a new demand for countervailing duties. On 29 March 1965, two days before the auto pact legislation was introduced in the House of Representatives, another assault against the agreement was made by an alliance of parts makers and the Modine Company. The Industrial Committee of Paducah, Kentucky, filed a petition with the commissioner of customs asking for the imposition of countervailing duties against all imports of parts from Canada. The petition claimed that the automotive agreement was 'a continuation in different garb of the motor vehicle and motor vehicle parts export subsidy scheme introduced in 1963.' In April, having little choice in the matter given the publicity surrounding it, the commissioner of customs announced that there would be an opportunity for concerned parties to submit opinions on this new round of countervail demands.[29]

The U.S. Automotive Service Industries Association launched a publicity campaign criticizing the pact. Harold T. Halfpenny, ASIA's legal counsel, delivered well-received speeches across the United States decrying the impact it would have on American parts makers. Halfpenny called it a grave threat to the future of the auto parts industry and insisted that it would result in 'substantial layoffs and injury to American industries.'[30] ASIA also claimed that the adjustment assistance provisions being worked out in Congress would amount to 'disaster assistance,' necessary to offset the debilitating effects that the new regime would have on displaced workers and 'bankrupt manufacturers.'[31] Legislators such as Gore and Hartke took up the parts makers' cause, and newspaper editorials became increasingly critical of the plan, as parts industry associations began their massive letter-writing campaign.[32]

ASIA also made their case in the Congress. ASIA president Allan Levine voiced the association's objections at the Senate Finance Committee's hearings in September 1965. He argued that the auto pact would 'definitely' weaken the competitive position of independent parts manufacturers. Halfpenny was even more direct, telling the committee that the legislation threatened 'the very existence of hundreds of small parts manufacturers throughout the country.'[33] The American parts manufacturers were convinced that U.S. automakers would transfer all of their captive production (non-replacement parts such as axles or specific engine parts) to Canadian companies in order to meet their production requirements, and this would gravely hurt rival American producers.[34]

By mid-1965 Washington was concerned that ASIA's efforts could be having some effect on public opinion and perhaps on legislators on Capitol Hill. The State Department went so far as to ask Ottawa to supply it with evidence of complaints from Canadian companies to show that the agreement was not as one-sided as the American parts makers were claiming.[35] At this point, the Johnson administration moved into high gear to ensure that the agreement passed and mobilized the influence of Wilbur Mills to push the bill through. When the Automotive Products Trade Agreement was signed into law by Johnson in October 1965, it left parts makers and their allies deeply embittered by what they saw as the president's strong-armed tactics.[36] Unable to convince enough legislators in Congress to oppose the agreement, the parts industry's battle against the auto pact came to a quiet end.[37]

The UAW's position was somewhat more complex than that of the parts makers. In an era before parts makers had become cross-border entities and before the UAW had broken into two, the union was an 'international' and as such was expected to protect the interests of members on both sides of the border. However, the UAW was rife with factionalism among the international leadership and between the leadership and rank and file in both Canada and the United States. Publicly, the UAW's position was in support of the agreement, as long as adequate adjustment assistance packages were created for any dislocated workers in either country. In a joint statement, international president Walter Reuther and Canadian director George Burt had announced in January 1965 that the UAW supported the principles of the agreement.[38]

Privately, sharp conflicts erupted among the union's leadership at Solidarity House in Detroit. Burt had demanded in 1964 that the UAW officially declare in favour of the Canadian duty-remission program, a position considered completely unreasonable by senior UAW officials such as Nat Weinberg, the union's director of research. Weinberg was adamant that the remission program was hurting American auto workers, and he complained to Reuther that Burt's demands were unrealistic. Weinberg was also convinced that the remission plan was indeed a bounty under U.S. law, a judgment he expressed in no uncertain terms to Canadian consular officials in Detroit. Fortunately, for the union leaders, events overtook them. In the summer of 1964, Paul Martin had asked Burt to keep a low profile on the auto issue because of the then-secret negotiations being conducted in Ottawa and Washington. Burt agreed to do so, and the question of official union support for the Drury remission plan was dropped.[39]

With the announcement of the auto pact, conflict within the UAW leadership re-emerged. Weinberg was sure that any price cuts on cars in Canada were a long way off and that the immediate tariff savings that the companies were to enjoy would simply not be passed onto Canadian consumers. He was even more concerned about the potential shift of employment between the two countries. Since the auto pact would have the effect of 'transferring to the US any unemployment which would result from a decrease in Canadian sales below the base period,' it would be running directly against the safeguards that the union had recommended be instituted to counter this very possibility. The 1964 base period used in the automakers' side agreement was a peak period, and Weinberg therefore believed that it was 'not only possible but highly likely' that such an unemployment shift would indeed occur. He also thought it unlikely that the UAW would be getting satisfactory adjustment assistance from the Congress – but did not concern himself with the plight of UAW members in the union's Canadian section. When the AFL-CIO research department submitted its critical assessment of the agreement, some members of the UAW's international hierarchy became deeply worried. Reuther, however, was determined to wait and see the legislation that Washington tabled and how the agreement affected the industry in the short term.[40]

Many American UAW locals were unhappy about the agreement. Like the American parts makers, UAW locals in the United States were fearful of the practical implications of the agreement's Canadian production guarantees. When Al Gore began his anti-auto pact crusade in 1965, Warren Mika, president of Local 368 in Muncie, Indiana, sent his heartiest congratulations to the senator from Tennessee for his 'forthright and perceptive opposition' to the pact. Mika was certain that the recent loss of 350 of jobs at the local Eaton Manufacturing Company could be directly attributable to the agreement and, furthermore, that those jobs were being transferred to Canada. Local 368's membership was pulling for Gore and hoped that he would continue his 'noble endeavor' to achieve Senate rejection of the agreement.[41] Notwithstanding the opposition of those few locals who feared a job drain northwards, the American UAW leadership remained supportive of the agreement, if sometimes reluctantly.[42]

Many Canadian UAW locals also opposed the agreement, but on ideological rather than practical grounds. Militant and left-leaning locals such as Oshawa's Local 222 (GM) and Windsor's Local 444 (Chrysler) saw it as a betrayal of Canada and of a distinctly Canadian way of life.[43] Swept up by the nationalism engulfing the country in the 1960s and early 1970s, these locals demanded that their union oppose any continental agreement that they saw as a sell-out of the national interest. Instead, they called for the creation of a government-owned crown corporation that would produce an 'all-Canadian car.' Failing that, the locals hoped for the imposition of heavy Canadian content requirements, which was a path that countries such as Brazil and Australia had taken.[44] Between January 1965 and the early 1970s, militant union locals provided some of the loudest opposition to the agreement in Canada, and this created deep divisions within the union. The Canadian UAW leadership's support for the pact further mobilized nationalist elements in the union.[45] They branded the Canadian director and his supporters as mere lackeys of the American-dominated international. 'Canadians

Prime Minister Lester Pearson and President John Kennedy in 1963.

Simon Reisman led Canadian efforts in developing the automotive industry in the 1960s and was the chief auto pact negotiator.

Although a committed economic nationalist, Walter Gordon felt that the auto pact was the best solution to the challenges facing the Canadian auto industry.

External Affairs Minister Paul Martin and Secretary of the Treasury Douglas Dillon face the press following another difficult round of negotiations in Ottawa, April 1964.

SIAMESE TWINS

The cross-border automotive problem was one of the most difficult issues between Canada and the United States in the 1960s and reflected the growing interdependence of the two nations.

As minister of trade and commerce, Mitchell Sharp supported the agreement's signing.

UAW International President Walter Reuther supported the auto agreement as a way to achieve wage parity between Canadian and American auto workers, a long-standing goal of the union.

The Canadian UAW's leadership were strong supporters of the auto agreement, even if their membership sometimes was not. By the 1970s, however, the union was solidly behind the auto pact. (l to r) UAW Canadian Director George Burt meets with Paul Martin, Charles Drury, and Labour Minister Allan MacEachen, April 1965.

Henry Ford II (on left) played a key role in the auto pact's creation. Here he examines the Oakville assembly line in 1960 with Mike Cochrane, the plant manager at the time.

Prime Minister Lester Pearson and President Lyndon Johnson prior to signing the auto pact.

During the trip to Texas to sign the agreement, President Johnson took Prime
Minister Pearson on a tour of the LBJ Ranch.

Martin, Pearson, Johnson, and Secretary of State Dean Rusk sign the agreement in front of the press, 16 January 1965.

Johnson, Martin, Pearson, and Pearson's wife, Maryon, write their names in cement at the LBJ Ranch following the signing of the auto pact, January 1965.

A photo from Paul Martin to Undersecretary of External Affairs Ed Ritchie,
'without whose help this meeting would not have been possible.'

The auto pact led to a massive building boom in the Canadian auto industry after 1965. Here, the opening of Ford's St Thomas Assembly Plant in 1967 is a cause of celebration.

By the 1970s, Canadian auto plants were completely geared towards North American production. This 1984 image from the Ford assembly operation in St Thomas, Ontario, illustrates the plant's continental approach.

Against the Auto Pact,' a union group based in Oshawa, argued that the agreement not only signalled the economic enslavement of Canada to the United States, but also the subservience of the Canadian UAW to the sinister U.S.-based international: 'The UAW has always worked hand-in-glove with U.S. foreign policy – imperialism – in Canada.'[46]

Yet, in spite of this opposition from locals on both sides of the border, and uncertainty at Solidarity House in Detroit, the UAW accepted the agreement. Canadian UAW director Burt was pivotal in ensuring that union support for it was maintained. Hardened by years of battles both inside and outside the UAW, Burt was able to face down the difficulties of being virtually ignored during the process that brought the auto agreement into being. White House officials had made efforts to keep Reuther and the American UAW leadership informed and involved, but Burt had been shut out of the process entirely.[47] Nevertheless, Burt battled Ottawa over the issue of adequate adjustment assistance for Canadian workers should they be faced with unemployment resulting from the rationalization of the North American auto industry.[48]

Drawing on decades of experience in the industry, Burt was convinced that the UAW's future lay with the auto pact. Since the days of the Bladen Commission, Burt had been arguing that the continental option was the best route for ensuring that Canadian auto workers would have jobs in a healthy auto industry. The Canada–U.S. auto pact also held out the possibility of wage parity with American UAW members – Canadian members were paid considerably less than their counterparts across the border. Wage parity had long been a goal of Canadian auto workers. Reuther, also convinced that a continental industry was the best bet for the union persuaded the American UAW leadership to endorse the auto agreement.[49]

Even with the support of the international leadership, the auto pact still faced criticism from a number of UAW locals in both Canada and in the United States. At the same time, September 1965, that Nat Weinberg was testifying before the Senate's Finance Committee that the UAW supported the pact's principles, Al Gore was on the Senate floor reading the testimony of UAW locals that condemned the agreement.[50] While Burt battled the Canadian government for better provisions under any transitional assistance benefits plan that might be proposed to the union, militant UAW locals in Oshawa and Windsor attacked both Burt and the auto pact. At the June 1965 meeting of the Canadian Council of the UAW, Burt had clearly stated his position. The UAW was in support of the auto agreement, as long as it was accompanied by adjustment assistance legislation to protect workers. But there was no use, Burt had argued, in demanding that an all-Canadian car be produced in Canada, something that the militant sections of the union were again demanding. This was simply unrealistic. Nor was there any use in UAW affiliates and locals launching independent actions against the government; such uncoordinated protests only made the union 'look somewhat ridiculous.' Burt's old nemesis, Charles Brooks of Windsor's Local 444 stood up at this point and attacked the agreement, claiming that 50,000 to 60,000 jobs (nearly three-quarters of all auto jobs in Canada) would be lost under its regime. Burt was forced to admit that barring any forthcoming legislation, the council should seriously consider opposing the entire program at their next quarterly meeting, to be held in September.[51]

Although the assistance program that Ottawa offered was not as generous as the Canadian UAW leadership had hoped for, in the end Burt concluded that it was the best that could be expected. By autumn 1965, Burt was more convinced than ever that the future of the UAW lay with the new deal and that it was senseless for it to launch a full-scale attack on the agreement, as many members were calling on the union to do. Burt was certain that 'the plusses [of the agreement] far outweigh the minuses,' and that the union, now faced with a 'massive and complicated accomplished fact' should simply make the best of it. The agreement was actually benefiting the union: At the September council meeting, Burt restated the union's support of the principles behind the auto pact and argued that, contrary to Brooks's dire predictions of mass layoffs, employment was rising dramatically in the auto industry, even in those locals that had most vociferously attacked the program.[52] In a final effort to convince the council to tone down its opposition, Burt made an impassioned plea for wage parity, which was, of course, impossible without the agreement:

I have been in the UAW in Canada since its start, and at the head of it nearly all those years. I have led more charges than most, and not much cared for the odds. But I think that I have learned to recognize an accomplished fact [the agreement] when I see one. And I know that it is better, when faced with one, to see what can be done about it than go banging your head against the wall.

I see a tremendous advantage in the present situation for our Canadian UAW members. We have in our hands for the first time in our history, and with the courtesy of the governments of the U.S. and Canada, if you please, the key to perhaps the oldest and greatest collective bargaining objective of our union: the right to equal pay for equal work with our American brothers.[53]

Although some segments of the union continued to denounce the agreement even after 1965, in Congress and the House of Commons supporters could rightfully claim that the UAW had endorsed it. In the United States, locals saw the Canada–U.S. auto pact as a political deal that unfairly exported American jobs northward, while in Canada nationalist locals saw it as evidence that their country's economy was being overwhelmed by the United States. But by the early 1970s opposition from the UAW had ebbed considerably. Indeed, in the years to come, the UAW and its Canadian successor, the Canadian Auto Workers (CAW), proved to be the auto pact's greatest supporters.[54]

By the end of 1965, the opposing parts makers and elements of the UAW that were against the pact had failed to block or alter it. In both cases, these segments of the North American auto industry were fragmented in their opposition. With difficulties in both their countries surmounted, Canada and the United States now needed only to ensure that the agreement obtain the consent of the international trade community. The battle to implement the auto pact shifted to Geneva, headquarters of the General Agreement on Tariffs and Trade.

Although Washington and Ottawa had effectively ratified the treaty, approval by the GATT was no sure thing. The pact's provisions were a clear violation of the most-favoured-nation principle, which required that any preferential treatment given to one country must be accorded to all members of the organization, and both sides realized early on that successful passage would require a delicate touch. The asymmetric provisions of the agreement necessitated that the United States obtain a waiver, because it was granting preferential treatment to only one country, Canada. The provisions did not require Canada to seek a GATT waiver, because the agreement said that companies from any country could gain auto pact status as long as they fulfilled the stated requirements. Initially, the United States pushed the Canadians to join them in a waiver request, under Article XXV of the GATT, which allowed members to breach the MFN principle under exceptional circumstances. The two sides would cite the proximity of the two auto industries, the similarity of markets and consumption patterns in the two counties, and the continuity of U.S. ownership in the auto industry on both sides of the border. U.S. officials were unwilling to grant zero duties on vehicles and parts on an MFN basis since they believed that to extend such benefits to the Europeans would be grossly unfair given the punitive attitude in Europe, especially in terms of non-tariff barriers, regarding U.S. automobiles.[55]

During the negotiations, Canadian representatives ensured that the provisions of the agreement reflected Canada's desire to gain the benefits of the close bilateral ties to the United States without isolating itself – a long-standing concern of the makers of Canadian trade policy.[56] In particular, Canada was worried about the reaction of the United Kingdom and Japan, countries with a large trade with Canada.[57] To avoid such criticism, the Canadians argued that the auto agreement was open to all companies; the restriction of duty-free status to certain bona fide manufacturers was an 'end use' measure that had been in place since before the advent of the GATT. The end use measure meant that while a company from any country could, in theory, come under the auto pact in Canada, Ottawa could restrict membership to certain companies. The Canadians were confident that the Japanese and European companies had no interest in setting up in Canada and were unlikely to do so, given the overwhelming preponderance of the American Big Three in North America. In the Canadian line of reasoning, non–North American companies were welcome to build plants and begin production in Canada whenever they had the inclination to do so, and if they did, they would be subject to the same safeguards to which the American automakers had agreed. Feeling secure that this would not occur in the foreseeable future, the Canadians could argue that they were not restricting access based on nationality, and therefore, they did not need to join the United States in asking for an MFN waiver.[58]

Washington agreed to Ottawa's position only because it was expedient to do so. Although perturbed at the Canadian refusal to seek a joint waiver, circumstances forced the Americans to act alone. First, time was crucial. The threat of countervailing duties had not been lifted by the fall of 1964, when the issue of GATT acceptance first arose, and the danger of a trade war sparked by the Modine Company's petition was still very real. Second, the U.S. Big Three were in full support of the auto agreement, which gave Washington incentive to obtain the waiver and consummate the agreement. Third, American prestige was on the line. The Johnson administration had twisted arms to ensure that Congress passed the auto pact. As the leader of the Western world and a long-time advocate of freer trade, the United States was embarking on a tariff-reducing experiment with its closest ally and trading partner, and this would be a litmus test of its influence at the international trading body. Thus, the United States put its full weight behind obtaining a waiver.[59]

In Geneva, the American request for a waiver was met with serious opposition. The auto agreement became a lightning rod for numerous conflicts that threatened to interrupt world trade. Japan and Britain demanded concessions from the United States for its 'infringement' on the MFN rule.[60] The European Economic Community (EEC, now the European Union) saw in the auto pact implicit U.S. approval of further trade regionalism, a position that neither the United States nor the GATT secretariat endorsed. The auto pact reopened the very bitter debate over preferences. Countries such as Australia had lobbied extensively for permission to grant preferential treatment only to certain countries, instead of across-the-board tariff reductions to all members of the GATT. It was felt that the Canada–U.S. auto pact would have the effect of creating tiers of trading relationships, which might slow and complicate further efforts to lowering trade barriers – another position that neither the United States nor the GATT secretariat supported.[61] Since the United States was providing a preference for Canada, many countries found the long-standing American opposition against preferential treatment to be hypocritical.[62]

These conflicts almost defeated the waiver request. At working sessions to examine the auto agreement, the U.S. and Canadian representatives came under heavy pressure from the other contracting parties to the GATT to justify the claim that the exceptional circumstances of the North American auto industry required such measures. The Canadians could avoid direct criticism by claiming that their part of the agreement was open to any country, but the United States was left to defend the preferential nature of the agreement. The Americans tried to mollify the unhappy GATT members by promising that the United States was prepared to make more and deeper cuts at the upcoming Kennedy Round of tariff negotiations. In late December 1965, however, it was not yet clear whether the U.S. waiver request would be granted.[63]

In the end, the waiver passed, on 19 December 1965. The most important reasons for this outcome begin with the fact that the U.S. government put its full weight behind the request and used the Kennedy Round as a carrot to push other countries towards further tariff reductions. At the same time, other GATT members found the auto pact waiver useful for their own purposes. EEC countries, seeking justification for strengthening their trading bloc, voted for it, as did countries who favoured preferential trade. Japan abstained. The British, in return for voting for the waiver, exacted changes to the Canadian tariff laws to provide easier access to their own automotive exports. And so, Canada managed to have the auto pact passed without being party to the waiver request, and by the end of 1965, the Canada–U.S. auto pact had been deemed acceptable by the world trade community.[64]

Opposition to the Automotive Products Trade Agreement failed for four key reasons. First, the opposition to it was diffuse and fragmented. The auto pact's detractors were a heterogeneous group, with little common ground and an international border that hampered cooperation. Auto parts makers, UAW locals, opposition political parties, consumer groups, and various others never coalesced in mounting an effective force against the agreement. For example, a Conservative MP like Alfred Hales worked with disgruntled parts makers and used their plight to cause as much of a stir as possible, but this alliance amounted to little. It was not an effective challenge to the Liberal government, and Hales did not seek allies from other parties (at the time the federal New Democratic Party was opposed to the agreement) or interest groups. Eventually (as we shall see) Canadian auto parts makers were either effaced by the competition, or they flourished under the new regime.[65]

Second, and more significantly, opponents such as Gore, Hales, and the parts makers failed to develop a credible alternative plan. Equivocal platitudes about average workers or protective tariffs did little to inspire support from uncommitted legislators in either country. Many Canadian UAW locals had long called for the nationalization of the Canadian auto industry through the creation of a crown corporation to build 'all-Canadian' cars. But this option was deemed unrealistic and too costly by government officials.[66] In Canada, the official Opposition in the House of Commons was hamstrung by the fact that the auto pact had emerged, however loosely, out of a plan that they themselves had constructed while in government. Moreover, the plan looked to be very beneficial from the Canadian perspective. The Canadian negotiators seemed to have achieved all they had wanted, and it was difficult to imagine a better arrangement.[67]

The nature of the auto agreement itself hampered organized resistance to it. Opposition was kept fragmented by an international border and further divided by regional, provincial, and national concerns. Although the border separating Canada from the United States had disappeared for the auto companies, it remained as salient as ever for opponents to the agreement, and they rarely considered trawling for cross-border allies. A discourse of national interests practised by the many opponents to the pact was unable to coalesce into a continental opposition to it.[68] Congressional and parliamentary members might use news from the other legislature's proceedings to attack the agreement, but they never formed alliances with each other. The suggestion by Senator Symington that he might consider working with Canadians to fight the agreement was greeted with reluctance by Opposition Leader John Diefenbaker.[69] When J.D. Loveridge of the Ingersoll Tool and Machine Company, of Ingersoll, Ontario, visited ASIA's annual meeting in Chicago to drum up support for his fight against the pact, he found an association that was indeed committed to fighting the agreement – but only on its own terms. Loveridge was told that ASIA planned to make its fight in Congress, and there was no inclination from ASIA that it would support a joint cross-border approach to the problem.[70]

Third, the pact's proponents, in addition to having the advantage of being unified in their purpose, were able to access vast resources and communications networks in both Canada and the United States to defend the agreement. The governments that had negotiated it remained steadfast in their support. In Canada, the Liberal government was able to use the parliamentary process to control the agreement's passage and to hobble its opponents. In the United States, the Democratic administration of Lyndon Johnson mobilized to convince a disinterested Congress that the auto agreement was useful to America. Both governments worked in tandem to maximize communication, and secrecy, during the agreement's gestation period, making opposition more difficult later on. When critics on either side of the border demanded to see the letters of undertaking signed by the Canadian manufacturers, for example, civil servants in both countries kept each other abreast of efforts to keep these provocative documents out of their opponents' hands.[71] Non-elected Canadian and American officials were much better informed about what was transpiring in each country's legislative process than were the elected representatives who opposed the agreement. This was also apparent in Geneva, where Canadian and American officials worked together, although sometimes reluctantly, to ensure passage of the agreement at the GATT.

Importantly, both governments left potentially hostile sectors of the industry out of the policymaking process, while the automakers – the heart of the industry – were given a negotiating status almost equal to that of the governments. Ottawa senior civil servants framed the dual negotiations as being equally important, and when they met with the small group of men who ran some of Canada's largest industrial concerns, they understood that the automakers themselves were as essential to the consummation of the agreement as was the U.S. government. With such a compact, powerful network acting in a relatively united fashion, it is not surprising that Ottawa and Washington could respond so quickly to the auto industry's demands, and vice versa.[72] Parts makers associations and disgruntled auto workers could never hold the governments' attention in the same manner. As Ford of Canada president Karl Scott stated so plainly at a meeting of the Ottawa chapter of the Canadian Club, he and his colleagues in the auto industry were 'not strangers in the capital city.'[73]

Successful negotiations between the automakers and the Canadian government were essential in fashioning the deal, and these private enterprises took on an importance hitherto unprecedented in the creation of a Canada–U.S. treaty. Relations between the automakers and the governments were of paramount importance in the negotiations. In Washington, administration officials kept in close contact with the U.S. parent companies, and when negotiations reached their most sensitive stage in the fall of 1964, Henry Ford II personally made certain that President Johnson was thoroughly aware that the Ford Motor Company was enthusiastic about the proposed agreement.[74] As Henry Ford was the controlling shareholder of one of the largest industrial entities on the planet, Johnson was sure to listen attentively to the man's advice. American Ford officials also kept the State Department abreast of developments between the Canadian government and Ford of Canada as the two sides negotiated the crucial 'letters of undertaking.'[75] The influence of the auto companies' on implementation of the agreement, both in Canada and the United States, was absolutely critical.

Finally, the automakers were very influential in convincing both governments and legislators – an important distinction in the American case – to support the agreement because of the vastness of their enterprises and the economic and political impact of their decisions. To a large degree, the Canada–U.S. auto pact was passed and survived early opposition to it because the auto companies themselves found the pact useful. Indeed, the role that the automakers played is key in explaining why the agreements' opponents were rendered ineffective. As we shall see in the following chapter, the auto companies remained generally satisfied with the agreement's performance. Operating as an oligopoly in close contact with both Ottawa and Washington, they could throw their considerable weight behind the agreement. Furthermore, with their largely integrated continental hierarchies, the automakers could react quickly to developments, on either side of the border – helping governments and hindering opponents. With no real pressure from the Big Three to change or terminate the agreement, the pact's opponents faced grave difficulties in trying to create a constituency to challenge the deal. Conversely, the automakers' compliance allowed the governments to ignore the opposition. Allan Levine of the ASIA was candid in admitting before the U.S. Senate that 'the Big Three have endorsed this plan. The independent parts manufacturer does not dare to oppose it openly.'[76] While many of the pact's opponents did not dare oppose the agreement openly, U.S. Senator Al Gore and his allies were the one group of people that were neither cowed into submission nor incapable of challenging the agreement from a position of strength. But they found too little support to kill the pact.

The power of the governments, working in tandem with the automakers, proved irresistible. The executive branches of both the Canadian and the U.S. governments dictated the terms of the negotiations and implementation of the agreement, and it was they who dissuaded the majority of senators and representatives from challenging the deal. The automakers' influential position ensured that as long as they supported the pact, opposition would always prove ineffective. In the end, the opponents' failure is less a reflection of their own abilities or influence and more of the new North American economic reality of the automotive industry that was produced by the rise of continental auto politics. Without a coherent cross-border organization, there was little that the opposition could do to the auto pact. Al Gore's case is instructive: a 'national' politician like Senator Albert Gore was an anachronism in the face of the newly constituted auto industry, and he could do little to an agreement that had simply erased the very borders he was fighting to protect.

5

Managing the Borderless North American Auto Industry, 1965–1968

The Canada–U.S. Automotive Products Trade Agreement had an immediate impact on the Canadian auto industry. The Big Three quickly rationalized their administration and production on a North American basis: Canadian firms and workers were subjected to dramatic changes. By 1968 joint industry-government management of the auto industry was well established. Ottawa was eager to see that the automakers fulfilled their commitments while the automakers sought to better their position under the agreement. A delicate balance between the automakers and the government emerged: As each side brought pressure on the other to gain better terms in implenting the auto pact, both gained a better understanding of its benefits – and limitations. As the mandated 1968 review of the agreement approached, questions as to how and whether they had indeed fulfilled their obligations generated problems between the Big Three and the Canadian government. More ominously, the declining overall American automotive trade surplus raised concerns in Washington, causing difficulties between the United States and Canada. Along with boosting the Canadian industry significantly, the auto pact had satisfied its intended objective of increasing Canada's automotive exports, and thus lowering Canada's chronic trade deficit – but at a rate far more impressive than the architects of the agreement could have foreseen. This new reality would test the resilience of the auto pact, as relations between the principals deteriorated.

With the advent of the new regime in operation, the industry mobilized to fulfil its obligations in order to achieve duty-free status. The agreement required the automakers to maintain the same ratio of production to sales as they had achieved in 1963–4 (the ratio), and the same level of Canadian value added (CVA) as in the base year 1963–4 – when their total CVA had had been more than $600 million. Under the letters of undertaking, the automakers were collectively required to invest a further $260 million in the Canadian auto industry by 1968 and to increase their CVA by 60 per cent, if there was any increase in the Canadian market. In other words, on top of the extra investment, if the Canadian market grew by, for example, 10 per cent in any year between 1965 and 1968, the Canadian automakers were required to increase their in-car CVA by 6 per cent.

Initially, the stipulations that the companies should boost their investment in Canada and maintain their base 1963–4 CVA were easily satisfied. In the first two years after 1965, expansion in the industry was boosted by a number of factors. Economic indicators pointed to a growing demand for autos in the immediate post-pact years, by a proportion that was greater in Canada than in the U.S. market.[1] Aware of this forecast, the Big Three factored the increased demand into their planning up to 1965.[2] Furthermore, the additional $260 million of investment stipulated by the agreement, on top of normal capital expenditures, ensured that the Canadian sector would be in an expansionary phase until at least 1968, the date by which the investment targets were to have been met.

The Big Three greatly expanded their Canadian facilities after 1965. One Department of Industry official estimated that more than fifty major projects had been announced by October 1965, nearly half of them by U.S. subsidiaries. In many instances, the companies specifically declared that the additional spending was because of the auto agreement, although many expansions had been planned before 1965 already to meet the growing Canadian demand.[3] General Motors had already added to its St Catharines plant, to build transmissions, and it opened an entirely new assembly plant in October 1965 at Ste Thérèse, just outside of Montreal. In 1966, GM announced new expansion plans for one of its Oshawa plants.[4] By the end of 1965, Ford, too, had announced major plans for expansion, at Oakville and Windsor, and for a new plant at St Thomas, Ontario.[5] Chrysler expanded its passenger vehicle plant in Windsor, a move that company officials admitted would not have happened without the pact.[6] Even tiny American Motors Corporation, with no assembly facilities in Canada at all before 1961, opened a new plant in Brampton in 1966 and that year produced 33,000 cars in Canada.[7] In the first two years under the auto pact, every major auto manufacturer had opened or expanded at least one major facility in Canada, which would account for much of the $260 million investment target.[8] So great was the growth in the Canadian auto industry that *Motor Age*, the U.S. parts industry's trade magazine noted, 'American auto makers, one by one, have announced plans to expand Canadian subsidiaries ... All Detroit seems to be [shifting towards Canadian production].'[9]

In spite of *Motor Age's* criticism of the Big Three, U.S. parts makers expanded their capacity in Canada as well. Many major American firms took steps to boost their facilities to gain the benefits of duty-free trade, and companies such as MacKinnon Industries of St Catharines (already a GM subsidiary) announced plans for growth, after experiencing some initial dislocation.[10] Even the Modine Manufacturing Company (which had instigated the countervailing duty petition) mused publicly about setting up new facilities in Canada so that it could take advantage of the agreement.[11] Canadian firms were taking similar steps. SKD, Fabricated Steel Products of Windsor, and ITL Industries of Hamilton all confirmed that the auto agreement had played a key role in their own 1965 expansions.[12] In late 1966 a Canadian consular official posted in Detroit made a tour of southwestern Ontario, and he was able to report that Canadian parts companies in the area 'were doing extremely well under the Auto Pact ... plant expansions seem to be the rule, not the exception.'[13]

The enormous growth in facilities showed in the production figures. In October 1965 the Motor Vehicle Manufacturers Association (MVMA) announced that the automotive industry in Canada was setting new production records.[14] Canadian manufacturers built nearly 700,000 vehicles that year. Parts production also increased dramatically, reaching a total annual value of almost $1 billion in 1968. Most of these parts, along with a sizeable proportion of the increased vehicle production, were headed to the United States. Midway through 1966 auto industry analysts at the Bank of Nova Scotia in Toronto commented on this greatly increased production, seeing in it the 'initial fruits of the Canada–U.S. automotive agreement which boosted not only completed vehicle exports but also exports of engines and parts.' They also predicted that the Canadian car market would continue to grow into the 1970s.[15] Department of Industry figures a year later, confirmed the dramatic results: 87 new plants and 164 plant expansions, accounted for a total investment of at least $506.5 million, and more than 20,000 new jobs – all thanks to the auto agreement.[16]

Economists concur that, on balance, the agreement considerably boosted Canada's economy and increased efficiency and productivity

Table 5.1 Motor vehicle production in Canada, Big Three and total industry, 1963–1968, (000s)

Year	GM	Ford	Chrysler	Big Three total	AMC	All others	Total industry
1963	265	142	87	494	30	8	532
1964	246	153	105	504	35	18	557
1965	351	169	136	656	31	19	706
1966	286	198	173	657	33	2	692
1967	312	178	187	677	33	–	710
1968	338	287	219	844	42	–	886

Source: Committee on Finance, U.S. Senate, *Canadian Automobile Agreement: U.S. International Trade Report on the U.S.-Canada Automotive Agreement; Its History, Terms and Impact* (Washington, DC, 1976), Chart A-28, 240. The table was compiled from data published in *Automotive News, Ward's*, and material supplied to the ITC by the MVMA and individual manufacturers.

Table 5.2 Original equipment parts production in Canada, 1963–1968 (U.S.$ millions)

Year	Automakers	Independent parts producers	Total
1963	85	321	406
1964	85	377	462
1965	137	504	641
1966	258	598	856
1967	185	686	871
1968	402	939	1,341

Source: Committee on Finance, U.S. Senate, *Canadian Automobile Agreement: U.S. International Trade Report on the US-Canada Automotive Agreement; Its History, Terms and Impact* (Washington, DC, 1976), Chart A-82, 294. The table was compiled from industry estimates and firms' responses to an ITC questionnaire.

in its automotive sector (see Table 5.1 and Table 5.2).[17] David Emerson contends that the impact of the auto pact cannot be understated. He estimates that Canada's gross national product in 1969 would have been 4.72 per cent lower in 1961 dollars if not for the auto pact, and exports and employment levels lower by 21.37 per cent and 2.84 per cent, respectively. The auto pact 'provided a substantial stimulus directly to the [automotive] industries themselves and, indirectly, to the Canadian economy.'[18] Parts firms and automakers pointed to the agreement in explaining their own increased production levels, as can be seen, for example, in GM's 1967 annual report.[19] In 1969, for the first time ever, the Canadian auto industry produced more than one million vehicles, a tremendous increase over the 325,000 produced in 1960.

At the same time that the Canadian industry was expanding, the Big Three were rationalizing their operations. Administratively, they reorganized their subsidiaries so that the once-independent Canadian entities became completely integrated into their parents' North American operations. Each of the Big Three shifted decision-making for their Canadian facilities to their corporate headquarters in Michigan. Chrysler reorganized its operations, putting Canada under 'U.S. and Canadian Operations' – run from its Detroit offices. In a special letter to shareholders in 1967, GM explained that because of the Canada–U.S. auto pact, the company had realigned its production facilities between the United States and Canada, with a resulting increase in production and some dislocation.[20]

Reorganization was most apparent, however, on the ground, as the automakers and parts makers integrated their Canadian plants into their overall operations. GM had less to gain through rationalization because of its immense size than Ford or Chrysler – it had already been achieving considerable economies of scale. Therefore, GM focused on increased parts production, although it did decrease its products assembly mix.[21] It produced fewer Pontiacs, Buicks, and Oldsmobiles in Canada, but increased its production of Chevrolets, so that in the post-pact period GM reduced by half the number of vehicle models that it made in Canada.[22] As part of its rationalization efforts, GM moved all boxing operations to Canada for the entire North American market. This meant shipping vehicles to Canada, repackaging them for transport, and then reshipping them back through the port of New York, allowing GM to boost its Canadian value added – as per the agreement.[23]

The other automakers could take even better advantage of the new opportunities for production. Chrysler decided to make the Valiant in Canada (called the Dodge Dart in the United States) for export to the United States; by 1965, more than 30,000 Valiants had been shipped south. Now Chrysler was able to import previously unavailable Plymouth Belvederes and Dodge Coronets to Canada.[24] AMC, with very little production in Canada prior to 1965, was in the best position to capitalize on the agreement. AMC completely phased out production of its Ambassador and Javelin lines and greatly expanded its production of Rebels and Ramblers. In 1969, the year that the Hornet was first introduced, AMC's Brampton operation produced for the entire eastern half of the continent, while its Kenosha, Wisconsin, plant built for the western half.[25] The reorganization of smaller U.S. parts companies operating in Canada was also profound. In southwestern Ontario, government officials reported that most of the companies selling under the Canada–U.S. auto pact were reducing or had reduced their lines significantly. It was also reported that 'many of the U.S. subsidiaries are undertaking significant intra-company rationalization with their parents to achieve economies of production through re-allocation of given product lines between Canadian and U.S. plants.'[26]

The case of the Ford Motor Company of Canada is particularly instructive. Before 1965 Ford of Canada was largely independent of its parent corporation, having retained a degree of autonomy unique in the Ford empire. In 1904, Henry Ford created the Canadian company with 51 per cent control held by other Ford stockholders, although the parent company did not own any shares itself. Ford of Canada developed as a separate entity, boasting its own Canadian-born management. Indeed, while the parent company had launched its Commonwealth strategy through Canada – because of the tariff, Ford of Canada owned Ford subsidiaries in a number of Commonwealth countries including Australia and South Africa – much of the decision-making had been left to the Ford of Canada management. But by the 1960s, by purchasing a majority of the company's outstanding shares, the parent company effectively gained control of Ford of Canada and appointed three Americans to its board, while taking over more of Ford of Canada's research and development and marketing programs. But Ford of Canada still retained a lot of independence regarding its operations, and in 1964 even offered the parent company its own plan for continental integration.[27]

When the auto agreement became operational, the parent company undertook to absorb Ford of Canada into a new North American organization. Ford's international division was reorganized so that Ford of Canada was subsumed within the North American automotive operations section under an executive vice-president responsible for continental operations. The president of Ford of Canada, although retaining his by-then largely symbolic title, would now report to the head of the sales group for North American operations, while the director of the Canadian overseas group became responsible to the parent company's executive vice-president in charge of overseas operations. Ford of Canada's purchasing and personnel operations were closely tied to the parent company, with Detroit having the final say on every major decision. Ford of Canada remained a separate profit centre within North America (a tiny number of its shares still traded on the Toronto Stock Exchange). However, all production decision-making was now done on a continental basis, and the Canadian company was to draw heavily on the parent's expertise in meeting its performance targets. What had formerly been an independent company, with its own hierarchy and structure, was by the end of 1967 merely a division within the Ford Motor Company's North American operations.[28]

On the ground, changes to Ford of Canada's operations were equally dramatic. Whereas Ford plants in Canada had been producing an entire range of vehicles for the Canadian market, they now produced only a few products for all of North America. The Windsor engine plant was modernized at the cost of $50 million. Previously, Windsor had produced nine basic engines in eighty-six different versions for various models for sale in Canada. Now, only one engine, a V-8 model (in about fifteen versions) was being built there – for shipment to plants in both Canada and the United States. The Windsor transmission and chassis plant was upgraded, to the tune of $20 million. Instead of producing more than 200 different products, as it had been doing before 1965, the plant now had only four main lines: compact car axles, transmissions, hubs and drums, and stampings. Windsor and the expanded plant in Oakville, in conjunction with two Ford plants in New Jersey, now produced and distributed for all of northeastern Canada and the United States. According to Ford of Canada's president Karl Scott, duplication was gradually reduced based on production and local economic factors.[29] In 1968 Rodney W. Markley, testifying before a congressional committee in Washington on behalf of his company, reported that, in the three years since the pact, Ford had drastically reduced the number of car and truck models it was producing in Canada, from seventy-one and 227 to forty-nine and sixty-four.[30]

Purchasing for Ford components in Canada was shifted to Detroit, which caused a stir in May 1965. About 125 people from the Oakville purchasing operation were moved to Michigan or absorbed elsewhere in the company. The Canadian value added that the operation represented, which to that point had been included in Canadian content valuations, was to be made up with further production so that Ford could meet its obligations under the Canada–U.S. auto agreement. Canadian critics pointed to the loss of Ford's purchasing operation as evidence that the auto pact was eroding Canadian plant and jobs, while

Ford and officials in Ottawa defended the action as a necessary aspect of the rationalization occurring under the new regime.[31]

These immense changes in the Canadian automotive industry marked a dramatic departure. From 1965 onwards, the Canadian auto industry was subsumed within the North American auto sector – and directed from Detroit. Over time the Canadian industry fulfilled and even surpassed many of the production targets set out in the agreement and the letters of undertaking, as the industry was integrated with its U.S. counterpart. A 1969 Canadian government report indicated that 1967 production was 29 per cent higher than in 1964, automotive exports were up from $82 million in 1964 to $1.2 billion in 1967 (an increase of 1,370 per cent), and annual additional investment between 1964 and 1967 was $174 million. Canadian efficiency, which had traditionally lagged far behind that of the Americans, had improved to 84 per cent of U.S. figures by 1967. Ottawa was satisfied that the auto pact had substantially fulfilled all of its objectives – increased production, exports, and employment – by 1968.[32] The long-term consequences of this continental rationalization were only slowly becoming apparent in those first few years of the agreement's operation. The immediate impact that integration of the Canadian auto industry into the U.S. industry had was most keenly felt by those most affected by changes in North America's auto industry: auto workers in Canada.

From the outset, it was obvious that some auto workers would lose their jobs as the industry reorganized on a continental basis. The Canadian UAW protested the lack of protection for its membership, which had been the price of the UAW's acceptance of the agreement. News that 1,600 Ford workers at Windsor would be laid off indefinitely reached Canadian UAW director George Burt in June 1965. Incensed; Burt complained to Labour Minister Allan MacEachen, reminding him that the UAW had been promised some sort of program to alleviate dislocation and protesting that though the agreement had been signed in January nothing was as yet in place to protect these workers.[33] Without additional protection for its dislocated members, Burt would be hardpressed to maintain already tenuous support of the union's rank-and-file.

Ottawa seemed in but little hurry to develop any such a program, and Burt was forced to badger MacEachen constantly, until finally, in June 1965, the minister announced the government's new transitional assistance benefits (TAB) program for auto industry workers. It fell far short of the UAW's expectations, with benefits of 62 per cent of the laid-off worker's weekly earnings, a dependence allowance of 2.5 per cent of weekly earnings per dependent, and a total weekly benefit that could not exceed 65 per cent of the average weekly wages and salaries in the automotive and parts industries. In other words, the most a worker thrown out of a job because of the auto pact could receive would be $75 a week. The labour minister praised the program and claimed that, since the automotive agreement was a great benefit to the national economy, it was only reasonable to expect other Canadians and their employers would help displaced auto workers.[34]

Union members, however, viewed the program as nothing but a clever sleight of hand, since the TAB merely replaced the already existing supplemental unemployment benefits (SUB) negotiated by the union – and could not exceed those levels. By some union estimates, the program cut a worker's earnings almost in half. In fact, because most of the automakers never agreed to sign onto the TAB, the programs' funds were used only by those companies where no SUB existed.[35] Dislocated auto workers, especially those at the Big Three, received the employee-employer funded SUB instead of the TAB, and this turn of events did not sit well with the major automakers.[36] Compared with U.S. transitional assistance legislation, which had been passed promptly and put in place long before the Canadian legislation, Ottawa's bill offered less compensation, a fact that was immediately exploited by both union representatives and opposition members in the House of Commons as an opening from which to attack the auto agreement.[37]

Burt saw no reason for which auto workers should lose their jobs because the government had entered into the auto pact (even though he was a supporter of it), and he was determined to get better protection for his members. In August 1966 it was announced that there would be 2,600 layoffs at GM in Oshawa. Burt led a delegation to Ottawa to again try to persuade the government to rework the TAB to provide more and better benefits. The union submitted a brief and met with the new minister of labour, John Nicholson, but left Ottawa with no firm commitments. For all of Burt's protestations, the government remained unmoved, as senior officials such as Simon Reisman were advising that the benefits of the agreement for auto workers were becoming increasingly apparent and would thus render such further measures unnecessary. By the end of the year, with more than 3,000 auto workers put out of their jobs because of the auto agreement, Ottawa had paid out a minuscule $4,559 through its program of transitional assistance ben-

Table 5.3 Employment in the auto industry in Canada, 1963–1968

Year	Parts and accessories	Assembly	Total
1963	26,100	34,200	60,300
1964	30,500	38,800	69,300
1965	34,600	45,400	80,000
1966	38,800	46,100	84,900
1967	37,100	47,000	84,100
1968	35,400	48,000	83,400

Source: Carl Beigie, *The Canada–U.S. Automotive Agreement* (Montreal: Canadian-American Committee, 1970), 83.

efits. The Canadian UAW had made virually no impact on government officials, and the TAB remained unchanged.[38]

By 1967 the question of worker dislocation was becoming a less prominent issue for the UAW, as by then the benefits of the agreement were indeed being realized through increased employment in the industry. Although there had been significant rationalization, as the Big Three integrated production into their larger North American operations, increased Canadian demand and the expansion required by the letters of undertaking meant that employment in the automotive industry reached new heights in the late 1960s (see Table 5.3). In 1968, total employment in the automotive industry was at 83,400, which represented an increase of nearly 15,000 jobs since 1964.[39]

The auto pact's obviously beneficial impact on employment silenced the UAW with regard to the worker protection legislation, and it turned its attention to criticizing domestic car prices. The UAW leadership in both Canada and the United States had made lower car prices another condition for its support of the agreement. This was particularly important on the Canadian side, as car prices in Canada were substantially higher than in the United States. Since the Canadian industry had most to gain from rationalization of the industry, it made sense that Canadian car prices should most dramatically reflect this new economy. During the congressional hearings on the auto pact in April 1965, UAW's Leonard Woodcock urged the U.S. administration to push Ottawa to ensure that Canadian car prices were lowered, which placed the Liberal government in a difficult position. In the House of Commons, Opposition members could not help but take advantage of the delicious irony – American unionists were demanding that the American government force the Canadian government to protect Canadian consumers![40] Since early 1965 there had also been pressure from the press demanding that the government ensure that consumers received some of the benefits of the agreement.[41] But the Liberal government held fast and said little on the issue, even after Chrysler Canada president Ron Todgham explained that car prices would not decrease in the foreseeable future.[42]

The battle over car prices peaked in September 1966. The Big Three announced that there would be no price cuts for the 1967 model year – there would actually be price increases – and the UAW took action. From the consumers' perspective, the auto agreement should have led to a narrowing of the price gap, since cars built in Canada were being sold in the United States, and vice versa. When the $50 million tariff savings was factored in, there was no obvious reason for prices to be actually rising. The union had commissioned a study which pegged the price differential at around $150 for a standard-sized, high-volume Chevrolet or Ford.[43] Other studies indicated that for the more expensive models, the difference was even greater.[44]

The union took their case directly to the government. Burt challenged Finance Minister Sharp and Industry Minister Drury to force automakers to roll back the announced price increases. Productivity and efficiency *had* improved, argued Burt, so it was nonsense for the manufacturers to claim increased costs – even when the new mandatory safety features such as seat belts were factored in. Burt claimed that there was no real price competition within the Big Three, as evidenced by the refusal of Ford and Chrysler to place price tags on their products until industry leader GM unveiled its prices for the new model year. This was an outrage, Burt argued, and he demanded that the Consumer Credit Committee be instructed to investigate the situation. Neither Sharp nor Drury agreed to the request, and Burt lobbied the committee himself the following month.[45] When committee members, too, rejected his plea, Burt was infuriated. Even Senator David Croll, long considered a staunch ally of labour, suffered from Burt's attack.[46] He accused Croll and the committee of being afraid of the government, and of General Motors – an accusation that Croll found unwarranted. Burt did not apologize, and the Consumer Credit Committee did not investigate auto prices.[47] By the end of the decade car prices were still higher (in some cases significantly higher) in Canada than in the United States.[48] As with the issue of legislation protecting dislocated workers, Ottawa remained immovable on car prices.

Government officials were far more concerned about the actual functioning of the agreement than about worker protection or car prices.

After 1965 relations between business and government in the auto industry became more complex. The automakers were responsible for implementing the changes brought about by the new agreement, and the government was determined to ensure that they met their new responsibilities under the pact and as stipulated in the letters of undertaking. This required Ottawa to closely monitor the progress in the industry to determine whether the companies were indeed fulfilling their obligations. Industry-government consultation was not new. The auto companies and the federal government had a long history of cooperating on various issues. The motor vehicle assemblers' lobby group, the Motor Vehicle Manufacturers Association (MVMA), had often met with government officials to propose ideas and gather information. The Bladen Commission, the 1962–3 transmission duty, and the Drury duty-remission plan had all been developed after close discussion with industry leaders. The auto pact itself had come into being only after intense negotiations with the MVMA and the Big Three automakers.

After the agreement was signed, the MVMA and the auto companies met regularly with government officials to chart the course for the industry's development under the new program. To achieve duty-free status, the automakers were to meet four goals under the 1965 Motor Vehicle Tariff Order (MVTO), which established the rules for the companies under the auto pact. The companies were required to achieve the stipulated production-to-sales ratios for both passenger and commercial vehicles (that is, the 1964 level for established producers, which was approximately 1:1 and could not be less than 75:100).[49] They had to meet the 1964 base CVA floor, which was calculated to be $679 million for the entire industry. Missing these targets – by even one dollar – meant a company no longer met the specified definition of a bona fide manufacturer under the agreement and would result, technically, in the company being forced to pay duties on the entirety of its imports, a massive amount of money. Furthermore, the letters of undertaking required the automakers to invest an additional $260 million in the Canadian auto industry and to ensure that they increased the value of their Canadian content by 60 per cent in passenger cars and 50 per cent in commercial vehicles of any increases in their production. The practical implications of these commitments can be seen in Tables 5.4 and 5.5 which outline the CVA and ratio requirements as agreed to by each company.

Following implementation of the Canada–U.S. auto pact, the MVMA

Table 5.4 Canadian production-to-sales ratio requirements, Big Three and American Motors (base year 1963–4 = 100)

	Passenger vehicles	Trucks	Commercial vehicles
GM	97.9	100.19	91.7
Ford	99.4	108.1	89.8
Chrysler	99.6	100.5	86.1
AMC	108.3		

Note: The companies' exact ratios were never made public during the life of the auto agreement. The documents on which this table is based were released only recently. Source: 'Base Year Ratios and/or Minimum Ratios Required,' Company Reports to Dept. of Industry, Trade and Commerce, National Archives of Canada, RG 19, Vol. 5959, File 8705-8-15, Statistics.

Table 5.5 Canadian value added (CVA) requirements, Big Three and American Motors, base year (1963–4), and additional requirements for the years 1965–6, 1966–7, 1967–8 ($ millions)

	Canadian value added				
	Base year CVA (1963–4)	Three-year base CVA	Annual additional CVA	Three-year additional CVA	Total three-year CVA
GM	315.73	947.19	40.33	121.00	1068.19
Ford	231.20	693.60	24.73	74.20	767.80
Chrysler	85.64	256.62	11.00	33.00	289.62
AMC	27.16	81.48	3.73	11.20	92.68
Total	659.73	1,978.89	79.79	239.40	2,218.29

Note: These figures do not include the growth in market requirement from the letters of undertaking, which stipulated that these companies were required to boost their CVA by 60% of the growth in the market for passenger vehicles and 50% of the growth in the market for trucks.
Source: Various letters of undertaking; Committee on Finance, U.S. Senate, *Canadian Automobile Agreement: U.S. International Trade Report on the U.S.-Canada Automotive Agreement; Its History, Terms and Impact* (Wasghington, DC, 1976), 455; James F. Keeley, 'Constraints on Canadian International Economic Policy' (PhD diss., Stanford University, 1980), 265.

and the individual automakers constantly sought to alter their requirements, particularly for the ratio. According to the auto agreement, the ratio was to be maintained for each class of vehicles, that is, the automakers were prohibited from shifting ratio requirements between classes of vehicles. This meant, for example, that if a company produced cars and trucks in 1964, it was required to continue producing both types of vehicles at the same rate that it sold them in order to maintain its duty-free status. Thus, for example, while it made more sense for a company such as Ford to discontinue production of trucks in Canada, and then simply import trucks and concentrate on producing only cars, the agreement forced Ford of Canada to continue (and indeed to increase) its production of trucks in order to meet the ratio requirements. This explains the addition of truck assembly operations at Ford's Oakville plant in 1966.[50] It also explains why the base CVA and additional $260 million required was so easily met by the producers and achieved, to a very large degree.[51]

Furthermore, because the sales-to-production ratio was based on production – that is, the companies were required to produce as many units as they sold, as opposed to selling as many as they produced – Canadian sales had a profound effect on ratio and Canadian content targets. For example, if Canadian sales increased, but those cars that represented the increase in sales were mostly imported models with no Canadian content, then the cars built in Canada had to achieve higher Canadian content levels to meet the CVA and 60 per cent targets, or the companies had to build more cars in Canada to satisfy the 60 per cent CVA threshold. Should a car built only in the United States become very popular in Canada, for example, this could have a tremendous impact on a company's ratio – as happened in the mid-1960s with the introduction of the Ford Mustang. Conversely, if there were a slump in U.S. demand of Canadian-made units, yet high Canadian demand for products originating in the United States, the ratio would be difficult to meet, since the sales value of Canadian cars might be unexpectedly high in relation to the production value of Canadian-made products. If the automakers could avoid meeting these ratio targets, they could manage their production more efficiently, with less emphasis on the need to meet Canadian content and production targets. The automakers disagreed with the method employed by the government to determine the sales-to-production ratio. Imported vehicles were valued at the sales price, which was considerably higher than the actual production value of vehicles made in Canada. Even if the Big Three continued to produce the same number of vehicles as they sold, the valuation differential resulted in a deterioration of the ratio. And so, in the words of MVMA president James G. Dykes, the ratio calculation became 'a king-sized headache.'[52]

The automakers' efforts to ease the burdens imposed on them by what had been intended to be the agreement's safeguards became apparent very soon after the auto pact went into operation. At a meeting in January 1965, the MVMA's chairman presented the government with a number of proposals. People throughout the industry were upset, claiming that they had not been informed of the full extent of the regulations under the new arrangement which hampered their performance, particularly concerning the ratio. First, the companies attacked the provision prohibiting them from importing a vehicle duty-free and later, if necessary, amending the terms by paying duty on that vehicle in order to meet the ratio requirement. Hypothetically, companies wanted to maintain some flexibility by being able to import vehicles duty-free and, if they did not meet their production to sales targets, pay duties on some of those cars in order to lower their ratio. Second, the automakers were unhappy with the exact calculation of the ratio. Since the ratio's numerator was based on the *sales value* of vehicles produced in Canada, it required special calculations for vehicles produced but not sold. This also made it more difficult for the companies to reach their ratio targets. Instead, they hoped to change the ratio to include the value of vehicles *produced and sold* in Canada. The industry wished to remedy these problems, a position which the government agreed to consider, although it did not commit itself to making any of the changes.[53]

By June 1965 many of the initial administrative problems surrounding the operation of the auto agreement had been solved, although the vehicle manufacturers still voiced a number of concerns primarily with regard to meeting the required ratios. Ottawa would not alter its expectations for the sales-to-production ratio, but it did agree to ease some of the reporting requirements from the companies.[54] Moreover, the government signalled to the automakers that it would try to be as flexible as possible when it came to meeting the ratio targets. Simon Reisman told the MVMA, 'If, at the end of a model year, it is determined that a firm has not achieved its ratio because of special circumstances which were beyond its control, I am satisfied that the Government would take this into consideration.'[55] Nevertheless, the following February, the MVMA was still lobbying for significant changes concerning the determination of the entry of parts and vehicles under the Motor Vehicle Tariff Order and to the calculation of the ratio. The association warned that unless the ratio calculations were eased to allow more flexible reporting, some companies might not meet the ratio requirements for the 1966 model year.[56]

In the spring of 1966 it could be seen that automakers were indeed having difficulties under the new Automotive Products Trade Agreement. A downturn in the Canadian market was especially troublesome for the smaller ones. AMC and Volvo both had problems making the ratio for the 1965 model year.[57] More ominously, rumours were beginning to circulate about the performance of the Big Three under the pact. A slowdown in the U.S. market threatened to cool their expected export programs.[58] In the autumn, it was reported that General Motors was behind in its investment targets, which had been slowed by a strike at its plant in Ste Thérèse. GM had expected to export 75,000 vehicles from the new factory, but the strike scrubbed most of that plan.[59] Ford and Chrysler were said to be well on their way to meeting the CVA stipulation, but their slow reporting left Ottawa unsure of their exact position. Only Chrysler president R.W. Todgham was willing to predict that the company would meet its targets before the 1968 deadline.[60]

Industry Minister Drury met with the presidents of the manufacturing companies in the second half of 1966 to ascertain the automakers' views on how things were going under the auto agreement. The meetings were candid, and they exposed many of the new tensions between the industry and the government since the agreement had been put into operation.[61] Some MVMA members were pleased with the auto agreement, while others, particularly GM, did not hide their dissatisfaction with it. The manufacturers pressed for an end to taxes on machinery. They claimed that the taxes were unfair and deterred them from sourcing more production in Canada, an issue that had been raised by the MVMA previously on a number of occasions, both private and public.[62] Drury told them that the matter would be considered by his and other departments. Eventually, the taxes on production machinery were lifted. This was one of the few concrete – and public – measures that Ottawa took in response to the automakers' demands.[63]

Drury asked the automakers to submit up-to-date reports on their operations for the years 1964–6 and their plans and projections for 1967 and 1968. The other firms complied, except GM. It withheld its plans for 1968 and did not report its purchases from parts firms, as had also been requested. Based on the information that they did have, the Canadian officials who studied the automakers' reports were relatively optimistic about the progress that the companies were making. Because of its smaller size and smaller target, Chrysler had already exceeded its 'bogey' of CVA by a large margin. Thus, Reisman was happy to say that apart from a few problems with the specific commitments, most of the firms 'had been working with considerable success to meet the objectives of the program.'

Table 5.6 Big Three Canadian value added (CVA), required and produced ($millions), and total CVA as a percentage of sales, by model year, 1965–1972

Year	General Motors CVA			Ford CVA			Chrysler CVA		
	Required	Produced	% of sales	Required	Produced	% of sales	Required	Produced	% of sales
1965	391.9	436.9	63	259.7	288.3	64	166.2	188.8	72
1966	428.1	506.9	67	290.7	349.2	69	195.1	238.5	77
1967	409.5	459.8	63	295.5	405.6	79	216.5	234.5	68
1968	597.4	567.6	67	403.5	424.5	75	290.7	309.2	74
1969	645.2	699.7	75	420.1	519.7	87	289.8	343.5	83
1970	585.5	687.9	84	371.0	535.6	103	264.8	361.1	97
1971	514.6	674.3	97	409.0	601.7	103	295.4	375.3	88
1972	649.8	818.2	87	464.6	677.1	99	319.9	436.4	93

Source: Company Reports to Dept. of Industry, Trade and Commerce, National Archives of Canada, RG 19, Vol. 5959, File 8705-8-15, File, Statistics.

The biggest problem remained the performance of General Motors. Based on the given information, it was anticipated that GM would fall far short regarding its ratio commitment in the 1967 model year. GM had met its CVA requirements for 1965 and 1966 (see Table 5.6), but Reisman wondered whether it would be able to make its total target of $121 million by 1968. He observed that GM had exported only $50 million CVA in parts in 1967, while Chrysler, a much smaller company, had exported $94 million CVA in parts in 1967. Overall, GM's Canadian production was expected to be considerably lower than required to meet its sales ratio and thus it wasn't going to be able to meet one of the key requirements of the agreement.[64] As Reisman had predicted, the following year more problems appeared as the automotive industry's slowdown in the United States began to cause difficulties for the larger producers. In early 1967 both GM and Ford asked Drury whether it would be possible to adjust the ratio calculation so that they would not miss their target. GM's president Walker explained to Drury that his company had a large carryover from 1966, had experienced the Ste Thérèse strike, and faced a decline in its exports because of the slowdown in the United States.[65]

Less surprising was Ford's notice to the Canadian government that there was a real chance that the company would miss its CVA requirement for 1967 (see Table 5.6). Even before the agreement had been signed in January 1965, Ford officials had explained to the government

Table 5.7 Big Three ratio required (in parentheses) and achieved, cars and trucks, by model year, 1965–1972

Year	General Motors ratio		Ford ratio		Chrysler ratio	
	Cars (97.9)	Trucks (100.1)	Cars (99.4)	Trucks (108.1)	Cars (99.6)	Trucks (100.5)
1965	102.5	111.5	101.9	111.5	99.7	101.9
1966	102.8	112.2	102.8	156.5	112.6	106.6
1967	98.4	103.3	101.1	208.9	110.9	101.8
1968	101.2	112.2	106.9	218.3	127.9	106.8
1969	122.5	122.3	160.1	238.7	143.0	105.0
1970	133.6	129.5	220.7	236.4	168.2	102.7
1971	127.5	103.5	184.1	202.1	137.3	102.2
1972	126.4	101.2	189.8	162.2	137.6	101.5

Source: Company Reports to Dept. of Industry, Trade and Commerce, National Archives of Canada, RG 19, Vol. 5959, File 8705-8-15, File, Statistics.

that the company would have a difficult time meeting the in-vehicle CVA requirement because it was rationalizing engine production so that many Canadian-made vehicles no longer had Canadian-built engine parts in them, a large obstacle to achieving the 60 per cent requirement.[66] Company officials predicted a $22 million shortfall in their CVA in the early years of the agreement. Because of this possibility, Ford had signed an additional letter of undertaking stating that it would make great efforts to further boost its production over the 1965–8 period. Government officials were inclined to 'give sympathetic consideration' to Ford because of these particular circumstances.

Ford of Canada's Karl Scott echoed GM's reasoning for his own company's failure to meet the ratio, namely, slowing U.S. sales. Adding to Scott's problems was the fact that Canadian buyers were snapping up the very popular U.S.-built Mustangs and Cougars, which further eroded the ratio. Ford just topped its 1965 ratio but had come close to missing it (see Table 5.7). Achieving its Canadian ratio target would require Ford to run its Canadian plants at capacity while plants sat idle in the United States, a proposition the company would not entertain as a given. Such a development, warned Scott, 'would raise problems in Congress and with the unions in the U.S.' Ford asked for two changes in the operation of the agreement. First, it asked that the ratio be determined on the basis of units rather than sales. This meant that less expensive Canadian-built cars would increase the ratio against the more pricey sports cars. The sales side of the ratio was higher per unit because of the more expensive imports, whereas the production side of the ratio was based on cheaper Canadian vehicles produced at Ford's Canadian plants. Basing the figures on units would go a long way to lowering the company's requirements, but it would still build as many cars as they sold in Canada. Second, Ford requested whether, in the event of a shortfall in the ratio for 1967, the company could make it up in 1968 in an aggregate surplus for all three categories of vehicles (passenger, commercial, and buses) in 1967 and 1968. The effect would be to allow Ford to ease its responsibility by stretching its ratio requirements over two years, instead of the normal one year production-to-sales ratio.[67]

Ottawa turned down both of Ford's requests. Government officials sternly warned Walker and Scott that 'they must meet their commitments in order to qualify for duty free privileges.' However, the stick was, of course, followed by a carrot. The government would not necessarily impose penalties on the companies if it were seen that they each had made the greatest efforts to meet their requirements: 'If a firm does not meet a particular commitment, the matter should be examined in relation to the company's overall performance.' Furthermore, Drury was sure that each company would indeed make these efforts and that would be taken into account. Drury informed Scott that he was 'impressed with the progress' Ford had made under the CVA and that he felt certain that it was possible for Ford to improve its ratio.[68]

The government did make one unique concession that enabled Ford to meet its requirements, while easing the threat of penalties should Ford miss them. Ottawa knew in advance that Ford was going to miss its CVA, and so it agreed to allow Ford to make up the shortfall by purchasing a greater supply of parts from Canadian vendors. The amount purchased would be determined by the shortfall in CVA in the period. In this way, Ford would purchase from independent parts makers the dollar value of whatever CVA target it missed in the given year. But in 1967 the government modified the company's obligations. If Ford missed its CVA, it could adopt a consignment program, and this would have the effect of reducing sales and, accordingly, increasing Canadian value added as a percentage of Canadian sales. Practically, this meant that Ford could consign sales in a given year over to the next year, when its production might be greater, and thereby boost production for the given year. When, in 1965, Ford came close to missing its CVA target, auditors from the Department of National Revenue allowed such a consignment and agreed, in 1967, that Ford had complied content with the operation of the agreement. At the very least, the auto pact was a much more desirable arrangement than the alternatives that the manufacturers had feared might otherwise ensue, namely, greater protectionism and greater Canadian content regulations. Government-industry relations, however, were strained to the breaking point by the end of the 1960s, as each side sought to gain what it could in its management of the automotive industry. With the pact-mandated 1968 review rapidly approaching, both faced difficulties in determining how their relationship should continue to develop. But this was just one of the problems that both the Canadian government and the industry faced. After 1968 American discontent with the implementation of the Automotive Products Trade Agreement of 1965 would threaten this already delicate balance.

with the new regulations. Privately, Ford officials admitted that without the concessions, it was liable to approximately $165 million in penalties.[69] This astounding figure illustrated the value of the automotive trade agreement to the manufacturers: Not only did they save on the actual duties (although in the absence of the agreement, the duties would not have been as high), their integrated production and rationalization provided further economic savings, as reflected in their parents companies' impressive financial results for the period.

Notwithstanding the exception granted Ford, the government was determined to hold the automakers to their commitments by keeping them uncertain about the implications for any failure to meet the requirements. Ottawa's strategy was to warn them of the consequences of failure under the program and encourage them to continue their efforts. By doing so, the government kept the manufacturers 'honest.' That is, by being kept in the dark of the consequences of failure to meet the targets, the companies were inclined to do their best to meet them. James Dykes of the MVMA summed up the industry group's frustration with the Canadian government: If a company was in trouble under the agreement, Dykes complained, 'the answer from the government was, Silence. In unspoken words it was, "do your best because we will not promise you relief if you miss fulfilling all requirements – but if you do, we will consider your special situation; if you are hurt come and see us and maybe we will help." This was a realistic, even a realistically entrepreneurial-like position, but large corporations are not amenable to operating with "ifs," "ands" and "buts" in government regulations.'[70]

Yet Dykes and the automakers remained circumspect. They did not voice their criticisms too loudly for fear of jeopardizing their position. For its part, the government remained determined to ensure that the companies met their requirements, and any weakening of those requirements would compromise their position.

Moreover, the ratio requirement, which was proving the most difficult to meet for the companies, held out the possibility of further investment in the future. Reisman admitted to Drury in the summer of 1967 that 'the ratio requirement is probably the main bargaining lever available for obtaining further production commitments from the motor vehicle companies.' Any relaxation of the ratio would be contingent on future levels of investment in Canada. According to Reisman, the same was true for the Canadian value added stipulation. 'Like the ratio, the present CVA requirement for vehicle assembly is one of the few bargaining counters available to the Government. It is desirable, therefore, that the vehicle producers clearly understand that this requirement will be waived on an annual basis only for those companies which realize the new objectives of the program.'[71] In other words, the ratio and the CVA were to be held in reserve, not only to hold the companies accountable for their Canadian production levels, but to provide leverage for further investment in Canada. The most noteworthy example of this occurred in the early 1970s, when Chrysler agreed to build the Pilette Road assembly plant in Windsor to make up for several years of missing its ratio targets.[72]

The Big Three understood the severity of missing the ratio, and they governed themselves accordingly. A little luck helped, as well. In June 1967, demand for cars in Canada reached an all-time high, as did Canadian production. Between them, GM and Ford produced over 100,000 vehicles, allowing them to avoid the penalties that might otherwise have been imposed. Despite each company's dire warnings, GM and Ford both achieved their ratio and CVA requirements under the agreement, as did Chrysler and virtually all of the other companies with auto pact status (see Table 5.7). Indeed, by 1968, it was clear that the auto pact was working exactly as its negotiators had hoped it would. Canadian content and value added in the automotive industry were growing visibly, and the boost to the industry was undeniable, not only in numbers of jobs but in the massive amounts of new investment and Canadian production: Total CVA in the industry was 69 per cent by 1967, well above the 58 per cent requirement (see Table 5.8). Collectively, automakers would continue to far surpass their CVA and ratio requirements for the period after 1965. While the impressive growth in the Canadian market for automobiles eased the difficulties they faced in meeting the ratio requirements, the constant threat that they might fail to meet their ratio continued to complicate industry-government relations. In spite of improvement in their production levels, the companies continued to press for the end of the ratio and the CVA requirements.[73] The government rejected these demands, once again, and suggested to the companies that they continue to do their best to meet the requirements.

By the late 1960s a clear pattern had developed between the government and the automakers regarding the operation of the Automotive Products Trade Agreement. The concessions made to Ford showed that while the government was willing to temporarily ease some of the restrictions (and demand future concessions in return), it was determined to hold companies to their commitments for as long as possible.

Table 5.8 Canada's auto industry, total Canadian value added, 1965–1972 ($ millions)

	CVA		Cost of vehicles sold	Cost of sales less CVA produced	CVA ratio: to cost of sales (%)	CVA ratio required to cost of sales (%)
	Required	Produced				
1965	891	992	1,534	542	65	58
1966	988	1,186	1,716	530	69	58
1967	1,002	1,200	1,738	538	69	58
1968	1,395	1,420	1,977	557	72	71
1969	1,471	1,703	2,110	407	81	70
1970	1,341	1,743	1,891	148	92	71
1971	1,350	1,825	1,911	86	96	71
1972	1,592	2,145	2,371	226	90	67

Source: Company Reports to Dept. of Industry, Trade and Commerce, National Archives of Canada, RG 19, Vol. 5959, File 8705-8-15, File, Statistics.

Reisman admitted that the ratio and CVA safeguards were the only leverage Ottawa had to keep the companies 'honest' in their operation and the only way that it might exact from them further investments in Canada. The threat of reimposing duties on missed targets was enough to net the government the required levels of investment and production. This provides a strong illustration of the impact of interventionist policies on the functioning of the marketplace. State-directed production goals were now the order of the day. As the results became apparent, Reisman and his colleagues could have no doubt that with the auto pact, Canada had successfully accrued its 'fair share' of North American automotive production.

The automotive industry, for its part, continued to demand a loosening of its obligations in an effort to reap the most benefits possible under the duty-free nature of the agreement. Understandably, the industry also sought to gain as much freedom from these state-directed targets as possible, without losing the benefit of duty-free trade. While the automakers continually threatened to miss their targets thereby hoping to get them reduced, they almost always achieved them. In fact, by the late 1960s it was becoming evident that the companies were shifting far more production to Canada than was actually required, a situation that held out the possibility of a distinctly negative response from the U.S. government.

In spite of their constant complaints, the automakers were generally

6

Consolidating the Borderless North American Auto Industry, 1968–1971

Despite a rapidly shifting relationship between Canada and the United States, and significant changes in political leadership and governmental personnel, the operation of the Canada–U.S. auto pact continued undisturbed until 1968. Thereafter, as the cross-border automotive trade balance swung rapidly in Canada's favour, the administration of President Richard Nixon grew ever more frustrated, until it demanded that all the Canadian 'transitional' production safeguards in the agreement be removed. U.S. pressure reached a breaking point, and the Canadians offered to make concessions. But by then it was nearly too late, and the Americans refused the offer. Instead, in August 1971, Washington threatened to unilaterally abrogate the 1965 Automotive Products Trade Agreement, as part of the drastic shift in American economic policy known as the 'Nixon shocks.' These measures were designed to strengthen the progressively weakened U.S. trade position, in which the effects of the auto pact played no small role.

In this uncertain and quickly changing economic environment, the automotive companies were caught between the two governments. Although the greatest profits would come if the safeguards were ended, and the companies were thereby free to conduct the continental auto industry as they saw fit, the automakers still feared the potential alternatives to the new regime. In Canada, the nationalism of Walter Gordon and his allies had not subsided, and harsh protectionist measures to be imposed by the Canadian government were the auto pact regime to flounder remained a possibility. Nevertheless, the companies continued to resist Ottawa's demands for greater production commitments by arguing that such increases would lead to renewed American attacks on the auto pact. In this way, the auto companies used the governments against each other: they told U.S. trade representatives that greater pressure to lift the safeguards would lead to a Canadian abrogation and a harsh new regime that would set back the movement towards freer trade and critically wound the industry; they told the Canadians that new or additional demands on them to meet Canadian state-directed production targets would arouse further U.S. criticism, and threaten the very basis of Canada–U.S. relations. For the auto companies, then, the status quo was a satisfactory end result.

The operation of the auto pact continued unaffected by changes in both national governments. In the United States, Lyndon Johnson, humbled by mounting economic problems and the Vietnam conflict, and facing increasing criticism and declining popularity, made the dramatic decision not to seek a second term as president.[1] Republican Richard Nixon was swept into office in 1968. Although White House staff and the administration's senior posts changed hands with the arrival of a new president, there was no desire to change the U.S. position on the automotive agreement, at least not initially. The appointment of Treasury Secretary John Connally in 1971, however, changed the tenor of Washington's attitude towards Canada considerably. Otherwise, many of the officials in the State Department who had negotiated the agreement, such as Philip Trezise and Julius Katz, continued to be responsible for Canadian issues.

In Canada, Pierre Trudeau won the 1968 federal election with a solid Liberal majority. While Trudeau's landslide victory signified new attitudes on some issues in Ottawa, there was no change in the government's position on the auto sector.[2] Nor did later changes in personnel or the structure of government ministries affect Canada's auto policy. In 1968 Bud Drury was replaced as industry minister by Ottawa MP Jean-Luc Pepin. After an academic career at the University of Ottawa, Pepin came into politics in 1963, and like Drury favoured a strong role for Ottawa in the progress and evolution of the Canadian auto sector. Although Pepin was not an 'industry man,' industry leaders came to respect his abilities and his determination to secure a strong position for the federal government in the development of the industry. Other notable cabinet changes made by Prime Minister Trudeau were the appointments of Edgar Benson to Finance and Mitchell Sharp to External Affairs.

There were changes in the staff and structure of the civil service. In 1967 Simon Reisman left his position as deputy minister of industry to become assistant to the president of the Treasury Board of Canada. He

was replaced by J.H. Warren, who had been involved in the auto negotiations as a representative of the Finance Department. Although he
changed positions, Reisman continued to be a key player on the auto
file until well into the 1970s; in 1978 he was made head of the Royal
Commission of Inquiry into the Canadian Automotive Industry.[3] In
April 1969, as an effort to streamline government operations, the departments of Industry and Trade and Commerce were folded into a
new Department of Industry, Trade and Commerce (ITC), which continued to oversee the government's auto policies; Pepin was minister of
the newly merged department until 1972.

After 1968, however, the new Canadian players on the cross-border
auto issue faced a dramatically changed atmosphere, as the United
States became more and more critical of the operation of the auto
agreement. In 1967 and 1968 the declining U.S. trade surplus brought
out intense attacks on it, especially in the U.S. Congress. Democratic
senators Al Gore (Tennessee) and Vance Hartke (Indiana), the
agreement's most visible congressional critics, renewed their complaints.
Under the enabling legislation that Congress passed in 1965, the auto
pact required the president to submit an annual report to Congress on
the progress of the agreement and the industry. This concession was
exacted by the legislative branch to keep some check on the
administration's trade initiatives and to remind the president that Congress had final authority over trade matters.[4]

The administration was tardy in submitting its initial report. In September 1966 the Commerce Department notified State Department
official Robert McNeill that the brief would not be submitted until
October. The team drafting the report, it was explained, had been
bogged down in other projects and had then been delayed by the
report's complexity. Furthermore, officials claimed that 'green' personnel had been responsible for the statistical analysis and that this also
slowed progress. Even with a promise that officials would work over-
time until the report was complete, the White House did not receive a
draft until mid-February 1967.[5] This delay provided an opportunity for
Senator Gore to renew his attacks, and he demanded a repeal of the
agreement.[6]

White House officials had been convinced that the senator was on a
lone crusade, with few supporters in Congress. Francis Bator, President
Johnson's congressional relations chief, thought that the auto pact's
performance had satisfied all of the main stakeholders in the sector and
that Gore's protests were unwarranted.[7] All the same, the White House

moved quickly to quell the latest opposition to the agreement. In March 1967 the administration released the *President's First Annual Report to the Congress on the Implementation of the Automotive Products Trade Act of 1965.*[8] The government had avoided a major embarrassment, and with a report in hand, the Finance Committee to which Gore's repeal had been referred felt under no pressure to submit his bill to the Senate for consideration.[9]

The *President's First Annual Report* was a brief, statistics-laden document detailing progress under the auto agreement. The initial results were encouraging, but the report was cautious, as 'this initial period is too short a time on which to base firm conclusions regarding the extent to which the agreement is fulfilling its basic objectives.' Nonetheless, the report showed that there was a massive upsurge in the total trade between the two countries, from U.S.$730 million in 1964 to U.S.$2,086 million in 1966. Both exports and imports between the two countries had increased. The U.S. trade surplus, however, was down – from U.S.$692 million in 1965 to U.S.$486 million in 1966. The report did point out that the U.S.$1.2 billion surplus in 1965–6 was larger than it had been in the previous two-year period. Overall, production and employment were up dramatically in both countries, although production increases had been greater in Canada. The report played down the increases in Canadian production, but clearly the U.S. auto trade surplus had fallen.[10]

The appearance of the *First Annual Report* only temporarily muted criticism of the agreement. In the spring of 1968 Gore demanded that the administration produce a second report. When that finally appeared, in May, it managed only to arouse critics further: the favourable balance of trade projected at the time of the agreement was 'less than anticipated,' according to the second report. Gore argued that America's balance of payments were being unwisely diminished by its own government's hand, something that could have easily been predicted – because the Canadians had proposed the pact in the first place to solve their own balance-of-payments problems.[11] With the government's own damaging admission, Gore was able to trigger a Senate analysis of the report, a new round of Senate Finance Committee hearings on the deal, and a new attempt to have it terminated.

The Senate Finance Committee's analysis confirmed Gore's suspicions. The committee concluded that 'the agreement has created a dramatic shift in U.S.–Canadian automotive trade, not to the U.S. advantage.' Yet the analysis did not prove to be the smoking gun that Gore

Table 6.1 Canada–U.S. automotive vehicle production (000s of units) and each country's share of total, 1965–1971

Year	Canada–U.S. Total units	Canada Units	Share (%)	United States Units	Share (%)
1965	11,960	846	7.2	11,114	92.9
1966	11,265	902	8.0	10,363	92.0
1967	9,939	947	9.5	8,992	90.5
1968	11,974	1,180	9.9	10,794	90.2
1969	11,535	1,353	11.7	10,182	88.3
1970	9,456	1,193	12.6	8,263	87.4
1971	12,023	1,373	11.4	10,650	88.6

Note: These figures for Canada differ slightly from the statistics cited in the appendices, because they do not include off-road vehicles.
Source: *Ward's Automotive Reports*, as cited in Canada, *1983 Report on the Canadian Automotive Industry* (Ottawa: Queen's Printer, 1983), 68.

had hoped for. Another spirited defence by government witnesses and auto company representatives diffused any advantage that Gore had gained. Pact negotiator Julius Katz bluntly told questioning senators that the U.S. trade surplus 'has not disappeared.'[12] One Canadian diplomat, quietly taking in the proceedings, noted that the hearings were disorganized and sparsely attended and that Senator Gore seemed inadequately prepared: 'The net effect' may have simply been to add to the record of support for the agreement by the administration and the major U.S. vehicle producers.'[13] Again, critics in Congress had failed to effectively challenge the Automotive Products Trade Agreement.

Publicly, Johnson administration officials were determined to defend the pact, but privately U.S. representatives were beginning to have some reservations as the deadline for the review mandated for 1968 approached. American officials had anticipated that the impact of the auto pact on cross-border trade would be relatively minimal in its first few months of operation. Although State Department analysts expected that by 1968 American manufacturers would increase their Canadian production by about U.S.$500 million over their 1964 level, they did not foresee a decline in the U.S. surplus from its 1964 level of approximately U.S.$580 million.[14] Canadian production increased dramatically by the end of 1965. In 1963 Canada had produced 702,000 motor vehicles. By 1967 that figure had reached 947,000 (see Table 6.1). In 1968 the Canadian industry had its most impressive year ever and for the first time surpassed one million vehicles produced. These huge in-

Table 6.2 Canada's trade with the United States in automotive products, 1964–1969
($ millions)

Year	Exports			Imports			Balance		
	Vehicles	Parts	Total	Vehicles	Parts	Total	Vehicles	Parts	Total
1964	26	79	105	67	655	723	−41	−576	−617
1965	90	147	237	170	852	1,022	−80	−705	−785
1966	493	361	854	409	1,103	1,511	84	−741	−657
1967	1,105	494	1,600	807	1,310	2,117	298	−816	−518
1968	1,686	758	2,444	1,093	1,818	2,910	593	−1,060	−466
1969	2,367	950	3,317	1,154	2,344	3,498	1,213	−1,394	−181
1970	2,127	1,142	3,269	934	2,131	3,065	1,193	−989	+204
1971	2,536	1,504	4,040	1,321	2,521	3,842	1,215	−1,017	+198
1972	2,752	1,801	4,553	1,551	2,957	4,508	1,201	−1,156	+45
1973	3,060	2,240	5,300	2,082	3,620	5,702	978	−1,380	−402

Note: Figures may not add because of rounding. The figures for imports include a
valuation adjustment. Because both the U.S. and Canada used 'foreign country price'
(as opposed to the foreign country export price), it was decided that the two countries
would revalue their imports based on the latter, since both imports and exports could
now be presented as a transaction value. Information on the export price was provided
to both governments by the automotive companies themselves after 1965.
Source: 'Report of the Subcommittee on Statistics to the Committee on the U.S.–
Canadian Automotive Agreement,' March 1970, National Archives of Canada, RG 19,
Vol. 5624, File 8705-01, part 4, Auto Agreement 1969–1970.

creases were not solely a response to increased Canadian demand.
Under the auto pact regime, Canadian exports to the United States had
increased enormously (see Table 6.2), far more than American government officials expected. The deficit, which was more than U.S.$700
million in 1965, had been reduced by over U.S.$200 million by 1967.

When U.S. Treasury Secretary John Connor (Connally's predecessor)
discussed the deteriorating U.S. trade balance with Canadian ambassador A.E. Ritchie, in August 1966, he expressed great concern that the
surplus had declined by $70 million and that the American government
could be exposed to criticism should the surplus drop further.[15] The
administration's discomfort was further exacerbated that month when
American trade journals reported that for the first time the United
States was now a net importer of Canadian motor vehicles, although it
was maintaining its overall automotive trade surplus.[16] Then, in September 1967, U.S. Commerce Department officials reported that the
Canadian deficit in autos and parts had been slashed by more than

U.S.$100 million, although they admitted to some inaccuracies in their figures because of the different reporting practices between the two countries.[17]

American concern over the operation of the agreement was understandable. The increasingly discouraging trade figures made U.S. officials especially nervous knowing, as they did, that the auto pact required a congressionally mandated joint review by 1 January 1968 to determine whether the agreement's objectives were being met. Furthermore, Congress's enabling legislation required the president to submit a special report on the review by 31 August 1968. The review and the special report would not be able to hide the declining U.S. trade surplus, which would expose the agreement to further attacks and scrutiny. Although both sides might wish to avoid them, these reviews were required by the treaty itself: While the creation of the Automotive Products Trade Agreement had forestalled the difficulties generated by the Drury remission plans, the agreement itself was to become a new point of contention between the two countries that were parties to it. Following sporadic consultation throughout 1967, review discussions began in earnest between the two sides in the late fall of 1967.[18]

These talks reflected the two countries' differing views. As leader of the U.S. delegation, Assistant Secretary of State for Economic Affairs Anthony M. Solomon made a determined case for an end to the safeguards and challenged the very basis of the Canadian position on the auto trade. At the time that the auto pact was signed, Solomon argued, 'we of course concluded that various transitional measures were required in the short run, but we should now take a hard look at these to see whether they are still necessary.' But, Solomon contended, the 'present conditions for free entry into Canada such as sales ratio and value-added provisions should be examined carefully during this review. Indeed, we would hope also to examine whether limitation of free entry to Canadian manufacturers cannot be dispensed with.'

Speaking for the Canadian side, Simon Reisman countered by discussing the progress made under the pact and asserting that the review certainly provided the two sides an opportunity to assess every aspect of the agreement, one of these being the difficulties that Canadian producers had faced in gaining fair entry into the U.S.-dominated market. Reisman was not to be cowed on the issue of the safeguards. Instead, he took the offensive with the position that the Canadians had their own problems with the operation of the agreement. Surely a review of the safeguards 'might well be desirable,' Reisman argued, but all aspects of the pact should be considered, beginning with its expansion to include other products in the automotive field such as tubes and tires and the thorny questions of accurate statistics and parity of wages and prices. Little immediate movement was expected by either side on these contentious issues. With the context of the talks set, both sides agreed to further meetings in the new year with a view to completing the joint review by the summer of 1968.[19]

A federal election was called for April 1968. In March Drury updated Finance Minister Mitchell Sharp on the review of the auto pact. The pact had resulted in 'substantial progress' in the industry, with increases in Canadian production, exports, investment, productivity, and employment. Drury further informed Sharp that despite these improvements the government was consulting with the manufacturers regarding their plans beyond 1968 with an eye towards exacting even further production guarantees: 'We believe that they should not only maintain the levels of output reached in model year 1968, but that they should continue to increase their Canadian value added.'[20] This position was in keeping with a cabinet decision of the previous December to seek new commitments from the Big Three for increased Canadian value added.[21] In spite of the obvious and growing U.S. complaining over the operation of the agreement, state-directed planning remained the primary Canadian goal under the auto pact regime.

To that end, in March and April of 1968 the Canadians held meetings with the auto manufacturers to try to determine their plans for future production. The Big Three were extremely reluctant to reveal anything about their planned undertakings. Canadian officials told them that they would be expected to increase their Canadian value added by a factor commensurate with the growth in the Canadian market, which would amount to approximately $850 million annually by 1974. The Canadian assumption was that the safeguards in the auto pact would ensure that the companies would boost their minimum CVA to 75 per cent of Canadian production by 1971 and to 80 per cent by 1974.[22] The manufacturers responded by saying that they were satisfied by the terms of the agreement and felt under no obligation to assume additional commitments. Knowing that the U.S. administration and Congress would be against further commitments, and understanding that the Canadians were very reluctant to reopen the agreement, the automakers were determined to resist any such additional demands. In spite of the companies' expressed unwillingness to agree to new commitments, Canadian officials maintained that the companies were simply 'delaying coming to grips with the problem as long as possible' and would eventually agree to further commitments.[23] No final decisions were made, however, as talks were interrupted by the 1968 Canadian federal election.

Soon after Trudeau's landslide victory, new ITC Minister Pepin and his civil servants returned to the joint U.S.–Canada review. In keeping with the Canadian policy of seeking to obtain new commitments from the manufacturers and in conjunction with the approaching review, the new minister quietly met with the Canadian producers in July to assess their willingness to consider further commitments beyond 1968. Response to Pepin's overtures was decidedly cool. The companies were extremely reluctant to go beyond oral guarantees about their plans after 1968. Written statements, they claimed, could be highly damaging to them in the United States, where congressional opponents would use any new letters to reopen their attacks on the agreement, which would be especially injurious in a U.S. election year. The executives reminded Pepin of the congressional amendment exacted at the time of the auto pact's passage which required any new undertakings after 1968 to be reported directly to the U.S. government. Such undertakings would undoubtedly provoke a firestorm in both Congress and the administration. Industry representatives informed Canadian officials that, to avoid such difficulties, the parent companies had instructed their Canadian affiliates not to give Ottawa any indication of their intentions in writing. Unbowed by this veiled threat, Pepin remained determined to obtain such written statements from the manufacturers. He made the case that the Canadian industry was still underperforming in comparison with its U.S. counterpart, and although much progress had been made, there was room for improvement. Despite serious protest from industry representatives, Pepin informed those at the meeting that he expected written statements of intentions from each manufacturer within two to three weeks.[24]

Thus, the major manufacturers finally submitted letters to the Canadian government. These letters, as Finance official R.B. Bryce admitted to Minister Sharp, were 'in themselves, fairly meaningless.' As opposed to the detailed plans that had been provided in the original letters, the new ones were simply general statements of the companies' desire to be productive corporate citizens of Canada. However, the automakers also agreed to submit their plans for the 1969 model year, and these showed a 'striking increase' of approximately 13 per cent over 1969 production levels. These plans, government officials admitted, were the best that could be extracted from the companies at the present time, and they represented only a partial achievement of the Canadian objectives. According to their written projections, General Motors' production would increase by approximately 15 per cent, Ford's by 13 per cent, and Chrysler's by 8 per cent. The corresponding increase in CVA as a proportion of the costs of sales for each company was given for GM as 7 per cent, Ford, 6 per cent, and Chrysler, 2 per cent, amounting to a total expansion in output over 1968 of $175 million.[25]

While Pepin was pleased with the 1969 targets, the lack of any figures after 1969 was unsettling. Ottawa wished to ensure that the manufacturers increased their CVA for the foreseeable future. But the companies were not proving cooperative: representatives of the Big Three did state orally that they had plans beyond 1969 for increasing production in Canada, but they flatly refused to give government officials any concrete indications of those plans. Moreover, in order to protect their position (to 'forestall any false rumours about their contents'), the companies made copies of the letters available to their parent companies and to various U.S. government departments. GM even sent copies of its letter to the Senate Finance Committee, where Al Gore had again been hammering the agreement.[26] Such a gesture illustrated the willingness of the companies to play the two governments off each other in their effort to maintain the status quo.

In the White House, presidential adviser W.W. Rostow submitted the auto pact review – completed, although the process had been interrupted by the Canadian election – to President Johnson for signature. Rostow told the president that the Canadians had wanted further commitments, but 'we made it clear this was no longer necessary and we couldn't go along.' Instead, the Canadians had 'settled' for letters from the Canadian companies regarding their future plans. Rostow informed the president that the companies had stated publicly that the letters were not commitments. Although there was a chance that the review (and the letters contained therein) might stimulate new attacks from Gore and Hartke, Rostow believed that the two senators were relatively alone in their campaign and suggested that increased employment in the industry, especially in Indiana, might also serve to dissuade Hartke from further attacks.[27]

The *Special Report on the Joint Review of the of the Canada–United States Automotive Products Agreement* was submitted to the U.S. Congress by the Johnson administration in September 1968. The very brief report stated that while 'considerable progress' had been made towards achiev-

Table 5.8 Canada's auto industry, total Canadian value added, 1965–1972 ($ millions)

| | CVA | | | | | |
	Required	Produced	Cost of vehicles sold	Cost of sales less CVA produced	CVA ratio: to cost of sales (%)	CVA ratio: required to cost of sales (%)
1965	891	992	1,534	542	65	58
1966	988	1,186	1,716	530	69	58
1967	1,002	1,200	1,738	538	69	58
1968	1,395	1,420	1,977	557	72	71
1969	1,471	1,703	2,110	407	81	70
1970	1,341	1,743	1,891	148	92	71
1971	1,350	1,825	1,911	86	96	71
1972	1,592	2,145	2,371	226	90	67

Source: Company Reports to Dept. of Industry, Trade and Commerce, National Archives of Canada, RG 19, Vol. 5959, File 8705-8-15, File, Statistics.

Reisman admitted that the ratio and CVA safeguards were the only leverage Ottawa had to keep the companies 'honest' in their operation and the only way that it might exact from them further investments in Canada. The threat of reimposing duties on missed targets was enough to net the government the required levels of investment and production. This provides a strong illustration of the impact of interventionist policies on the functioning of the marketplace. State-directed production goals were now the order of the day. As the results became apparent, Reisman and his colleagues could have no doubt that with the auto pact, Canada had successfully accrued its 'fair share' of North American automotive production.

The automotive industry, for its part, continued to demand a loosening of its obligations in an effort to reap the most benefits possible under the duty-free nature of the agreement. Understandably, the industry also sought to gain as much freedom from these state-directed targets as possible, without losing the benefit of duty-free trade. While the automakers continually threatened to miss their targets thereby hoping to get them reduced, they almost always achieved them. In fact, by the late 1960s it was becoming evident that the companies were shifting far more production to Canada than was actually required, a situation that held out the possibility of a distinctly negative response from the U.S. government.

In spite of their constant complaints, the automakers were generally

content with the operation of the agreement. At the very least, the auto pact was a much more desirable arrangement than the alternatives that the manufacturers had feared might otherwise ensue, namely, greater protectionism and greater Canadian content regulations. Government-industry relations, however, were strained to the breaking point by the end of the 1960s, as each side sought to gain what it could in its management of the automotive industry. With the pact-mandated 1968 review rapidly approaching, both faced difficulties in determining how their relationship should continue to develop. But this was just one of the problems that both the Canadian government and the industry faced. After 1968 American discontent with the implementation of the Automotive Products Trade Agreement of 1965 would threaten this already delicate balance.

6

Consolidating the Borderless North American Auto Industry, 1968–1971

Despite a rapidly shifting relationship between Canada and the United States, and significant changes in political leadership and governmental personnel, the operation of the Canada–U.S. auto pact continued undisturbed until 1968. Thereafter, as the cross-border automotive trade balance swung rapidly in Canada's favour, the administration of President Richard Nixon grew ever more frustrated, until it demanded that all the Canadian 'transitional' production safeguards in the agreement be removed. U.S. pressure reached a breaking point, and the Canadians offered to make concessions. But by then it was nearly too late, and the Americans refused the offer. Instead, in August 1971, Washington threatened to unilaterally abrogate the 1965 Automotive Products Trade Agreement, as part of the drastic shift in American economic policy known as the 'Nixon shocks.' These measures were designed to strengthen the progressively weakened U.S. trade position, in which the effects of the auto pact played no small role.

In this uncertain and quickly changing economic environment, the automotive companies were caught between the two governments. Although the greatest profits would come if the safeguards were ended, and the companies were thereby free to conduct the continental auto industry as they saw fit, the automakers still feared the potential alternatives to the new regime. In Canada, the nationalism of Walter Gordon and his allies had not subsided, and harsh protectionist measures to be imposed by the Canadian government were the auto pact regime to flounder remained a possibility. Nevertheless, the companies continued to resist Ottawa's demands for greater production commitments by arguing that such increases would lead to renewed American attacks on the auto pact. In this way, the auto companies used the governments with the new regulations. Privately, Ford officials admitted that without the concessions, it was liable to approximately $165 million in penalties.[69] This astounding figure illustrated the value of the automotive trade agreement to the manufacturers: Not only did they save on the actual duties (although in the absence of the agreement, the duties would not have been as high), their integrated production and rationalization provided further economic savings, as reflected in their parents companies' impressive financial results for the period.

Notwithstanding the exception granted Ford, the government was determined to hold the automakers to their commitments by keeping them uncertain about the implications for any failure to meet the requirements. Ottawa's strategy was to warn them of the consequences of failure under the program and encourage them to continue their efforts. By doing so, the government kept the manufacturers 'honest.' That is, by being kept in the dark of the consequences of failure to meet the targets, the companies were inclined to do their best to meet them. James Dykes of the MVMA summed up the industry group's frustration with the Canadian government: If a company was in trouble under the agreement, Dykes complained, 'the answer from the government was, Silence. In unspoken words it was, "do your best because we will not promise you relief if you miss fulfilling all requirements – but if you do, we will consider your special situation; if you are hurt come and see us and maybe we will help." This was a realistic, even a realistically entrepreneurial-like position, but large corporations are not amenable to operating with "ifs," "ands" and "buts" in government regulations.'[70]

Yet Dykes and the automakers remained circumspect. They did not voice their criticisms too loudly for fear of jeopardizing their position. For its part, the government remained determined to ensure that the companies met their requirements, and any weakening of those requirements would compromise their position.

Moreover, the ratio requirement, which was proving the most difficult to meet for the companies, held out the possibility of further investment in the future. Reisman admitted to Drury in the summer of 1967 that 'the ratio requirement is probably the main bargaining lever available for obtaining further production commitments from the motor vehicle companies.' Any relaxation of the ratio would be contingent on future levels of investment in Canada. According to Reisman, the same was true for the Canadian value added stipulation. 'Like the ratio, the present CVA requirement for vehicle assembly is one of the few bargaining counters available to the Government. It is desirable, therefore, that the vehicle producers clearly understand that this requirement will be waived on an annual basis only for those companies which realize the new objectives of the program.'[71] In other words, the ratio and the CVA were to be held in reserve, not only to hold the companies accountable for their Canadian production levels, but to provide leverage for further investment in Canada. The most noteworthy example of this occurred in the early 1970s, when Chrysler agreed to build the Pilette Road assembly plant in Windsor to make up for several years of missing its ratio targets.[72]

The Big Three understood the severity of missing the ratio, and they governed themselves accordingly. A little luck helped, as well. In June 1967, demand for cars in Canada reached an all-time high, as did Canadian production. Between them, GM and Ford produced over 100,000 vehicles, allowing them to avoid the penalties that might otherwise have been imposed. Despite each company's dire warnings, GM and Ford both achieved their ratio and CVA requirements under the agreement, as did Chrysler and virtually all of the other companies with auto pact status (see Table 5.7). Indeed, by 1968, it was clear that the auto pact was working exactly as its negotiators had hoped it would. Canadian content and value added in the automotive industry were growing visibly, and the boost to the industry was undeniable, not only in numbers of jobs but in the massive amounts of new investment and Canadian production: Total CVA in the industry was 69 per cent by 1967, well above the 58 per cent requirement (see Table 5.8). Collectively, automakers would continue to far surpass their CVA and ratio requirements for the period after 1965. While the impressive growth in the Canadian market for automobiles eased the difficulties they faced in meeting the ratio requirements, the constant threat that they might fail to meet their ratio continued to complicate industry-government relations. In spite of improvement in their production levels, the companies continued to press for the end of the ratio and the CVA requirements.[73] The government rejected these demands, once again, and suggested to the companies that they continue to do their best to meet the requirements.

By the late 1960s a clear pattern had developed between the government and the automakers regarding the operation of the Automotive Products Trade Agreement. The concessions made to Ford showed that while the government was willing to temporarily ease some of the restrictions (and demand future concessions in return), it was determined to hold companies to their commitments for as long as possible.

which commended the progress under the agreement, the third one was much less forthcoming in its praise. A decrease in the U.S. automotive trade surplus from U.S.$580 million in 1964 to U.S.$164 million in 1968 (on a wholesale basis) was noted with a comment that the Canadian automotive industry had shown impressive growth and was expanding rapidly. 'In view of these industry and trade developments,' the report went on, 'it would seem timely to move toward elimination of the transitional restrictions on Canadian imports of motor vehicles and parts from the United States.' All that was promised were further consultations 'with a view toward working to achieve fully the objectives of the automotive agreement.'[33]

Reluctant to enter into consultations in which the Americans would undoubtedly demand an end to the safeguards, the Canadians put off further talks. The Americans were not to be denied, however, and the Canadians finally agreed to a November meeting in Washington. These proved a preview of U.S.–Canada talks on the auto pact for the next two years. Philip Trezise, who had led the Americans during the original auto pact negotiations in 1964, headed the American delegation. Trezise opened 'vigourously' and maintained the same line throughout the meetings: Canada had undertaken an obligation in 1965 to move towards free trade, and the transitional safeguards were to last for three years – before full free trade became operational. Five years had now passed. 'By all economic indicators the Canadian industry had met and indeed surpassed its goals,' and the time had come, Trezise announced, to move to automotive free trade in North America. Not only was the United States not interested in expanding the automotive agreement to include replacement parts, there would be no more discussion of expansion until the present safeguards had been removed. The United States was showing a $6 million auto trade *deficit* with Canada for the first six months of 1969, which was unacceptable, Trezise told the Canadians. At the very least, Ottawa was to present a timetable indicating when the transitional measures would end, or at least some criteria to be fulfilled to end them. Trezise was emphatic: 'The end had to come sooner or later. There was no time better than the present, given the high production and employment levels.'[34]

Canada's response was measured. The Canadian delegates at the meeting repeated that Canada had not yet attained a fair and equitable share of the North American auto industry. Significant institutional factors, such as U.S. ownership in the industry, meant that Canada could not yet count on continued expansion based solely on market forces. The increased rationalization in the industry meant that Canadian concerns were far removed from the day-to-day operations of the U.S. automakers. In some cases the Canadian subsidiaries were now reporting directly to their heads in the United States, without any consideration being given to the Canadian management structure that remained.

Ottawa was concerned that the safeguards were not offering Canada adequate protection in the event either of possible downturns in the automotive industry or the continued institutional factors which, it claimed, worked unfairly against Canadian companies. The Canadian industry was still less productive than the U.S. industry, and Canada's share of North American production was still less than its share of consumption. This situation, claimed the Canadians, necessitated keeping the safeguards in place until these obstacles to true free trade had been overcome. Although the safeguards were 'partly' out of date (the letters of undertaking had expired in 1968), Ottawa was eager to see them 'further strengthened.' Unless this was done, there might be a reduction of CVA in the 1970 production year: 'If this happened, there would be implications in terms of the public attitude in Canada towards the automotive agreement.' Concerns were also raised about section 205 of the U.S. legislation, which required the president to make a special report to Congress should it be established that the automakers had made further commitments to the Canadian government. To the Canadians, this 'was an overt influence affecting the performance of the companies and was a form of extra territorial intervention by the U.S.' Their positions staked out, the two sides ended the November meetings without any movement.[35]

Canadian officials met for consultations with the Big Three automakers in January 1970. In a wide-ranging discussion, the Big Three told ITC Minister Pepin that, given U.S. complaints over its worsening trade balance, this was a most inopportune time for negotiations. They strongly recommended that 'Canada should make every effort to postpone reaching a meaningful decision until the atmosphere improves.' When it came to the operation of the program itself, Pepin was disappointed to find that the automakers refused to give the government any idea of their plans after 1970. He was determined to secure some measure of control over the auto agreement and wondered why Canada should not be entitled to production capacity equal to its consumption. The auto companies were not averse to a production floor, but they were very reluctant to see any more production targets after 1970. They were most strongly opposed to any change in the auto regime that would result in unrestricted free trade on a multinational basis. They believed that duty-free imports from other countries (especially from Japan) in the absence of any reciprocal action from those countries would be 'patently unfair' and harmful. With no significant movement with the automakers, the Canadians made plans to meet with them again in the near future.[36]

The failure of industry and intergovernmental talks by early 1970 marked a new phase in the discussions – the emergence of efforts by the United States to link other issues to the auto pact negotiations. Since the November 1969 discussions, Washington had become even more frustrated by the lack of developments in the talks on the automotive industry, as well as by Prime Minister Trudeau's actions in other fields of the Canada–U.S. relationship. In February 1970 it was reported to the White House that Trudeau had publicly 'expressed displeasure' at Nixon's decision to expand the U.S. anti-ballistic missile (ABM) system. Nixon's response was swift. National Security Advisor John R. Brown III immediately informed Secretary of State Henry Kissinger that the president was greatly unimpressed by Trudeau's comments and instructed him to 'find a way to "slap Trudeau a bit" on an economic issue which Canada is interested in and where Trudeau's prestige is involved.' Whether or not the auto pact was specifically chosen by the U.S. administration as the economic issue over which to hit back at Trudeau is not clear, but there is no doubt that for whatever reason after 1970 the auto pact became increasingly linked to other issues in the Canada–U.S. relationship.[37]

The first indication of this new policy came during the next round of Canada–U.S. talks in February 1970. Trezise told the Canadians that their attitude during the last discussions had been 'completely negative.' Furthermore, he let it be known that the matter was so serious that it 'could poison relations in other fields' and could even lead to the termination of the agreement, although such an outcome was not inevitable. Trezise proposed that the safeguards be suspended temporarily, as a sign of goodwill on Canada's part. Pepin was not intimidated by this U.S. threat. He reminded the American team that an alternative to the auto pact was 'some form of national policy as in the case of Australia.' Perhaps, he suggested, the safeguards could be replaced by new commitments from the companies, which might take a different form than the current safeguards. Trezise and Julius Katz, the other chief American negotiator, expressed 'serious disappointment' at the

Canadian idea of further safeguards. 'Expansion in Canada,' Trezise stated, 'was a Canadian government objective but not an objective of the agreement.' Discussions continued throughout the following months, but, unable to make any headway on the agreement, the two sides again broke off talks.[38]

The Americans almost gave up. Frustrated by Ottawa's' unwillingness to move on the file, by the end of 1970 they informed the Canadians that, unless they offered new proposals in the near future, there would be no further talks. Congressional pressure had reached a boiling point. A House Ways and Means Committee, under the chairmanship of Wilbur Mills, who had once been a pact supporter, had recommended that unless the safeguards were removed the United States should unilaterally terminate the agreement. The Senate Finance Committee, long a focus for pact critics, agreed with Mills. While no one in Washington as yet believed that the administration would abrogate the treaty, U.S. officials warned Canadian staff at the embassy in Washington that frustration over the auto pact impasse was again giving the administration reason to consider linking the safeguards to other issues in the Canada–U.S. relationship. Worried Canadian officials reported to Ottawa of American hints that the interest equalization tax (IET) exemption, which had been granted to Canada in 1963 when it was desperate in the face of a rapidly disintegrating fiscal position, was not written in stone – especially since it did not seem necessary to protect Canada's balance of payments any more than the 'transitional' safeguards did. Again, the United States was willing to link the auto pact discussions to other aspects of the Canada–U.S. relationship.[39]

By May 1971 the U.S. administration had lost all patience with Ottawa. During informal discussions in Washington, the Canadians reiterated that it was economically and politically unrealistic for Canada to give up the safeguards without anything being put in their place. Both Trezise and Katz reminded the Canadians that the two countries had entered into an agreement in 1965, one which required the removal of the transitional safeguards within a trial period, which was now concluded. Canada's failure to end the safeguards was, in effect, 'welching on an undertaking.' Trezise and Katz also told the Canadians that they represented the most sympathetic views in Washington on the issue, and apart from the congressional hostility towards the agreement that had always been present, great pressure was building in the Treasury and Commerce departments for something to be done – including abrogation of the pact. The debate had become 'barren,' and unless the

Canadians committed to alleviating the pressure, there was no saying what might happen.[40]

The administration's attitude was articulated by tough-talking Texan John Connally, Nixon's treasury secretary since February 1971. The first-quarter U.S. trade deficit was at U.S.$5.6 billion, which Connally announced was 'clearly not sustainable.' In his view, the auto pact was a key factor in this deficit, and testifying before the Senate subcommittee hearings on foreign trade, he stated – in response to a question on the auto pact – that the United States should have taken action to improve its position on the agreement 'yesterday.' The auto pact was, to his mind, a classic case where American largesse had made it too easy for the country's trading partners. Two days later, Treasury Under-secretary Paul Volker echoed these remarks, saying that the State Department had 'been soft' in trade negotiations and that it was now time to restore the balance. There had to be a way to remove 'some of the irritations' that were causing the United States so many difficulties.[43]

In the face of this quickly worsening situation, Canadian officials met to formulate recommendations for government action. The problem had become, in Simon Reisman's words, an 'open sore.' Based on Connally's comments and their own recent discussions with their counterparts in Washington, 'U.S. authorities were approaching a position where they could be prepared to terminate the Agreement.' Canadian officials recommended that Ottawa unilaterally suspend the safeguards. Along with deflating pressure over the auto pact, this would lead to better relations with the United States more generally. Minister Pepin, however, was not willing to give up so easily. He announced that, in return for Canada's action on the safeguards, Washington was expected to make a public statement (preferably a presidential proclamation) to the effect that the United States accepted that Canada should continue to receive a fair share of the North American automotive production. Pepin also wanted a joint consultative committee on the agreement. In spite of his desire for U.S. concessions before Canada unilaterally suspended the safeguards, Canadian officials arranged to have further meetings in Washington in July 1971. During the meetings, the Canadian proposals were met with scepticism. Washington submitted that if the Canadians did suspend the safeguards, there could be no insinuation that the United States had 'paid' for these concessions by agreeing to the presidential proclamation and the joint committee.[42]

At this point, events overtook the negotiators. By summer 1971 the balance-of-payments situation had deteriorated considerably further,

and the United States had a trade deficit for the first time since 1959.
Trade with Europe and the rest of the world was in a positive balance.
But with Japan and Canada the United States was in a deficit position,
and the size of that deficit had increased dramatically since 1968.[43] The
position of the U.S. dollar was becoming very precarious as well. Since
the end of the Second World War and the creation of the Bretton Woods
system, the U.S. dollar had acted as the international currency and
remained tied to a set gold standard of U.S.$35. By 1971 European
countries had accumulated U.S. dollars to such an extent that the administration in Washington was unsure whether it could cover gold
convertibility requests. Connally told Nixon at Camp David in August
1971 that 'we are meeting here today because we are in trouble overseas. The British came in today to ask us to cover $3 billion, all their
dollar reserves. Anybody can topple us – anytime they want – we have
left ourselves completely exposed.'[44] At the same time, the United
States was facing increasing inflation at home, a result of the massive
expenditures of the Vietnam War. With a large and growing deficit and
an unstable dollar, action was necessary.

The Nixon administration's response was called the 'new economic
policy,' and known worldwide as the Nixon shocks, or *shokku* in the
Japanese lexicon. It represented a seismic shift in U.S. policy. On 15
August, Nixon informed the world that the United States was imposing
austerity measures to regain control of its economy. First, a 10 per cent
surcharge was to be imposed on all imports coming into the United
States. While the surcharge did not apply to new cars and parts coming
from Canada, officials in Ottawa estimated that $80 million in replace-
ment parts would be affected by the new tax. Nixon also cut taxes and
froze wages and prices for three months. The job development tax
credit (JDTC) and the Domestic International Sales Corporation (DISC)
were two incentives designed to spur industrial growth in the United
States. They, too, had an impact on the Canadian auto industry, especially in terms of new investment. More shockingly, President Nixon
signalled the end of the Bretton Woods system by announcing that the
U.S. dollar was no longer to be convertible to gold but would now
float freely, which resulted in its devaluation compared with other
currencies.[45]

These measures had a profound effect on America's trading partners,
especially Canada. Since the Second World War, the Canadian economy
had been helped by U.S. willingness to embrace Canadian
'exemptionalism.'[46] Although not always prompt in allowing Canada

an exemption (witness the IET affair in 1963), the United States had given Canada preferential treatment under many of its policies. The auto pact was, of course, an exceptional measure, although the new automotive regime was really more a reflection of the unique structure of the auto industry, the particular circumstances surrounding the Canadian measures taken between 1962 and 1964, and the position of the Big Three automakers in wishing to avoid further onerous content requirements in Canada, than it was an exemption based on the potential damage that a U.S. policy would do to the Canadian economy. Now, Washington was ending Canada's exceptional status in the U.S.-dominated world economy. Many Canadian products (including autos) entering the United States were not affected by the surcharge,[47] but the economic impact on Canada was still undeniable. Canadians were shocked by the severity of the new U.S. policy. Quickly, they sought talks with the Americans to blunt some of the more onerous measures, such as the surcharge, JDTC, and DISC.[48]

The Canadians did not know that, as part of its austerity measures, the United States also planned to unilaterally terminate the auto pact. For the Nixon administration, the 1965 Automotive Products Trade Agreement was a key source to the troubling trade deficit, and after talks reached another standstill in July 1971, the U.S. government dug in its heels. The American deficit in automotive products with Canada had reached U.S.$197 million, a staggering sum to Washington officials.[49] The departments of Commerce and Treasury had never had any liking for the Canadian deal, and since 1968 had made it known that unless Canada offered concessions on the implementation of the agreement, it should be terminated. When Nixon announced his austerity measures, unilateral cancellation of the auto pact was intended to be one of his 'shocks.' Only a last-minute plea by State Department official Julius Katz kept it off the scrap heap. When Katz realized that abrogation of the auto pact was part of Nixon's new economic policy speech, he begged White House officials to reconsider. He was convinced that such an abrupt move would utterly disrupt the North American auto industry and irreparably damage Canada–U.S. relations. Undoubtedly, the automakers themselves would have taken exception to such a disruptive move made without prior consultation with them. Katz's intervention required annoyed White House staff to hurriedly redraft Nixon's speech only hours before he was to deliver it.[50]

Although this last-minute reprieve for the auto pact was not something that the Canadian officials knew about at the time,[51] it was nevertheless abundantly clear to them that U.S. dissatisfaction with its balance of payments could have devastating effects on Canada–U.S. relation, particularly regarding the trade balance and even more specifically the trade in automotive products. Shaken by the severity of the U.S. reaction to its international payments problem, Canadian officials agreed that Ottawa could no longer seek a quid pro quo in suspending the safeguards.[52] They entered into further discussions with the Americans, but they now faced a much less patient partner, for after 15 August 1971 the auto negotiations took place within the context of the Nixon shocks.

But further meetings on the auto pact did not result in any substantial movement towards resolution. Talks in September between U.S. Treasury Secretary Maurice Stans and ITC Minister Pepin resulted in Pepin's offer to suspend the CVA and ratio, linked to hopes that the United States would consider striking a joint committee to study the agreement. The Canadians had stopped pushing for a presidential proclamation stating that Canada deserved a fair share of North American production. Washington's response was cautious. Although the administration was pleased that Canada would be removing the safeguards, if Canada did not move quickly in doing so, the White House could not avoid harsh criticism of the agreement in the already-delayed annual report on its progress. Moreover, as a sign of their continued willingness to link other economic issues to the auto pact talks, the United States would not consider removal of the 10 per cent import surcharge imposed in August until the safeguards were removed. Publicly, however, Prime Minister Trudeau stated that the auto pact safeguards were in no way linked to the surcharge talks. When Canadian representatives met with U.S. officials in November, it was obvious that negotiations would drag on for some time.[53]

By 1971 the impasse over future changes to the auto pact issue had become what one stakeholder described as a 'temporary state of equilibrium.'[54] Despite the intense pressure from the United States on Canada to alter the auto pact, its operation continued unchanged. In the House of Commons, the prime minister reiterated that continuation of the safeguards was not a determining factor in the wider trade talks between the two countries and that Canada would not unilaterally alter the auto agreement.[55] The Canadians were able to maintain the safeguards as long as discussions continued. When yet another round of meetings in December 1971 resulted only in agreement to hold further meetings in the new year, an exasperated John Connally declared that Canada was the only country that had not taken any substantive steps towards an agreement with the United States on the American balance-of-payments situation.[56]

Although remaining an irritant in Canada–U.S. relations after 1971, the auto pact stopped being a major cross-border issue. A number of factors relieved the enormous pressure that the United States exerted on Canada. First, the safeguards no longer acted as an incentive for further production in Canada; instead, they now operated as a floor. Safeguards remained symbolically important to Canadians, but for all practical purposes mattered little, and to some in the U.S. administration, they were not worth a major international incident. State Department officials and National Security Council advisers wanted to avoid any such conflict and recommended that the Treasury Department hawks – who were determined to see an end to the safeguards – be reined in.[57] In their view, further agitation on the issue would provoke 'an unnecessary foreign policy crisis with adverse domestic implications.'[58] In preparing Nixon for Trudeau's December 1971 visit to the White House, Kissinger informed the president that although the prime minister would offer to suspend the safeguards, the issue had become more a political than an economic imperative. If the United States were willing to live with the safeguards, there was no reason to force their termination, or even their suspension. Certainly, it did not justify a major incident.[59]

Second, the automakers were not against the safeguards. To them, the current regime remained much more desirable than increased content and/or safeguards or, alternatively, an unrestricted free-trade regime in which they had to compete against offshore imports on a duty-free basis. Indeed, the most important factor in the political decisions regarding the safeguards and the auto pact was the viewpoint of the Big Three. 'The U.S. companies,' Kissinger told Nixon, 'say that removal of the safeguards would have little economic effect and have asked that the U.S. government place a low priority on their removal.'[60] Fearful of the Canadian reaction (especially the threat of Canadianization) were the United States to terminate the agreement, the Big Three intentionally de-emphasized the importance of the safeguards in their talks with the administration. By 1971 the companies were out-producing the requirements under the safeguards by far, and they had obviously come to the conclusion that production in Canada was not merely a necessity under the auto pact, it was also profitable (see Table 6.1). The automakers saw no need to provoke Washington further over the safeguards and thereby threaten their increasingly lucrative operations in

Canada. Instead, they very quietly suggested that safeguards were not, in fact, a problem for them, and thus not a problem for the U.S. government, either. The end of the auto pact, on the other hand, would be seriously damaging. In February 1972, William R. Pearce, the U.S. government's deputy special representative for trade negotiations, summed up the major automakers' view to John Connally, saying; 'Ford, General Motors and Chrysler have stated that termination [of the auto pact] would cause them severe hardship.'[61] Connally would have been willing to terminate the agreement unilaterally in August 1971, but the opposition of the Big Three to doing so was enough to give the administration pause. Without pressure from the automakers to remove the safeguards, and with little appetite for any disruption in the auto industry, the U.S. government was less inclined to press the Canadians as vigourously as they had in the past on the 'transitional' safeguards.

Third, removing the safeguards would create its own problems. Should Ottawa unilaterally suspend all of the safeguards, including the bona fide manufacturer requirement, the Canadian market would be open to Japanese and German imports. The United States, on the other hand, was protected by its own auto pact stipulation stating that vehicles imported from Canada must have 50 per cent North American content. Moreover, if Canada did suspend safeguards and then create a preferential market for North American cars alone, it would be required to seek a waiver from the General Agreement on Tariffs and Trade, as the United States had done in 1965. This, Canadian officials believed, would be very difficult.[62] Nor did the Big Three wish to see increased competition in the North American market from Japanese or European manufacturers. Again, William Pearce's analysis is insightful: 'Enlargement of this duty-free privilege is not supported by the major U.S. manufacturers, would not benefit U.S. exports if accorded on an MFN basis, and could not be granted by Canada without a waiver from its GATT obligations.'[63] The original GATT negotiations on the auto pact had not been easy, and Washington would surely face further difficulties in Geneva if it reopened it to scrutiny. With a radically changed international economy, as a result of the 15 August measures, America's economic partners would be in no mood to grant easy passage to changes in the Canada–U.S. auto agreement. Given these problems, Julius Katz admitted in early 1972 that 'the present time would not be propitious for Canada to seek a waiver.'[64]

Fourth, the U.S. trade surplus with Canada in automotive products improved significantly after 1972. The deficit had decreased to U.S.$99 million, and in 1973 the United States was once again in a surplus position, with a positive balance in automotive trade with Canada of U.S.$426 million. By 1974 this surplus had reached beyond U.S.$1.2 billion. The trade surplus had been the most visible indicator of what many in the U.S. Congress and administration saw as the unfair nature of the auto agreement, and its spectacular recovery by the mid-1970s greatly alleviated U.S. pressure for the removal of the safeguards.[65] In Simon Reisman's view, the return to a balance in America's favour 'served to ease some of the pressure from the U.S. for removal of the safeguards,' although they still remained a 'bone of contention.'[66] The positive shift in the trade balance did, however, silence the auto pact's most vocal critics, at least in the United States.[67]

The shift in the balance-of-payments account was partly caused by the relative values of the Canadian and U.S. currencies. In May 1970 Ottawa's Minister of Finance Edgar Benson announced that the Canadian dollar was to float against the U.S. currency instead of being fixed at 92.5 cents. The Canadian dollar rose almost immediately to 97 cents, further dampening U.S. imports from Canada. In December 1971 Canada declared its unwillingness to enter into the U.S.-sponsored Smithsonian agreement, submitted as a last-ditch effort to maintain the fixed currency regime and shore up the U.S. dollar. Canada's response further influenced the exchange rate, and by 1973 all major currencies had flexible rates. As a result, by April 1974, the Canadian dollar had increased in value to U.S.$1.04, which further handicapped Canadian imports from the United States.[68]

There remains the question of whether the auto companies themselves manipulated the cross-border trade to alleviate the pressure coming from the U.S. administration. As the automakers repeatedly admitted, the 1965 Automotive Products Trade Agreement had proved to be far more beneficial to them than any other imaginable regime (save continental unrestricted free trade) and any abrupt change to the operation of the North American automotive trade was, from their viewpoint, distinctly unwelcome. No available evidence suggests that the Big Three themselves actively interfered with the auto trade or manipulated their intracompany transfer pricing in an effort to bring the cross-border exchange into a less provocative balance. Nevertheless, it is not unreasonable to suggest that some element of self-preservation may have been in play as the three companies managed the North American industry. After all, the Canadian automotive trade surplus, which had so angered the Nixon administration, fortuitously reversed itself in favour of the United States just as American pressure – and the threats of abrogation – reached their height (see Table 6.2). A more recent case, involving Ford of Canada, indicates that such a practice is probably not entirely unknown to the major auto manufacturers. During court proceedings over Ford's privatization of its Canadian subsidiary in 2001, it was suggested that in the late 1980s and early 1990s Ford had manipulated its own intracompany transfer pricing system to render Ford of Canada unprofitable (while during the same period wholly-owned General Motors Canada and Chrysler Canada were making record profits). This allegedly had the effect of driving down the share price in an effort to ease the pending buyout of the remaining independent Ford shareholders by the parent company so that it could take the Canadian company private.[69] Again, there is no evidence to suggest that under the auto pact these companies did, or could, collude to manipulate the North American automotive trade on such a large scale.

Fifth, U.S. policymakers became more and more focused on the impact of offshore imports on the American market. Increased Japanese imports were one of the targets of Nixon's austerity measures, a situation that deteriorated further after 1972, and especially after the 1973 oil embargo by the Organization of Petroleum Exporting Countries. As American consumers snapped up inexpensive and fuel-efficient Japanese compact cars, Washington became less concerned with problems stemming from Canadian trade questions. In 1973 the United States imported 1.7 million overseas vehicles, compared with 569,000 in 1965. The 1973 imports constituted nearly 16 per cent of U.S. sales, whereas in 1965 'foreign' imports (non–North American cars) accounted for barely 6 per cent of the American market.[70] Nixon's inaccurate 1972 remark that Japan was America's largest trading partner reflected the growing U.S. preoccupation with the Japanese.

Finally, political issues on both sides of the Canada–U.S. border helped to ease the pressure. President Nixon was re-elected in November 1972; soon after the U.S. government apparatus became consumed with the Watergate affair. A distracted administration had little time to effectively pursue a matter that seemed minor in comparison. In Canada, after a lacklustre campaign in 1972, Trudeau was able to form only a minority government, dependent on the support of the New Democratic Party. As a consequence, Ottawa's policies tacked leftward, and nationalistic measures such as the Foreign Investment Review Agency were passed. As in 1964, Canadian government officials hinted to their U.S. counterparts that a detrimental outcome for Canada on the auto talks could very well lead to the collapse of the Liberal minority government, and then further difficulties between the two countries.[71] The sheer repetitiveness of the talks played a role in wearing down the American side: during yet another round of talks in 1972, Assistant Treasury Secretary Paul Volker stated that the 'divergent positions of their governments had been reviewed ad nauseum and there was nothing to be gained from rehashing them again.'[72]

As the auto agreement receded from the U.S. administration's view, it became apparent that it had survived its most challenging and vulnerable period. With the help of the Big Three multinational automakers, which increasingly found the auto pact to be a boon to their operations, Canada had managed to hold onto the safeguards that protected its auto industry. While Ottawa had agreed to major concessions (including temporary suspension of the safeguards), it had not been forced to publicly announce these measures and thus could avoid having to implement them. For the United States, the automotive industry continued to function in a manner that negatively affected the U.S. balance-of-payments account, and the auto pact continued to be a reminder of its weakening economic situation. The auto pact also reminded Washington of what it considered to be the inherent unfairness of the agreement and of Ottawa's unwillingness to embrace 'true' free trade – as was intended by the pact. The Nixon administration's desire to unilaterally abrogate the auto agreement marked the nadir of its difficult early years. But the auto pact survived because both the Canadian government and especially the U.S.-based auto industry were satisfied with its impact on the industry, and wished to see it continue in operation. After 1971 implementation of the Automotive Products Trade Agreement continued unchanged – with the Canadian safeguards intact – until the early 1980s, when more fundamental changes to the auto industry worldwide and to the economic relationship between Canada and the United States required a reworking of the automotive trade regime between the two countries and the U.S. multinationals. By then the Canada–U.S. auto pact become one of the foundations of the North American economy and was seen to be one of the most successful trade agreements in history.

Conclusion: The Borderless North American Auto Industry, 1971–2001

After surviving the difficulties to do with President Nixon's austerity measures, the Automotive Products Trade Agreement of 1965 continued to function undisturbed as the pre-eminent Canada–U.S. agreement on trade and the organizing mechanism facilitating the steadily growing continental trade in automotive products. Cars and parts continued to flow across the border unmolested by tariffs: in some years more flowed south than north, but in most years the reverse was true. The vast majority of Americans remained entirely unaware of this chronic imbalance, most likely few even knew of the auto pact's very existence, let alone its place in the North American economy.[1] By the mid-1980s, when free trade again became an issue under debate in Canada, the auto pact was a cornerstone of economic life in North America.

Fundamental changes in the Canadian, North American, and global auto industries and to the Canada–U.S. trade relationship significantly influenced operations under the agreement. Total automotive trade between Canada and the United States grew from $10 billion in 1973 to $60 billion in 1986. Canadian producers went on fulfilling their requirements under the auto pact, and in most cases, surpassed the pact's safeguard stipulations.[2] The process begun in 1965 was completed, as Canada's auto industry was rationalized and fully integrated into the larger North American auto industry. A new 'continental auto politics' developed, as the borderless industry spawned by the Canada–U.S. auto pact allowed the Big Three automakers to take advantage of their new capital mobility and play off states and provinces against each other for investment incentives and tax breaks.[3]

Meanwhile, the global auto industry was being transformed. By the late 1970s the U.S. multinationals were in sharp decline, as imports from

Japan flooded the North American market, prompting the United States to impose 'voluntary' export restrictions. When Japanese automakers built U.S. plants, in an effort to mollify Washington (and to maintain profits resulting from a high Japanese yen), Canadians wanted a piece of the action as well. By the early 1980s Japanese automakers had been lured to Canada with the promise of duty-remission plans called special remission orders (SROs), which were, essentially, the same type of scheme that had caused so much strain in Canada–U.S. relations in the mid-1960s. Japanese frims such as Toyota and Honda set up plants in southwestern Ontario. Not surprisingly, the new remission plans provoked the displeasure of elected officials from adjacent U.S. states such as Michigan, who believed that Canada was providing unfair incentives to Japan. The Canada–U.S. auto trade, which by the mid-1980s tilted heavily in favour of Canada, further influenced U.S. legislators.[4]

Protectionism in the United States and the shortcomings of stalled negotiations of the General Agreement on Tariffs and Trade prompted Canadian policymakers to cast around for alternatives for Canada's trading future. Brian Mulroney and the Progressive Conservative party came to power in Ottawa in 1984. They soon took up the recommendation of the Royal Commission on the Economic Union and Development Prospects for Canada (appointed by Prime Minister Trudeau and headed by D.S. Macdonald) for a free trade agreement (FTA) with the United States.[5] The trade difficulties caused by Canada's new round of remission schemes gave the undertaking a sense of urgency. By 1987, after intense and often acrimonious negotiations – led on the Canadian side, once again, by 1965 auto pact negotiator Simon Reisman – a comprehensive free trade deal was consummated.[6]

The automotive provisions of the free trade agreement were a particularly sore spot during the negotiations.[7] The Canada–U.S. auto agreement had been enormously beneficial for some segments of the Canadian polity and economy. Indeed, the auto pact had become a fundamental plank of Canada's industrial policy and an article of faith for many Canadian politicians – especially those from auto-dependent Ontario – and auto workers.[8] Surprisingly, the auto pact had also become something of a touchstone for economic nationalists opposed to the deal, who ignored the obvious continentalism of the new agreement and instead feared that jobs and safeguards for a production 'fair share' might be threatened.[9] Because of its continental, tariff-removing aspects, the auto agreement was held up by Prime Minister Mulroney as evidence of the benefits of free trade.[10] Thus, by the mid-1980s, the auto pact was much more than a mere trade mechanism. From the cold realities of dry trade statistics and complex production ratios, the auto pact was now in the realm of myth, and as such, a symbol for both the advocates and detractors of free trade.

The fate of the auto pact became a flashpoint in negotiating the Canada–U.S. Free Trade Agreement. After all these years, Washington was demanding that the protectionist elements of the auto agreement be eliminated, while true to form, Reisman and the Canadian team were reluctant to allow any changes to the pact. But, when it became clear that difficulties over the auto sector might scuttle the entire free trade deal,[11] a somewhat uneven compromise was worked out.[12] While officially the auto pact remained untouched under the 1989 free trade agreement, in actuality the operating rules of the auto industry were altered fundamentally. With the FTA, auto products were imported duty-free between the two countries regardless of a company's status under the auto pact. The FTA rules of origin, which were slightly more stringent, replaced auto pact rules of origin for duty-free entry into the United States and Canada and vice versa. Now, 50 per cent of the direct costs of parts and vehicles had to include North American content to achieve duty-free status.[13] Thus, although Canada retained its own auto pact provisions in a new 1988 Motor Vehicle Tariff Order (MVTO), the U.S. auto pact provisions became redundant. Even without the auto pact, FTA rules applied regarding entry of autos and parts into the United States. Moreover, these changes gave the new agreement's critics justification to say that the auto pact had been 'gutted.'[14] Under the new rules, the U.S.-based multinationals were no longer legally required to fulfil Canadian safeguard provisions in order to import duty-free into Canada – the 'transitional' safeguards that the Americans had railed against for years had finally been terminated. The new regime provided the multinationals all the benefits of production in Canada, such as lower labour costs, excellent productivity, and the discounted Canadian dollar, without having to maintain the 1965 safeguards, although they did continue to satisfy auto pact requirements. After the Canada–U.S. FTA, companies were required to achieve 50 per cent North American content only, and (obviously) this did not necessarily include Canada.[15]

Certain compromises were made by Ottawa to subdue the outcry from U.S. auto-producing states. The Canadian auto pact measures continued under the 1988 MVTO, with two fundamental concessions exacted from the Canadians. First, the new duty-remission programs, which benefited Japanese transplants, were to be phased out over a ten-year period (by 1998). Second, and more damaging given Ottawa's assurances during the original GATT discussions, membership under the auto pact was frozen to the Big Three automakers plus CAMI (a joint GM-Suzuki venture) and Volvo. Japanese companies such as Honda and Toyota were excluded from the tariff savings that had come with auto pact status, even if they met the production levels that the original auto pact companies had achieved.[16] However, unlike the Japanese transplants, the original auto pact companies continued to import duty-free into Canada from third countries, as long as they maintained their safeguard requirements.[17] In other words, Honda Canada could import and export to the United States, since it satisfied the Canada–U.S. free trade requirements, but it was not able to import duty-free from Japan directly to Canada, even though it achieved production and content levels equivalent to those of the original auto pact companies.

The North American Free Trade Agreement, passed in 1993, boosted the content requirement to 62.5 per cent, and set tariff levels for the import of vehicles from Mexico into Canada and the United States. It did not, however, substantially alter the course of events, which had been pretty much determined under the Canada–U.S. agreement on free trade.[18] The auto pact list remained frozen, and the duty-remission orders were still phased out. What in 1965 had been a tactical move by Canadian negotiators to avoid scrutiny at the GATT – the claim that the auto pact would be administered on a most-favoured-nations basis, and thus open to companies from any country – had become inconsistent with the provisions of the CUSFTA in 1989 and NAFTA four years later. Instead, after 1998, the auto pact was seen to discriminate against Japan and to provide a major benefit for North American producers. In real terms, this meant that the Japanese (and European companies) were forced to pay a duty when they imported from non–North American countries, while the U.S.-owned Canadian companies could import from third countries duty-free. In dollar values, the duties amounted to approximately $150 million a year on the import of Japanese and European luxury cars which were not built in North America. When Canada eliminated tariffs on parts imports from third countries, but without substantially lowering let alone ending the 6.1 per cent duty on completed vehicles (the MFN rate following the GATT's Uruguay Round reductions), the response from Japan and Europe was predictable.[19]

In mid-1998, with the end of the special remission orders, the Japanese and Europeans complained to the World Trade Organization that they were being discriminated again under the auto pact, since the agreement created an unfair two-tiered automotive industry. There were North American-based companies that were included in the original auto pact list, and offshore companies frozen out by the 1989 CUSFTA (and although the European companies were not producing in Canada, they had been frozen out as well). The first tier could import cars from outside North America duty-free, while the second could not. In their submissions to the WTO, the two complainants argued that the granting of auto pact status was contrary to the GATT MFN, that the Canadian value-added requirement of the auto pact was inconsistent with the GATT, and that the production-to-sales ratios in the auto pact were also inconsistent with GATT provisions. The submissions to the WTO made much of the letters of undertaking, submitted in 1965 by the automakers to the Canadian government, claiming that these letters represented continued Canadian content requirements for duty-free entry up to the present day.[20] They also argued that the Canadian promises at the GATT in 1965 that companies from countries other than the United States would be allowed to join had not been kept.[21]

The WTO ruled that Canada was in violation of international trade rules and had struck out on almost all the Japanese-European claims. The WTO panel found that Canada discriminated by not affording products from non-auto pact countries similar treatment 'immediately and unconditionally' and that Canada was thus in violation of Article I of the GATT. Similarly, the CVA requirements under the MTVO of 1988 were also in violation of the GATT. The panel even found the 1965 letters of undertaking, which had been a requirement for auto pact status, to be in violation of the GATT. However, the panel did not find in favour of the European claim that the ratio requirement was inconsistent with the GATT rules, but this was of little consolation to the Canadians.[22] Ottawa replied that it would not appeal the WTO's decision, and with that the Canada–U.S. Automotive Products Trade Agreement quietly passed away in February 2001.

It is ironic that the auto pact died at the hands of the World Trade Organization three and a half decades after its enactment. In 1965 the Canadian provisions of the pact had been negotiated by the two countries party to it and accepted by the GATT, whose members agreed to grant the United States a waiver for its preferential treatment of Canada. Yet in 1999–2000 the Canada–U.S. auto pact was in violation of numerous clauses under international trade law. What had happened? Three significant changes contributed to the agreement's demise.

First, and perhaps most ironic, was the Canadian position on the acceptability of the auto pact under the GATT's MFN rule. To some degree, it passed in 1965 because the auto pact was new, untested, and unique. No one was entirely sure how it would work – or work out, for that matter. In 1965 Canada had claimed that its provisions did not violate the MFN principle because, it assured the GATT, any and all countries were eligible to take advantage of the auto pact simply by setting up shop in Canada. This was not entirely true even then, as Canadian officials had nervously admitted to themselves at the time. It became patently untrue following the 1989 CUSFTA, which forever froze new companies out of the Canadian duty-free regime regardless of their nationality. In hoping to avoid isolating themselves further in the bilateral relationship with the United States in 1965, Canada had placed itself in a very awkward position on autos when the time came for it to finally take the plunge in 1989 and join the United States in a free trade agreement.

Second, and this was significant, the United States had changed dramatically in its view of the place of the Canadian automotive industry in North America. In 1964–5 Washington was determined to avoid a trade war with its largest trading partner, one that might have had serious implications both domestically and internationally.[23] When its attempt to negotiate unrestricted free trade in the automotive sector failed, it threw its full weight behind the auto pact and the waiver request, and thus succeeded in attaining its goals, goals that benefited the United States, its auto industry, and not incidentally, Canada and its auto industry, as well. As long as this state of affairs existed, Washington could not amend or end the auto pact, as became glaringly apparent when Nixon sought to abrogate the pact unilaterally in 1971. But the Canada–U.S. Free Trade Agreement of 1989 marked a turning point. With the new auto provisions, the United States no longer had to keep Canada's concerns in mind. Although the North American auto industry remained tightly managed even after 1989 (largely for the benefit of the U.S. multinationals), under the new arrangement Canada could no longer point to an intergovernmental agreement that essentially required U.S. production at Canadian sites. The automakers continued to produce in Canada not because it was necessary to do so to achieve duty-free treatment, but for other reasons. At the World Trade Organization panel, the U.S. government acted as a disinterested third party. The United States had no incentive to support a position that benefited only Canada.[24]

Third, the horizontal integration of the automotive industry world-wide had an impact on North American trade rules. No one could have prophesied in 1965 that one day Ford would own Jaguar or that Daimler-Benz would essentially take over Chrysler. With this U.S.–European cross-ownership, American-based multinationals could import cars from Europe duty-free while the Japanese could not, only because in 1965 the Canadians had insisted that the third-country MFN clause be inserted into the agreement. This discrimination formed the heart of the Euro-pean-Japanese case at the WTO. But in 1965 no one could have pre-dicted such an outcome. Nor would one have taken many wagers predicting that Canada, the United States, and Mexico would someday share a free trade agreement and that it would enable U.S. multination-als to import 'foreign' cars in all corners of North America duty-free. From the vantage point of 1965, it would have been exceedingly diffi-cult to predict the shape of the global auto industry in the year 2000.

The WTO ruling leaves many unanswered questions about the terms of the Canada–U.S. auto pact's past at the GATT and the future of the Canadian automotive industry. What if the Canadians had joined the U.S. waiver request in 1965, instead of insisting that auto pact status would be extended to new countries? The Canadians had not requested a waiver in 1965 because they feared that other aspects of the agree-ment would not pass MFN scrutiny and because they did not want to expose themselves to further demands from the other GATT countries, as would turn out to be the case for the United States.[25] In the end, both Japan and the European Union, which in 1965 questioned but did not aggressively pursued the legitimacy of the Canadian provisions at the GATT, brought suit against Canada at the WTO more than three de-cades later – on the same points. Nevertheless, the unpredictable changes in the global auto industry, as well as in Canada's trade policies, make it difficult to argue that in 1965 Ottawa's strategy should have been different.

There is the question of the long-range impact of the end of the auto pact on Canada's auto industry. While the newspaper headlines an-nouncing the WTO decision may make one think of it as the death-knell for the Canadian automotive industry, this would be far from the case.[26] The closure of auto plants in Windsor, Oakville, and Ste Thérèse follow-ing the pact's demise are no indication that the Canadian industry is on its last legs. The Canada–U.S. auto pact was effectively hollowed out in 1989. An end to duty-free treatment for third-country imports only for the Big Three automakers is of little real economic significance to them, and it is not likely to prompt their sudden wholesale exodus.[27] Had the U.S. parent companies wanted to leave Canada, they could have done so following the implementation of the CUSFTA. They have not yet done so because assembling and producing cars in Canada has been economically beneficial and politically prudent for them and will remain so as long as the Canadian dollar is discounted, Canadian automotive productivity is high, and the Big Three continue to value their status as good Canadian corporate citizens. Although it remains to be seen what long-term impact the entry of Mexico into the North American free trade shpere will have on the Canadian automotive industry, a report from 1999 suggests that under NAFTA, Canada's automotive industry can more than hold its own.[28]

What, then, is the legacy of the auto pact? Was the 1965 Automotive Products Trade Agreement a misguided attempt at state intervention in the automotive industry that had the effect of hindering Canadian economic development? Did the agreement simply transform Canadians from hewers of wood and drawers of water into makers of auto parts and assemblers of automobiles, in some sort of industrialized version of Harold Innis's staples thesis? Did Canada become even more of an automotive backwater, with none of the true benefits of the industry? Canadian automotive trade grew by leaps and bounds from the 1960s onwards, but generally, the Canadian economy benefited only as long as American demand remained high. To be sure, employment and production in the automotive sector increased, but profits went and stayed south, as did the managers and the research and development divisions.[29] With complete ownership of the Canadian 'subsidiaries' in the hands of the American multinationals, Canada had obviously not been receiving the full benefits of its labour.

But was that necessarily a bad thing? Without the auto pact, what kind of automotive industry would Canada now have? The cost of maintaining 'national' ownership in the auto industry turned out to be too high for countries such as the United Kingdom and Sweden that tried to go it alone after the 1960s.[30] Canadians would not have tolerated the higher prices that an 'all-Canadian car' would have meant, especially when they could easily cast their eyes south of the border and see equivalent vehicles available at a far lower cost. Canadians have shown time and time again that they are more comfortable with the less expensive American option than the more expensive Canadian alternative when it comes to industrial, consumer, and cultural goods. A national Canadian car industry was a possibility given the nationalist rhetoric of the 1960s, but it would probably not have survived long in the rapidly changing global auto industry.

Canadian policymakers negotiating the Canada–U.S. auto pact of 1965 were successful, given the political and economic constraints of the North American context in the 1960s. The benefits gleaned from the 'fair share' achieved under the pact – a large auto employment sector and constant and massive investment in Canada – were far greater, it can be assumed, than what would have been had alternative paths been followed. The unique form of Canada's state-directed investment and production targets in the automotive sector proved the wisdom of Reisman's (and his team's) bargaining strategy. Canadian vehicle assembly grew disproportionately to Canada's consumption, while Canada's parts industry also enjoyed the benefits of the agreement. Many Canadian companies such as Magna International, Wescast Industries, ABC Group, and the Woodbridge Group, for example, became giants and innovators in the industry, enabled by the Canada–U.S. auto pact. While their initial successes were largely derived from selling to the Big Three automakers in Canada under the terms of the pact, in time they thrived against global competition, as well.[31]

By the late 1990s, Canadian automotive plants were regularly producing more than double the country's consumption with regard to units of automotive vehicles, and they accounted for almost one-fifth of North American output. Production and employment in the Canadian automotive sector were far in excess of the fair share in 1964 that Canadian negotiators had argued Canada should have. In 1999 Canada produced three million vehicles, and that was double the country's sales of 1.5 million vehicles. Pundits went so far as to predict (incorrectly) that, for the first time in history, Ontario might produce more vehicles than Michigan, the historic home of the North American auto industry. If one were to judge the long-term results of the agreement, based on the goals pursued by Reisman and his colleagues in 1964 – ending 'institutional barriers' to increased automotive productivity and exports, stable employment, improvement in Canada's balance of payments on auto products with the United States – Canadian policymakers would be seen to have been highly successful.[32]

The effectiveness of the auto agreement, especially the sales-to-production ratio safeguards, were most evident after it ceased to exist. In 2001 and 2002, General Motors, Ford, and DaimlerChrysler all announced that production facilities in Canada would be closed down after 2003 – GM's Ste Thérèse plant in Quebec, Ford's Oakville, Ontario, truck plant, and DaimlerChrysler's Windsor Pillette assembly plant (which built delivery trucks). These plants, especially the Ford and DaimlerChrysler facilities, were initially built to ensure that the automakers maintained their ratios under the 1965 agreement. Their closure illustrates how effective the ratio policy was, and although the closures are a loss to Canada's automotive industry, they do not mark its death, but rather a realignment that is, actually, closer to Canada's 'fair share' of assembly in North America. In the words of one leading automotive analyst, the plants facing closure are 'fringe' facilities in Canada and not the core of Canada's automotive production.[33]

Criticism of Canadian policymakers for the continental aspects of the 1965 Automotive Products Trade Agreement, which meant foreign control over the auto industry and a dearth of white-collar jobs or research and development in Canada, should be seen to be unfair. Civil servants understood at the time that with the continental deal Canada would be foregoing such aspects of the automotive industry forever. But Canada, at the time, could not really boast of any automotive research and development sector, nor could it be said that the Canadian management of the Big Three provided any great benefits, since most of the Canadian subsidiaries were run by Americans.[34] Canadians and their policymakers chose the continental path because of conditions unique to Canada: U.S. ownership predominating in the industry, the proximity of the Canaidan and American markets to each other, the similar tastes of Canadian and American consumers, and the comfort with which Canadians embraced American consumer products and culture. That the Canadians were able to exact some protection for their domestic industry in the form of the safeguard guarantees and the letters of undertaking resulted from two factors: The particular circumstances of the period, namely, the evolution of Canadian tariff policies and the creation of the duty-remission schemes, coupled with the political and economic realities faced by Canadian and American politicians and planners in the mid-1960s, provided an environment conducive to the managed trade regime that emerged. Furthermore, the determination of the Canadians to hold out for an acceptable fair share and their willingness to threaten the United States with alternative paths (the 'sombrero under the table') gave the American government and the automotive multinationals the incentive to cooperate with the Canadians. The willingness of the Big Three to avoid more onerous restrictions was key to ensuring their participation in the new regime. Regardless of the reasons behind its creation, implementation, and survival, the

Canada–U.S. auto pact is an obvious example showing that 'fair trade' can be achieved, even when negotiating with the most powerful country and the most powerful economic sector in the world.

Yet the Automotive Products Trade Agreements of 1965 did set Canada along a particular, continental path. When the heavy weight of continentalism in the auto sector was brought to bear on the rest of Canada's economic prospects, it enforced a framework on Canada's economic options from which it was difficult to break free. With so much of Canada's well-being bound up in such an influential economic sector, it was almost impossible for policymakers to ignore the importance of the continental precedent set by the automotive agreement. This explains the constant use of the auto pact as a rhetorical device espousing the benefits of free trade by the Mulroney Conservatives during the 1988 election campaign. It was obvious that although Canadians had taken on a host of economically nationalistic initiatives (from the Foreign Investment Review Agency to the National Energy Policy) at a time when the auto pact was locking Canada's economy tightly into that of the United States, this unsteady asymmetry would eventually come to be questioned, as it was in 1988. Any country would find it challenging to have continentalism in its most important economic sector with the most powerful economy in the world and to have the rest of its economic policy remain on the outside of such a domineering imperative. It was a difficult task to erect or maintain economic barriers within the borderless North American auto industry.

In the long run, however, the auto pact turned out to be so beneficial to Canadians (and to the American multinationals) as much because of chance as because of the foresight of those on the Canadian side of the negotiations. Canadian policymakers sought to achieve immediate and short-term benefits for the Canadian auto industry that would be similar to those available under the 1962–4 duty-remission schemes. These included the safeguards in the intergovernmental agreement and all the targets set out in the letters of undertaking between the Canadian government and the Canadian subsidiaries of the Big Three automakers. But the Canada–U.S. auto agreement worked better than had been expected by the Canadians, and by the late 1960s automotive production had shifted northward to a greater degree than either of the two governments had imagined, or anticipated. When Washington sought to end the safeguards, Ottawa resisted. Eventually, the Canadian government did agree to suspend them. By the early 1970s domestic and foreign political and economic events had distracted the United States, and cross-border difficulties over the auto agreement faded. The auto pact may have benefited Canada, but it created difficulties in Canada–U.S. relations, especially during the Nixon administration. These difficulties were finally resolved only with the gutting of the auto agreement following the negotiations regarding the Canada–U.S. Free Trade Agreement in the mid-1980s. In the 1990s further Canadian difficulties with Japan and the European Union over the operation of the automotive agreement were only resolved after they took recourse to the World Trade Organization. Created as a 'free trade' alternative to national policies, the 1965 Automotive Products Trade Agreement met its death at the hands of the WTO in 2001, which declared that the pact violated international trade rules[35] – and was not enough like free trade.

Appendix A
Text of the Automotive Products Trade Agreement, 1965

The Government of the United States and the Government of Canada,

Determined to strengthen economic relations between their two countries;

Recognizing that this can best be achieved through the stimulation of economic growth and through the expansion of markets available to producers in both countries within the framework of the established policy of both countries of promoting multilateral trade;

Recognizing that an expansion of trade can best be achieved through the reduction or elimination of tariff and all other barriers to trade operating to impede or distort the full and efficient development of each country's trade and industrial potential;

Recognizing the important place that the automotive industry occupies in the industrial economies of the two countries and the interests of industry, labour and consumers in sustaining high growth in the automotive industry;

Agree as follows:

Article I

The Governments of the United States and Canada, pursuant to the above principles, shall seek the early achievement of the following objectives:

a) The creation of a broader market for automotive products within which the full benefits of specialization and large-scale production can be achieved;

b) The liberalization of United States and Canadian automotive trade in respect to tariff barriers and other factors tending to impede it, with a view to enabling the industries of both countries to participate on a fair and equitable basis in the expanding total market of the two countries;

c) The development of conditions in which market forces may operate efficiently to attain the most economic patter of investment, production and trade.

It shall be the policy of each Government to avoid actions which would frustrate the achievements of these objectives.

Article II

a) The Government of Canada, not later than the entry into force of the legislation contemplated in paragraph b) of this Article, shall accord duty-free treatment to imports of the products of the United States described in Annex A.

b) The Government of the United States, during the session of the United States Congress commencing on January 4, 1965, shall seek enactment of legislation authorizing duty-free treatment of import of the products of Canada described in Annex B. In seeking such legislation, the Government of the United States shall also seek authority permitting the implementation of such duty-free treatment retroactively to the earliest date administratively possible following the date upon which the Government of Canada has accorded duty-free treatment. Promptly after the entry into force of such legislation, the Government of the United States shall accord duty-free treatment to the products of Canada described in Annex B.

Article III

The commitments made by the two Governments in this Agreement shall not preclude action by either Government consistent with its obligations under Part II of the General Agreement on Tariffs and Trade.

Article IV

a) At any time, at the request of either Governments, the two Governments shall consult with respect to any matter relating to this Agreement.

b) Without limiting the foregoing, the two Governments shall, at the request of either Government, consult with respect to any problems which may arise concerning automotive producers in the United States which do not at present have facilities in Canada for the manufacture of motor vehicles, and with respect to the implications for the operation of this Agreement of new automotive producers being established in Canada.

c) No later than January 1, 1968, the two Governments shall jointly undertake a comprehensive review of the progress made towards achieving the objectives set forth in Article I. During this review the Governments shall consider such further steps as may be necessary or desirable for the full achievement of these objectives.

Article V

Access to the United States and Canadian markets provided for under this Agreement may by agreement be accorded on similar terms to other countries.

Article VI

This Agreement shall enter into force provisionally on the date of signature and definitively on the date upon which notes are exchanged between the two Governments giving notice that appropriate action in their respective legislatures has been completed.

Article VII

This Agreement shall be of unlimited duration. Each Government shall however have the right to terminate this agreement twelve months from the date on which that Government gives written notice to the other Government of its intention to terminate the Agreement.

In witness thereof the representatives of the two Governments have signed this Agreement.

Done in duplicate at Johnson City, Texas, this 16th day of January, 1965, English and French, the two texts being equally authentic.

For the Government of the United States of America:
L.B. Johnson   D. Rusk
For the Government of Canada:
L. B. Pearson   P. Martin

Annex A

1.

1)   Automobiles; when imported by a manufacturer of automobiles.

2)   All parts, accessories and parts thereof, except tires and tubes, when imported for use as original equipment in automobiles to be produced in Canada by a manufacturer of automobiles.

3)   Buses, when imported by a manufacturer of buses.

4)   All parts, and accessories and parts thereof, except tires and tubes, when imported for use as original equipment in buses to be produced in Canada by a manufacturer of automobiles.

5)   Specified commercial vehicles, when imported by a specified manufacturer of commercial vehicles.

6)   All parts, accessories and parts thereof, except tires and tubes, and any machines or other articles required under Canadian tariff item 438a to be valued separately under the tariff items regularly applicable thereto, when imported for use as original equipment in specified commercial vehicles to be produced in Canada by a manufacturer of specified commercial vehicles.

2.

1)   'Automobile' means a four-wheeled passenger automobile having a capacity for not more than ten persons;

2)   'Base year' means the period of twelve months commencing on the 1st day of August, 1963 and ending on the 31st day of July, 1964;

3)   'Bus' means a passenger motor vehicle having a seating capacity for more than ten persons, or a chassis thereof, but does not include any of the following vehicle or chassis therefore, namely an electric trackless trolley bus, amphibious vehicle, tracked or half-tracked vehicle or motor vehicle designed primarily for off-highway use;

4)   'Canadian value added' has the meaning assigned by regulation made under section 273 of the *Canadian Customs Act*;

5)   'Manufacturer' vehicles has the meaning assigned by regulation made under section 273 of the *Canadian Customs Act*;

   i) produced vehicles of that class in Canada in each of the four consecutive three month's periods in the base year, and

   ii) produced vehicles of that class in Canada in the period of twelve months ending on the 31st day of July in which the importation was made

A) The ratio of the net sales value of which the net sales value of all vehicles of that class sold for consumption in Canada by the manufacturer in that period is equal to or higher than the ratio of the net sales value of all vehicles of that class produced in Canada by the manufacturer in the base year to the net sales of all vehicles in that class sold for consumption in Canada by the manufacturer in the base year, and is not in any case lower than seventy-five to one hundred, and

The Canadian value added of which is equal to or greater than the Canadian value added of all vehicles of that class produced in Canada by the manufacturer in the base year;

6) 'Net sales value' has the meaning assigned by regulation made under section 273 of the *Canadian Customs Act*;

7) 'Specified commercial vehicle' means a motor truck, motor truck chassis, ambulance or chassis therefor, or hearse or chassis therefor, but does not include:.

   a) any following vehicle or chassis designed primarily therefor, namely a bus, electric trackless trolley bus, golf or invalid carrier, straddle carrier, amphibious vehicle, tracked or half-tracked vehicle or motor vehicle designed primarily for off-highway use or motor vehicle specially constructed and equipped to perform special services or functions, such as, but not limited to, a fire engine, mobile crane, wrecker, concrete mixer or mobile clinic, or

   b) any machine or other article required under Canadian Tariff item 438a to be valued separately under the tariff item regularly applicable thereto.

3) The Government of Canada may designate a manufacturer for not falling within the categories set out above as being entitled to the benefit of duty-free treatment in respect of the goods described in this Annex.

Annex B

1) Motor vehicles for the transport of persons or articles as provided for in items 962.05 and 692.10 of the *Tariff Schedules of the United States* and chassis therefor, but not including electric trolley buses, three-wheeled vehicles, or trailers accompanying truck tractors, or chassis therefor.

2) Fabricated components, not including trailers, tires, or tubes for

tires, for use as original equipment in manufacture of the motor vehicles of the kinds described in paragraph 1) above.

3) Articles of the kinds described in paragraphs 1) and 2) above include such articles whether finished or unfinished but do not include any article produced with the use of materials imported into Canada which are products of any foreign country (except materials produced within the customs territory of the United States), if the aggregate value of such imported materials when landed at the Canadian port of entry, exclusive of any landing cost and Canadian duty, was –

a) with regard to the kinds described in paragraph 1), not including chassis, more than 60 percent until January 1, 1969, and thereafter more than 50 percent of the appraised custom value of the article imported into the customs territory of the United States, and

b) with regard to chassis of the kinds described in paragraph 1) and articles of the kinds described in paragraph 2), more than 50 percent of the appraised customs value of the article imported into the customs territory of the United States.

Appendix B
Sample Letter of Undertaking, Ford
Motor Company of Canada

Ford Motor Company of Canada, Ltd.
Oakville, Ontario
14 January 1965

Dear Mr Minister:

We are writing with respect to the agreement between the governments of Canada and the United States concerning production and trade in automotive products.

Ford Motor Co. of Canada, Ltd., welcomes the agreement and supports its objectives. In this regard, our company notes that the Governments of Canada and the United States have agreed 'that any expansion of trade can best be achieved through the reduction or elimination of tariff and all other barriers to trade operating to impede or distort the full and efficient development of each country's trade and industrial potential.' In addition, we note that the Governments of Canada and the United States shall seek the early achievement of the following objectives:

a) The creation of a broader market for automotive products within which the full benefits of specialization and large-scale production can be achieved;
b) The liberalization of United States and Canadian automotive trade with respect to tariff barriers and other factors tending to impede it, with a view to enabling the industries of both countries to participate on a fair and equitable basis in the expanding total market of the two countries; and
c) The development of conditions in which market forces may operate

effectively to attain the most economic patter of investment, production, and trade.

Our company also notes that the right to import motor vehicles and original equipment parts into Canada under the agreement is available to vehicle manufacturers in Canada who meet the conditions stipulated in the Motor Vehicles Tariff Order of 1965. These conditions are, in brief, that vehicle manufacturers shall maintain in each model year their production of motor vehicles in Canada in the same ratio to sales of motor vehicles for consumption in Canada and the same dollar value of Canadian value added in the production of motor vehicles in Canada, as in the period August 1, 1963 to July 31, 1964.

We understand that –

i) in ascertaining whether Ford qualifies as a motor vehicle manufacturer and whether the requirements of paragraphs 1 and 2, below, are satisfied, production of automotive vehicles in Canada by Ford Motor Co. of Canada, Ltd. ('an associated person') will be taken into account, whether sold in Canada or exported;

ii) in determining whether the requirements of paragraphs 1 and 2, below, are satisfied, export sales of original equipment parts by Ford Motor Co. of Canada, Ltd., and by any associated person in Canada (as well as production of automotive vehicles in Canada by Ford Motor Co. of Canada, Ltd., and by any associated person, whether sold in Canada or exported), and purchases of original equipment parts by any affiliated Ford company outside of Canada from Canadian vendors, will be taken into account. An 'affiliated Ford company' is one that controls, or is controlled by, or is under common control with, Ford Motor Co. of Canada, Ltd.

iii) for the purpose of computing the ratios referred to in paragraph 2 1) e) ii) A) of the order in council of the definition of manufacturer, the numerators of the fractions will consist of the net sales value of all passenger automobiles (or specified commercial vehicles or buses) produced by the motor vehicle manufacturer in Canada, including those sold in Canada and those sold in export, and the denominators of the fractions will consist of the net sales values of all passenger automobiles (or of specified commercial vehicles or buses) sold by the motor vehicles manufacturer for consumption in Canada, including imported passenger cars (or specified commercial vehicles or buses) but excluding passenger cars (or specified commercial vehicles or buses) that are produced by the motor vehicle manufacturer in Canada and sold in export.

The undertakings in this letter are based on the definition of 'Canadian value added' in your present regulations.

We understand that in the computation of Canadian value added for vehicle assembly in Canada, section 2 A (I) of the regulations would prevent us from including the cost of parts produced in Canada that are exported from Canada and subsequently imported into Canada as components of original equipment parts; this provision reduces the incentive to source in Canada parts that would be incorporated in U.S. engines and other original equipment parts. Accordingly, we request that you give careful consideration to the revision of this clause.

In addition to meeting these stipulated conditions in order to contribute to meeting the objectives of the agreement, Ford Motor Co. of Canada, Ltd., undertakes:

1. To increase in each model year over the preceding model year Canadian value added in the production of vehicles and original equipment parts by an amount equal to 60 percent of the growth in the market for automobiles sold by our company for consumption in Canada and by an amount equal to 50 percent of the growth in the market for commercial vehicles specified in Tariff Item 950 sold by our company for consumption in Canada, it being understood that in the event of a decline in the market a decrease in Canadian value added based on the above percentage is acceptable. For this purpose, growth or decline in the market shall be measured as the difference between the cost to our company of vehicles sold in Canada during the current model year and the cost to our company of vehicles sold in Canada during the preceding model year net of Federal sales taxes in both cases.

    We understand that in the event that the total passenger car and / or total truck sales of our company in any model year fall below the total passenger car and/or total truck sales of our company during the base period, Canadian value added requirements would be reduced below the base period amendments for the purpose of this section, and for the conditions stipulated in the Motor Vehicles Tariff Order of 1965.

    We believe that the definition of growth is unfair because it includes as growth the difference between the cost of the vehicles produced in Canada and the cost to us of identical imported vehicles. In the event that we rationalize our vehicle production in Canada so as to concentrate our production in Canada on high volume models for the North American market with other models being imported, the difference in cost as defined above would result in substantial growth even though there was no change in the number and models of vehicles sold in Canada. We request your careful consideration of a change in the definition that would eliminate this inequity. This inequity is compounded by the fact that Ford Motor Co. of Canada, Ltd., is compelled by the Canadian antidumping law to import vehicles at dealer price, and we request that your Government also give careful consideration to a change in the antidumping law in respect of vehicles imported under the Motor Vehicles Tariff Order of 1965.

2   To increase Canadian value added over and above the current amount that we achieved in the period August 1, 1963 to July 31, 1964, and that which we undertake to achieve in 1) above, by an amount of $74.2 million during the period August 1, 1967 to July 31, 1968.

The undertakings given in this letter are to be adjusted to the extent necessary for conditions not under the control of the Ford Motor Co. of Canada, Ltd., or of any affiliated Ford company, such as acts of God, fire, earthquake, strikes at any plant owned by Ford or by any of our suppliers, and war.

The Ford Motor Co. of Canada, Ltd., also agrees to report to the Minister of Industry, every 3 months beginning April 1, 1965, such information as the Minister of Industry requires pertaining to progress achieved by our company as well as plans to fulfill our obligations under this letter. In addition, Ford Motor Co. of Canada. Ltd., understands that the Government will conduct an audit each year with respect to the matters described in this letter.

We understand that before the end of the model year 1968 we will need to discuss together the prospects for the Canadian automotive industry and our company's program.

Yours sincerely,

Ford Motor Co. of Canada, Ltd.,
by K.E. Scott, President.

Appendix C
Automotive Statistics, 1960–1999

Table C1 North American vehicle production summary, 1960–1999 (units)

Year	U.S.	Canada	Mexico	All North America	Cdn. % of U.S.	Cdn. % of North America
1960	7,894,220	395,855	49,807	8,339,882	5.01	4.74
1961	6,643,822	390,459	62,563	7,096,844	5.87	5.50
1962	8,189,402	508,667	66,637	8,764,716	6.21	5.80
1963	9,100,585	632,172	69,135	9,801,892	6.94	6.44
1964	9,245,678	669,549	90,752	10,005,979	7.24	6.69
1965	11,114,213	853,931	97,395	12,056,539	7.68	7.08
1966	10,363,254	896,119	114,521	11,373,894	8.64	7.87
1967	8,992,269	939,635	126,991	10,058,895	10.44	9.34
1968	10,793,744	1,178,186	146,781	12,118,701	10.91	9.72
1969	10,182,562	1,350,481	165,811	11,698,854	13.26	11.54
1970	8,262,657	1,189,461	189,986	9,642,104	14.39	12.33
1971	10,649,666	1,373,108	211,393	12,234,167	12.89	11.22
1972	11,297,509	1,471,392	229,791	12,998,692	13.02	11.31
1973	12,662,919	1,589,499	285,568	14,537,986	12.55	10.93
1974	9,983,934	1,563,850	350,947	11,898,731	15.66	13.14
1975	8,965,413	1,442,076	356,642	10,764,113	16.08	13.39
1976	11,485,536	1,646,824	324,979	13,457,339	14.33	12.23
1977	12,699,086	1,764,987	280,813	14,744,886	13.89	11.97
1978	12,895,286	1,818,378	384,127	15,097,791	14.10	12.04
1979	11,475,737	1,629,855	444,426	13,550,018	14.20	12.02
1980	8,010,563	1,369,697	490,006	9,870,176	17.09	13.87
1981	7,940,781	1,280,499	597,118	9,818,398	16.12	13.04
1982	6,985,313	1,235,668	472,637	8,693,618	17.68	14.21
1983	9,225,698	1,502,325	285,485	11,013,508	16.28	13.64
1984	10,939,058	1,835,074	357,998	13,132,135	16.77	13.97
1985	11,653,956	1,934,110	458,680	14,046,746	16.59	13.76
1986	11,335,241	1,854,418	341,052	13,530,711	16.35	13.70
1987	10,925,605	1,635,151	395,258	12,956,014	14.96	12.62
1988	11,237,947	1,976,896	512,776	13,727,619	17.59	14.40
1989	10,875,574	1,965,480	641,275	13,482,329	18.07	14.57
1990	9,783,433	1,946,542	820,558	12,550,533	19.89	15.50
1991	8,811,808	1,887,537	989,373	11,688,754	21.42	16.14
1992	9,731,478	1,950,646	1,080,863	12,762,987	20.04	15.28
1993	10,891,740	2,242,186	1,080,687	14,221,613	20.58	15.76
1994	12,249,990	2,320,403	1,109,338	15,679,731	18.94	14.79
1995	11,974,616	2,407,155	934,733	15,316,504	20.10	15.71
1996	11,831,225	2,397,166	1,222,711	15,451,102	20.26	15.51
1997	12,149,987	2,622,278	1,356,360	16,128,625	21.58	16.25
1998	12,001,864	2,570,321	1,459,891	16,032,076	21.41	16.03
1999	13,024,010	3,048,693	1,532,623	17,605,326	23.40	17.31

Source: *DesRosiers Automotive Yearbook 2000* (Richmond Hill, ON: DesRosiers Automotive Consultants, 2000), 112.

Table C2 North American production-to-sales ratios, vehicles, 1960–1999 (%)

Year	U.S.	Canada	Mexico	North America
1960	104.3	75.7	91.0	102.4
1961	97.1	76.3	101.5	95.7
1962	100.4	86.9	104.0	99.5
1963	101.7	96.5	91.5	101.3
1964	97.8	92.2	97.2	97.4
1965	102.3	102.8	101.1	102.3
1966	97.3	108.3	101.2	98.1
1967	91.1	115.2	100.9	93.1
1968	94.5	132.5	100.7	97.3
1969	88.9	147.2	100.3	93.3
1970	81.9	153.6	102.3	87.2
1971	87.6	146.0	103.0	92.0
1972	85.1	138.1	99.5	89.2
1973	88.1	129.6	110.2	91.6
1974	87.9	125.2	106.3	92.0
1975	84.1	109.5	103.1	87.4
1976	89.7	127.5	107.1	93.4
1977	88.6	131.2	97.1	92.3
1978	86.5	133.1	106.4	90.7
1979	83.0	116.7	104.5	86.6
1980	71.3	108.4	105.5	76.1
1981	74.4	107.5	104.6	79.2
1982	68.6	134.2	101.3	75.1
1983	77.5	139.0	104.6	83.1
1984	77.2	143.0	108.4	83.2
1985	74.9	126.4	117.1	80.3
1986	71.1	122.3	131.8	76.4
1987	72.4	107.0	159.4	76.8
1988	71.6	126.5	150.0	78.0
1989	72.7	132.5	143.8	79.9
1990	69.2	148.1	150.6	78.4
1991	70.3	146.7	153.9	80.8
1992	74.2	158.9	152.9	84.8
1993	77.0	188.7	179.2	89.1
1994	79.7	184.9	185.7	91.9
1995	79.5	207.1	503.3	93.3
1996	76.9	199.8	348.8	91.2
1997	78.7	184.6	272.5	92.9
1998	75.4	180.5	226.9	89.2
1999	75.0	198.2	230.2	91.2

Source: *DesRosiers Automotive Yearbook 2000* (Richmond Hill, ON: DesRosiers Automotive Consultants, 2000), 113.

Table C3 Canada's automotive trade with the United States, 1960–1999
(Can$ millions)

Year	Exports			Imports			Balance		
	Vehicles	Parts	Total	Vehicles	Parts	Total	Vehicles	Parts	Total
1960	0	4	4	90	317	407	–90	–313	–403
1961	0	9	9	71	327	398	–71	–318	–389
1962	3	13	16	78	441	519	–75	–428	–504
1963	4	36	40	49	555	604	–46	–518	–564
1964	26	79	105	67	655	723	–41	–576	–617
1965	90	147	237	170	852	1,022	–80	–705	–785
1966	493	361	854	409	1,103	1,511	84	–741	–657
1967	1,105	494	1,600	807	1,310	2,117	298	–816	–518
1968	1,686	758	2,444	1,093	1,818	2,910	593	–1,060	–466
1969	2,367	950	3,317	1,154	2,344	3,498	1,213	–1,394	–181
1970	2,127	1,142	3,269	934	2,131	3,065	1,193	–989	204
1971	2,536	1,504	4,040	1,321	2,521	3,842	1,215	–1,017	198
1972	2,752	1,801	4,553	1,551	2,957	4,508	1,201	–1,156	45
1973	3,060	2,240	5,300	2,082	3,620	5,702	978	–1,380	–402
1974	3,408	2,027	5,435	2,517	4,110	6,627	891	–2,083	–1,192
1975	3,790	2,113	5,903	3,125	4,599	7,724	665	–2,485	–1,821
1976	4,774	3,105	7,879	3,287	5,588	8,875	1,487	–2,483	–996
1977	5,996	3,865	9,861	3,952	7,001	10,953	2,044	–3,136	–1,092
1978	7,048	4,945	11,993	4,360	8,222	12,582	2,688	–3,277	–589
1979	6,709	4,723	11,432	5,699	8,821	14,520	1,010	–4,098	–3,088
1980	6,670	3,636	10,306	4,605	7,746	12,351	2,065	–4,110	–2,045
1981	8,287	4,437	12,724	5,066	9,395	14,461	3,221	–4,958	–1,737
1982	11,116	5,308	16,424	3,748	9,823	13,571	7,368	–4,515	2,853
1983	13,410	7,475	20,885	6,015	11,584	17,599	7,395	–4,109	3,286
1984	18,965	10,885	29,850	8,124	15,791	23,915	10,841	–4,906	5,935
1985	21,699	12,104	33,803	10,552	17,752	28,304	11,147	–5,648	5,499
1986	22,232	12,525	34,484	11,452	17,862	29,314	10,780	–5,610	5,170
1987	20,343	12,240	32,583	11,973	16,707	28,680	8,370	–4,467	3,903
1988	23,689	12,272	35,961	11,681	20,307	31,988	12,008	–8,035	3,973
1989	23,515	12,051	35,566	10,856	17,840	28,696	12,659	–5,789	6,870
1990	24,153	10,697	34,850	9,621	16,694	26,315	14,532	–5,997	8,535
1991	24,025	9,340	33,365	9,909	15,702	25,611	14,116	–6,362	7,754
1992	27,709	10,812	38,521	9,869	18,853	28,722	17,847	–8,041	9,799
1993	35,245	11,448	46,693	12,152	19,964	32,116	23,093	–8,516	14,577
1994	43,229	13,193	56,422	15,717	23,739	39,456	27,152	–10,546	16,966
1995	47,021	13,212	60,233	16,009	26,056	42,065	31,012	–12,844	18,168
1996	46,979	14,825	61,804	16,865	26,283	43,148	30,114	–11,458	18,656
1997	50,686	16,208	66,894	20,347	29,949	50,295	30,339	–13,741	16,599
1998	57,040	18,922	75,962	21,146	34,658	55,803	35,894	–15,735	20,159
1999	70,239	22,248	92,487	22,757	39,941	62,698	47,482	–17,693	29,789

Source: *DesRosiers Automotive Yearbook 2000* (Richmond Hill, ON: DesRosiers
Automotive Consultants, 2000), 190.

Table C4 Canadian automotive trade with all countries, 1960–1999 (Can$ millions)

Year	Exports			Imports			Balance		
	Vehicles	Parts	Total	Vehicles	Parts	Total	Vehicles	Parts	Total
1960	28	24	52	247	332	579	−219	−308	−528
1961	21	29	50	183	343	527	−163	−314	−477
1962	29	34	62	179	463	642	−150	−430	−580
1963	37	60	97	117	575	692	−80	−516	−595
1964	82	105	187	164	673	836	−82	−567	−649
1965	183	182	364	285	868	1,154	−103	−687	−789
1966	603	402	1,005	507	1,124	1,631	96	−722	−626
1967	1,205	541	1,745	912	1,346	2,259	293	−806	−513
1968	1,833	816	2,650	1,269	1,849	3,118	564	−1,033	−469
1969	2,488	1,035	3,523	1,398	2,399	3,797	1,091	−1,364	−273
1970	2,268	1,244	3,512	1,174	2,280	3,454	1,094	−1,036	58
1971	2,650	1,593	4,243	1,695	2,681	4,376	955	−1,088	−133
1972	2,869	1,892	4,761	2,015	3,190	5,205	854	−1,298	−444
1973	3,186	2,364	5,550	2,459	3,889	6,348	727	−1,525	−798
1974	3,612	2,174	5,786	2,967	4,440	7,407	645	−2,266	−1,621
1975	4,211	2,298	6,509	3,535	4,887	8,422	676	−2,589	−1,913
1976	5,201	3,284	8,485	3,809	5,898	9,707	1,392	−2,614	−1,222
1977	6,610	4,067	10,677	4,544	7,346	11,890	2,066	−3,279	−1,213
1978	7,759	5,269	13,028	5,254	8,630	13,884	2,505	−3,361	−856
1979	7,267	5,179	12,446	6,426	9,388	15,814	841	−4,209	−3,368
1980	7,304	4,087	11,391	5,764	8,309	14,073	1,450	−4,222	−2,682
1981	8,943	5,038	13,981	6,665	9,924	16,589	2,278	−4,886	−2,608
1982	11,556	5,738	17,294	5,161	10,317	15,478	6,395	−4,579	1,816
1983	13,691	7,747	21,438	7,641	12,325	19,966	6,050	−4,578	1,472
1984	19,311	11,189	30,500	10,300	17,326	27,626	9,011	−6,137	2,874
1985	21,915	12,456	34,371	13,659	19,418	33,077	8,256	−6,962	1,294
1986	22,454	12,712	35,166	15,406	19,843	35,249	7,048	−7,131	−83
1987	20,530	12,654	33,184	16,053	18,799	34,852	4,470	−6,145	−1,668
1988	23,992	12,651	36,643	15,617	22,180	37,797	8,375	−9,529	−2,254
1989	23,882	12,499	36,381	14,866	20,558	35,424	9,016	−8,059	957
1990	24,395	11,201	35,596	13,725	19,850	33,575	10,670	−8,649	2,021
1991	24,273	9,909	34,182	14,886	19,196	34,082	9,387	−9,287	100
1992	27,956	11,289	39,245	14,842	22,468	37,310	13,114	−11,179	1,935
1993	36,006	12,454	48,460	16,483	23,375	39,858	19,523	−10,921	8,601
1994	44,173	14,278	58,450	19,808	28,008	47,815	24,365	−13,730	10,635
1995	48,468	14,664	63,132	20,110	30,266	50,376	28,358	−15,602	12,756
1996	47,932	15,937	63,869	21,071	30,394	51,465	26,861	−14,457	12,404
1997	51,446	17,768	69,214	26,228	34,211	60,439	25,218	−16,443	8,775
1998	57,674	19,990	77,665	27,294	39,358	66,652	30,382	−19,369	11,013
1999	71,061	23,334	94,395	30,230	45,579	75,809	40,832	−22,246	18,586

Source: *DesRosiers Automotive Yearbook 2000* (Richmond Hill, ON: DesRosiers Automotive Consultants, 2000), 189.

Table C5 Big Three Canadian value added (CVA), required and produced (Can$ millions), and total CVA as a percentage of cost of sales, by model year, 1965–1979

	General Motors			Ford			Chrysler		
Year	CVA required	CVA produced	CVA to sales (%)	CVA required	CVA produced	CVA to sales (%)	CVA required	CVA produced	CVA to sales (%)
1965	391.9	436.9	63	259.7	288.3	64	166.2	188.8	72
1966	428.1	506.9	67	290.7	349.2	69	195.1	238.5	77
1967	409.5	459.8	63	295.5	405.6	79	216.5	234.5	68
1968	597.4	567.6	67	403.5	424.5	75	290.7	309.2	74
1969	645.2	699.7	75	420.1	519.7	87	289.8	343.5	83
1970	585.5	687.9	84	371.0	535.6	103	264.8	361.1	97
1971	514.6	674.3	97	409.0	601.7	103	295.4	375.3	88
1972	649.8	818.2	87	464.6	677.1	99	319.9	436.4	93
1973	864.7	979.6	75	575.8	792.5	90	421.8	469.3	73
1974	959.2	1,120.5	75	667.4	765.6	73	489.3	451.9	59
1975	1,172.8	1,318.1	70	774.9	782.8	63	561.6	497.8	56
1976	1,370.9	1,592.2	72	909.0	939.1	63	687.1	689.4	62
1977	1,601.8	1,923.2	73	983.1	1,148.2	71	734.7	840.4	70
1978	1,807.0	2,244.2	75	1,150.2	1,399.9	73	717.5	787.6	68
1979	2,365.3	2,620.4	66	1,380.6	1,495.8	64	770.9	740.1	59

Source: Company Reports to Dept. of Industry, Trade and Commerce, NAC, RG 19, Vol. 5959, File 8705-08-15, File, Statistics.

Table C6 Big Three ratio required (in parentheses) and achieved, cars and trucks, by model year, 1965–1978

	General Motors		Ford		Chrysler	
Year	Cars (97.9)	Trucks (100.1)	Cars (99.4)	Trucks (108.1)	Cars (99.6)	Trucks (100.5)
1965	102.5	111.5	101.9	111.5	99.7	101.9
1966	102.8	112.2	102.8	156.5	112.6	106.6
1967	98.4	103.3	101.1	208.9	110.9	101.8
1968	101.2	112.2	106.9	218.3	127.9	106.8
1969	122.5	122.3	160.1	238.7	143.0	105.0
1970	133.6	129.5	220.7	236.4	168.2	102.7
1971	127.5	103.5	184.1	202.1	137.3	102.2
1972	126.4	101.2	189.8	162.2	137.6	101.5
1973	102.2	100.8	171.8	159.5	109.4	68.6
1974	115.1	101.5	142.6	112.4	101.4	53.8
1975	107.9	101.3	155.0	109.6	117.2	64.2
1976	98.6	114.3	163.4	112.9	126.5	111.1
1977	118.0	136.3	158.7	112.4	106.0	182.4
1978	121.9	141.4	154.5	159.0	115.6	195.8

Source: Company Reports to Dept. of Industry, Trade and Commerce, NAC, RG 19, Vol. 5959, File 8705-08-15, File, Statistics.

Table C7 Canadian auto industry, Canadian value added (Can$ millions), both required and produced, and also as a proportion of sales, 1965–1979

Year	CVA required	CVA produced	Cost of vehicles sold	Cost of sales less CVA produced	CVA produced to cost of sales (%)	CVA required to cost of sales (%)
1965	891	992	1,534	542	65	58
1966	988	1,186	1,716	530	69	58
1967	1,002	1,200	1,738	538	69	58
1968	1,395	1,420	1,977	557	72	71
1969	1,471	1,703	2,110	407	81	70
1970	1,341	1,743	1,891	148	92	70
1971	1,350	1,825	1,911	86	95	69
1972	1,592	2,145	2,371	226	90	66
1973	2,056	2,522	3,200	678	79	64
1974	2,373	2,687	3,795	1,108	71	62
1975	2,787	2,987	4,545	1,558	66	61
1976	3,249	3,606	5,345	1,739	67	61
1977	3,611	4,337	6,001	1,664	72	60
1978	4,010	4,951	6,727	1,776	74	59
1979	5,002	5,491	8,554	3,063	64	58

Source: Company Reports to Dept. of Industry, Trade and Commerce, NAC, RG 19, Vol. 5959, File 8705-08-15, File, Statistics.

Notes

Introduction

1 On the development of the postwar auto industry, see Lawrence J. White, *The Automobile Industry since 1945* (Cambridge, 1971); John B. Rae, *The American Automobile Industry* (Boston, 1984); George Maxcy, *The Multinational Automobile Industry* (New York, 1981).

2 The idea of free trade re-emerged forcefully in the 1950s and 1960s and was espoused by numerous academics, think tanks, and business leaders. For example, the Canadian-American Committee, a cross-border research association dedicated to studying the close relationship between the two countries, was instrumental in kindling the free trade flame in the 1960s. Soon after its creation in 1957, the committee began publishing studies emphasizing the free trade option, including a 1963 book that thrust the idea boldly onto the public agenda, *A Canada–U.S. Free Trade Arrangement: Survey of Possible Characteristics* (Montreal, 1963). On Canada and the GATT in this period, see Michael Hart, 'Canada at the GATT: Twenty Years of Canadian Tradecraft, 1947–1967,' *International Journal* 52 (Autumn 1997), 581–604.

3 Stephen Azzi, *Walter Gordon and the Rise of Canadian Nationalism* (Montreal and Kingston, 1999).

4 From 1965 to 1968, the companies were to increase their Canadian investment by $260 million and to increase the Canadian content in their production by 60 per cent of whatever increase might occur in their sales in a given year. The U.S. government, which was not privy to the details of the letters initially, found the terms exceedingly generous to the Canadians. One American official complained, 'We knew about the Canadian plan to blackjack the companies, but we expected the companies to be harder

bargainers. They didn't have to give away so much. It must have been profitable for them.' Quoted from Robert O. Keohane and Joseph S. Nye, *Power and Interdependence* (New York, 1989), 207.

5 For the text of the agreement and a sample letter of undertaking, see Appendixes A and B.

6 For Canadian employment, production, and trade statistics from 1965 onwards, see Chapters 5 and 6, and Appendix C.

7 For other views on the auto pact, see James G. Dykes, *Background on the Canada–United States Automotive Products Trade Agreement* (Toronto, 1979); Carl Beigie, *The Canada–U.S. Automotive Agreement: An Evaluation* (Montreal, 1970); Paul Wonnacott and R.J. Wonnacott, 'The Automotive Agreement of 1965,' *Canadian Journal of Economics and Political Science* 33, 2 (1967), 269–84; Leonard Waverman and Melvyn Fuss, *The Canada–U.S. Auto Pact of 1965: An Experiment in Selective Trade Liberalization* (Toronto, 1986).

8 Studies that focus largely on the role of state planners in the creation of the agreement include Greg Donaghy, 'A Continental Philosophy: Canada, the United States and the Negotiation of the Auto Pact, 1963–1965,' *International Journal* 52, 3 (1998), 441–64; John Kirton, 'The Politics of Bilateral Management: The Case of the Automotive Trade,' *International Journal* 36, 1 (1980–1), 39–69; James F. Keeley, 'Cast in Concrete for All Time? The Negotiation of the Auto Pact,' *Canadian Journal of Political Science* 16, 2 (1983), 281–98.

9 During the negotiations, the Canadians continually referred to the farm implements agreement, the only other sectoral trade agreement. Government studies reported the steady Canadian decline in this industry. The studies include Walter Gordon's 1957 *Report of the Royal Commission on Canadian Economic Prospects* and Vincent Bladen's 1961 *Report of the Royal Commission on the Automotive Industry*.

10 See, e.g., Thomas Zeiler, *Free Trade, Free World: The Advent of GATT* (Chapel Hill and London, 1999).

11 Studies on intervention into the auto industry in the period include: Peter Stubbs, *The Australian Motor Industry: A Study in Protection and Growth* (Melbourne, 1972); Rich Kronish and Kenneth S. Mericle, *The Political Economy of the Latin American Motor Vehicle Industry* (Boston, 1984); John P. Truman and John T. Morris, *Transforming the Latin American Auto Industry: Unions, Workers and the Politics of Restructuring* (Armonk, NY, 1998).

12 Helen Shapiro, *Engines of Growth: The State and Transnational Auto Companies in Brazil* (Cambridge, 1994), 4–24.

13 Douglas C. Bennett and Kenneth E. Sharpe, *Transnational Corporations versus the State: The Political Economy of the Mexican Auto Industry* (Princeton, NJ, 1985), 41–2, 245–71.

14 Joseph S. Nye, 'Transnational Relations and Interstate Conflicts: An Empirical Analysis,' *International Organization* 28 (Autumn 1974), 987 n43.

15 For views on the Canadian state and economic development, see H.G. Aitken, 'Defensive Expansion: The State and Economic Growth in Canada,' in W.T. Easterbrook and M.H. Watkins, eds., *Approaches to Canadian Economic History* (Toronto, 1967); Philip Mathias, *Forced Growth: Five Studies of Government Involvement in the Development of Canada* (Toronto, 1971); Keith Banting, ed., *The State and Economic Interests* (Ottawa, 1986).

16 For a view on the interaction of developed countries and multinationals, see A.E. Safarian, 'Policy on Multinational Enterprises in Developed Countries,' *Canadian Journal of Economics* 11, 4 (1978), 641–55.

17 Lorraine Eden and Maureen Appel Molot discuss three stages of Canada's national policies (defensive expansionism, 1867–1940; compensatory liberalism 1941–82; and market liberalism beginning in 1982) in 'Canada's National Policies: Reflections on 125 Years,' *Canadian Public Policy* 19, 3 (1993), 232–51; Michael Bliss, *The Evolution of Industrial Policies in Canada: A Historical Survey* (Ottawa, 1982).

18 See, e.g., Greg Donaghy, *Tolerant Allies: Canada and The United States, 1963–1968* (Montreal and Kingston, 2002). In the chapter, 'A Continental Philosophy: The Autopact and the Kennedy Round,' there is virtually no mention of the pivotal role of the auto companies in facilitating the creation of the agreement.

19 For views on business-government relations in Canada, see W.T. Stanbury, *Business-Government Relations in Canada: Grappling with Leviathan* (Toronto, 1986); William Coleman, 'Canadian Business and the State,' in Banting, ed., *State and Economic Interests*, 245–87; V.V. Murray, ed., *Theories of Business-Government Relations* (Toronto, 1985); Mark C. Baetz and Donald H. Thain, eds., *Canadian Cases in Business-Government Relations* (Toronto, 1985), esp. W.T. Stanbury, 'A Framework for the Analysis of Business-Government Relations in Canada,' 1–35. For business-government relations in the United States, see Kim McQuaid, *Uneasy Partners: Big Business in American Politics, 1945–1990* (Baltimore, 1994); McQuaid, *Big Business and Presidential Power from FDR to Reagan* (New York, 1982). On U.S. multinationals, see Raymond Vernon, *Sovereignty at Bay: The Multinational Spread of U.S. Enterprises* (New York, 1971); Mira Wilkins, *The Maturing of the Multinational Enterprise: American Business Abroad from 1914 to 1970* (Cambridge, MA, 1974); Jack N. Behrman, *U.S. International Business and Governments* (New York, 1971).

20 For an excellent analysis of relations between multinationals and nations, see Isabel Studer-Noguez, *Ford and the Global Strategies of Multinationals: The North American Auto Industry* (New York, 2002).

21 Gilbert R. Winham, 'Choice and Strategy in Continental Relations,' in Andrew Axline et al., eds., *Continental Community? Independence and Integration in North America* (Toronto, 1974), 237.

22 A.D.P. Heeney and Livingston T. Merchant, *Canada and the United States: Principles for Partnership* (Ottawa, 1965).

23 For more on the Temple speech and the Canada-US relationship during this period, see Donaghy, *Tolerant Allies.*

24 Richard Leach, 'Canada and the United States: A Special Relationship,' *Current History* (April 1977), 143–9; Elliot J. Feldman and Lily Gardner Feldman, 'The Special Relationship between Canada and the United States,' *Jerusalem Journal of International Relations* 4, 4 (1980), 56–85; John Kirton and Robert Bothwell, 'A Proud and Powerful Country: American Attitudes toward Canada, 1963–1976,' *Queen's Quarterly* 92, 1 (1985), 108.

25 Ian Lumsden, ed., *Close the 49th Parallel Etc.: The Americanization of Canada* (Toronto, 1970); Stephen Clarkson, ed., *An Independent Foreign Policy for Canada?* (Toronto, 1968); and Robert Laxer, ed., *(Canada) Ltd.: The Political Economy of Dependency* (Toronto, 1973).

26 For Accounts using the cooperation/conflict approach, see: Donaghy, *Tolerant Allies;* J.L. Granatstein and Norman Hillmer, *For Better or for Worse: Canada and the United States to the 1990s* (Toronto, 1991); J.L. Granatstein, 'Cooperation and Conflict: The Course of Canadian-American Relations since 1945,' in Charles F. Doran and John H. Sigler, eds., *Canada and the United States: Enduring Friendship, Permanent Stress* (Englewood Cliffs, NJ, 1985); and John Herd Thompson and Stephen J. Randall, *Canada and the United States: Ambivalent Allies* (Montreal and Kingston, 1994). Thompson and Randall summarize the approach, stating, 'If the past is our guide, the U.S.-Canada relationship in the future cannot be other than intense, close, and cooperative, yet conflictual in both its details and its fundamentals.'

27 Keohane and Nye, *Power and Independence,* 179.

1 The Canadian Auto Industry, 1900–1963

1 E.E. Mahant, *Free Trade in American-Canadian Relations* (Malabar, FL, 1993); Donald Creighton, *John A. Macdonald: The Old Chieftain* (Toronto, 1955).

2 R.C. Brown and R. Cook, *A Nation Transformed: Canada, 1896–1921* (Toronto, 1974).

3 Tom Traves, *The State and Enterprise: Canadian Manufacturers and the Federal Government, 1917–1931* (Toronto, 1979), 101.

4 For views of the early Canadian auto industry, see Tom Traves, 'The Development of the Ontario Automobile Industry to 1939,' in Ian

Drummond, ed., *Progress without Planning: The Economic History of Ontario from Confederation to the Second World War* (Toronto, 1987); Donald F. Davis, 'Dependent Motorization: Canada and the Automobile to the 1930s,' in Douglas McCalla, ed., *The Development of Canadian Capitalism* (Toronto, 1990); O.J. McDiarmid, 'Some Aspects of the Canadian Automobile Industry,' *Canadian Journal of Economics and Political Science* 6 (Feb.–Nov. 1940), 258–74.

5 On the impact of American producers on the indigenous Canadian auto industry, see Robert E. Ankli and Fred Frederiksen, 'The Influence of American Manufacturers on the Canadian Automobile Industry,' *Business and Economic History* 9 (1981), 101–16.

6 For the development of the early American auto industry, see Douglas Brinkley, *Wheels for the World: Henry Ford, His Company, and a Century of Progress, 1903–2003* (New York, 2003); Alfred D. Chandler, *Giant Enterprise: Ford, General Motors and the Automobile Industry* (New York, 1964); Charles K. Hyde, 'The Dodge Brothers, the Automobile Industry, and Detroit Society in the Early Twentieth Century,' *Michigan Historical Review* 22, 2 (1996), 49–82; Charles K. Hyde, *Riding the Roller Coaster: A History of the Chrysler Corporation* (Detroit, 2003).

7 On the emergence of Ford in Canada, see Mira Wilkins and Frank Ernest Hill, *American Business Abroad: Ford on Six Continents* (Detroit, 1964); Dimitry Anastakis, 'From Independence to Integration: The Corporate Evolution of the Ford Motor Company of Canada, 1904–2004,' *Business History Review* 78, 2 (2004), 213–53; James Mays, *Ford and Canada: 100 Years Together* (Montreal, 2003).

8 Heather Robertson, *Driving Force: The McLaughlin Family and the Age of the Car* (Toronto, 1995); Michael Moritz, *Going for Broke: The Chrysler Story* (Garden City, NY, 1981); Vincent W. Bladen, *Report of the Royal Commission on the Automotive Industry* (hereafter, Bladen Report) (Ottawa, 1961), 101.

9 'Brief Presented by the Ford Motor Company of Canada, Ltd., to Tariff Inquiry Commission, Nov. 30, 1920,' Benson Ford Research Center (BFRC), Acc. 284, Henry Ford Office, Box 13, File 7, Branches-Canada.

10 For more on Ford in Canada, see Wilkins and Hill, *American Business Abroad*.

11 Bladen Report, 101; Canada, *Debates of the House of Commons*, 16 March 1925, 1179 (hereafter *Debates*).

12 Ford of Canada's prevalence in this field was a result of the original agreement between Henry Ford and Gordon McGregor, which stipulated that Ford of Canada would have the rights to all the Commonwealth countries save the United Kingdom and Ireland. By the mid-1920s, Ford of

Canada, which had a large Canadian minority ownership, had established subsidiaries in Australia, New Zealand, and South Africa. As GM's and Chrysler's Canadian subsidiaries were wholly owned and had not been established as the result of any partnership arrangement, they were mostly focused on the Canadian domestic market.

13 Reductions were also made to the intermediate and British preferential tariff. *Debates*, 15 April 1926, 2450; McDiarmid, 'Some Aspects of the Canadian Automobile Industry,' 261; Traves, *State and Enterprise*, 104. See Table 1.1 above.

14 The Bennett government also added a third category of tariff for cars valued at over $2,200, which was set at 40 per cent. See Table 1.1 above.

15 In August 1945, Order-in-Council C 5623 modified the 40 per cent content bracket by raising the level to 15,000 units. This was intended to ease the way for Nash (later American) Motors, which began production in Canada in 1946.

16 James G. Dykes, *Background on the Canada – United States Automotive Products Trade Agreement* (Toronto, 1979), 24.

17 On recognition of the UAW by the Canadian industry, see Sam Gindin, *The Canadian Auto Workers: The Birth and Transformation of a Union* (Toronto, 1995), esp. Chapter 4, 'The Union Arrives.'

18 Dominion Bureau of Statistics (DBS) figures cited from Sun Life Assurance Company of Canada, *The Canadian Automotive Industry* (Ottawa, 1956), 3.

19 For the post–Second World War labour issues surrounding the auto industry, see Charlotte Yates, *From Plant to Politics: The Autoworkers Union in Postwar Canada* (Philadelphia, 1993) and Don Wells, 'The Impact of the Postwar Compromise on Canadian Unionism: The Formation of an Auto Worker Local in the 1950s,' *Labour / Le Travail* 36 (Fall 1995), 147–73. See also, Dimitry Anastakis, 'Between Nationalism and Continentalism: State Auto Industry Policy and the Canadian UAW, 1960–70,' *Labour / Le Travail* 53 (Spring 2004), 87–124.

20 On the postwar suburbanization trend, see Doug Owram, *Born at the Right Time* (Toronto, 1997), esp. Chapter 3, 'Safe in the Hands of Mother Suburbia,' and Paul-André Linteau, 'Canadian Suburbanization in a North American Context: Does the Border Make a Difference?' *Journal of Urban History* 13 (1986/7), 252–74.

21 See Anastakis, 'From Independence to Integration.'

22 On the elections of 1957 and 1958, see J. Murray Beck, *Pendulum of Power: Canada's Federal Elections* (Scarborough, 1968). On the Liberal party of the 1950s and the Gordon Commission, see Stephen Azzi, *Walter Gordon and the Rise of Canadian Nationalism* (Montreal and Kingston, 1999) and Reg

Whitaker, *The Government Party: Organizing and Financing the Liberal Party of Canada, 1930–1958* (Toronto, 1977).

23 On Diefenbaker and his government, see Peter C. Newman, *Renegade in Power: The Diefenbaker Years* (Toronto, 1973) and John Diefenbaker, *One Canada: Memoirs of the Right Honourable John G. Diefenbaker*, vol. 1, *The Years of Achievement* (Toronto, 1975).

24 The Diefenbaker government's economic policies are discussed by Donald Fleming, *So Very Near: The Political Memoirs of Donald M. Fleming*, vol. 2, *The Summit Years* (Toronto, 1985) and by Robert Bothwell, Ian Drummond, and John English, *Canada since 1945: Power, Politics, and Provincialism* (Toronto, 1989), Chapter 20.

25 John Holmes, 'Industrial Reorganization, Capital Restructuring and Locational Change: An Analysis of the Canadian Automobile Industry in the 1960s,' *Economic Geography* 59 (1983), 265.

26 Ralph Young, 'Imported Cars Taking Almost 30% of Market,' *Financial Post*, 6 Aug. 1960.

27 'UAW Proposes Probe of Jobless Causes,' *Globe and Mail*, 4 April 1960; 'How Canadians Can Get a Made-in-Canada Car They Want and Can Afford,' ibid., 5 July 1960; National Archives of Canada (NAC), RG 33/45, Royal Commission on the Automobile Industry (hereafter Bladen Commission), Vol. 4, File 33, UAW, Confidential Correspondence.

28 Bladen Commission, ibid.

29 A second parts lobby group, the Canadian Automotive Wholesalers and Manufacturers Association (CAWMA), represented smaller independent and Canadian firms that produced for the automotive aftermarket. D.S. Wood (APMA) and James G. Dykes (CACC) to A.F.W. Plumptre, 15 May 1957, NAC, RG 19, Department of Finance, Vol. 4620, File 8705-04-3. Summary of correspondence, CACC to Fleming and Diefenbaker, Dec. 1959–June 1960, Bladen Commission, Vol. 1, Public Briefs, Summaries.

30 Vincent Bladen, *Bladen on Bladen* (Toronto, 1978), 146–47. 'P.M. Offers Royal Probe of Automobile Industry,' *Globe and Mail*, 6 July 1960; Harold Greer, 'Bladen One-Man Prober of Auto Industry,' ibid., 3 Aug. 1960.

31 McLuhan suggested that the Americanization of Europe had diluted the humanity of the car, saying, 'In an American car, you are not on the road, but in the car.' Bladen responded, 'Luckily I do not have to submit a design for a car but a design for an industry.' Lower was much more practical, suggesting that a car built for Canadian conditions might have a market outside of Canada. Bladen Commission, Vol. 3, File 110, Marshall McLuhan.

32 For the various submissions to the commission, see Bladen Commission,

Vol. 3, Briefs Submitted to the Commission; Bladen, *Report*, Chapter V, 'Proposals Made in the Briefs Presented to the Commission,' 39–55.

33 Bladen, *Bladen on Bladen*, 152–3.

34 Bladen to various, 8 Nov. 1960; D.S. Wood (APMA) to Bladen, 17 Jan. 1961; Ford Motor Car Co. to Bladen, 30 Jan. 1961. Bladen Commission, Vol. 18, Confidential Correspondence. Burt to Bladen, 'Proposed Methods of Integrating Production of Canadian and Foreign Automobile Manufacturers,' 30 Nov. 1960, Walter Reuther Library (WRL), UAW, Region 7, Box 9, File 14.

35 Bladen Report, 51–2; Bladen actually received three submissions from the UAW, one from Burt representing the union's leadership, one from Local 444, and one from the GM Intra-Corporation Council.

36 Bladen, Report, 42–4, 50–1.

37 These measures included repealing the 7.5 per cent excise tax and ending British preferential treatment in the Canadian market by increasing the tariff on U.K. imports from zero to 10 per cent.

38 Bladen, Report, 57–73.

39 A.F.W. Plumptre to Fleming, 7 Feb. 1961, NAC, MG 32, Donald Fleming Papers (hereafter Fleming Papers), Vol. 99, Bladen Commission.

40 See Walker to Fleming, 18 May and 15 June 1961; Fleming to Diefenbaker, 25 April 1961. Ibid.

41 S.S. Reisman to Fleming, 30 March 1961; E.H. Walker to Fleming, 30 March 1961; Fleming to Walker, 4 April 1961; Walker to Fleming, 6 April 1961; Fleming to Walker, 10 April 1961. Ibid.

42 The following account of the Finance Department's analysis of the Bladen Report is taken from: Plumptre to Fleming, 'Report of the Royal Commission on the Automotive Industry,' 28 April 1961; Fleming to Diefenbaker, 4 May 1961; Plumptre to Fleming, 'Bladen Report – Budget,' 11 May 1961; Plumptre to Fleming, 'U.K. Considerations,' 12 May 1961; Plumptre to Bladen, 'Bladen Report- Recommendation #2,' 18 May 1961. Ibid.

43 Michael Hart, *A Trading Nation: Canadian Trade Policy from Colonialism to Globalization* (Vancouver, 2002), 224–5.

44 *Debates*, 20 June 1961, 6652–4, 6662–5; Ronald Anderson, 'Tax on Cars Repealed: Sub-Par Dollar Soon,' *Globe and Mail*, 21 June 1961.

45 Plumptre to Fleming, 26 June, 1961; Plumptre to Fleming, 28 June 1961; Plumptre to Fleming, 29 June 1961. Fleming Papers, Vol. 99, Bladen Commission.

46 Karl E. Scott (Ford of Canada) to Fleming, 22 June 1961; Ron W. Todgham (Chrysler Canada) to Fleming, 23 June 1961; Plumptre to Fleming, 23 June 1961. Ibid. 'Hassle Brews in Car Industry: Auto Makers vs the Parts Men,' *Financial Post*, 4 Nov. 1961.

47 W.L. Ginsburg to Burt, 10 Aug. 1961, WRL, UAW Region 7, Box 9, File 15; UAW to Donald Fleming, 10 Jan. 1962, ibid., File 14.

48 D.S. Wood to Diefenbaker, 15 Oct. 1961; Wood to Fleming, 20 and 22 Nov. 1961, NAC, MG 26M, Diefenbaker Papers, Vol. 320, Reel M-7993 (hereafter Diefenbaker Papers). 'Car Parts Makers Ask an Export Credit Plan,' *Financial Post*, 3 Feb. 1962.

49 Irving Brecher and Simon Reisman, *Canada–United States Economic Relations* (Ottawa, 1957).

50 In 1978 Reisman was appointed to head his own royal commission on the auto industry. Eventually he would gain widespread fame as the chief negotiator for Canada during the 1987–8 free trade negotiations with the United States.

51 Like Reisman, both Warren and Golden had very successful careers. In 1971 Warren became Canadian high commissioner to the United Kingdom, and in 1975 he became ambassador to the United States. Golden became the president and chairman of Telesat Canada.

52 Biographical information from *Who's Who in Canada*, Vol. 12 (1970/2), Vol. 35 (2000). Author's interviews with S.S. Reisman, C.D. Arthur, J.H. Warren, Dec. 1997 and Nov. 1999.

53 Plumptre to Fleming, 28 Nov. 1961. Fleming Papers, Vol. 99, Bladen Commission.

54 See Bothwell et al., *Canada Since 1945*, particularly Chapter 20, 'Managing the Economy: Budgets, the Bank, and the Diefenbuck.'

55 On the 1962 election, see Beck, *Pendulum of Power*; Newman, *Renegade in Power*, 322–32, and Bothwell et al., *Canada since 1945*, 211–14.

56 The monthly sales of imported cars reached nearly 10,000 in July 1961. By August 1962 that number had fallen to under 4,000. John Saywell, *Canadian Annual Review for 1962* (Toronto, 1963), 221–2.

57 As cited in John Holmes, 'From Three Industries to One: Towards an Integrated North American Automobile Industry,' in Maureen Appel Molot, ed, *Driving Continentally: National Policies and the North American Auto Industry* (Ottawa, 1993), 27.

58 See, e.g., Lester Pearson's comments in *Debates*, 1 Oct. 1961, 71, and in 'Should Not Bury Bladen Report,' editorial *Windsor Star*, 14 Oct. 1961. 'Five Car Firms Back Bladen's Recommendations, Two with Reservations,' *Globe and Mail*, 31 Oct. 1961.

59 The account of the Bladen Committee's meetings and conclusions comes from correspondence and documents found in NAC, RG 20, Department of Industry, Vol. 1714, File 1105-01.

60 *Ward's Automotive Reports* (hereafter *Ward's*), 15 Oct. 1962; Charles Brooks to Diefenbaker, 12 Nov. 1962. Diefenbaker Papers, Vol. 519, Reel M-8894.

61 Cabinet Conclusions, 23 Oct. 1962. NAC, RG 2, Privy Council, Vol. 6193, 1962.
62 *Debates*, 29 Oct. 1962, 1007–8.
63 'Ottawa Aims to Raise Car Parts Exports,' *Globe and Mail*, 29 Oct. 1962; 'Jolt For the Auto Makers,' editorial ibid., 1 Nov. 1962.
64 'Canada Puts 25% Levy on Automatic Transmissions as Spur to Own Industry,' *Ward's*, 5 Nov. 1962; Carlyle Dunbar, 'Pry First Auto Parts to U.S.' *Financial Post*, 15 Dec. 1962.
65 *Ward's*, 25 Feb. 1963; Saywell, *Canadian Annual Review for 1962*, 222; 'GM of Canada Will Make Automatic Transmissions,' *Financial Post*, 16 Feb. 1961.
66 'PM Announces Finish of All Tariff Surcharges,' *Globe and Mail*, 1 April 1963; *Ward's*, 15 April 1963.
67 See, e.g., the CAWMA's complaints about the remission plan in 'Where Bladen Report Overlooked an Industry,' *Financial Post*, 17 Nov. 1962, and Thomas H. Whellams (CAWMA) to Diefenbaker, 19 March 1963 Diefenbaker Papers, Vol. 320, Reel M-7993.
68 'Meeting of the Committee to Study Possible Further Applications of the Principles Recommended in the Bladen Report,' 5 Dec. 1962; 'Extension of Export Incentive Scheme to Automotive Parts Producers,' C.D. Arthur to S. Reisman, 1 Feb. 1963. NAC, RG 20, Vol. 1714, File 1105-01.
69 Ibid.
70 See Jocelyn Ghent, 'Did He Fall or Was He Pushed? The Kennedy Administration and the Collapse of the Diefenbaker Government,' *International History Review* 1, 2 (1979), 246–70.

2 Canada State Intervention and the Failure of Automotive Free Trade, 1963–1964

1 On Pearson, see his *The Memoirs of the Right Honourable Lester B. Pearson*, vols. 1–3 (Toronto, 1972–5); John English, *The Worldly Years: The Life of Lester Pearson, 1949–1972* (Toronto, 1992); Norman Hillmer, ed., *Pearson: Unlikely Gladiator* (Montreal and Kingston, 1999); Peter Stursburg, *Lester Pearson and the Dream of Unity* (Toronto, 1978) and *Lester Pearson and the American Dilemma* (Toronto, 1980). On Pearson's government and its policies, see Greg Donaghy, *Tolerant Allies: Canada and the United States, 1963–1968* (Montreal and Kingston, 2002); P.E. Bryden, *Planners and Politicians: Liberal Politics and Social Policy, 1957–1968* (Montreal and Kingston, 1997); Peter C. Newman, *The Distemper of Our Times: Canadian Politics in Transition, 1962–1968* (Toronto, 1968).

2 There has been a tremendous amount written about Walter Gordon. Gordon's own works include *A Political Memoir* (Toronto, 1977); *Troubled Canada: The Need for New Domestic Policies* (Toronto, 1961); *Storm Signals: New Economic Policies for Canada* (Toronto, 1975); *What Is Happening to Canada* (Toronto, 1978). See also, Dennis Smith, *Gentle Patriot: A Political Biography of Walter Gordon* (Edmonton, 1973), and Stephen Azzi, *Walter Gordon and the Rise of Canadian Nationalism* (Montreal and Kingston, 1999).

3 Azzi, *Walter Gordon*, 59–61. Azzi observed that Gordon was at times rather hypocritical when it came to foreign control (ibid., 24–6, 67–8). Not only did he raise capital in the United States, but he sold a number of companies to American investors. 'Gordon's concern over foreign ownership,' argues Azzi, 'was secondary to his goal of accumulating capital' (at 26).

3 Sharp had been Deputy Minister of Trade and Commerce. See his *Which Reminds Me ... A Memoir* (Toronto, 1994), 184–5.

4 On Paul Martin Sr, see his *A Very Public Life*, vol. 2, *So Many Worlds* (Toronto, 1985), 23.

5 *Canadian Directory of Parliament* (Ottawa, 1963); Introduction to C.M. Drury, 'The Canadian Department of Industry,' in the Empire Club of Canada, *Addresses 1963–1964* (Toronto, 1964).

6 On Walter Gordon's ideas and the Liberal party, see Azzi, '"It was Walter's View": Pearson, the Liberal Party and Economic Nationalism,' in Hillmer, *Pearson: Unlikely Gladiator*.

8 Speech from the throne, Canada, *Debates of the House of Commons* (hereafter *Debates*) 16 May 1963, 6–7.

9 The speech from the throne also talked about the Canada Development Corporation, which was not established until 1971.

10 Budget speech, *Debates*, 13 June 1963, 996–1006; Stanley Westfall, 'Aim to Keep Firms Canadian' and 'Bid to Halt U.S. Takeovers: Tax Levied on Sale of Firms,' *Globe and Mail*, 14 June 1963.

11 On the June 1963 budget debacle, see Newman, *Distemper of Our Times*, 15–25; Azzi, *Walter Gordon*, Chapter 4; 'The Full Story: Experts Tell Why 30% Tax Flopped,' *Financial Post*, 29 June, 1963.

12 Reisman referred to the new department as Gordon's 'hobby-horse,' author's interview with author, 13 Dec. 1997.

13 *Debates*, 27 June 1963, 1641–50. On 25 July 1963, Drury was officially sworn in as minister of industry.

14 Ibid.

15 Organizational Chart, 1 April 1964. NAC, RG 20, Department of Industry, Vol. 1793.

16 Reisman to Gordon, 7 May 1963, NAC, RG 19, Department of Finance, Vol. 3946, File 8705-1, part 1; 'Memorandum for Discussion with Auto Companies,' to Drury, 9 May 1963, ibid., Vol. 3947, File 8705-8-16, part 1.
17 J.G. Dykes (CACC) to Drury, 7 June 1963, ibid.
18 John A. Gibson, 'Production Record Set by Automakers: Expect Continued Rise,' *Globe and Mail*, 2 July 1963; Bruce Macdonald, 'Cut Imports Again, Plea to Auto Men,' ibid., 29 Aug. 1963.
19 Drury to Martin, 29 July 1963, NAC, MG 32 B12, Paul Martin Papers, vol. 241, File 28-3-1, Auto Industry, 1963–6; Reisman to Gordon, 31 July 1963, NAC, RG 19, Vol. 5624, File 8705-4-02. Eventually, Chrysler decided against building a stamping plant in Canada see Annis to Reisman, 26 Sept. 1963, NAC, RG 20, Vol. 2066, File 8001-260-A4, part 1.
20 Drury to Dykes, 15 Aug. 1963, NAC, RG 19, Vol. 3947, File 8705-8-16, part 1.
21 'GM Chief Predicts Record Spending: Car Price Rise Feared if Parts Imports Cut,' *Globe and Mail*, 21 Aug. 1963; 'Discussions with Auto and Parts Firms,' Bryce to Gordon, 28 Aug. 1963, NAC, RG 19, Vol. 3947, File 8705-8-16, part 1; 'Car Men Near Agreement on Cutting Parts Imports,' *Financial Post*, 31 Aug. 1963; Carlyle Dunbar, 'Why All Canada Will Feel Decision on Cars,' ibid., 7 Sept. 1963.
22 Information in the following paragraphs on the development of the extended duty-remission scheme is from: 'Memorandum to Ministers: Proposals to Reduce Trade Deficit in Automobile Industry,' 28 Aug. 1963; 'Notes for Minister of Industry in Announcing New Measures to Foster Greater Production and Trade in Motor Vehicles and Parts, September, 1963,' Bryce to Gordon, 1 Oct. 1963; 'Proposal to Reduce the Trade Deficit in Motor Vehicles and Parts,' 3 Oct. 1963; 'Cabinet Agenda: The Automotive Industry,' Bryce to Gordon, 9 Oct. 1963. NAC, RG 19, Vol. 3946, File 8705-1, part 1, Dec. 1964. Bryce to Gordon, 28 Aug. 1963, ibid., Vol. 3947, File 8705-8-16, part 1.
23 Section 303 of the U.S. Tariff Act of 1930 states: 'Whenever any country ... shall pay or bestow, directly or indirectly, any bounty or grant upon the manufacture or production for export of any article or merchandise manufactured or produced in such country, ... then upon the importation of any such article ... there shall be levied and paid, in all such cases ... an additional duty equal to the net amount of such bounty or grant, however the same shall be paid or bestowed.' 19 USC S1303.
24 'Memorandum of Conversation,' Robert Moore (Ford Motor Co.) and Francis Linville (U.S. Embassy, Ottawa), 15 July 1963; 'Discussions with Auto and Parts Firms,' Bryce to Gordon, 28 Aug. 1963. NAC, RG 19, Vol. 3947, File 8705-8-16, part 1.

25 On the difficulties of the Diefenbaker-Kennedy relationship, see Knowlton
   Nash, *Kennedy and Diefenbaker: The Feud that Helped Topple a Government*
   (Toronto, 1990) and Peter C. Newman, *Renegade in Power: The Diefenbaker
   Years* (Toronto, 1963), 353–8.
26 'Text of Kennedy Pearson Communiqué on 2–Day Meeting,' *New York
   Times*, 12 May 1963.
27 'Memorandum of Conversation,' Charles Drury and Griffith Johnson,
   6 June 1963, U.S. National Archives and Records Administration (hereafter
   NARA), RG 59, State Department, Central Foreign Policy Files, 1963, Box
   3474, Free Trade (FT), Canada–U.S.
28 Patrick Michael Grady, 'The Canadian Exemption from the United States
   Interest Equalization Tax' (doctoral dissertation, University of Toronto,
   1973), 94–5; Gerald Wright and Maureen Appel Molot, 'Capital Movements and Government Control,' *International Organization* 28 (1976), 671–
   88; J.L. Granatstein, 'When Push Comes to Shove: Canada and the United
   States,' in Thomas G. Patterson, ed., *Kennedy's Quest for Victory: American
   Foreign Policy, 1961–1963* (New York, 1989), 102–3.
29 Donaghy, *Tolerant Allies*, 25–9.
30 Ibid.; and Azzi, *Walter Gordon*, 113–14.
31 'Memorandum of Conversation: U.S. Proposed Interest Equalization Tax,'
   5 Aug. 1963, NARA, RG 56, Treasury Department, Entry 198, Papers of
   Douglas Dillon, 1961–1965 (hereafter Dillon Papers), Box 15C-ES.
32 'Memorandum,' Moore and Linville, 15 July 1963. 'Memorandum of
   Conversation,' Dillon, Fowler, Donner, and Roach, 12 Sept. 1963, NARA,
   RG 59, Entry 5299, Box 2, File, Auto Parts (hereafter Auto Parts File);
   'Briefing of Meeting with Frederic Donner, Chairman of General Motors,'
   9 Sept. 1963, NARA, Dillon Papers, Box 15 C-ES.
33 'Canadian Export Promotion Policies,' 12 Sept. 1963. NARA, RG 59,
   Conference Files, 1949–72 (hereafter Conference Files), Box 326.
34 'Memorandum of Conversation,' B.G. Barrow and Francis Linville, 17 Sept.
   1963, NARA, Auto Parts File.
35 Donald Barry, 'Eisenhower, St Laurent and Free Trade, 1953,' *International
   Perspectives* (March/April, 1987), 8–11.
36 'Summary Record of Joint United States–Canadian Committee on Trade
   and Economic Affairs, Sept. 20–21, 1963,' NAC, RG 19, Vol. 3943, File
   8522/U585-7 1963. 'Record of Meeting: Joint United States–Canadian
   Committee on Trade and Economic Affairs, Eighth Meeting, Washington,
   Sept. 20–21, 1963,' NARA, Conference Files, Box 326.
37 'U.S. Regrets Trade Plan: Canadian Idea "Screwy,"' *Ottawa Citizen*, 21 Sept.
   1963; 'Auto Parts Plan Fails to Win Support in U.S.,' *Globe and Mail*, 21 Sept.

1963. Editorial courments on the plan can be found in 'Canadian Protectionism,' *New York Times*, 26 Sept. 1963; and 'Canada Proposes to Cut Imports of Autos, Parts,' *Wall Street Journal*, 23 Sept. 1963.

38 Ball to Bundy, 11 Oct. 1963, NARA, RG 56, Entry 198F, Undersecretary Henry H. Fowler, 1961–1964 (hereafter Fowler Papers), Box 1C-F, State Department to U.S. Embassy Ottawa, 17 Oct. 1963. 'Memorandum of Conversation: Canadian Plans for Trade in Automotive Field,' 17 Oct. 1963, NARA, RG 59, Box 3474.

39 'Memorandum, Canadian Rebate Plan: GATT Aspects of United States Countervailing Duty on Canadian Auto Plan,' Margaret Shea Coates to Mr Rains, 21 Oct. 1963, NARA, Fowler Papers, Box 1C-F.

40 Bullitt to Dillon, 18 Oct. 1963, ibid. 'Memorandum of Conversation: Canadian Motor Vehicle Export Expansion Scheme,' 21 Oct. 1963, NARA, RG 59, Box 3474; 'Fight Ottawa Auto-Parts Plan, U.S. Industry Urged: Threaten Retaliation if Trade Rules Broken,' *Globe and Mail*, 23 Oct. 1963.

41 U.S. Embassy, Ottawa to State Department, 23 Oct. 1963. John F. Kennedy Library (hereafter JFK), Christian Herter Papers (hereafter Herter Papers), Box 7; State Department to U.S. Embassy Ottawa, 24 Oct. 1963, NARA, RG 59, Box 3474; 'Fight Ottawa Auto-Parts Plan, U.S. Industry Urged: Same Policy Planned Elsewhere: Gordon,' *Globe and Mail*, 23 Oct. 1963.

42 *Debates*, 1 Oct. 1963, 3069–70, 3 Oct., 3152, 18 Oct. 3737, 22 Oct., 3855, 25 Oct., 1963, 3999–4001.

43 U.S. Consulate Toronto to State, 1 Nov. 1963, NARA, RG 59, Box 3474.

44 'Auto Plan Supported by UAW' and 'UAW, Parts Makers Cautious, Back Drury,' *Globe and Mail*, 29 and 31 Oct. 1963.

45 'Lengthening the Lines,' *Globe and Mail*, editorial, 15 Nov. 1963; Carlyle Dunbar, 'Watch the Car Parts Manufactures Go Out after that Business,' *Financial Post*, 2 Nov. 1963.

46 U.S. Embassy Ottawa to State Department, 28 and 29 Oct. 1963, JFK, Herter Papers, Box 7; George Bain, 'Ottawa Proposal Called Low Blow,' *Globe and Mail*, 26 Oct. 1963.

47 'Canada Acts to Grab Off Big U.S. Auto Sales Slice,' *New York Journal of Commerce*, 28 Oct. 1963; 'U.S. Voices "Concern" as Canada Announces Tariff Rebate Plan for Its Auto Industry,' *Wall Street Journal*, 28 Oct. 1963; Raymond Daniell, 'Canada to Remit Auto-Part Duties,' *New York Times*, 26 Oct. 1963.

48 John C. Wagner (Office of the General Counsel, State Department) to Robert L. McNeill, 28 Oct. 1963; Robert E. Baldwin to Christian Herter, 30 Oct. 1963; Robert E. Hudec to Herter, 30 Oct. 1963. JFK, Herter Papers, Box 7.

49 James A. Reed to Fowler, 30 Oct. 1963, NARA, Dillon Papers, Box 16C-ES; John C. Bullitt to Fowler, 30 Oct. 1963, NARA, Fowler Papers, Box 1C-F.

50 'Reply to United States Aide-Memoire on Automobiles,' Reisman to Gordon, Bryce, 4 Nov. 1963, NAC, RG 19, Vol. 3946, File 8705-1, part 1, Dec. 1964. Ritchie to Economic Division, 6 Nov. 1963, Ottawa, Department of Foreign Affairs and International Trade, File 37-7-1-USA-2, Vol. 1, USA, Auto Pact (hereafter DFAIT). State Department to U.S. Embassy Ottawa, 8 Nov. 1963, JFK, National Security File (hereafter NSF), Box 19. Gordon to Drury, 8 Nov. 1963, and Robertson to Martin, 12 Nov. 1963, DFAIT.

51 On Lyndon Johnson and his foreign policies, see H.W. Brands, *The Foreign Policies of Lyndon Johnson: Beyond Vietnam* (College Station, TX, 1999); and Warren I. Cohen and Nancy Berkhopf Tucker, eds., *Lyndon Johnson Confronts the World: American Foreign Policy, 1963–1968* (New York, 1994).

52 'Talking Points for Meeting of 21–22 Jan., 1964: Auto Parts,' 16 Jan. 1964, and 'Background Paper on Auto Tariff Changes,' 17 Jan. 1964, Lyndon B. Johnson Library (hereafter LBJ), NSF, Country File, Canada, Visits, (hereafter NSF Canada) Box 167. 'Your Meeting with PM Pearson, 21–22 Jan. 1964,' Rusk to LBJ, 17 Jan. 1964, NARA, RG 59, Entry 5297, Box 2, Pearson Visit; 'Pearson-Johnson Talks,' Bullitt to Dillon, 22 Jan. 1964, NARA, Dillon Papers, Box 22C-ES, Presidential Correspondence; 'Memorandum: Meeting between PM and President, Auto Parts,' 23 Jan. 1964, Canadian Embassy Washington to External Affairs (hereafter DEA), 27 Jan. 1964, DFAIT.

53 Reisman to Bryce and Gordon, 12 Feb. 1964, NAC, RG 19, Vol. 3946, File 8705-2, part 1.

54 Reisman to Land, 23 March 1964, ibid., File 8705-1, part 1.

55 Devon Smith, 'Auto Exports from Canada to U.S. Rise Embarrassingly,' *Globe and Mail*, 21 Feb. 1964.

56 Carlyle Dunbar, 'Car zparts Spreading Prosperity All Over'; Knowlton Nash, 'U.S. Twitches over Our Auto Exports' and 'Auto Export 'Carrot' Gets Many Nibbles.' *Financial Post*, 4 April 1964.

57 *Ward's*, 4 May 1964. Reisman to Land, 23 March 1964, and N.B. Macdonald to Drury, 23 March 1964, NAC, RG 19, Vol. 3946, File 8705-1, part 1.

58 Memorandum of Conversation, 17 Feb. 1964, NARA, RG 59, Box 991.

59 Reisman to Plumptre, 4 March 1964, and Canadian Embassy Washington to External Affairs, 9 March 1964, NAC, RG 19, Vol. 3947, File 8705-8-16, part 1.

60 Vance Hartke to L.B. Johnson (copy), 19 March 1964, NAC, RG 20, Vol. 2052, File 1021-10, part 2.

61 Jerry Flint, 'Canadian Car Push: Dominion Tempts U.S. Auto Firms to Move Parts Output to North,' *Wall Street Journal*, 26 March 1964; Canadian

Embassy Washington to DEA, 26 March 1964, DFAIT; P. Trezise to Rusk, 27 March 1964, NARA, RG 59, Box 1050.

62 J.F. Shaw to S. Erdkamp, 7 April 1964, NARA, RG 59, Auto Parts File; Modine Manufacturing Co., *Annual Report for 1964, 1965*, Historical Collections, Baker Library, Harvard Business School.

63 Kenneth C. Mackenzie, *Tariff-Making and Trade Policy in the U.S. and Canada: A Comparative Study* (New York, 1969).

64 'History of the Modine Manufacturing Co.,' Modine Manufacturing Co., Racine, Wisconsin (unpublished corporate history, n.d.); Canadian Embassy Washington to External Affairs, 16 April 1964, NAC, RG 20, Vol. 2052, File 1021-10, part 2; Martin Goodman, 'Americans Blast Our Auto Policy,' *Toronto Daily Star*, 10 April 1964.

65 'UAW Local Blasts Tariff Benefit for Canada Parts,' *New York Journal of Commerce*, 15 April, 1964.

66 *Congressional Record (Senate)*, 28 April 1964, 9291–2.

67 'Memorandum of Conversation, Canadian Auto Parts Scheme,' 24 April 1964, NARA, RG 59, Country Directory for Canadak, Box 1249, International Trade, Canada. 'U.S.-Canadian Trade and Balance of Payments Relations,' U.S. Embassy Ottawa to State Dept., 15 April 1964, ibid. Box 991, FT-Canada-US.

68 'Position Paper: Canadian Automotive Duty Remission Plan.' Joint U.S.–Canadian Committee on Trade and Economic Affairs, 29–30 April, 1964, ibid., Entry 5297, Box 2, File, For. 1.

69 Brubeck to Bundy, 9 Jan. and 9 April 1964, LBJ, NSF Canada, Box 164, File, Canada Memos; 'Auto Parts Straining U.S.-Canada Relations,' *New York Journal of Commerce*, 7 May 1964.

70 Brubeck to LBJ, 27 April 1964, and LBJ to the Secretaries of State, Treasury and Commerce, 28 April 1964, LBJ Library, NSF Canada, Box 164.

71 LBJ to Secretaries, 28 April, 1964, ibid.

72 'Memorandum to the Minister, Joint U.S.-Canadian Committee on Trade and Economic Affairs, Ottawa, April 29–30, 1964,' 23 April 1964, NAC, RG 20, Vol. 2053, File 1021-11.

73 Reisman to Gordon, 30 April 1964, NAC, RG 19, Vol. 3947, File 8705-8-16, Part 1; Cabinet Conclusions, 27 April 1964. NAC, RG 2, Vol. 6264.

74 The account of the joint cabinet meeting is taken from the following documents: 'Record of the Joint U.S.-Cabinet Committee on Trade and Economic Affairs, April 29–30, 1964.' NARA, RG 59, Conference Files, Box 346; 'Telephone Conversations: Ball and Dillon, 13 May 1964,' LBJ, George Ball Papers, Canada I; Telephone Conversations (hereafter Ball Papers)

75 Hodges suggested this plan at the post-meeting press conference. He

argued that under the TEA, the duties on autos and parts could be cut by 50 per cent, which would bring the tariff for such items down to around 4 per cent. The Canadians could, he pointed out, immediately reduce their tariffs.

76 Ball, telephone conversation with Philip Trezise, 14 May 1964, LBJ, Ball Papers. G. D'Andelot Belin to George Ball, 19 May 1964; 'Canadian Auto Parts,' George S. Springsteen to Johnson, 20 May 1964; Belin to Dillon, 25 May 1964. NARA, Dillon Papers, Box 22C-ES.

77 This account is based on: Ball, telephone conversation with Paul Martin, 5:15 p.m., 29 May 1964; Ball, telephone conversation with Dillon, 6:20 p.m., 29 May, 1964. Ball telephone conversation with Martin, 6:30 p.m., 29 May 1964. LBJ, Ball Papers; Gordon to File, 1 June 1964, NAC, RG 19, Vol. 3947, File 8705-8-16, part 2.

78 Gordon to File, 31 May 1964, ibid., File 8705-1, part 1; 'Auto Tariff Retaliation Moves Step Closer in U.S.,' *Globe and Mail*, 1 June 1964.

79 'Canadian Automotive Program,' Memo for the Cabinet Committee on Finance and Economic Policy, 9 June 1964, NAC, RG 19, Vol. 3946, File 8705-1, part 1.

80 Ibid.

81 The account of the 17 Aug. 1964 meeting is taken from: R.Y. Grey to Cabinet, 21 Aug. 1964, ibid.; Cadieux to Martin, 19 and 24 Aug., 1964, DFAIT, Vol. 3; 'Free Trade Arrangement for Automobiles and Automotive Products,' Memorandum of Conversation, 17 Aug. 1964, NARA, RG 59, Box 1249; Ottawa Embassy to Washington, Airgram, 31 Aug. 1964, ibid.

82 Grey to Bryce, 19 Aug. 1964 and Grey to Gordon, 24 Aug. 1964, NAC, RG 19, Vol. 3946, File 8705-1, part 1.

83 Sharon Erdkamp to Maynard Glitman, 19 Aug. 1964, NARA, Auto Parts File.

84 Telephone conversation, Bill Brubeck and George Ball, 26 Aug. 1964, LBJ, Ball Papers.

85 Author's interview with Philip Trezise, 24 Nov. 1999.

86 'Position Paper: Canadian Automotive Remission Plan,' 25 June 1964, NARA, Auto Parts File.

87 Douglas C. Bennett and Kenneth E. Sharpe, *Multinational Corporations versus the State: The Political Economy of the Mexican Auto Industry* (New Brunswick, NJ, 1987).

88 Peter Stubbs, *The Australian Motor Industry: A Study in Protection and Growth* (Melbourne, 1971).

89 Helen Shapiro, *Engines of Growth: The State and Transnational Auto Companies in Brazil* (Cambridge, MA, 1994); Helen Shapiro, 'The Determinants of

Trade and Investment Flows in L.D.C. Auto Industries: The Cases of Brazil and Mexico,' in Maureen Appel Molot, ed., *Driving Continentally: National Policies and the North American Auto Industry* (Ottawa, 1993), 101–34.

90 S.L. Terry was assistant to the vice-president of the international division at Chrysler. 'Statement on Canadian Duty Remission Program, 9 March 1964,' Detroit Consulate to Ottawa, Telex, 9 July 1964, NAC, RG 20, Vol. 2053, Vol. 1021–11, part 1.

91 Memo of conversation, John Meininger (Ford Motor Company) and John Shaw assistant chief, trade agreements division), NARA, RG 59, Box 990, FT 13, Duties, Canada; J.M Roche (executive vice-president, GM) to Commissioner of Customs, 19 June 1964, NAC, RG 19, Vol. 3947, File 8705-8-16, part 2.

92 Brubeck to LBJ, 8 May 1964. LBJ, NSF Canada, Box 164; Keohane and Nye, *Power and Independence*, 204–5.

93 Telephone conversation, Bill Brubeck and George Ball, 26 Aug. 1964, LBJ, Ball Papers; Philip Hart to Dean Rusk, 8 May 1964, NARA, RG 59, Box 1050, FT-Canada–U.S.

94 'Canadian Auto Parts,' G. D'Andelot Belin to Dillon, 31 Aug. 1964, NARA Dillon Papers Box 22C-ES.

3 The Big Three and the Creation of a Borderless Auto Industry, 1965

1 Hugh Monroe, 'Time Bomb May Lie under Auto-Parts Exports as Opposition to Plan Intensifies in U.S.' and 'U.S.-Canada Trade War Feared in Wake of Auto-Part Export Row,' *Globe and Mail*, 3 July and 4 Aug. 1964; Richard Lawrence, 'U.S.-Canada Auto Parts Row Rages,' *New York Journal of Commerce*, 8 Sept. 1964.

2 Arthur R. Upgren and William J. Waines, *The Midcontinent and the Peace: The Interests of Western Canada and Central Northwest United States in the Peace Settlements* (Minneapolis, 1943).

3 Ibid., 36–7.

4 Keenleyside was then chair of the B.C. Hydro Commission, and he played a key role in the Columbia River Treaty negotiations a few years later. Hugh Keenleyside, 'Treatment for Our Lopsided U.S. Trade,' *Financial Post*, 7 May 1960.

5 'How Canadians Can Get a Made-in-Canada Car They Want and Can Afford,' UAW, 5 July 1960, NAC, RG 45/33, Royal Commission on the Automotive Industry (hereafter Bladen Commission), Vol. 4, File 33, UAW.

6 'Chrysler submission to the Bladen Royal Commission,' 1960. Ibid., Vol. 16. File 42, Confidential Correspondence.

7 'Review of Corporate Profit Improvements Attainable through Increased Integration of Ford U.S. and Ford of Canada Automotive Operations,' 30 Jan. 1964; 'Supplemental Study of Corporate Profits Improvements Attainable through Increased Integration of Ford U.S. and Ford of Canada Operations,' 27 Feb. 1964. Ford Company of Canada Archives, Oakville, Ontario (hereafter Ford Archives).

8 Henry Ford II to Arjay Miller, et al., 6 March 1964; L.A. Iacocca to K.E. Scott, 19 March 1964; Ben D. Mills to K.E. Scott, 17 March 1964; C.R. Beacham to Arjay Miller, 18 March 1964; 'Washington D.C. Implications of Contemplated Changes in Ford of Canada Operations,' 13 March 1964. All correspondence in: Comments to the Executive Office from Ford U.S. Staffs and Divisions Concerning the Proposed Increase in Integration of the Canadian and U.S. Automotive Operations, Ford Archives.

9 Canadian civil servants were well aware of the impact of free trade in farm implements. By the 1950s, this once-booming sector had fallen far behind its American counterpart. Royal Commission on Canada's Economic Prospects, J.D. Woods and Gordon, Ltd., *The Canadian Agricultural Machinery Industry* (Hull, QC, 1956).

10 For more on the growing nationalism of the period, and its impact on the Canadian UAW, see Dimitry Anastakis, 'Between Nationalism and Continentalism: State Auto Industry Policy and the Canadian UAW,' *Labour/Le Travail* 53 (Spring, 2004) 94–6.

11 See the introduction to Thomas Zeiler, *Free Trade, Free World: The Advent of GATT* (Chapel Hill and London, 1999); William S. Borden, 'Defending American Hegemony: American Foreign Economic Policy,' in Thomas G. Paterson, ed., *Kennedy's Quest for Victory: American Foreign Policy, 1961–1963* (New York, 1989), 69–71; Kenneth C. Mackenzie, *Tariff-Making and Trade Policy in The U.S. and Canada: A Comparative Study* (New York, 1969), 35–41.

12 Brubeck to Bundy, 11 April 1963, NARA, RG 59, State Department, Central Foreign Policy Files, 1963, Box 3852, Political 15–Canada Government.

13 George Ball, 'Interdependence: The Basis of Canada-U.S. Relations,' 26 April 1964, United States Information Service Text, NAC, RG 20, Vol. 2052, File 1021-10, part 2. For an interesting view of the speech and Canadian reaction to it, see George Ball, 'The Problem of Nationalism in a Shrinking World,' in R.H. Wagenberg, ed., *Canadian-American Interdependence: How Much? Proceedings of the 10th Annual Seminar on Canadian American Relations, 1968* (Windsor, ON, 1970); Don Hanright, 'U.S. Offering Customs Union?' *Ottawa Citizen*, 28 April 1964; Bruce Macdonald, 'Tension High for Canada-U.S. Meet,' *Globe and Mail*, 29 April 1964.

14 At a conference twenty years after the agreement was signed, Reisman recalled the initial breakthrough: 'It is not clear who was the real driver in finding the qualified free trade solution. I have always been prepared to give Phil Trezise all the credit and he has always insisted that I must share the blame.' In separate interviews with the author, each man agreed that the other had played a key role in developing the idea. Simon Reisman. 'The Relevance of the Auto Pact for Other Sectoral Trade Agreements,' *Canada–United States Law Journal* 10 (1985), 77, author's interviews with Simon Reisman and Philip Trezise, 19 Dec. 1997 and 24 Dec. 1999; U.S. Embassy Ottawa to State Department, 4 Sept. 1965, and 21 Jan. 1965, NARA, RG 59, Box 1248, File International Trade 7–12, Canada; Washington to Ottawa, 8 Sept. 1964, NAC, RG 19, Vol. 3946, File 8705-2, part 1.

15 Henry Ford II to L. Johnson, 16 Sept. 1964, LBJ Library (LBJ), National Security Files (NSF), Country File, Canada (hereafter LBJ, Canada), Box 164, Canada Memos.

16 'Memorandum for the President: Your Meeting with Prime Minister Pearson, September 16, 1964,' Ball to L. Johnson, 14 Sept. 1964, ibid.; Brubeck to L. Johnson, 15 Sept. 1964, ibid., Box 167.

17 'Memorandum to the President,' Dillon to L. Johnson. Brubeck to L. Johnson, 15 Sept. 1964, ibid., Box 164.

18 Brubeck to Bundy, 12 Sept. 1964; 'Memorandum for the President,' Rusk to L. Johnson, 18 Sept. 1964; Brubeck to Bundy, 18 Sept. 1964. Ibid.

19 'Memorandum for the President,' Dillon to L. Johnson, 22 Sept. 1964, ibid.

20 The account of the 15 Sept. meeting is taken from: 'Proposals to Reduce the Trade Deficit in the Auto Industry,' Sept. 1964; 'Auto Industry Program Proposals Regarding Alternative Measures,' D.F. Wall secretary of Cabinet Committee on Finance and Economic Policy, 16 Sept. 1964. Drury to Cabinet, 17 Sept. 1964. NAC, RG 19, Vol. 3946, File 8705-1, part 1.

21 Ibid.

22 J.F. Grandy to R.K. Joyce, 17 Sept. 1964; 'Draft: Trade Agreement between the Government of Canada and the Government of the United States,' J.F. Grandy to A.E. Ritchie, S.S. Reisman, J.H. Warren, etc., 17 Sept. 1964. Ibid. File 8705-2, part 1, Jan. 1964 to 15 Jan. 1965. 'Proposed Program for the Auto Industry,' Sept. 1964, NAC, RG 20, Vol. 2053, File 1021-11, part 2.

23 In his recollections of the negotiations, Philip Trezise has stated that 'the companies were consulted, as were the parts makers, but not until after the initial discussions with the Canadians had shown that agreement might be possible.' Philip Trezise, 'The Relevance of the Auto Pact for Other Sectoral Trade Agreements,' *Canada–United States Law Journal* (1985), 66.

24 Greg Donaghy Insists there were greater divisions within the cabinet as
to which approach to take with the Americans. See his 'A Continental
Philosophy: Canada, the United States and the Negotiation of the Auto
Pact, 1963–1965,' *International Journal* 52, 3 (1998), 459; Cabinet Conclu-
sions, 17 Sept. 1964, NAC, RG 2, Vol. 6265; R.B. Bryce to J.F. Grandy, 17
Sept. 1964; D.J. Leach to Cabinet, 22 Sept. 1964. NAC, RG 19, Vol. 3946,
File 8705-2, part 1.

25 The account of the meeting is taken from 'Notes of Meeting of September
19th in the House of Commons between Mr Drury and Presidents of the
Six Leading Automotive Manufacturers,' 21 Sept. 1964, NAC, RG 20, Vol.
2053, File 1021–11, part 2.

26 The account of the 24–5 September talks comes from the following documents: Grandy to Gordon, 24 Sept. 1964; 'Notes on the Possible Content
of an Inter-Governmental Agreement,' 24 Sept. 1964; Grandy to Gordon,
Bryce, 25 Sept. 1964; Stoner to Gordon, Grandy, Warren, Reisman, 29 Sept.
1964. NAC, RG 19, Vol. 3946, File 8705-2, part 1. Drury to Reisman, 25 Sept.
1964, ibid. RG 20, Vol. 1802, File 114-115, part 2. 'Draft Report to Ministers:
Auto Industry Program,' 28 Sept. 1964, RG 20, Vol. 2053, File 1021-11, part
2. US Embassy Ottawa to State Department, 25 Sept. 1964, NARA, RG 59,
Box 990, FT 13–2, Tariffs, Canada. 'Possible Free Trade Arrangement in
Automotive Products,' 24–5 Sept. 1964, ibid. Box 1249, File IT 7-12,
Canada.

27 A few Canadian companies that produced parts for military vehicles were
able to 'double dip' by getting credit under the Defence Production Sharing Agreements (which was designed to allow Canadians companies
access to U.S. military spending) and again under the remission program.
U.S. representatives were unhappy with the situation and had pointed to
the loophole as another reason to challenge the duty-remission program.
For more on the DPSA, see John Kirton, *The Consequences of Integration: The
Case of the Defence Production Sharing Agreements* (Ottawa, 1972); US embassy Ottawa to State Department, 25 Sept. 1964, NARA, RG 59, Box 990.

28 'Negotiations with Canada on Automobile Trade,' Trezise and McNeill to
Ball and Hodges, 29 Sept. 1964, NARA, RG 56, Entry 198, Papers of Dou-
glas Dillon, 1961–1965 (hereafter Dillon Papers) Box 23C-ES, Presidential
Correspondence.

29 'Discussion of Canadian Auto Problem with Foreign Secretary Martin,'
Trezise to Ball and Rusk, 11 Sept. 1964, NARA, RG 59, Entry 5297, Box 3,
File, Politics 15.

30 Brubeck to Bundy, 23 Sept. 1964; Bundy to Record (White House), 24 Sept.
1964. LBJ NSF Canada, Box 164.

31 J.F. Grandy to Gordon, Bryce, 25 Sept. 1964, NAC, RG 19, Vol. 3946, File 8705-2, part 1.

32 Throughout the auto talks, GM remained the least forthcoming of the Big Three. Canadian officials felt that the company's attitude stemmed from its position as the largest company and leader of the industry. 'Auto Industry: Canada–U.S. Meeting,' 24–5 Sept. 1964, ibid.

33 'Draft Letter of Undertaking,' 22 Sept. 1964; 'Auto Program: Objectives and Company Commitments, Meeting of 29 Sept. 1964,' Reisman to Drury, 22 Sept. 1964; 'Meeting with Motor Vehicle Producers, 29 Sept. 1964,' Reisman to Barrow, 25 Sept. 1964; 'Meeting with Motor Vehicle Manufacturers,' Reisman to Drury, 29 Sept. 1964; 'Auto Industry Program,' Drury to Pearson, 21 Oct. 1964, NAC, RG 20, Vol. 2053, File 1021-11, part 2.

34 For the government–parts makers discussions and their views, see the following documents: 'Meeting with APMA, 2 October,' Reisman and Barrow to Drury, 1 Oct. 1964; 'Notes on Meeting Between Parts Manufacturers and Minister of Industry,' 6 Oct. 1964. Ibid., Proposed New Automotive Program, Sept.–Oct. 1964. J.W. Marshall (Ontario Steel Products, Ltd., President of APMA) to Barrow, 19 Nov. 1964; R.M. Foote (Auto Specialties Manufacturing) to A.E. Ritchie, 20 Nov. 1964; D.S. Wood (APMA) to Drury, 27 Nov. 1964; J.W. Marshall to Drury, 30 Nov. 1964. Ibid., part 3. 'Auto Industry Program: Meeting with Parts Makers,' Cadieux to Martin, 24 Nov. 1964, NAC, Department of Foreign Affairs and International Trade (DFAIT), Vol. 3, Aug.–Dec. 1964.

35 On the Canadian decision to proceed with the negotiations, see McKinney to Ritchie, 6 Nov. 1964, ibid. 'Auto Industry Program,' 16 Nov. 1964; 'CCFEP,' O.G. Stoner, 10 Nov. 1964. NAC, RG 19, Vol. 3946, File 8705-1, part 1. 'Principle Questions Requiring an Early Cabinet Decision,' 16 Nov. 1964, NAC, RG 20, Vol. 2053, File 1021-11, part 3, Oct.–Dec. 1964. 'Cabinet Conclusions,' 19 Nov. 1964 ibid. RG 2, Vol. 6265.

36 On the American decision to proceed with the negotiations, see 'Canada: Status Report,' Brubeck to Bundy, 9 Nov. 1964, LBJ, NSF Canada, Box 164. Hendrick to Dillon, 20 Nov. 1964, NARA, Dillon Papers, Box 23C-ES. 'Proposed Free Trade Arrangement with Canada for Auto Products,' Trezise and McNeill to Dillon, Hodges, Wirtz, Herter, and Ball, 20 Nov. 1964, NARA, RG 59, Entry 5299, Box 2, File Auto Parts (hereafter Auto Parts File). Henry Wilson to Bill Moyers, 25 Nov. 1964; 'Memo for the President: Subject: Canada–American Free Trade in Autos and Parts,' Trezise to Wilson, 25 Nov. 1964. LBJ, Henry H. Wilson Papers, Box 1. Francis Bator to Bundy, 25 Nov. 1964. Ibid., Francis M. Bator Papers, Box 1.

37 Washington to External Affairs, 4 Dec. 1964; 'Draft Trade Agreement

between the Government of Canada and the Government of the United States of America,' 5 Dec. 1964, NAC, RG 19, Vol. 3946, File 8705-2, part 1.

38 Grandy to Gordon and Bryce, 9 Dec. 1964, ibid., 'Canada–U.S. Discussions on Auto Products,' M. Cadieux to P. Martin, 10 Dec. 1964; Canadian Embassy Washington to Department of External Affairs (hereafter DEA), 10 Dec. 1964, DFAIT, Vol. 3.

39 'Memorandum to Cabinet: Auto Industry Program,' 17 Dec. 1964; 'Memorandum for the Prime Minister: Canada–USA Negotiations on Automobiles,' 17 Dec. 1964, NAC, RG 19, Vol. 3946, File 8705-2, part 1.

40 During the negotiations, the role of replacement parts had been hotly contested. The Canadian team had successfully resisted American demands that replacement parts be included in the agreement, arguing that the Canadian parts industry would never be able to survive under such an arrangement.

41 'Cabinet Conclusions,' 21 Dec. 1964, NAC, RG 2, Vol. 6265. 'Record of Cabinet Decision: 21 Dec. 1964,' 28 Dec. 1964, NAC, RG 19, Vol. 3946, File 8705-2, part 1.

42 Interviews of Alexander Vuillemin and Edward Stanger, Corporate Planning Division, GM, John F. Kennedy Library (hereafter JFK), Jack Behrman Papers, Box 14.

43 R.K. Joyce to C.D. Arthur, 2 Dec. 1964; 'Auto Company Talks, 11 Dec.,' R.Y. Grey to Joyce, 15 Dec. 1964. NAC, RG 10, Vol. 5642, File 8705-4-02. 'Motor Vehicle Manufacturers' Commitments,' n.d., Dec. 1964. E.K. Brownridge (American Motors) to Reisman, 24 Dec. 1964; Reisman to Brownridge, 31 Dec. 1964; Drury to Reisman, 22 Dec. 1964. NAC, RG 20, Vol. 2053, File 1021–11, part 3.

44 George Ball telephone conversation with P. Trezise, 6 Jan. 1965, LBJ, George Ball Papers, Canada I: Telephone Conversations (hereafter Ball Papes).

45 Keohane and Nye also observe that it was reported that Drury 'went over the head' of the Canadian firm and negotiated directly with the senior U.S. GM officials. Robert O. Keohane and Joseph S. Nye, *Power and Interdependence: World Politics in Transition* (New York, 1989), 182, note at bottom of page. U.S. Embassy Ottawa to State Department, 8 Jan. 1965, NARA, RG 59, Box 991, FT-4, Trade Agreements, Canada–U.S.

46 E.H. Walker to Drury, 13 Jan. 1965, NAC, RG 19, Vol. 5175, File 8705-1, part 3.

47 Washington to DEA, 6, 7, and 8 Jan. 1965, Ibid., File 8705-2, part 1.

48 The total 1963–4 base year dollar amount for the Big Three was Can$ 679 million.

49 Annex A did, however, include a part that stipulated that the government of Canada could designate a manufacturer 'not falling within the categories' in the Annex as being entitled to duty-free treatment. This allowed the government to designate Volvo under the agreement at a 40 per cent Canadian content rate, which was in keeping with the company's previous content commitments.

50 D.J. Leach to Cabinet, Record of Cabinet Decision of Meeting of 6 Jan. 1965, NAC, RG 19, Vol. 3946, File 8705-2, part 1. Robertson to Stoner, 4 Jan. 1965, DFAIT, Vol. 4.

51 Ball telephone Conversation with Bundy, 6 Jan. 1965, LBJ, Ball Papers.

52 Department of State, Administrative History, 'The Department of State during the Administration of President Lyndon B. Johnson,' Vol. 1, Part II, NARA, RG 59, Executive Secretariat.

53 George Ball telephone conversation with P. Trezise, 6 Jan. 1965, LBJ, Ball Papers.

54 In this correspondence, Cooper was referring to the auto pact and the Civil Air Treaty, which was not signed by the two leaders. Chester L. Cooper to Bundy, 12 Jan. 1965, LBJ, NSF Canada, Box 167.

55 John E. Merriam to S. Little, 13 Jan. 1965, NARA, RG 59, Conference Files, 1949-1972, Box 369.

56 Ibid.

57 'Prime Minister's Statement,' Washington to External Affairs, 16 Jan. 1965; 'White House Press Release,' Washington to External Affairs, 19 Jan. 1965. NAC, RG 19, Vol. 3946, File 8705-2, part 2.

58 'Dief Fears Pact Faulty,' Montreal Gazette, 18 Jan. 1965; 'Sharp Shrugs Off PC Criticism of Auto Plan,' Hamilton Spectator, 19 Jan. 1965.

59 The first mention of the auto pact in Congress came from Senator Philip Hart, a Democrat from Michigan, who gave the agreement a resounding endorsement on 25 Jan. 1965.

60 Press release, 'UAW Hails U.S.–Canada Move to End Auto Tariffs but Insists on Protection for Workers Adversely Affected,' 16 Jan. 1965, Walter Reuther Library (hereafter (WRL), UAW Region 7, Box 8, File 6; Reuther to Lyndon B. Johnson, 15 Jan. 1965, ibid., Walter Reuther Papers, Box 49 (hereafter Reuther Papers), File 3.

61 Weinberg to Irv Bluestone, 'Canadian Auto Trade Agreement,' 20 Feb. 1965, ibid.

62 Burt and UAW Council of Canada to MacEachen, 18 March 1965. WRL, UAW, Region 7, Box 42, File 2; 'UAW Worried over Tariff Pact,' Globe and Mail, 19 March, 1965; Burt to Canadian Council, 27 and 28 March 1965, WRL, Reuther Papers, File 4.

63 Washington to DEA, 12 Jan. 1965, DFAIT, Vol. 5; 'Court to Hear U.S. Auto Parts Incentives Suit,' *New York Journal of Commerce*, 13 Jan. 1965.

64 'ASIA vs the USA,' *Motor Age*, Jan. 1965, W5; 'Auto Parts Industry Sure Congress Will Sink Treaty,' *Montreal Star*, 29 Jan. 1965.

65 'Risks and Rewards,' 'Prices Will Tell the Story,' editorials, *Globe and Mail*, 18 and 19 Jan. 1965. U.S. press reaction can also be found in 'Canada in the U.S. Press,' NAC, MG 26 N3, Pearson Papers, Vol. 260, File 749.3, Automobiles.

66 'Free Trade for Whom?' *Washington Post*, editorial 17 Jan. 1965. Bundy to L.B. Johnson, 18 Jan. 1965, LBJ, Bator Papers, Box 1.

67 See, e.g., 'Close Up on You, Canada and Free Trade,' *Windsor Star*, 11 Jan. 1965; 'Common Market Ahead?' *New York Times*, 17 Jan. 1965; 'Sir Wilfrid Has the Last Word,' *Globe and Mail*, 22 Jan. 1965; 'What Would Free Trade with the U.S. Do for and to Canada?' *Toronto Star*, 30 Jan. 1965.

68 See, e.g. Ian Lumsden, ed., *Close the 49th Parallel, Etc.: The Americanization of Canada* (Toronto, 1970); Stephen Clarkson, ed., *An Independent Foreign Policy for Canada?* (Toronto, 1968); Robert Laxer, ed., *(Canada) Ltd.: The Political Economy of Dependency* (Toronto, 1973).

69 After all, the new arrangement would have very little effect on the American auto industry – the Canadian auto sector would simply be integrated *into* the American. Few American plants would change their production, distribution, or research and development plans because of the new regime. In the context of American foreign policy in the 1960s, the auto pact is a very minor topic, while it is a significant and noted achievement for Canadian policymakers.

70 One U.S. official remarked during another auto negotiation at GATT that 'while we recognize that Reisman may well be disappointed that the U.S. has not accepted his proposal as presented, we believe it would be a mistake to take too seriously what appears to have been an emotional reaction from a volatile man whose first response was to pick up the phone but who in franker moments admits to using table-thumping as a negotiating ploy.' U.S. Embassy Geneva to State Department, 6 Oct. 1966, NARA, RG 59, Box 990.

71 M. Glitman to file, 27 Jan. 1965, NARA, RG 59, Entry 5299, Box 6, File Foreign Trade, FT 4 Agreements, US-Canada Automotive Products.

72 L.B. Johnson Briefing Book for Pearson Visit, 15 Jan. 1965, LBJ, Canada, Box 167.

73 'Memo for the President: Subject: Canada-American Free Trade in Autos and Parts,' Trezise to Wilson, 25 Nov. 1964, ibid. Wilson Papers, Box 1.

74 George Ball, 'The United States and Canada: Common Aims and Common

Responsibilities' (Speech to the Canadian and Empire Clubs, 22 March 1965), *Department of State Bulletin* 52, no. 1347 (19 April 1965), 573–4.

75 'Statement of Fred G. Secrest, Vice President and Controller of the Ford Motor Company before the Committee on Ways and Means, U.S. House of Representatives, On H.R. 6960,' 28 April, 1965, NAC, RG 19, Vol. 3946, 8705–2, part 4.

76 See Chapter 2.

77 Philip Trezise, 'The Relevance of the Auto Pact for Other Sectoral Trade Agreements,' *Canada–United States Law Journal* 10 (1985), 66.

78 Walter L. Gordon, *A Political Memoir* (Toronto, 1977), 169.

79 'Remarks of PM, Uplands Airport,' 17 Jan. 1965, DFAIT, Vol. 5.

80 Keohane and Nye, *Power and Interdependence*, 178–93.

4 The Implementation of the Auto Pact, 1965–1966

1 For Senator Gore's political ideas and his legislative battles, see his *The Eye of the Storm: A People's Politics for the Seventies* (New York, 1970) and *Let the Glory Out: My South and Its Politics* (New York, 1972). For his defeat in 1970, see Gene Graham, 'Gore's Lost Cause,' *New South* 26, 1 (1971), 26–34; David Halberstam, 'The End of a Populist,' *Harper's*, no. 242 (Jan., 1971), 25–45. For a more academic analysis of Gore's loss, see David Price and Michael Lupfer, 'Volunteers for Gore: The Impact of a Precinct Level Canvass in Three Tennessee Cities,' *Journal of Politics* 35 (1973), 410–38; David Price and Michael Lupfer, 'On the Merits of Face-to-Face Campaigning,' *Social Science Quarterly* 53, 1 (1972), 534–43.

2 Following his defeat in 1970, one thoughtful reporter attributed the loss to the fact that Gore 'had remembered the challenge to be a statesman but forgotten the necessity to be a politician.' Wilma Dykeman, *Tennessee: A Bicentennial History* (New York, 1975), 115.

3 The Subcommittee on Canadian Affairs was dominated by senators from small border states. Senate Committee on Foreign Relations (SCFR), *Automotive Products Agreement between the United States and Canada: Hearing before a Subcommittee of the Committee on Foreign Relations, 10 February, 1965* (hereafter SCFR *1965*) (Washington, DC, 1965), 12, 21.

4 Ibid., 26–7.

5 U.S. Congress, *The Congressional Record (Senate)* (Washington, DC, 1967), 14 March 1967, 6499.

6 The House passed the bill by a vote of 280 to 113 on 31 Aug. 1965. Voting was largely non-partisan, although Canadian observers thought that the administration expected fewer dissenting votes by Democrats. Washing-

ton Embassy to DEA, 2 Sept. 1965, NAC, RG 19, Vol. 4844, File 8705-2, part 6, Auto Agreement.

7 Senate Committee on Finance (SCF), United States–Canadian Automobile Agreement: Hearings before Committee on Finance, United States Senate, on H.R. 9042, September 14, 15, 16, 20, and 21, 1965 (hereafter SCF *1965*) (Washington, D.C., 1965); in particular see Gore's interrogations of Thomas Mann, Undersecretary of State for Economic Affairs, 81–9, and Secretary of Labor Willard Wirtz, 366. See also Hartke's interrogation of the representatives of the Big Three; *Congressional Record (Senate)*, 14 March, 1967, 6469, and 15 May 1968, 13382.

8 See, e.g., SCF *1965*, 274–290.

9 Gore's defence of auto jobs would stand him well during his last election campaign though, as most of those polled at the Ford plant in Nashville threw their support behind the farmer from Carthage. Paul R. Wells, 'Blood and Gore,' *New Republic*, 24 Oct. 1970, 11–12; SCF, *1965*; *Congressional Record (Senate)*, 15 Feb. 1967, 3352.

10 Gore's amendment to delay the Senate's decision until the new year was defeated 43 to 31, while Hartke's motion which would have allowed the legislation to come into force unless subsequently rejected by Congress on the basis of a further tariff commission study was defeated 40 to 34; Bruce Macdonald, 'Filibuster Threatened on Car Pact,' *Globe and Mail*, 21 Sept. 1965.

11 For the Senate debate on the legislation, see *Congressional Record (Senate)*, 30 Sept. 1965, 24569–79, 24597–622. For the political manoeuvring over the adjustment assistance provisions, see the correspondence of the SFC, NARA I (Washington, DC), Legislative Records Center.

12 Lawrence Bator to LBJ, 4 June, 1965, LBJ Library, National Security Files (NSF), Country Files, Canada (hereafter NSF Canada), Box 166; various 1965 documents, NARA I, Records of the U.S. House of Representatives, 89th Congress, Committee on Ways and Means, Legislative Files on House Bills (hereafter NARA I, 89th Congress), Box 49–50.

13 Key was the April testimony of witnesses such as Undersecretary of State for Economic Affairs Thomas Mann, the UAW's Leonard Woodcock, Secretary of Commerce John T. Connor, Secretary of Labor W. Willard Wirtz, Ford Motor Co. vice president Fred G. Secrest, Chrysler vice-president David W. Kendall, American Motors Corp. vice-president Bernard A. Chapman, and General Motors vice president James M. Roche. NAC, RG 19, Vol. 3946, File 8705-2, part 4, 28 April 1965. 'Some Surprising Answers to Questions on the U.S.–Canada Auto Pact,' *New York Journal of Commerce*; 6 May 1965. See also, SCF 1965.

14 In the House, Michigan representatives voted on the auto agreement as follows: 13 for (7 Republicans, 6 Democrats), 3 against (all Democrats), and 2 Democrats abstained. In the Senate, both Michigan senators, Patrick McNamara and Philip Hart (both Democrats) voted for the agreement. Overall, in the Senate, 36 Democrats and 18 Republicans voted for the agreement, while 17 Democrats and only one Republican (Carl Curtis of Nebraska) voted against it. Twenty-eight senators abstained or were not able to vote (16 Democrats and 12 Republicans). In particular, Senator Hart's early and considerable support for the agreement was noted by Canadian observers. Hart was one of the most respected politicians on the Hill at the time. Washington to External Affairs, 25 Jan. 1965, NAC, RG 19, Vol. 8705–2, part 2, 16 Jan.–Feb. 1965; *Congressional Record (Senate)*, 25 Jan. 1965, 14282.

15 'Release: Office of the White House Press Secretary,' 22 Oct. 1965, NAC, RG 19, Vol. 4844, File 8705-2, part 7, Auto Agreement, 1965–1968.

16 Gore cited the petitions of 7,752 former auto workers who were now unemployed because of the agreement. He also noted that auto industry employment in Canada had grown by more than 20,000 since 1965. *Congressional Record (Senate)*, 14 March 1967, 6497–8.

17 The Presidential *Report* was a brief and rather dry rendering of statistics which Gore condemned as utterly useless. 'Canada-U.S. Auto Pact,' n.d., Albert Gore Papers, Albert Gore Research Center, Middle Tennessee State University, Murfreesboro, Tennessee (hereafter Gore Papers); Senate Committee on Finance, *Canadian Automobile Agreement: First Annual Report of the President to the Congress on the Implementation of the Automotive Products Trade Pact of 1965, March 22, 1967* (hereafter SCF *1967*) (Washington, DC, 1967).

18 *Congressional Record (Senate)* 1967: 15 Feb., 3349–55; 3 March, 5383–84; 14 March, 6496–6500; 21 March, 7449; 'Canadian Auto Scheme,' various dates, Gore Papers.

19 Most Conservatives did not openly criticize the agreement, either in the House of Commons or privately. If anything, Opposition MPs thought it proved how successful the Tory transmission/engine duty-remission scheme had been.

20 The Alfred Hales Papers at the NAC consist largely of files devoted to criticism of the auto pact.

21 Canada, *House of Commons Debates* (hereafter *Debates*), 5 May 1966, 4759. The NDP also criticized the agreement as a sell-out. '"Yankee Traders" Fooled Us on Auto Pact, Douglas,' *Toronto Telegram*, 11 May 1965.

22 *Debates*, 8 April 1965, 144–5.

23 Debates and questions about the auto pact were part of proceedings in the House of Commons throughout 1965 and 1966. On the issues of the $50 million rebate, car prices, and the auto company layoffs, see *Debates* in particular (for 1965), April, 13 297–8; April 26, 401–3; April 30, 971; (for 1966) Feb. 28, 1873–75. And *Globe and Mail* (1965): 'Auto Price Cuts: Start in 1966?' 16 March 1965; 'Handling of Layoff Notice by Ford Upsets Martin,' 24 April; 'Ford Plans to Shift Canadian Purchasing to U.S. HQ,' 19 May; Bruce Macdonald, 'Urges Price Cuts on Cars: "Not Trying to Aid Tories,"' 15 Sept.

24 *Debates*, 5 May 1966, 4760, 4762.

25 There is considerable correspondence among government officials regarding the timing of the auto pact bill. See, e.d., J.G. Hawden to J.R. McKinney, 16 Feb. 1965; 'Memorandum to the Cabinet: Canada–U.S. Automotive Agreement, Timing of Parliamentary Debate,' 16 Feb. 1965. Department of Foreign Affairs and International Trade (DFAIT), Vol. 6, Jan.–March 1965. 'Timing of Parliamentary Debate,' J.R. McKinney to R. Latimer, R.Y. Grey, B.G. Barrow, 12 Feb. 1965; NAC, RG 19, Vol. 3946, File 8705-2, part 2; 'Memo to Martin: Parliamentary Resolution,' Cadieux to Martin, 10 Jan. 1966, DFAIT, Vol. 10, Oct. 1965–Jan. 1966.

26 D.S. Wood to Walter Gordon, 26 Jan. 1965, NAC, RG 19, Vol. 3946, File 8705-2-2; 'Firms Fear Monopoly on Car Parts,' *Globe and Mail*, 2 Feb. 1965. The Canadian Tooling Manufacturers' Association also requested that the agreement be reworked in order to better compete with the U.S. tooling industry. 'Tool Firms Ask Rewrite of Car Pact,' ibid., 17 Aug. 1965.

27 See, e.g., D.S. Wood to Walter Gordon, 26 Jan. 1965, NAC, RG 19, Vol. 3946, File 8705-2, part 2. J.D. Loveridge (Ingersoll Machine and Tool Co.) to H. Gray, 13 May, 1965; Loveridge to Gray, 4 June 1965; Gray to Loveridge, 14 June 1965; Gray to Drury, 30 June 1965; Drury to Gray, 9 Aug. 1965. NAC, RG 20, Vol. 1826, File 1022-17, part 3, Automotive Agreement. 'Meeting with Directors of APMA,' N.B. Macdonald to file, 8 Nov. 1965, ibid., Vol. 2063, File 8001-260/A46, part 2, APMA, 1965–1967.

28 Days before the agreement was officially signed at Johnson City, Texas, ASIA and a group of independent parts makers had filed suit against the secretary of the treasury in U.S. District Court. The motion asked that a writ in the nature of mandamus be issued compelling the secretary to levy countervailing duties against the Canadian remission scheme. When the Canadian government passed an order-in-council providing that duty remissions would no longer be paid after 17 January, the Treasury Department ended its investigation the next day, and the case was eventually null and void. U.S. Tariff Commission, 'Report to the Committee on Ways

and Means on HR 6960, 89th Congress, The Automotive Products Trade
Act of 1965,' 23 April 1965, NARA I, Box 49–50; 'Court to Hear U.S. Auto
Parts Incentives Suit,' *New York Journal of Commerce*, 13 Jan. 1965; 'LBJ's
Great Automotive Market: Congress Cool – Parts Makers Hot,' *Motor Age*
(Feb. 1965).

29 It was clear that Gore was working closely with ASIA and the other parts
makers (see n36). Washington Embassy to DEA, 30 March, 2 and 14 April
1965, NAC, RG 19, Vol. 3946, File 8705-2, part 3; Francis Bator to Lee
White, 15 April 1965, LBJ, White House Central Files (WHCF), Legislation,
Box 156; Marcel Cadeuix to Martin, 26 April, 1965, DFAIT, Vol. 8, March-
April, 1965; Richard Lawrence, 'U.S.–Canadian Auto Pact Hits New
Obstacle,' *New York Journal of Commerce*, 23 March, 1965; Richard
Lawrence, 'U.S.–Canada Auto Pact Being Probed,' ibid., 21 April 1965.

30 Harold T. Halfpenny, 'United States–Canadian Agreement on Automotive
Parts,' *Legal News and Views (ASIA)*, 21 Jan. 1965.

31 'Automotive Industry to Fight U.S.–Canadian Auto Parts Pact,' ASIA
News Release, 9 Feb. 1965.

32 'Free Trade for Whom?' *Washington Post*, editorial, 17 Jan. 1965; 'ASIA vs
the USA,' *Motor Age* (Jan. 1965); 'ASIA Knocks Heads with Big Three' and
'Canada Auto Pact Triggers "Write Your Congressman" Move,' *Motor Age*
(Feb. 1965).

33 SCF, *1965*, 189, 275.

34 'Auto Pact Worries U.S. Parts Suppliers,' *Toronto Telegram*, 1 Feb. 1965;
Testimony of Allan Levine and Harold T. Halfpenny, NAC, RG 19, Vol.
3946, File 8705-2, part 4.

35 M. Glitman to S.E. Erdkamp, 21 April, 1965, NARA, RG 59, Bureau of
European Affairs, Country Director for Canada, Records Relating to
Economic Matters, 1956–1966, Entry 5299, Box 6, File Foreign Trade (FT), 4,
Agreements, U.S.–Canada Automotive Products.

36 Neil Regeimbal, editor of the pro-ASIA *Motor Age*, wrote after the pact was
passed that notwithstanding the 'screams of anguish' from the Congress
over the bill, Johnson's 'arm twisting' was extremely successful in silenc-
ing the agreement's critics. 'Sore Arms in Washington,' *Motor Age* (Nov.
1965). In the same issue, a caption under a picture of failed pact opponents
Gore, Halfpenny and Levine reads; 'Smiling – But Not Happy ... All three
opposed the Administration's tariff agreement with Canada. But LBJ
wanted it; and LBJ got it. That's hardly news. The hotly debated tariff Bill
is now law.'

37 Modine officials lamented their defeat when the agreement was passed
into law: 'All in all, our challenge to the "Canadian Scheme" was a bad

move ... We lost in one way but won in another. We never lost a penny of business to Canada. Somehow, and we don't know exactly how, our interests had been protected in negotiating the 1965 Auto Pact. It was "high politics."' Unpublished History, n.d. Modine Manufacturing Co., Racine Wisconsin, 8.

38 Press release, 'UAW Hails U.S.-Canada Move to End Auto Tariffs but Insists on Protection for Workers Adversely Affected,' 16 Jan. 1965, Walter Reuther Library (WRL), UAW, Region 7, Box 8, File 6.

39 Burt to Reuther, Weinberg, July 1964; Reuther to Commissioner of Customs, 30 June 1964, WRL, Walter Reuther Papers, Box 49, File 2. Weinberg to Reuther, 9 and 11 July 1964, ibid., UAW Region 7, Box 8; Weinberg to Reuther, 9 July 1964, ibid., Reuther Papers, Box 49; Detroit Consulate to External Affairs, 20 July 1964, NAC, RG 20, Vol. 2053, File 1021, part 1. Burt to Martin, 20 July 1964, DFAIT, Vol. 2; Burt to Martin, 8 Oct. 1964, ibid. Vol. 3.

40 Weinberg to Reuther, 'U.S.–Canadian Auto Free Trade Agreement,' 18 Jan. 1965; Weinberg to Reuther, 'Adjustment Assistance Provisions of Draft Bill to Implement U.S.–Canada Auto Trade Agreement,' 6 Feb. 1965; Weinberg to Irv Bluestone, 'Canadian Auto Trade Agreement,' 20 Feb. 1965, WRL, Reuther Papers, Box 49, File 3.

41 *Congressional Record (Senate)*, 24428, 20 Sept. 1965.

42 Both the Canadian and American leadership made it clear that support of the agreement would be conditional on the creation of worker protection plans. Reuther to Secretary of Labor Willard Wirtz, Senator Russell B. Long, 20 Sept. 1965; Reuther to LBJ, 15 Jan. 1965. WRL, Reuther Papers, Box 49; 'Asks for Worker Protection: UAW Worried Over Tariff Pact,' *Globe and Mail*, 19 March 1965.

43 Other Canadian locals such as Local 200 (Windsor) protested the auto agreement, as well. 'Local 200 Resolution to Prime Minister Pearson,' 14 May 1965, NAC, MG 26 N, Lester Pearson Papers, Vol. 260.

44 The left-leaning section of the union, which opposed the auto agreement, made its views – on continentalism, the 'all-Canadian car,' and higher Canadian content – apparent in its independent submissions to the Bladen Commission and in its attacks on the plan during the 1965 meetings of the UAW's Canadian Council. 'Submission of Local 444 UAW-AFL-CIO to the Royal Commission on the Automotive and Parts Industries,' Oct. 1960, NAC, RG 33/45, Bladen Commission; Burt to Canadian Council, 'Report of UAW Canadian Director,' 26 and 27 June 1965, WRL, UAW Region 7, Box 69, File 3; Burt to Canadian Council, 'Canada-U.S. Automotive Trade Agreement,' 25 and 26 Sept. 1965, ibid., Box 8, File 7.

45 For views on the factions in the Canadian UAW at the time, see Charlotte Yates, *From Plant to Politics: The Autoworkers Union in Postwar Canada* (Philadelphia, 1993), Sam Gindin, *The Canadian Auto Workers: Birth and Transformation of a Union* (Toronto, 1995), and Dimitry Anastakis, 'Between Nationalism and Continentalism: State Auto Industry Policy and the Canadian UAW,' *Labour/Le Travail* 53 (Spring 2004), 87–124.

46 '*New Canada* Special Supplement: The Auto Pact Is Destroying Canada's Auto Industry; May 1972,' p. 3, NAC, MG. 32–G63, Alfred Hales Papers, Vol. 4.

47 As late as the end of December, 1964, Burt demanded to know what was happening in the negotiations and complained to Martin and other ministers that the UAW was being left out in the cold. After the agreement passed, the government accepted none of the UAW's suggestions regarding the agreement, adjustment assistance, or the administration of the agreement. In the United States, the Johnson administration kept Reuther well informed of the progress of the agreement. Burt to Martin, 8 Oct. 1964, DFAIT, Vol. 3; Burt to Drury, 8 Oct. 1964, NAC, RG 20, Vol. 2053, File 1021-11, part 4; Martin to Burt, 30 Dec. 1964, DFAIT, Vol. 4; Reuther to LBJ, 15 Jan. 1965, Reuther Papers, Box 49, File 3.

48 In the United States, benefits for auto workers were about 85 per cent of the normal union-negotiated supplemental unemployment benefits, compared with approximately 65 per cent under the Canadian plan. Weinberg to Reuther, 23 June 1965, ibid., File 5; Burt, 'UAW Canadian Region, Administrative Letter, Vol. 1, No. 1.' 28 June 1965, WRL, UAW Region 7, Box 42, File 2; 'UAW Press Release: Transitional Assistance Benefits,' 28 June 1965, ibid., Box 8, File 6.

49 In March 1965 senior international members including Reuther, Leonard Woodcock, and Irv Bluestone agreed that wage parity would be a major goal for the UAW in the immediate future and promised to support such a resolution at the UAW's upcoming 20th Constitutional Convention in California. This was a defensive move, as well: Parity would ensure that production remained in the United States instead of being shifted to Canadian workers who were not as well paid. Weinberg to Bluestone, 22 March 1965, WRL, Reuther Papers, Box 49, File 4.

50 Senate Committee on Finance, *United States–Canadian Automobile Agreement, 1965*, 246.

51 Local 444 (Windsor) and Local 222 (Oshawa) to Pearson, 'Resolution Re: Worker Assistance/Dislocation,' 30 April 1965; Canadian UAW Council to Pearson, 5 May 1965. NAC, Pearson Papers, Vol. 260, File 749.32. P.J. Lavelle to Fred Wanklyn, 8 June 1965, NAC, MG 32 B12, Paul Martin

Papers, Vol. 260 File 1; Burt to Canadian Council, 'Report of UAW Canadian Director,' 26 and 27 June, 1965, WRL, UAW Region 7, Box 69, File 3; Burt to Canadian Council, 'Canada–U.S. Automotive Trade Agreement,' 25 and 26 Sept. 1965, ibid., Box 8, File 7.

52 Burt argued that at Local 444, Local 199, and Local 222 employment had increased from 4,568 to 9,059, from 6,300 to 7,997, and from 15,100 to 17,300, respectively. Burt to Canadian Council, 25 and 26 Sept. 1965. Ibid.

53 Ibid.

54 In 1999–2000, when the auto pact's legality under the WTO was questioned by the Japan and the European Union, the CAW was the strongest defender of the agreement.

55 The United States did not pursue the possibility of an Article XXIV waiver governing the creation of free trade areas beyond the point of speculation, as it was realized that the auto agreement did not in any way apply to 'substantially all the trade between the constituent territories in products originating in such territories.' For a good, brief analysis of Article XXIV, see Hart, 'GATT Article XXIV and Canada–U.S. Trade Negotiations,' *Review of International Business Law* 1 (1987), 319–36; M. Cadeiux to the Ministers of External Affairs, Finance, Trade and Commerce, and Industry. 19 Oct. 1964, NAC, RG 19, Vol. 3946, File 8705-1, part 1, to Dec. 1964.

56 For an excellent analysis of Canada and GATT, see Michael Hart, *Fifty Years of Canadian Tradecraft: Canada at the GATT, 1947–1997* (Ottawa, 1998).

57 British Prime Minister Harold Wilson made his concerns known to Pearson regarding the auto agreement well before the United States presented its waiver request at Geneva. Even before the pact was officially announced, Japan informed Canada that it was 'seriously concerned' and regretted that the two countries had embarked on such a scheme. London to DEA, 16 Dec. 1964; Messrs. Kimoto and Kusoka, Japanese Embassy to A.E. Ritchie; Ritchie to File, 30 Dec. 1964. NAC, RG 20. Vol. 2053, File V.1021-11, part 4, Proposed New Auto Program; Tokyo to DEA, 24 Dec. 1964, DFAIT, Vol. 3.

58 Economic Division, DEA to A.E. Ritchie, 18 Dec. 1964. DFAIT, Vol. 4. For a detailed explanation of the Protocol of Provisional Application, which governed the end use provisions, see Frank Stone, *Canada, the GATT and the International Trade System*, 2nd ed. (Montreal, 1992), 38–9, and Frank Swacker, Kenneth Redden, and Larry Wenger, *World Trade without Barriers: The World Trade Organization and Dispute Resolution* (Charlottesville, Va., 1995), 67–8; M. Cadeiux to the Ministers, 19 Oct. 1964.

59 McGeorge Bundy to Record, 24 Sept. 1964, LBJ, Canada, Box 164; Francis Bator to LBJ, 4 June 1965, ibid., Box 166; State circular to various embas-

sies, 1 July 1965, NARA, RG 59, Subject Numeric Files, 1964–1966, Box 990, FT Canada.

60 Sources informed the State Department that the British decision on the waiver vote would be 'extremely difficult' if the United Kingdom did not receive something in return. London to State Department, 18 Jan. 1965, LBJ, NSF Canada, Box 164.

61 John Jackson, 'The Puzzle of the GATT,' *World Trade Law Journal* 1 (1967), 154.

62 Geneva to DEA, 2 Nov. 1965, NAC, RG 19, Vol. 4844, File 8705-02.

63 The difficulties the United States faced can be seen in the account of the second working party struck to assess the agreement and taken from the following documents: 'U.S. – Imports of Automotive Products, Report of Working Party Submitted to the Council of Representatives on 19 Nov., 1965 (L/2509)' and 'U.S. – – Imports of Automotive Products, Decision of 20 Dec., 1965,' *Basic Instruments and Selected Documents (BISD) 14th Supplement* (Geneva, July 1966), 38–9; London to State Department, 5 Nov. 1964, NARA, RG 59, Subject Numeric Files, 1964–1966, Box 991; Geneva to External Affairs, 6 Nov. 1965, DFAIT, Vol. 10; Geneva to DEA, 9 and 12 Nov. 1965, NAC, RG 19, Vol. 4844, File 8705-2.

64 Geneva to DEA, 20 Dec. 1965, DFAIT, Vol. 10; Harold Wilson to Pearson, 7 April 1965, ibid., vol. 7; GATT, *BISD, 16th Supplement*, 1966, 23–31, 162–77.

65 Hales to D.S. Wood (APMA), 26 Feb. 1965, NAC, Alfred Hales Papers, Vol. J.D. Loveridge to Hales, 30 March 1965; Loveridge to Hales, 1 April, 1965; Hales to Loveridge 11 May, 1965; Hales to Loveridge, 2 June 1965. Ibid., Vol. 2.

66 'Memo to Ministers: Proposals to Reduce the Trade Deficit in Automobile Industry,' Simon Reisman to Walter Gordon, 28 Aug. 1963, NAC, RG 19, Vol. 3946, File 8705-1-1.

67 It is noteworthy that the auto pact did not become a major issue in the 1965 Canadian election campaign.

68 The most fascinating example of this is the UAW. Union locals in Canada and the United States were against the pact, but they never cooperated to work towards its defeat, primarily because many of the Canadian locals advocated a brand of nationalism which would have seen the Canadian industry not only end the auto pact, but have the Canadian UAW break from its 'international.' The break, of course, eventually happened.

69 'Dief Not Saying if He'll Accept U.S. Senator's Help,' *Toronto Star*, 16 Sept. 1965.

70 During his discussions with ASIA members, Loveridge found that 'With

one exception, all the members present were hostile to the plan and it was believed that the one member had been bought off with a hefty chunk of business,' presumably, by one of the major auto companies. Loveridge to Hales, 30 March 1965, NAC, Hales Papers, Vol. 1.

71 Hales led a long fight in the Canadian parliament to gain access to the Canadian government–Big Three letters of undertaking, which remained secret. U.S. officials, on the other hand, were well aware of their contents.

72 Only in the auto industry, with its few, very powerful companies, could an agreement such as the auto pact been created. In 1965, the Big Three, all American-owned, controlled more than 90 per cent of production in Canada.

73 Canadian Club of Ottawa, *Addresses* (Ottawa, 1969), 12 Feb. 1969.

74 Henry Ford II to LBJ, 16 Sept. 1964; McGeorge Bundy to Record, 24 Sept. 1964, LBJ, NSF Canada, Box 164.

75 William Brubeck to Bundy, 23 Sept. 1964, ibid.

76 SFC *1965*, 180.

5 Managing the Borderless North American Auto Industry, 1965–1968

1 A State Department analysis of the agreement forecast a consumption rise for Canada of 8 per cent a year. 'The Economic Effects of the Canadian Auto Agreement,' 20 April 1965, NARA, RG 59, Entry 5299 Box 14, File, Foreign Trade 4 (FT4), Trade Agreements Canada–U.S., Auto Products.

2 Kenneth P. Thomas, *Capital beyond Borders: States and Firms in the Auto Industry, 1960–1994* (New York, 1997), 113–4.

3 K.W. Burke (Officer, Mechanical Transportation Branch) to C.D. Arthur, 18 Aug. 1965; Burke to File, 19 and 20 Aug. 1965. NAC, RG 20, Vol. 1826, File 1022–17, part 3. 'Facts Relating to Expansion of Automotive Industry in 1964 and 1965,' 8 Oct. 1965, ibid., Vol. 1793, File Automotive Correspondence; Burke, 'Quarterly Report on the Auto Industry,' 19 Nov. 1965, ibid., Vol. 1775, File 8001-260/A4, part 2.

4 GM expansion can be in part explained by commitments made before the automotive agreement. Robert Rice, 'Opening of GM Plant in Quebec Hailed by Lesage as Milestone,' *Globe and Mail*, 13 Oct. 1965; 'GM Oshawa Project to Cost $2.5 Million,' ibid., 19 July, 1966.

5 For Ford's expansion and reorganization, see below.

6 Richard H. Courtenaye (U.S. Consul General, Windsor) to Joseph Scott, 23 Feb. 1966, NARA, RG 59, Entry 5299, Box 6, File FT4.

7 Carl Beigie, *The Canada–U.S. Automotive Agreement* (Montreal: Canadian–American Committee, 1970), 61–3; S. Watkins (U.S. Embassy Ottawa) to file, 25 Oct. 1966. NARA, RG 59, Box 14.

8 The exact nature of Big Three spending on plant and parts has never been publicly disclosed by the corporations. No company allowed access to these records, and company documents which contain such figures continue to be restricted by the public archives, reflecting the companies' wishes.

9 'Industry News,' *Motor Age* (May 1965), 10.

10 'MacKinnon Calls Back 450,' *Globe and Mail*, 8 Nov. 1966.

11 'At this moment it is difficult to assess what effect the new agreement and the proposed legislation will have on the company's future production; it may be necessary for the company to establish a facility in Canada.' Modine Manufacturing Co., *Annual Report for 1965*, (10 May 1965), 6 (in author's files).

12 John Fell, '3 Auto-Parts Firms Improve Facilities to Cash In on Pact,' *Globe and Mail*, 23 June 1965.

13 While many Canadian companies were benefiting from the auto agreement, some firms, particularly independent Canadian stampers, faced difficulties as the Big Three shifted their purchasing patterns to take better advantage of the auto pact. This became especially apparent in 1966, as orders for the 1967 model year were completed. Roger Newman, 'Stamping Firms Say Auto Makers Shifting Millions in Orders to U.S.,' *Globe and Mail*, 27 Jan. 1965; Roger Newman, 'Most Firms Believe Auto Pact Will Be Help, but Only Time and Buying Pattern Will Tell,' ibid., 9 Feb. 1966; 'Auto Pact Victim No. 1 Costs Town 218 Jobs,' ibid., 30 April 1966; 'Tour of South-Western Ontario, Sept. 19–Oct. 7 1966: H.S. Hay, Consul and Trade Commissioner, Detroit,' NAC, RG 19, Vol. 5175, File 8705-1, part 3; 'Canadians Have Parts, Will Sell,' *Globe and Mail*, 2 July 1965.

14 Roger Newman, 'Canadian Auto Production Sets Record for Nine Months,' *Globe and Mail*, 13 Oct. 1965.

15 'Monthly Review, The Bank of Nova Scotia: Changing Influences in Canada's Automobile Industry,' Toronto, July 1966, NAC, RG 19, Vol. 4620, File 8705-01, part 2.

16 'New Plants and Expanded Facilities Announced as a Result of Automotive Programs,' NAC, RG19, 10 Jan. 1967, Department of Foreign Affairs and International Trade (DFAIT), Vol. 12.

17 Ralph Cowan, 'Effects of the United States–Canadian Automotive Agreement on Canada's Manufacturing, Trade and Price Posture' (PhD diss., University of Michigan, 1972). Cowan (114–16) and Beigie (The Canada–U.S. Automotive Agreement, 77–93) agreed that the auto pact increased efficiency but noted that the safeguards did have distorting effects on the industry.

18 David L. Emerson, *Production, Location and the Automotive Agreement* (Ottawa, 1975), 18.

19 GM, *Annual Report, 1967*, Baker Library, Harvard Business School (hereafter Baker Library).

20 Chrysler Corporation, *Annual Report 1967* and GM, *Annual Report, 1967*, Baker Library.

21 Cowan, 'Effects of U.S.–Canada Automotive Agreement,' 133.

22 Beigie, *Canada–U.S. Automotive Agreement* 65.

23 Jack Behrman interviews with Alexander Vuillemin and Edward Stanger (Corporate Planning Division, GM), n.d., John F. Kennedy Presidential Library (hereafter JFK), Jack Behrman Papers, hereafter Behrman Papers, Box 14.

24 Beigie, *Canada–U.S. Automotive Agreement* 64; Cowan, 'Effects of U.S.–Canada Automotive Agreement,' 32.

25 Ibid.

26 'Tour of South-Western Ontario.

27 Mira Wilkins and Frank Earnest Hill, *American Business Abroad: Ford on Six Continents* (Detroit, 1964), 114, 131; I.A. Litvak, C.J. Maule, and R.D. Robinson, *Dual Loyalty: Canadian-U.S. Business Arrangements* (Toronto, 1971), 61–74; 'Review of Corporate Profits Attainable through Increased Integration of Ford U.S. and Ford of Canada Automotive Operations,' 30 Jan. 1964. Ford Company of Canada Archives, Oakville, Ontario (hereafter Ford Archives).

28 Officials at Ford described the changes, saying, 'Previously the Canadian company decided how it should meet the content requirements and what it should manufacture and assemble. Now, all of this is decided in Detroit simply because the U.S. company has to decide what the content in Canada shall be in order to integrate it with all the North American operations. Consequently, the Canadian company is really a division under the North American operations rather than being a separate company as it used to be.' Jack Behrman interviews with John Andrews (FMC, vice president in charge of European Auto Operations) and Percy Prance (formerly a director of Ford of Canada), 28 April, 1967, JFK, Behrman Papers, Box 14; Wilkins and Hill, *American Business Abroad*; Litvak et al. Dual Loyalty; FMC, *Annual Reports, 1965–1967*, Baker Library, Harvard Business School.

29 Joseph Scott (Minister, U.S. Embassy Ottawa) to W. Park Armstrong, Jr (U.S. Consul General, Toronto), 13 May 1965; Courtenaye to Scott, 23 Feb. 1966. NARA, RG 59, Entry 5299, Box 6.

30 U.S. Senate Committee on Finance (SCF), *Canadian Automobile Agreement: Hearing Before the Committee on Finance, U.S. Senate, July 19, 1968* (hereafter SCF *1968*) (Washington, DC, 1968), 48–9.

31 'Ford Plans to Shift Canadian Purchasing to U.S. Headquarters,' *Globe and Mail*, 19 May 1965; Cadieux to Martin, 19 May 1965, DFAIT, Vol. 8. For a more detailed view of the evolution of Ford of Canada, see Dimitry Anastakis, 'From Independence to Integration: The Corporate Evolution of the Ford Motor Company of Canada,' *Business History Review* 78 (Summer, 2004) 213–53.

32 *Annual Report, 1969* (Ottawa, 1969), 36.

33 Burt to MacEachen, 22 and 23 April 1965, (hereafter Walter Reuther Library WRL), UAW Region 7, Box 8, File 9; 'Handling of Layoff Notice by Ford Upsets Martin,' *Globe and Mail*, 24 April 1965; 'Ottawa to Aid Men Laid Off by Ford: UAW,' ibid., 30 April 1965.

34 *Canada, House of Commons Debates* (hereafter *Debates*) 28 June 1965, 2907–12; 'Press Release, Transitional Assistance Benefits.' 28 June 1965, DFAIT, Vol. 9.

35 Ford, which had laid off 1,600 workers, was the first to indicate that it would not sign on to the program. UAW leaders were perplexed, wondering why Ford wouldn't sign on to the TAB, which would cost the company only slightly more than the SUB. 'Ottawa Fund Plan for Car Workers Protested by Ford,' *Globe and Mail*, 30 June 1965. Henry Renaud, Local 200, Press Release, 'Ford and the TAB,' 27 July 1965; Renaud to Martin, 21 Sept. 1965, NAC, MG 32 B12, Paul Martin Papers (hereafter Martin Papers), Vol. 260, File 1.

36 'Ottawa Fund Plan for Car Workers Protested by Ford,' *Globe and Mail*, 30 June 1965.

37 Benefits for U.S. auto workers were about 85 per cent of their SUB. WRL, Walter Ruether Papers, Box 49, File 5. Weinberg to Reuther, 23 June 1965, ibid., UAW Region 7, Box 42, File 2, Burt, 'UAW Canadian Region, Administrative Letter, Vol. 1, No. 1,' 28 June 1965, ibid., Box 8, File 1; Burt, 'UAW Press Release: Transitional Assistance Benefits,' 28 June 1965, ibid. For a good example of the long debate over adjustment assistance benefits to workers, see *Debates*, 10 May 1965, 1110–76.

38 Burt to Canadian Council, 'Report of Canadian UAW Council Committee on the U.S.–Canadian Automotive Products Agreement,' 24–5 Sept. 1966, WRL, UAW Region 7, Box 42, File 5; 'Cabinet to Weigh Aid for Laid-Off GM Men,' *Globe and Mail*, 8 Oct. 1966; Dennis McDermott to Canadian Council, 'Brief on the Canadian–United States Automotive Products Agreement,' 20 Feb. 1969, WRL, UAW Region 7, Box 8, File 14.

39 See, e.g., Roger Newman, 'Fast-Growing Oshawa Quickly Overcomes the Shock of GM's 2,550–Man Layoff,' *Globe and Mail*, 4 Nov. 1966.

40 In the Commons, PC MP Donald MacInnis asked Drury for his comments

on 'statements emanating from union leaders in the U.S. to the effect that the U.S. Government has the right to insist that the Canadian Government impress upon the auto manufacturers that the advantages they received in the recent agreement be passed on to consumers.' Drury could only respond that the costs would eventually go down. *Debates*, 30 April 1965, 778–9; Bruce MacDonald, 'UAW Urges Johnson to Push Ottawa for Cut in Canadian Auto Prices,' *Globe and Mail*, 30 April 1965.

41 See, e.g., 'Prices Will Tell the Story,' editorial, and Bruce MacDonald, 'Auto Firms to Face Heavy Pressure for Price Cuts,' *Globe and Mail*, 19 Jan. 1965; 'Disparity Wide, Auto Price Cuts: Start in 1966?' ibid., 16 March, 1965.

42 PC MP Alfred Hales was the most consistent critic of the government on the auto agreement. When he read of Todgham's comments in the *Globe*, he challenged Drury on the issue. Drury's response was: 'The government has never taken the position that car prices will be the same ... The program is not designed to eliminate, nor can it affect, the difference in the cost of transportation in the two countries ... [The differences in the two countries] makes it difficult to achieve an eventual retail price parity.' *Debates*, 26 Jan. 1966, 281–2.

43 Another less scientific UAW study showed that in 1966 the Dodge Dart sold for $625 less in the United States than in Canada. 'Canadian and U.S. Car Prices,' 2 Sept. 1966, WRL, UAW Region 7, Box 6, Folder 7; Burt to Canadian Council, 2 and 3 April 1966, ibid., Box 69, File 4.

44 From 1964 to 1967, the price differential between a Buick Riviera sold in Canada and in the United States was on average approximately $1,100 (expressed at U.S. dollars where US$1 = Can$ 92.5). Even after 1968, the difference still remained around $400. Beigie, *Canada–U.S. Automotive Agreement*, 116.

45 Burt to Sharp, Drury, 26 Sept. 1966, WRL, UAW Region 7, Box 6, File 7; 'UAW urges Ottawa to Probe Prices, Profits of Car Makers,' *Globe and Mail*, 26 Sept. 1966; Drury to Burt, 5 Oct. 1966, WRL, UAW Region 7, Box 8, File 11; UAW Press Release, 'Wage Parity and Prices,' 7 Oct. 1966, ibid., Box 6, File 13.

46 Having resigned as Mitchell Hepburn's labour minister during the bitter Oshawa strike in 1937, Croll left the premier with the immortal line 'I'd rather walk with the workers than ride with General Motors.' The following year he was elected mayor of Windsor. S. Gindin, *The Canadian Autoworkers: The Birth and Transformation of a Union* (Toronto: Lorimer, 1995) 61.

47 'UAW Chides Decision,' *Globe and Mail*, 8 Oct. 1966; Burt to Saltsman, Croll, 27 Sept. 1966; Croll to Burt, 12 Oct. 1966. Burt to Croll, 24 Oct. 1966. WRL, UAW Region 7, Box 6 File 7.

48 Respectively, the average price differential percentage for the Valiant, Ford Custom, and Buick Riviera in 1969 was 4.2, 5.6, and 10. Beigie, *Canada–U.S. Automotive Agreement*, 116. In a letter to Prime Minister Pearson, the Consumer Association of Canada also demanded that the government ensure that car prices be monitored under the new regime. See the *Canadian Consumer* (March–April 1965), 106–7, and (May–June 1965), 142–3.

49 In correspondence with E.K. Brownridge (president of AMC), Industry Department officials explained the calculation of the company's ratio like this: In 1964 for instance, AMC had a production value of $65,011,941 (total production less value of imported cars). The company's sales that year totaled $65,166,666. This resulted in a ratio of 99.76 (sales divided by production). The officials elaborated: 'In the above example [the calculation of ratio], if sales increase by $1 million, then production must increase by slightly under $1 million to preserve the ratio established in the base period. This means that for every dollar of imported car, Canadian production (expressed as Canadian value added) must be increased by 99.76 cents.' These figures deal with 1964, not the 1963– base year, in which AMC production was much greater. E.K Brownridge to Reisman, 24 Dec. 1964. B.G. Barrow to E.K. Brownridge, 30 Dec. 1964. NAC, RG 20, Vol. 2053, File 1021–11, part 4.

50 Under the auto agreement, Ford was required to maintain its base 1963–4 CVA spending of $191.8 million on cars and $39.4 million on trucks. Cowan, 'Effects of U.S.–Canada Automotive Agreement,' 32; author's interview with Dennis DesRosiers, 20 March 2001.

51 James F. Keeley, in his dissertation, 'Constraints on Canadian International Economic Policy' (Stanford University, 1980), 265, estimates that the excess CVA (the total of CVA beyond the base and additional requirements) was as follows (all figures in U.S.$ millions):

	1965	1966	1967	1968
CVA Required	794.6	882.6	890.6	1,241.0
CVA Achieved	888.4	1,056.9	1,062.1	1,699.9
Excess CVA	93.8	174.3	171.5	458.9

52 Dykes, *Background on the Canada–U.S. Automotive Products Trade Agreement* (Toronto: MVMA, 1979), 57.

53 James G. Dykes (MVMA) to R.C. Labarge (deputy minister of national revenue), 28 Jan. 1965, NAC, RG 20, Vol. 2065, File 8001–240–M13, MVMA (hereafter 1964–1966 MVMA File), 'Meeting with MVMA,' Joyce to Grey, 28 Jan. 1965, ibid., RG 19, Vol. 5624, File 8705-4-02.

54 In September 1964 DOI submitted detailed plans for the manufacturers'

reporting under the pact. These included annual and quarterly reports on the levels of production, Canadian content, and non-Canadian content achieved. 'Proposed Programme for the Auto Industry,' n.d, NAC, RG 20, Vol. 2053, File 1021–11, part 2.

55 Dykes to Barrow, 9 June 1965, MVMA File; 'Ad Hoc Committee Meeting on the Automotive Programme, 23 June, 1965,' NAC, RG 19, Vol. 5624, File 8705-3, part 1.

56 'Notes on common industry problems relating to Canada–U.S. Automotive Trade Agreement,' MVMA to government, 9 Feb. 1966, ibid., 'Comments on Matters Relating to the Automotive Trade Agreement Submitted by the MVMA, Feb. 11, 1966,' 23 March 1966, MVMA File.

57 Because the base year 1963–4 was one in which AMC had set production records in Canada, AMC's passenger car ratio was 108.3. Since this ratio was only 103.5 in 1965, Ottawa officials thereafter only required a ratio of 95 from AMC, and thus the company avoided paying duties. In 1965, Volvo's passenger car ratio was 86.2, which was above its required ratio of 81.6. However, Ottawa had given the Swedish car maker significant additional incentives to produce in Canada, and the company's figures did not accurately reflect its actual output, which was much lower, especially in terms of the CVA. 'Production to Sales Ratios' and 'Base Year Ratios and/or Minimum Ratios Required,' Reports to Departments of Industry, Trade and Commerce, NAC, RG 19, Vol. 5959, File 8705-8-15, File, Statistics. For more on Volvo in Canada, see Dimitry Anastakis, 'Building a "New Nova Scotia": State Intervention, the Auto Industry, and the Case of Volvo in Halifax, 1963–1998,' *Acadiensis* 34 (Autumn 2004), 3–30.

58 Roger Newman, 'Auto Slump in U.S. May Curb Exports of Canadian Firms,' *Globe and Mail*, 22 June 1966.

59 Roger Newman, 'Market Uncertainty Could Spoil Fulfilment of Auto-Trade Pact,' *Globe and Mail*, 9 Nov. 1966.

60 Roger Newman, 'Chrysler May Reach Pact Target Early,' ibid., 16 Sept. 1966.

61 'Memorandum for File: MVMA Meeting on Auto Program,' J.A. McMillan (chief, motor vehicles division, mechanical transport branch [MTB], DOI), 28 July 1966, NAC, RG 20, Vol. 1775, File 8001-260/A4, part 2; 'Operations of the Canadian Motor Vehicle Producers under the Auto Program,' Reisman to Drury, 6 Feb. 1967, ibid., Vol. 1793, File, Automotive Program.

62 'Notes on common industry problems relating to Canada–U.S. Automotive Trade Agreement,' MVMA to government, 9 Feb. 1966, NAC, RG 19, Vol. 5624, File 8705-3, part 1; 'Canadian Auto Industry Working for Exemption from Sales Tax Now,' *Globe and Mail*, 15 April 1966; J.G. Dykes

(MVMA) to Sharp, 25 April 1966, NAC, RG 19, Vol. 5624, File 8705-4-02.
63 Anthony Westell, 'Canada Cutting Tariffs on Imported Machinery by over $50 Million a Year,' *Globe and Mail*, 13 Dec. 1967.
64 The automakers' slow reporting made the government's estimates of production difficult. Based on GM's information, Reisman calculated the following ratios for the company in early 1967, which were slightly off from the final figures:

GM Ratio	1964	1965	1966	1967
Passenger Cars	94.0	96.0	97.0	77.9
Trucks	99.7	100.2	101.5	66.0
Commercial Vehicles	91.7	93.2	95.8	90.5

'Operations of the Canadian Motor Vehicle Producers under the Auto Program,' Reisman to Drury, 6 Feb. 1967, NAC, RG 20, Vol. 1793, File, Automotive Program.
65 Ibid.; 'GM Request for Modification of Ratio Calculation,' Barrow to file, 15 March 1967, ibid., File Automotive Correspondence.
66 Scott to Drury, 14 Jan. 1965, DFAIT, Vol. 5; Keeley, 'Constraints,' 243.
67 Drury to Scott, 20 March 1967; 'Operations of the Ford Motor Company of Canada under the Automotive Program,' 22 March 1967, NAC, RG 20, Vol. 1793, File, Automotive Correspondence.
68 Ibid.
69 Ford achieved its base-year ratio targets of 99.4 for cars, 108.1 for trucks, and 89.8 for buses. Scott to Drury, 14 Jan. 1965, DFAIT, Vol. 5; 'File: Auto Pact, Ford Confidential' (response of FMC officials to questionnaire), n.d., 1975, Dennis DesRosiers Papers, Private Collection.
70 Dykes, *Background*, 59.
71 Reisman to Drury, 9 Aug. 1967, NAC, RG 20, Vol. 1793, File, Automotive Correspondence.
72 For 1973–5 Chrysler's annual ratio achieved for trucks was 68.5, 53.8, and 64.2, respectively, well below the 100.5 required ratio. To avoid the immense penalties for missing the targets, Chrysler agreed to build the truck plant and therefore boost truck production well beyond the ratio. When the Pillette facility came on line, building small vans, Chrysler's truck ratio increased dramatically to 182.4 in 1977 and 195.8 in 1978. Author's interview with Dennis DesRosiers, 20 April 2001; 'Production to Sales Ratios' and 'base Year Ratios and/or Minimum Ratios Required,' NAC, RG 19, Vol. 5959, File 8705-08-15, File, Statistics.
73 E.H. Walker (MVMA) to Drury, 22 June 1967; NAC, RG 20, Vol. 1793, File, Automotive Correspondence.

6 Consolidating the Borderless North American Automobile Industry, 1968–1971

1 See Robert M. Collins, 'The Economic Crisis of 1968 and the Waning of the "American Century,"' *American Historical Review* 101, 2 (April 1996), 396–422.

2 For views on Trudeau and his government, see Andrew Cohen and J.L. Granatstein, eds., *Trudeau's Shadow: The Life and Legacy of Pierre Elliott Trudeau* (Toronto, 1998); Christina McCall and Stephen Clarkson, *Trudeau and Our Times*, Vols. 1 and 2 (Toronto, 1990–4).

3 Simon Reisman, *The Canadian Automotive Industry: Performance and Proposals for Progress* (Ottawa, 1978).

4 Section 205(b) of the enabling legislation states, in part: 'Whenever the President is informed that any manufacturer has entered into any undertaking, by reason of governmental action, to increase the Canadian value added of automobiles, buses, specified commercial vehicles, or original equipment parts produced by such manufacturer in Canada after August 31, 1968, he shall report such finding to the Senate and the House of Representatives.'

5 Rodney L. Borum to Robert L. McNeill, 29 Sept. 1966, NARA, RG 476, Bureau of International Export Administration, Bureau of International Commerce, Subject Files, 1965–1966, File 496.1, Autos; Washington to External Affairs (hereafter DEA), 14 Feb. 1967, NAC, RG 19, Vol. 4844, File 8705-2, part 8.

6 See Chapter 4.

7 Bator to Johnson, 16 March 1967, Lyndon B. Johnson Presidential Library (hereafter LBJ), White House Central Files (WHCF), Trade, Auto parts.

8 Senate Committee on Finance (SCF), *Canadian Automobile Agreement: First Annual Report of the President to the Congress on the Implementation of the Automotive Products Trade Pact of 1965, March 22, 1967* (hereafter SCF, *First Annual Report*) (Washington, DC, 1967).

9 United States, *Congressional Record (Senate)*, 15 Feb. 1967, 3349–55; 3 March 1967, 5383–4; 14 March 1967, 6496–6500; 21 March 1967, 7449.

10 SCF, *First Annual Report*, 1–3, 11–13, 21–7.

11 The president's *Second Annual Report* indicated that while the total value of auto trade between the two countries had jumped from U.S. $730 million in 1964 to over U.S. $3.2 billion in 1967, the decline of the U.S. surplus was equally dramatic, from U.S. $578 million to U.S. $285 million, or a shift of almost U.S. $300 million. *Canadian Automobile Agreement: Second Annual Report of the President to the Congress on the Implementation of the Automotive*

Products Trade Pact of 1965, May 18, 1968 (hereafter SCF, *Second Annual Report*) (Washington, DC, 1968).

12 SCF, *Canadian Automobile Agreement: Hearing Before the Committee on Finance, July 19, 1968* (hereafter SCF 1968) (Washington, DC, 1968), 1, 5, 63, 65. The auto companies' representatives stated that the agreement was 'workable' (GM) 'the only course of action which can preserve for the United States a significant trade advantage in automotive products with Canada' (Chrysler), and 'the agreement has worked well ... we strongly favour its continuation' (Ford), ibid., 31, 42, 47.

13 Washington to DEA, 19 July 1968. NAC, RG 19, Vol. 5624, File 8705-2, part 9.

14 'The Economic Effects of the Canadian Auto Agreement,' 20 April 1965, NARA, RG 59, Entry 5229 Box 14, File, Foreign Trade (FT) 14, Trade Agreements Canada-U.S., Auto Products.

15 A.E. Ritchie to J.C. Langely, 10 Aug. 1966, Department of Foreign Affairs and International Trade (DFAIT), Vol. 11.

16 Richard Lawrence, 'U.S. Now net Importers of Autos from Canada,' *New York Journal of Commerce*, 12 Aug. 1966.

17 Bruce Macdonald, 'Auto Pact Closing Canada–U.S. Gap,' *Globe and Mail*, 22 Sept. 1967.

18 These discussions included direct meetings on the agreement and the 11th annual Joint Canada–United States Ministerial Cabinet Committee on Trade and Economic Affairs, which was held in Montreal in June 1967. The joint cabinet meetings provided an opportunity for both sides to stake out their positions, but did not result in any concrete movement on the review. NARA, RG 59, Conference Files, 1949–1972, Box 450; 'Canada–United States Ministerial Meeting: Briefing Paper on Exchange of Views on Progress under the Automotive Agreement,' May 1968, NAC, RG 19, Vol. 4844, File 8705-2, part 8.

19 'Review of Canada–USA Auto Agreement,' Washington to DEA, 14 Dec. 1967; 'Auto Agreement Review,' J.E.G. Howarth to Grey, Annis, 19 Dec. 1967, ibid.

20 Drury to Sharp, 8 March 1968, ibid., Vol. 5175, File 8705-1, part 3.

21 DEA to Washington, 4 Dec. 1967; Washington to DEA, 4 Dec. 1967; DEA to Washington, 5 Dec. 1967; Washington to DEA, 6 Dec. 1967. Ibid., Vol. 4844, File 8705-2, part 8. Minutes of Cabinet, 12 Dec. 1967, NAC, RG 2, Vol. 6323, 1967; 'Review of the Auto Program,' Cabinet Conclusions, 12 Dec. 1967, ibid.

22 These figures were given by Chrysler executives to the U.S. Senate Finance Committee hearings in 1968. It is assumed that similar figures were expected from GM and Ford. SCF 1968, 84.

23 Washington to DEA, 18 March 1968; 'Review of the Automotive Program,' Drury to Cabinet, 30 April 1968, NAC, RG 19, Vol. 4844, File 8705-2, part 8.

24 DEA to Washington, 24 July 1968; Bryce to Grey, 31 July 1968; Bryce to Sharp, 26 Aug. 1968; 'Memorandum to Cabinet: Review of the Automotive Program,' 28 Aug. 1969, ibid., Vol. 5624, File 8705-2, part 9.

25 Ibid.

26 'Record of Cabinet Committee on Economic and Policy Programs Decision, Meeting of May 1, 1968,' 9 May 1968, ibid., Vol. 5175, File 8705-1, part 3.

27 'Special Report on Joint Review of the Automotive Parts Trade Agreement,' W.W. Rostow to L.B. Johnson, 30 Aug. 1968, LBJ Library, NSF, Country File, Canada, Cables and Memos (hereafter LBJ, NSF Canada), Box 166.

28 U.S. House of Representatives, *Special Report on the Joint Review of the United States Canada Automotive Products Agreement*, Document No. 379, 4 Sept. 1968; *Congressional Record (Senate)*, 4 Sept. 1968, 25545; Canada, *Debates of the House of Commons* (hereafter *Debates*), 16 Sept. 1968, 39–40.

29 In one section of this unused speech, Gore called the report a 'little six page rag.' *Congressional Record (House)*, 4 Sept. 1968, 25545. 'Speech, October, 1968 (not used),' Albert Gore Research Center, Tennessee, Albert Gore Papers, File Canada-U.S. Auto Pact (hereafter Gore Papers). 'New auto Pact Deal,' *Financial Post*, 7 Sept. 1968. Gore to State and Treasury Departments, 16 Sept. 1968; William Macomber (State) to Gore, 1 Oct. 1968; (Commerce) to Gore, 11 Oct. 1968. Gore Papers. Washington to DEA, 3 Oct. 1968, NAC, RG 19, Vol. 5624, File 8705-2, part 9.

30 Washington to DEA, 6 Feb. 1969, ibid. SCF, *Canadian Automobile Agreement: Third Annual Report of the President to the Congress on the Operation of the Automotive Products Trade Act of 1965, July 17, 1969* (hereafter SCF, *Third Annual Report*) (Washington, DC, 1969), 25.

31 R.C. Monk to Howarth (Industry, Trade and Commerce), 28 Feb. 1969, NAC, RG 19, Vol. 5624, File 8705-2, part 9; 'Meetings with Presidents of the Big Four Automotive Companies,' J.H. Warren to Jean-Luc Pepin, March 1969; 'Briefing Notes for the Minister,' Warren to Pepin, March 1969; R.C. Monk to R. de C. Grey, 1 April 1969, ibid., Vol. 5175, File 8705-01, part 3.

32 Washington to DEA, 1 May, 18 June, and 19 Sept. 1969, ibid., Vol. 5624, File 8705-2, part 9; 'State Department Position Paper on the Automotive Agreement,' 20 June 1969, NARA, RG 59, Conference Files, Box 493; David Crane, 'Canada's Trade Views Outlined to U.S. Government Officials,' 26 June 1969, *Globe and Mail*, and 'Canada, U.S. Plan Talks on Auto Pact, Oil Sales,' ibid., 27 June 1969.

33 SFC *Third Annual Report*.
34 Washington to DEA, 14 Nov. 1969; M. Schwarzmann to J. Loomer, 22 Dec. 1969. NAC, RG 19, Vol. 5624, File 8705-2, part 10; 'Memorandum to Ministers: Automotive Trade Products,' 17 Nov. 1969, ibid., Vol. 5625, File 8705-8-16, part 5; Terrance Willis, 'U.S. Looks for Early Changes to Liberalize Auto Pact Terms,' 14 Nov. 1969, *Globe and Mail*; 'U.S. to Press for End to Pact Safeguards,' 17 Nov. 1969, ibid.
35 Ibid.
36 'Notes on the Minister's Meeting with the Big Three Presidents, Jan. 14–16, 1970,' n.d., NAC, RG 19, Vol. 5625, File 8705-8-16, part 5.
37 John R. Brown III to Henry Kissinger, 6 Feb. 1970, NARA, Nixon Presidential Files, NS Files Canada, Box 670.
38 'Auto Agreement: Meeting of Trezise with the Minister, Wed., Feb. 11, 1970,' 12 Feb. 1970, NAC, RG 19, Vol. 5624, File 8705-2, part 10.
39 Washington to DEA, 14 Dec. 1970, ibid., part 11.
40 Upon his departure from the State Department in Dec. 1971, Trezise publicly warned that a 'faction' was forming in the U.S. government which was determined to alter trade patterns so that Canada would be in a deficit position with the United States. Based on his comments, it was assumed by reporters that Treasury officials, who had usually taken a harder line with Canada, were behind the faction. Ross H. Munro, 'Canadian Deficit in Trade Called Aim of U.S. Faction,' *Globe and Mail*, 6 Dec. 1971; Latimer to Schwarzmann, 7 May 1971, NAC, RG 19, Vol. 5624, File 8705-2, part 11.
41 'U.S. Balance of Payments Deficit up Sharply,' *Globe and Mail*, 18 May 1971; Washington to DEA, 18 and 20 May 1971, NAC, RG 19, Vol. 5624, File 8705-2, part 11.
42 'Summary Record of Meeting of Senior Interdepartmental Committee on the Automotive Agreement, 25 May, 1971,' ibid., File 8705-3, part 1; DEA to Washington, 31 May 1971, ibid., File 8705-2, part 11; 'Brief for Consultations with U.S. Officials on the Automotive Agreement,' 16 June 1971; 'Automotive Agreement: Report on Washington Visit,' 4 Aug. 1971; Washington to DEA, 10 Aug. 1971, ibid. part 12.
43 'Commerce Department Trade Analysis,' C. Fred Fergsten to H. Kissenger, 8 Jan. 1971, NARA, Nixon Presidential Materials Project, WHCF, Subject Files, EX TA, Trade, Box 1, 1969–1974.
44 As quoted in Allan J. Matusow, *Nixon's Economy: Booms, Busts, Dollars and Votes* (Lawrence, KS, 1998), 153.
45 For views on Nixon and the New Economic Policy see, e.g. Matusow, *Nixon's Economy*, esp. chapters 5 and 6; Joanne Gowa, *Closing the Gold*

Window: Domestic Politics and the End of Bretton Woods (Ithaca, 1983); Richard Nixon, *U.S. Foreign Policy for the 1970s: Shaping a Durable Peace: A Report to the Congress*, 3 May 1973; Terrance Wills, 'U.S. Imposes 10% Import Surcharge,' *Globe and Mail*, 16 Aug. 1971.

46 See, e.g., R.D. Cuff and J.L. Granatstein, *American Dollars – Canadian Prosperity: Canadian–American Economic Relations 1945–1950* (Toronto, 1978).

47 Ironically, the U.S. measures included the imposition of a 6.5 per cent surtax on offshore vehicles and the removal of a 7 per cent excise tax on autos, which was intended to spur domestic consumption of U.S.-built vehicles. However, because the Big Three imported completed vehicles from Canada, it was speculated that the measure might actually have the affect of spurring more production and employment at Canadian car makers. 'U.S. Surcharge on Imports Termed "Holding a Gun to the Head of the Rest of World"' *Globe and Mail*, 16 Aug. 1971.

48 For a good explanation of 'exemptionalism,' see Charles Doran, *Forgotten Partnership: U.S.-Canada Relations Today* (Baltimore and London, 1984), 21–2; Stanley McDowell, 'Ottawa to Request Exemption from 10% U.S. Tax on Imports,' *Globe and Mail*, 17 Aug. 1971; John Rolfe, 'Cabinet Meets Today on Bid for Exemption from U.S. Tax,' ibid., 18 Aug. 1971; Terrance Wills and John Slinger, 'Further Talks Planned: Canada Fails to Win Escape from Surtax,' ibid., 20 Aug. 1971.

49 SCF, *Canadian Automobile Agreement: Seventh Annual Report of the President to the Congress on the Operation of the Automotive Products Trade Act of 1965, January 24, 1974* (hereafter SCF, *Seventh Annual Report*) (Washington, DC, 1974), 12.

50 For another account of this episode, see J.L. Granatstein and Robert Bothwell, *Pirouette: Pierre Trudeau and Canadian Foreign Policy* (Toronto, 1990), 64–6.

51 However, in late 1971 Assistant Secretary of the Treasury for International Affairs John R. Petty essentially told Canadian representatives how close the auto pact had been to being terminated. Discussing the latest impasse, Petty argued that the agreement was proving unworkable and if it required renegotiation, it should be terminated. This, he noted, 'was the solution commanding large support at Camp David for it had been proposed that one of the August 15 measures would be USA notice to terminate the agreement.' Washington to DEA, 13 Dec. 1971, NAC, RG 19, Vol. 5624, File 8705-2, part 12.

52 J.C. Oliver to file, 20 Aug. 1971, ibid.

53 John Rolfe, 'U.S. Demands an End to Pact Safeguards,' *Globe and Mail*, 29 Sept. 1971; Gordon McGregor, 'Ottawa Wants to Keep Bargaining Point,'

ibid., 29 Sept. 1971; 'Memorandum to the Cabinet: Canada-United States Automotive Products Trade Agreement,' 5 Nov. 1971, NAC, RG 19, Vol. 5625, File 8705-8-16, part 6.

54 Dykes, *Background*, 74.

55 Vianney Carriere, 'PM Reticent on Pact Safeguards,' *Globe and Mail*, 30 Sept. 1971.

56 'Canada-U.S. Trade Discussions, Dec. 16–17, 1971: Automotive Products Agreement,' n.d.; 'Memorandum to the Cabinet: Report on Automotive Products Agreement Discussions with the United States,' 5 Jan. 1972, NAC, RG 19, Vol. 5624, File 8705-2, part 13.

57 'Memorandum for the President: Canadian Trade Negotiations and Your Trip to Canada,' Connally to Nixon, 7 April 1972; 'U.S.–Canada Trade Discussions,' Robert Hormats to Kissinger, 25 April 1972. NARA, Nixon Presidential Files, NSF Canada, Box 671.

58 'Tough Treasury Position on Canada – A Pointless Crisis,' Helmut Sonnenfeldt and Robert Hormats to Kissinger, 4 Feb. 1972, ibid.

59 'Memorandum for the President: Visit of Canadian Prime Minister Trudeau,' Kissenger to Nixon, 4 Dec. 1971, ibid., VIP Visits, Box 912.

60 Ibid.

61 William R. Pearce to John Connally and Peter Flanagan (assistant to the president), 15 Feb. 1972, ibid., WHCF, Box 66.

62 J.H. Stone to Oliver, 29 June 1971, NAC, RG 19, Vol. 5624, File 8705-2, part 12; Grandy to Pepin, 6 Jan. 1972, ibid., part 13.

63 Connally to Flanagan, 15 Feb. 1972.

64 Washington to DEA, 5 Jan. 1972, NAC, RG 19, Vol. 5624, File 8705-2, part 13.

65 SFC, *Canadian Automobile Agreement: United States International Trade Commission Report* (hereafter JFC, *ITC Report*) (Washington, DC, 1976), 455. See also Appendices.

66 Reisman, *Canadian Automotive Industry*, 44.

67 In Canada, opposition to the agreement was rekindled by the return of the deficit, especially among nationalist auto workers. See, e.g., *New Canada*, a labour newspaper that called for the end of the agreement after 1972. Copies can be found in the Alfred Hales Papers at NAC.

68 For more on the Canadian currency in the period, see James Powell, *A History of the Canadian Dollar* (Ottawa, 1999).

69 On the issue of Ford's transfer pricing, see Richard Pound, 'Playing for More,' *CGA Magazine* 33 (Jan., 1999), 56; Greg Keenan, 'Ford Executive Queried Low Earnings,' *Globe and Mail*, 20 June 2001; 'Ford of Canada

Shares Undervalued by Transfer Pricing, Stockholders Complain,' *Canadian Press*, 30 April 2002.
70 SFC, *ITCR* 467.
71 'Memorandum of Conversation: Marcel Cadieux, William Porter, Rufus Smith,' 9 March 1973, NARA, Nixon Presidential Files, WHCF, Canada, CO 26, Box 15, File 1/1/1973.
72 'Memorandum of Conversation: Paul Volcker, Peter Towe,' 1 Feb. 1972, ibid.

Conclusion

1 Not surprisingly, the auto pact does not figure prominently in the historiography of U.S. foreign relations in the 1960s. Although it was considered by many to be one of the most successful trade treaties ever signed, one would be hard-pressed, for instance, to find any reference of the agreement in the copious materials about the pact's American progenitor, Lyndon B. Johnson. In his massive study on the Texan, *Flawed Giant: Lyndon Johnson and His Times* (New York, 1998), Robert Dallek does not even cite the auto agreement. Somewhat more surprising is how little coverage the auto pact receives in Lester Pearson's memoirs or in his official biography. In *The Worldly Years*, John English devotes exactly one line to the agreement. Given its stature as one of the most concrete accomplishments of the Pearson government and its tremendous impact on the Canadian economy and North American auto industry, it is curious indeed that its creators (and their biographers) failed to address the agreement more thoughtfully.
2 This is the conclusion of James F. Keeley, 'Cast in Concrete for all Time: the Negotiation of the Auto Pact,' *Canadian Journal of Political Science* 16, 2 (1983) 294 and Beigie, *An Evaluation*, 110–11. Also see Appendices.
3 For an excellent analysis of this new regime, see Kenneth Thomas, *Capital beyond Borders: States and Firms in the Auto Industry, 1960–1994* (New York, 1996). See also David Leyton-Brown, 'The Mug's Game: Automotive Investment Incentives in Canada and the United States,' *International Journal* 35 (1979–1980), 170–84.
4 Negative U.S. reaction to the new 'special remission orders,' which had been recommended by Reisman in his capacity as a royal commissioner in 1978, is noted by R. Wonnacott, 'The Canada–U.S. Free Trade Agreement and the Auto Pact,' *Trade Monitor* 2 (March, 1988), 6–7, and Gilbert R. Winham, 'The Auto Pact Is Running on Empty: Without the New Free-

Trade Deal, the Old One Will Be in Jeopardy,' *Globe and Mail*, 15 Nov. 1988. By the early 1980s, U.S. deficits in the auto trade reached an $5 billion. For a good, brief view of Canada's automotive relations with Japan, see Klaus Pringsheim, *The Car Wars between Canada and Japan: The State of Affairs in 1983 and the Outlook Beyond* (Toronto, 1983).

5 Canada, *Report of the Royal Commission on the Economic Union and Development Prospects for Canada*, vol. 1 (Ottawa, 1985).

6 For general treatments of the FTA negotiations, see Michael Hart, *Decision at Midnight: Inside the Canada–U.S. Free Trade Negotiations* (Vancouver, 1994); G. Bruce Doern and Brian W. Tomlin, *Faith and Fear: The Free Trade Story* (Toronto, 1991), and Gordon Ritchie, *Wrestling with the Elephant: The Inside Story of the Canada–U.S. Trade Wars* (Toronto, 1997).

7 See, e.g., Ritchie, *Wrestling with the Elephant*, 130–1.

8 Doern and Tomlin, *Faith and Fear*, 83–4.

9 Richard Gwyn noted the irony in the CAW, Canada's most nationalistic union, defending the auto pact, an agreement that utterly continentalized the auto industry. *Nationalism without Walls: The Unbearable Lightness of Being Canadian* (Toronto, 1995), 39–40.

10 During the 1988 free trade election, Mulroney called opponents of the agreement 'nervous Nellies' who had criticized the auto pact in the 1960s; Mulroney saw the auto pact as proof of the benefits that would come from free trade.

11 See, e.g., 'Congressman Wants Changes in Free Trade Auto Pact Provisions,' *Toronto Star*, June 15 1988; Andrea Gordon, 'Wilson Warns of Risk: "Auto Pact dies without trade deal,"' ibid., 1 Nov. 1988.

12 Contemporary commentator, and former Department of Industry official N.B. Macdonald, noted that 'when we read the fine print, it becomes clear that Canada gave way to American demands,' in 'Will the Free Trade Deal Drive a Gaping Hole through the Auto Pact?' *Policy Options* (Jan. 1989), 10.

13 FTA rules emphasized the direct costs of processing and did not include general or administrative expenses. Jon R. Johnson, 'The Effect of the FTA on the Auto Pact,' in Maureen Appel Molot, ed., *Driving Continentally: National Policies and the North American Auto Industry* (Ottawa, 1993), 262–3.

14 For a good discussion of the FTA and the auto pact, see ibid., 267–9.

15 Consequently, the United States allowed its 1965 GATT waiver to lapse following the full implementation of the FTA on 1 Jan. 1998.

16 The list of auto pact companies is found in Part One of Annex 1002.1 of the FTA.

17 For example, Ford of Canada could import Jaguars from the United

Kingdom duty-free under the pact, while Toyota Canada paid duties on any imports of Lexus into Canada.

18 After 1 Jan. 1994 Mexican trucks could enter Canada and the United States duty-free, while passenger vehicles and heavy trucks were subject to small duties (1.3 and 2.4 per cent, respectively). As of 1 Jan. 2003 all vehicles are duty-free as long as they meet the NAFTA rules of origin, which as stated, boosted North American content from 50 to 62.5 per cent. The content changes were viewed by the Japanese transplants as a further discriminatory measure implemented at the behest of the Big Three. For further views on the impact of NAFTA on the North American auto industry, see Lorraine Eden and Maureen Appel Molot, 'The NAFTA's Automotive Provisions: The Next Stage of Managed Trade,' *C.D. Howe Institute Commentary*, no. 53 (Nov. 1993); Jon R. Johnson, 'NAFTA and the Trade in Automotive Goods,' and Peter Morici, 'NAFTA Rules of Origin and Automotive Content Requirements,' in Steven Gooberman and Michael Walker, eds., *Assessing NAFTA: A Trinational Analysis* (Vancouver, 1993); Sidney Weintraub and Christopher Sands, *The North American Auto Industry under NAFTA* (Washington, DC, 1998).

19 For a good, brief explanation of tariff changes post-NAFTA, see Weintraub and Sands, *North American Auto Industry under NAFTA*.

20 World Trade Organization, *Canada – Certain Measures Affecting the Auto Industry, Report of the Panel* (WT/DS139/R, 11 Feb. 2000), 9–16 (hereafter WTO). A downloaded version of this document was minimized from 413 pages to 195 pages, thus the cited page numbers do not correspond to the actual official document.

21 Japan's argument read as follows: 'The effect of the CUSFTA was to prohibit new applicants from qualifying for auto pact status. As a result, contrary to statements made by the Government of Canada's representative before the GATT Working Party, eligibility of the Duty Waiver could no longer be extended to new manufacturers. Since 1 January, 1989, new manufacturers, including Japanese manufacturers, have been barred forever from enjoying the benefit of the duty waiver.' WTO, 18.

22 From the 'Findings' section of the Panel Report, WTO, 168–94.

23 Although one might find it hard to believe, top White House officials felt that the 'Canadian auto problem' might hurt Johnson's election chances in 1964. Bill Brubeck and George Ball, Telephone Conversation, 26 Aug. 1964, LBJ Library, George Ball Papers, Canada I: Telephone Conversations.

24 The U.S. submission to the WTO panel was inconsequential.

25 See Chapter 4.

26 Heather Scofield and Greg Keenan, 'Canada Told to Scrap Auto Pact,' *Globe and Mail*, 14 Oct. 1999; Tony Van Alphen, 'WTO Deals Canada 1–2 Punch: Tariff Changes Ordered to Historic Auto Pact,' *Toronto Star*, 14 Oct. 1999; 'Auto Pact Falls Victim to Globalization,' ibid., editorial, 15 Oct. 1999.

27 While it is unclear as to what the exact cost of the duty might be for the Big Three, numbers as low as $30 million have been cited. This would be a tiny fraction of the over $22 billion in completed vehicles that Canada had imported in recent years.

28 Pardeep Kumar and John Holmes, 'The Impact of NAFTA on the Auto Industry in Canada,' in Weintrub and Sands, *The North American Auto Industry under NAFTA*; Barrie McKenna, 'U.S. Study Concludes Canadian Auto Makers are Surviving NAFTA,' *Globe and Mail*, 12 Jan. 1999.

29 By the end of the 1990s, GM and Ford were wholly owned subsidiaries of their U.S. parents, while Chrysler Canada was a division of DaimlerChrysler, a German-American company.

30 In the United Kingdom, there are no more 'British' car companies, as all of them (notably Jaguar and Rolls Royce) have been bought by 'foreign' (American- and German-based multinationals) companies. In Sweden, which used to boast Saab and Volvo, both companies have been bought by American-based multinationals. Even the U.S. multinationals are not immune to this global concentration in the auto industry, as the takeover of Chrysler by Daimler shows.

31 Surprisingly, given its importance in the Canadian and North American auto sector, there has been no thorough assessment of the evolution of the Canadian parts industry.

32 See the Appendices for production statistics.

33 Steve Erwin, 'Canada "Got Away Light" in Ford Cuts, DesRosiers Says,' *National Post*, 14 Jan. 2002.

34 Notwithstanding continentalization, Canada has recently become an attractive centre for automotive research and development by the Big Three, especially in Windsor, Ontario, where industry-government-academic partnerships such as the AUTO21 initiative at the University of Windsor are proving to be very successful.

35 WTO.

Bibliography

Archival Sources: Canada

National Archives of Canada

Manuscript Records: Personal Papers
  John Diefenbaker
  Donald Fleming
  Walter Gordon
  Howard Charles Green
  Alfred Hayes
  Arnold Heeney
  Paul Martin
  George Nowlan
  Joseph Parkinson
  Lester B. Pearson
  E. Ritchie
  Basil H. Robinson
  Abraham Rotstein
  Mitchell Sharp
  Gerald Stoner

Government of Canada Records
  Department of External Affairs
  Economic Council of Canada
  Records of the Privy Council
  Ministry of Industry
  Ministry of Finance
  Ministry of Trade and Commerce

Other
  Royal Commission on Automobiles
  Royal Commission on Canada's Economic Prospects
  United Automobile Workers, Canadian Section (Canadian Automobile
  Workers)

The Department of Foreign Affairs and International Trade

  File 37-7-1-USA-2: Foreign Trade – Tariff Negotiations – Canada – and
  Canada with other countries – USA – Auto Pact; vols. 1–12, 1964–1968.

University of Toronto Archives

  Vincent Bladen Papers

Other Archives and Institutions

  Ford Motor Company of Canada, Oakville, Ontario
  Canadian Auto Workers Union, Toronto, Ontario
  Dennis DesRosiers Papers, DesRosiers Automotive Consultants, Richmond
  Hill, Ontario

Archival Sources: United States

National Archives of the United States of America
Archives I, Washington, D.C., Legislative Record Center
  U.S. House of Representatives, 89th Congress, Committee on Ways and
  Means

Archives II, College Park, Maryland
  Department of State
  Department of the Treasury
  Department of Commerce
  Bureau of Export Administration

Nixon Presidential Files
  National Security Council Files
  White House Central Files
  White House Confidential Files

White House Staff Papers
  Peter Peterson
  Peter Flanigan

Lyndon B. Johnson Presidential Library (University of Texas, Austin, Texas)

Administration Records
  National Security Files
  White House Central Files
  White House Confidential Files

White House Staff Office Files
  Mike Manatos
  Bill Moyers
  Henry Hall Wilson

Personal Papers
  George Ball
  Francis M. Bator
  Henry H. Fowler

John F. Kennedy Presidential Library (Columbia Point, Massachusetts)

Administration Records
  National Security Files
  Presidential Papers: President's Office Files
  White House Central Files

Other Archives and Manuscripts: Personal Papers
  George Ball
  Jack Behrman
  Douglas Dillon
  Christian Herter
  Luther Hodges
  Nicholas Katzenbach

Oral Histories
  Dean Acheson
  George Aiken
  Averill Harriman

John M. Kelly
Livingstone Merchant
Teno Roncailo
Walt W. Rostow
William R. Tyler
Stewart Udall

Presidential Recordings
Pre-Presidential Files

Harvard Business School, Baker Library (Cambridge, Massachusetts)

Historical Collections, Corporate Reports
   Studebaker Corporation
   Ford Motor Company, Limited
   General Motors Corporation
   Chrysler Corporation
   Borg-Warner Corporation

Walter P. Reuther Library: Archives of Labor and Urban Affairs (Wayne State University, Detroit, Michigan)

George Burt Collection
United Auto Workers: Canadian Regional Office Collection
UAW Presidents Office, Walter P. Reuther Collection
Toronto Sub Regional Office Collection

Albert Gore Research Center *(Middle Tennessee State University, Murfreesboro, Tennessee)*

Albert Gore Papers

Interviews

Simon Reisman, 19 and 20 Dec. 1997
J.F. Grandy, 26 Oct. 1999
Tom Kent, 30 Nov. 1999
C.D. Arthur, 29 Nov. 1999
Philip Trezise, 24 Dec. 1999
J. Warren, 20 April 2000

Walt W. Rostow, 5 May 2000
D. DesRosiers, 20 April 2001

Published Sources

Government Publications: Canada

Bladen, Vincent. *Royal Commission on the Automotive Industry.* Ottawa: Queen's Printer, 1961.
Brecher, Irving, and Simon Reisman. *Royal Commission on Canadian Economic Prospects: Canada–United States Economic Relations.* Ottawa: Queen's Printer, 1957.
– *Debates of the House of Commons.* Ottawa: Queen's Printer, various years.
– *Report of the Royal Commission on the Economic Union and Development Prospects for Canada,* vol. 1. Ottawa: Minister of Supply and Services, 1985.
Department of External Affairs. *External Affairs.* Ottawa: Queen's Printer, various years.
Department of Foreign Affairs and International Trade. *Documents on Canadian External Relations.* Ottawa: Queen's Printer, various years.
Gordon, Walter. *Royal Commission on Canadian Economic Prospects: Final Report.* Ottawa: Queen's Printer, 1957.
Industry Canada, Automotive Branch. *Automotive Industry: Overview and Prospects.* Ottawa: Minister of Supply and Services, 1995.
– *Statistical Review of the Canadian Automotive Industry.* Ottawa: Minister of Supply and Services, 1990.
Reisman, Simon S. *The Canadian Automotive Industry: Performance and Proposals.* Ottawa: Minister of Supply and Services, 1978.
Sun Life Assurance Co. of Canada. *The Canadian Automotive Industry.* Ottawa: Queen's Printer, 1956.
Woods, J.D., and Gordon Ltd. *Royal Commission on Canadian Economic Prospects: The Canadian Agricultural Machinery Industry.* Ottawa: Queen's Printer, 1956.
Young, John H. *Royal Commission on Canadian Economic Prospects: Canadian Commercial Policy.* Ottawa: Queen's Printer, 1957.

Government Publications: Province of Ontario

Ministry of Treasury, Economics and Intergovernmental Affairs (Ontario). *Canada's Share of the North American Automotive Industry: An Ontario Perspective.* Toronto: Queen's Printer of Ontario, 1978.

Government Publications: United States

House of Representatives. *Special Report on the Joint Review of the United States Canada Automotive Products Trade Agreement*. Document No. 379, 4 Sept. 1968. Washington, DC: Government Printing Office, 1968.

Senate Finance Committee. *Canadian Automobile Agreement: Annual Reports of the President to the Congress on the Implementation of the Automotive Products Trade Agreement*. Washington, DC: Government Printing Office, various years.

– *Canadian Automobile Agreement: Hearing Before the Committee on Finance, United States Senate*. Washington, DC: Government Printing Office, 1968.

– *Canadian Automobile Agreement: United States International Trade Commission Report on the US-Canadian Automotive Agreement: Its History, Terms and Impact*. Washington, DC: Government Printing Office, 1976.

– *United States–Canada Automobile Agreement: Hearings Before the Committee on Finance, United States Senate, on H.R. 9042, September 14, 15, 16, 20 and 21, 1965*. Washington, DC: Government Printing Office, 1965.

Senate Foreign Relations Committee. *Automotive Products Agreement Between the United States and Canada: Hearing Before a Subcommittee of the Committee on Foreign Relations, 10 February, 1965*. Washington, DC: Government Printing Office, 1965.

United States. *Congressional Record, Senate and House of Representatives*. Washington, DC: Government Printing Office, various years.

– *Department of State Bulletin*. Washington, DC: Government Printing Office, various years.

– *The Foreign Relations of the United States*. Washington, DC: United States Government Printing Office, various years.

– *United States Federal Register*. Washington, DC: Government Printing Office, various years.

Non-Governmental Organization Publications

General Agreement on Tariffs and Trade, *Basic Instruments and Selected Documents*. Geneva, various years.

Books, Articles, and Theses

Acheson, Dean. 'Canada: Stern Daughter of the Voice of God.' In Livingston Merchant, ed., *Neighbours Taken for Granted: Canada and the United States*. New York: Praeger, 1966.

Afza, Talat. 'The U.S.–Canadian Auto Pact of 1965: A case study of sectoral trade liberalisation.' PhD diss., Wayne State University, 1988.

Alexander, W.E. *An Econometric Model of Canadian–U.S. Trade in Automotive Products, 1965–1971.* Ottawa: Bank of Canada, 1974.

Alper, Donald K., and James Loucky, 'North American Integration: Paradoxes and Prospects.' *American Review of Canadian Studies* 26, 2 (1996), 177–82.

Anastakis, Dimitry. 'Between Nationalism and Continentalism: State Auto Industry Intervention and the Canadian UAW, 1960–1970.' *Labour / Le Travail* 53 (Spring, 2004), 87–124.

– 'Building a "New Nova Scotia": State Intervention, the Auto Industry and the Case of Volvo in Halifax, 1963–1998.' *Acadiensis* 34 (Autumn, 2004), 3–30.

– 'From Independence to Integration: The Corporate Evolution of the Ford Motor Company of Canada, 1904–2004.' *Business History Review* 78 (Summer, 2004), 213–53.

– 'Requiem for a Trade Agreement: The Auto Pact at the WTO, 1999–2000.' *Canadian Business Law Journal* 34, 3 (2000), 313–35.

Arnold, Samuel. 'The Impact of the Automotive Trade Agreement between Canada and the United States.' Master's Thesis. Montreal: McGill University, 1969.

Ankli, Robert E., and Fred Frederiksen. 'The influence of American Manufacturers on the Canadian Automobile Industry.' *Business and Economic History* 9 (1981), 101–16.

Armstrong, Christopher, and H.V. Nelles. *Southern Exposure: Canadian Promoters in Latin America and the Caribbean, 1896–1930.* Toronto: University of Toronto Press, 1988.

Armstrong, Willis C., 'The American Perspective.' In H. Edward English, ed., *Canada–United States Relations.* New York: Praeger, 1976.

Arnold, Samuel. 'The Impact of the Automotive Trade Agreement between Canada and the United States.' Master's thesis, McGill University, 1969.

Asher, Robert, and Ronald Edsforth, eds. *Autowork.* Albany: State University of New York Press, 1995.

Axline, Andrew, P.V. Lyon, M.A. Molot, J. Hyndman, eds. *Continental Community? Independence and Integration in North America.* Toronto: McClelland and Stewart, 1974.

Axworthy, Tom. 'Innovation and the Party System: An Examination of the Career of Walter L. Gordon and the Liberal Party.' Master's thesis, Queen's University, 1970.

Azzi, Stephen. *Walter Gordon and the Rise of Canadian Nationalism.* Montreal and Kingston: McGill-Queen's University Press, 1999.

Ball, George. *The Discipline of Power: Essentials of a Modern World Structure.* Boston and Toronto: Little, Brown, 1968.

- 'Overview of Canadian-U.S. Relations.' In Edwards R. Fried and Philip H. Trezise, eds., *U.S.–Canadian Economic Relations: Next Steps?* Washington, DC: Brookings Institution, 1984.
Barry, Donald. 'Eisenhower, St. Laurent and Free Trade, 1953.' *International Perspectives* (March/April, 1987), 8–11.
Beck, J. Murray. *Pendulum of Power: Canada's Federal Elections.* Scarborough, ON: Prentice-Hall, 1968.
Behrman, Jack N. 'International Sectoral Integration: An Alternative Approach to Freer Trade.' *Journal of World Trade Law* 6, 3 (1972), 269–83.
- 'The Automotive Agreement of 1965: A Case Study in Canadian-American Economic Affairs.' In Richard A., Preston, ed., *The Influence of the United States on Canadian Development: Eleven Case Studies.* Durham, NC: Duke University Press, 1972.
Beigie, Carl. *The Canada-U.S. Automotive Agreement.* Montreal: Canadian-American Committee, 1970.
Bennett, Douglas C., and Kenneth E. Sharpe. *Transnational Corporations versus the State: The Political Economy of the Mexican Auto Industry.* Princeton, NJ: Princeton University Press, 1985.
Berger, Carl. *The Writing of Canadian History.* Oxford: Oxford University Press, 1976.
Bladen, Vincent. *Bladen on Bladen.* Toronto: University of Toronto Press, 1978.
Blanchette, Arthur. *Canadian Foreign Policy, 1955–1965: Selected Speeches and Documents.* Toronto: McClelland and Stewart, 1977.
- *Canadian Foreign Policy, 1966–1976: Selected Speeches and Documents.* Toronto: Gage, 1980.
Bliss, Michael. *Northern Enterprise: Five Centuries of Canadian Business.* Toronto: McClelland and Stewart, 1987.
Boland, F.J., ed. *Fourth Seminar on Canadian-American Relations at Assumption University of Windsor, November 8, 9, 10, 1962.* Windsor: Assumption University, 1962.
Bothwell, Robert. *Lester Pearson: His Life and World.* Toronto: MHR 1978.
Bothwell, Robert, Ian Drummond, and John English. *Canada Since 1945: Power, Politics, and Provincialism.* Toronto: University of Toronto Press 1989.
Boyle, Kevin. *The UAW and the Heyday of American Liberalism, 1945–1968.* Ithaca, NY: Cornell University Press, 1995.
Brands, H.W. *The Foreign Policies of Lyndon Johnson: Beyond Vietnam.* College Station, TX: Texas A&M University Press, 1999.
Bryce, R.B. *Maturing in Hard Times: Canada's Department of Finance through the Great Depression.* Kingston and Montreal: McGill-Queen's University Press, 1986.

Bryce, R.B., and David W. Slater. *War Finance and Reconstruction: The Role of Canada's Department of Finance, 1939–1946*. Ottawa, 1995. (David W. Slater, self-published)

Canadian-American Committee. *Toward a More Realistic Appraisal of the Automotive Agreement*. Washington, DC: National Planning Association, 1970.

Canadian Automobile Chamber of Commerce. *Facts and Figures of the Automobile Industry*. Toronto: Canadian Automobile Chamber of Commerce, 1934–1957.

Canadian Who's Who. Toronto: Who's Who Canadian Publications, various years.

Clarke, Frank. 'Divided Within: Economic Nationalism within the Liberal Party of Canada, 1963–1968.' Master's thesis, University of Waterloo, 1992.

Clarkson, Stephen, ed. *An Independent Foreign Policy for Canada?* Toronto: McClelland and Stewart, 1968.

Clement, Wallace. *Continental Corporate Power: Economic Elite Linkages between Canada and the United States*. Toronto: McClelland and Stewart, 1977.

Cohen, Andrew, and J.L. Granatstein. *Trudeau's Shadow: The Life and Legacy of Pierre Elliot Trudeau*. Toronto: Random House Canada, 1998.

Cohen, Warren I., and Nancy Berkhopf Tucker, eds. *Lyndon Johnson Confronts the World: American Foreign Policy, 1963–1968*. New York: Cambridge University Press, 1994.

Conrad, Margaret. *George Nowlan: Maritime Conservative in National Politics*. Toronto: University of Toronto Press, 1986.

Cook, Ramsay, and R.C. Brown. *A Nation Transformed: Canada, 1896–1921*. Toronto: McClelland and Stewart, 1974.

Cooper, Richard. 'Trade Policy as Foreign Policy.' In Robert Stern, ed., *U.S. Trade Policy in a Changing World Economy*. Cambridge, MA: MIT Press, 1988.

Courchene, Thomas J., with Colin R. Telmer. *From Heartland to North American Region State: The Social, Fiscal and Federal Evolution of Ontario*. Toronto: University of Toronto Press, 1998.

Cowan, Ralph. 'Effects of the United States-Canadian Automotive Agreement On Canada's Manufacturing, Trade and Price Posture.' PhD diss., University of Michigan, 1972.

– ed. *The North American Automobile Industry: Shaping a Dynamic Global Posture*. Windsor: Institute for Canadian-American Studies, 1983.

Creighton, Donald. *John A. Macdonald: The Old Chieftain*. Toronto: Macmillan, 1955.

Crispo, John. *International Unionism: A Study in Canadian-American Relations*. Toronto: McGraw-Hill, 1967.

Critchlow, Donald T. *Studebaker: The Life and Death of An American Coroporation*. Bloomington: Indiana University Press, 1996.

Crosby, Ann Denholm. *Dilemmas in Defence Decision-Making: Constructing Canada's Role in NORAD, 1958–1996*. New York: St Martin's Press, 1998.

Cuff, R.D., and J.L.Granatstein. *American Dollars – Canadian Prosperity: Canadian-American Economic Relations, 1945–1950*. Toronto: Samuel-Stevens, 1978.

– *Canadian–American Relations in Wartime: From the Great War to the Cold War*. Toronto: Hakkert, 1975.

Dales, J.H. *The Protective Tariff on Canada's Development: Eight Essays on Trade and Tariffs When Factors Move with Special Reference to Canadian Protectionism, 1870–1955*. Toronto: University of Toronto Press, 1966.

Dallek, Robert. *Flawed Giant: Lyndon Johnson and His Times, 1961–1973*. New York: Oxford University Press, 1998.

Davis, Donald F. "Dependent Motorization: Canada and the Automobile to the 1930s." In Douglas McCalla, ed., *The Development of Canadian Capitalism: Essays in Business History*. Toronto: Copp Clark Pitman, 1990.

Diebold, William, ed. *Bilateralism, Multilateralism and Canada in U.S. Trade Policy*. Cambridge, MA: Ballinger, 1988.

Diefenbaker, John. *One Canada: Memoirs of the Right Honourable John G. Diefenbaker*, 2 vols. Toronto: Macmillan, 1975.

Donaghy, Greg. 'A Continental Philosophy: Canada, the United States and the Negotiation of the Auto Pact, 1963–1965.' *International Journal* 52, 3 (1998), 441–64.

– *Tolerant Allies: Canada and the United States, 1963–1968*. Kingston and Montreal: McGill-Queen's University Press, 2002.

Doran, Charles F. 'Coping with the "Shock Factor" in Canada-U.S. Commercial Relations.' In Earl H Fry and Lee H. Radebaugh, eds., *Canada–U.S. Economic Relations in the 'Conservative' Era of Mulroney and Reagan*. Provo, Utah: Brigham Young University, 1984.

– *Forgotten Partnership: U.S.–Canada Relations Today*. Baltimore: Johns Hopkins University Press, 1984.

Dykeman, Wilma. *Tennessee: A Bicentennial History*. New York: W.W. Norton, 1975.

Dykes, James G. *Background on the Canada–United States Automotive Products Trade Agreement*. Toronto: Motor Vehicle Manufacturers Association, 1979.

– *Canada's Automotive Industry*. Toronto: McGraw-Hill, 1970.

Eden, Lorraine, and Maureen Appel Molot. *Continentalizing the North American Auto Industry*. Ottawa: Centre for Trade Policy and Law, 1992.

Edwards, Charles E. *Dynamics of the United States Automobile Industry*. Columbia: University of South Carolina Press, 1965.

Emerson, David L. *Production, Location and the Automotive Agreement*. Ottawa: Economic Council of Canada, 1975.

Empire Club of Canada. *Addresses of the Empire Club of Canada.* Toronto: T.H. Best Printing Co., various years.

English, H. Edward. 'Foreign Investment in Manufacturing.' In H. Edward, English, ed., *Canada-United States Relations.* New York: Preager, 1976.

– *Industrial Structure in Canada's International Competitive Position: A Study of the Factors Affecting Economies of Scale and Specialization in Canadian Manufacturing.* Montreal: Private Planning Association, 1964.

– *International Economic Integration and National Policy Diversity.* Ottawa: Carleton University Press, 1990.

English, John. *The Worldly Years: The Life of Lester Pearson, 1949–1972.* Toronto: Knopf, 1992.

Feldman, Elliot J., and Lily Gardner Feldman. 'The Special Relationship between Canada and the United States.' *Jerusalem Journal of International Relations* 4, 4 (1980), 56–85.

Finlayson, Jock A. 'Canada, Congress and U.S. Foreign Economic Policy.' In Denis Stairs and Gilbert R. Winham, eds., *The Politics of Canada's Economic Relationship with the United States.* Toronto: University of Toronto Press, 1985.

– 'Canadian International Economic Policy: Context, Issues and a Review of Some Recent Literature.' Denis Stairs and Gilbert R. Winham, research coordinators, *Canada and the International Political/Economic Environment.* Toronto: University of Toronto Press, 1985.

Fleming, Donald. *So Very Near: The Political Memoirs of the Hon. Donald M. Fleming.* Toronto: McClelland and Stewart, 1985.

Flynn, David Michael. 'The Rationalization of the United States and Canadian Automotive Industry, 1960–1975.' PhD diss., University of Massachusetts, 1979.

Ford Motor Company of Canada, Ltd. *Some General Aspects of the Canadian Customs Tariff, the National Economy, and the Automobile Industry in Canada.* Windsor, Ontario, 1938.

Fox, Annette Baker, Alfred O. Hero, Jr, and Joseph S. Nye, eds. *Canada and the United States: Transnational and Transgovernmental Relations.* New York: Columbia University Press, 1976.

Frayne, A., A. Chumack, and R. MacDonald, *Perspectives on the Automobile in Canada.* Ottawa: Transport Canada, 1977.

Free Trade and the Auto Pact: Proceedings of the Seminar at the Centre for Canadian-American Studies, Windsor, Ontario. Windsor, ON: University of Windsor Press, 1988.

Fry, Earl H. 'Canada's Investment Policies: An American Perspective.' In Peter Karl Kresl, ed., *Seen From the South.* Provo, Utah: Brigham Young University, 1989.

– *The Politics of International Investment*. New York: McGraw-Hill, 1983.
Ghent, Jocelyn. 'Canada, the United States and the Cuban Missile Crisis.' *Pacific Historical Review* 58, 2 (1979) 159–84.
– 'Did He Fall or Was He Pushed? The Kennedy Administration and the Collapse of the Diefenbaker Government.' *International History Review* 1, 2 (1979), 246–70.
Gindin, Sam. 'Breaking Away: The Formation of the Canadian Auto Workers.' *Studies in Political Economy* 29 (Summer, 1989), 63–89.
– *The Canadian Auto Workers: The Birth and Transformation of a Union*. Toronto: Lorimer, 1995.
Globerman, Steven, and Michael Walker, eds. *Assessing NAFTA: A Trinational Analysis*. Vancouver: The Fraser Institute, 1993.
Godfrey, David, and Mel Watkins, eds. *Gordon to Watkins to You, Documentary: The Battle for Control of Our Economy*. Toronto: New Press, 1970.
Gordon, Walter L. *A Choice for Canada*. Toronto: McClelland and Stewart, 1966.
– *A Political Memoir*. Toronto: McClelland and Stewart, 1977.
– *Storm Signals: New Economic Policies for Canada*. Toronto: McClelland and Stewart, 1975.
– *Troubled Canada: The Need for New Domestic Policies*. McClelland and Stewart, 1961.
– *What Is Happening to Canada*. Toronto: McClelland and Stewart, 1978.
Gore, Albert. *The Eye of the Storm: A People's Politics for the Seventies*. New York: Herder and Herder, 1970.
– *Let the Glory Out: My South and Its Politics*. New York: Viking Press, 1972.
Gotlieb, Allan. *'I'll Be With You in a Minute, Mr. Ambassador': The Education of a Canadian Diplomat in Washington*. Toronto: University of Toronto Press, 1991.
Grady, Patrick Michael. 'The Canadian Exemption from the United States Interest Equalization Tax.' PhD diss., University of Toronto, 1973.
Graham, Gene. 'Gore's Lost Cause.' *New South* 26, 1 (1971), 26–34.
Granatstein, J.L. *Canada, 1957–1967: The Years of Uncertainty and Innovation*. Toronto: McClelland and Stewart, 1986.
– 'Cooperation and Conflict: The Course of Canadian-American Relations Since 1945.' In Charles F. Doran and John H. Sigler, eds., *Canada and the United States: Enduring Friendship, Permanent Stress*. Englewood Cliffs, NJ: Prentice-Hall, 1985.
– 'Free Trade between Canada and the United States: The Issue That Will Not Go Away.' In Denis Stairs and Gilbert R. Winham, eds., *The Politics of Canada's Economic Relationship with the United States*. Toronto: University of Toronto Press, 1985.
– *A Man of Influence*. Toronto: Deneau, 1981.

– *The Ottawa Men: The Civil Service Mandarins, 1935–1957*. Oxford: Oxford University Press, 1982.

– 'When Push Comes to Shove: Canada and the United States." In Thomas G. Patterson, ed., *Kennedy's Quest for Victory: American Foreign Policy 1961–1963*. New York: Oxford University Press, 1989.

– ed. *Canadian Foreign Policy: Historical Readings*. Toronto: Copp Clarke Pitman, 1986.

Granatstein, J.L., and Robert Bothwell. *Pirouette: Pierre Trudeau and Canadian Foreign Policy*. Toronto: University of Toronto Press, 1990.

Grant, George M. *Lament for a Nation: The Defeat of Canadian Nationalism*. Toronto: McClelland and Stewart, 1965.

Green, William C., and Ernest J. Yanarella, eds. *North American Auto Unions in Crisis: Lean Production as Contested Terrain*. Albany: State University of New York Press, 1996.

Grey, Rodney de C. *Trade Policy in the 1980s: An Agenda for Canada–U.S. Relations*. Calgary: C.D. Howe Institute, 1981.

Gwyn, Richard. *The 49th Paradox*. Toronto: McClelland and Stewart, 1985.

– *Nationalism Without Walls: The Unbearable Lightness of Being Canadian*. Toronto: McClelland and Stewart, 1995.

– *The Scope of Scandal: A Government in Crisis*. Toronto: Clarke-Irwin 1965.

Halberstram, David. 'The End of a Populist.' *Harper's* 242 (Jan. 1971), 25–45.

– *The Reckoning*. New York: Morrow, 1986.

Hart, Michael. 'Almost But Not Quite: The 1947–1948 Bilateral Canada–U.S. Negotiations.' *American Review of Canadian Studies* 19, 1 (1989), 25–58.

– 'Canada at the GATT: Twenty Years of Canadian Tradecraft, 1947–1967.' *International Journal* 52, 4 (1997), 581–608.

– *Fifty Years of Canadian Tradecraft: Canada at the GATT, 1947–1997*. Ottawa: Centre for Trade Policy and Law, 1998.

– 'GATT Article XXIV and Canada-United States Trade Negotiations.' *Review of International Business Law* 1 (1987) 317–55.

– *A Trading Nation: Canadian Trade Policy from Colonialism to Globalization*. Vancouver: UBC Press, 2002.

Hecht, Irene W.D. 'Israel D. Andrews and the Reciprocity Treaty of 1854: A Reappraisal.' *Canadian Historical Review* 44, 4 (1963), 313–29.

– 'Washington Under Two Presidents: 1953–1959; 1959–1962.' *International Journal* 22 (1967), 500–11.

Heeney, A.D.P., and Livingston T. Merchant, *Canada and the United States: Principles For Partnership*. Ottawa: Queen's Printer, 1965.

– *The United States–Canadian Automobile Agreement: A Study in Industrial Adjustment*. Ann Arbor: University of Michigan Press, 1967.

Hillmer, Norman, ed. *Partners Nevertheless: Canadian-American Relations in the Twentieth Century*. Toronto: Copp Clark Pitman, 1989.
– *Pearson: Unlikely Gladiator*. Montreal and Kingston: Queen's University Press, 1999.
Hodgetts, J.E. *The Canadian Public Service, 1867–1970*. Toronto: University of Toronto Press, 1973.
Holmes, John. *The Break Up of an International Labour Union: Uneven Development in the North American Auto Industry and the Schism in the UAW*. Kingston: Queen's University Press, 1990.
– *Divergent Paths: Restructuring Industrial Relations in the North American Auto Industry*. Kingston: Queen's University Press, 1992.
– 'Industrial Reorganization, Capital Restructuring and Locational Change: An Analysis of the Canadian Automobile Industry in the 1960s.' *Economic Geography* 59 (1983), 251–67.
Holmes, John W. *Life with Uncle: The Canadian-American Relationship*. Toronto: University of Toronto Press, 1981.
– 'Merchant-Heeney Revisited: A Sentimental Overview.' In Laure McKinsey and Kim Richard Nossal, eds., *America's Alliances and Canadian-American Relations*. Toronto: Summerhill, 1988.
Hood, Hugh. *The Motor Boys in Ottawa: A Novel*. Toronto: Stoddart, 1986.
Iacocca, Lee. *Iacocca: an Autobiography*. Toronto: Bantam Books, 1986.
Jackson, John. 'The Puzzle of the GATT.' *World Trade Law Journal* 1 (1967), 131–61.
James, Warren. *Wartime Economic Co-Operation: A Study of Relations Between Canada and the United States*. Toronto: Ryerson, 1949.
Johnson, Harry. 'The Bladen Plan or Increased Protection of the Canadian Automotive Industry.' *Canadian Journal of Economics and Political Science* 29 (May, 1963), 212–38.
Johnson, Jon R. 'The Effect of the Canadian-U.S. Free Trade Agreement on the Auto Pact.' In Maureen Appel Molot, ed., *Driving Continentally: National Policies and the North American Auto Policy*. Ottawa: Carleton University Press, 1993.
Kealey, Gregory S. *Toronto Workers Respond to Industrial Capitalism, 1867–1892*. Toronto: University of Toronto Press, 1980.
Keeley, James F. 'Cast in Concrete for All Time? The Negotiation of the Auto Pact.' *Canadian Journal of Political Science* 16, 2 (1983), 281–98.
– 'Constraints on Canadian International Economic Policy.' PhD diss., Stanford University, 1980.
Kent, Tom. *A Public Purpose: An Experience of Liberal Opposition and Canadian Government*. Montreal and Kingston: McGill-Queen's University Press, 1988.

Keohane, Robert O., and Joseph S. Nye. *Power and Interdependence: World Politics in Transition*. New York: HarperCollins, 1989.

Kirton, John. "The Consequences of Integration: The Case of the Defence Production Sharing Agreements." In W. Andrew Axline, ed., *Continental Community? Independence and Integration in North America*. Toronto: McClelland and Stewart, 1974.

– 'The Politics of Bilateral Management: The Case of the Automotive Trade.' *International Journal* 36 (1980–1), 39–69.

Kirton, John, and John Gerard Ruggie. 'The North American Political Economy in the Global Context: An Analytical Framework.' *International Journal* 42 (Winter, 1986–7).

Kronish, Rich, and Kenneth S. Mericle, eds. *The Political Economy of the Latin American Motor Vehicle Industry*. Cambridge, MA: MIT Press, 1984.

Krugman, Paul. *The Age of Diminished Expectations: U.S. Economic Policy in the 1990s*. Cambridge, Mass: MIT Press, 1990.

Kumar, Pradeep. *Change, But in What Direction? Divergent Union Responses to Work Restructuring in the Integrated North American Auto Industry*. Kingston: Queen's University Press, 1993.

– *Continuity and Change: Evolving Human Resource Policies and Practices in the Canadian Automobile Industry*. Montreal and Kingston: McGill-Queen's University Press, 1996.

LaMarsh, Judy. *Memoirs of a Bird in a Gilded Cage*. Toronto: McClelland and Stewart, 1969.

Lavelle, Patrick J., and Robert White. *An Automotive Strategy for Canada*. Ottawa: Ministry of Supply and Services, 1983.

Laxer, Robert, ed. *(Canada) Ltd.: The Political Economy of Dependency*. Toronto: McClelland and Stewart, 1973.

Lea, Sperry. *A Canada–U.S. Free Trade Agreement: Survey of Possible Characteristics*. Washington, DC, and Montreal: Canadian-American Committee, 1963.

Leach, Richard. 'Canada and the United States: A Special Relationship.' *Current History*, 12, 426 (1977), 145–9.

Levitt, Kari. *Silent Surrender: The Multinational Corporation in Canada*. Toronto: MAC, 1970.

Lichtenstein, Nelson. *The Most Dangerous Man in Detroit: Walter Reuther and the Fate of American Labour*. New York: Basic Books, 1995.

Lipsey, Richard G. 'Canada and the United States: The Economic Dimension.' In Charles F. Doran and John H. Sigler, eds. *Canada and the United States: Enduring Friendship, Persistent Stress*. Englewood Cliffs, NJ: Prentice-Hall, 1985.

Litvak, I.A., C.J. Maule, and R.D. Robinson. *Dual Loyalty: Canadian-U.S. Business Arrangements*. Toronto: McGraw-Hill, 1971.

Lumsden, Ian, ed. *Close the 49th Parallel Etc.: The Americanization of Canada*. Toronto: University of Toronto Press, 1970.

Lyon, Peyton. 'The Canadian Perspective.' In H. Edward English, ed., *Canada–United States Relations*. New York: Praeger, 1976.

Macdonald, N.B. 'A Comment: The Bladen Plan For Increased Protection for the Automotive Industry.' *Canadian Journal of Economics and Political Science* 29, 4 (1963).

– 'Will the Free Trade Deal Drive a Gaping Hole through the Auto Pact?' *Policy Options* 10, 1 (1989), 10–17.

Mackenzie, Kenneth C. *Tariff-Making and Trade Policy in the U.S. and Canada: A Comparative Study*. New York: Praeger, 1969.

Mahant, E.E. *Free Trade in American-Canadian Relations*. Melbourne: Krieger, 1993.

Mahant, E.E., and G.S. Mount. *An Introduction to Canadian-American Relations*. Toronto: Methuen, 1984.

Malmgren, Harald B. 'The Evolving Trade System.' In H. Edward English, ed., *Canada-United States Relations*. New York: Praeger, 1976.

Martin, Lawrence. *The Presidents and the Prime Ministers, Washington and Ottawa Face to Face: The Myth of Bilateral Bliss, 1867–1982*. Toronto: Doubleday Canada, 1982.

Martin, Paul. *A Very Public Life*, vol. 2, *So Many Worlds*. Toronto: Deneau, 1985.

Masson, Francis, and H. Edward English. *Invisible Trade Barriers between Canada and the United States*. Washington, DC: National Planning Association, 1963.

Masson, Francis, and J.B. Whitley. *Barriers to Trade between Canada and the United States*. Montreal: Canadian-American Committee, 1960.

Mathias, Philip. *Forced Growth: Five Studies of Government Involvement in the Development of Canada*. Toronto: Lewis and Samuel, 1971.

Matusow, Allan J. *Nixon's Economy: Booms, Busts, Dollars and Votes*. Lawrence: University of Kansas Press, 1998.

Maxcy, George. *The Multinational Automobile Industry*. New York: St. Martin's, Press, 1981.

McCall, Christina, and Stephen Clarkson. *Trudeau and Our Times*, 2 vols. Toronto: McClelland and Stewart, 1990, 1994.

McCalla, Douglas, ed. *The Development of Canadian Capitalism*. Toronto: Copp Clark Pitman, 1990.

McDiarmid, O.J. 'Some Aspects of the Canadian Automobile Industry.' *Canadian Journal of Economics and Political Science* 12 (1948).

– *Commercial Policy in the Canadian Economy*. Cambridge: Harvard University Press, 1946.

McGraw-Hill. *McGraw-Hill Directory and Almanac of Canada*. Toronto: McGrawHill, various years.

Metzger, Stanley. 'The United States-Canada Automotive Products Agreement of 1965.' *World Trade Law Journal* 1, 1 (1967), 104–9.

Middlemiss, Danford W. 'Defence Co-Operation.' In Norman Hillmer, ed., *Partners Nevertheless: Canadian-American Relations in the Twentieth Century*. Toronto: Copp Clark Pitman, 1989.

Milkman, Ruth. *Farewell to the Factory: Auto Workers in the late Twentieth Century*. Berkeley: University of California Press, 1997.

Molot, Maureen Appel, ed. *Driving Continentally: National Policies and the North American Auto Industry*. Ottawa: Carleton University Press, 1993.

Molot, Maureen Appel, and Lorraine Eden. 'The NAFTA's Automotive Provisions: The Next Stage of Managed Trade.' *C.D. Howe Institute Commentary* 53 (Nov. 1993), 1–24.

Morici, Peter, Arthur J.R. Smith, and Sperry Lea. 'Canadian–U.S. Trade Relations.' In Peter Karl Kresl, ed., *Seen From the South*. Provo, Utah: Brigham Young University, 1989.

Moritz, Michael. *Going for Broke: The Chrysler Story*. Garden City, NY: Doubleday, 1981.

Moroz, Andrew R. *Canada–United States Automotive Trade and Trade Policy Issues*. University of Western Ontario, Department of Economics, 1983.

Nash, Knowlton. *Kennedy and Diefenbaker: The Feud that Helped Topple a Government*. Toronto: McClelland and Stewart, 1990.

National Liberal Federation. *Report of the Proceedings of the National Liberal Convention 1958*. Ottawa: National Printers Ltd., 1958.

Neisser, Albert C. 'The Impact of the Canada-United States Automotive Agreement on Canada's Motor Vehicle Industry: A Study in Economies of Scale.' PhD dissertation, University of Michigan, 1966.

Newman, Peter C. *The Distemper of Our Times: Canadian Politics in Transition, 1963–1968*. Toronto: McClelland and Stewart, 1968.

– *Renegade in Power: The Diefenbaker Years*. Toronto: McClelland and Stewart, 1963.

Norrie, Kenneth, and Douglas Owram. *History of the Canadian Economy*. 2nd ed. Toronto: Harcourt Brace, 1996.

Nossal, Kim Richard. 'Economic Nationalism and Continental Integration: Assumptions, Arguments and Advocacies.' In Denis Stairs and Gilbert R. Winham, eds., *The Politics of Canada's Economic Relationship with the United States*. Toronto: University of Toronto Press, 1985.

Owram, Douglas. *The Government Generation: Canadian Intellectuals and the State, 1900–1945*. Toronto: University of Toronto Press, 1986.

Patterson, Thomas G., ed. *Kennedy's Quest for Victory: American Foreign Policy 1961–1963*. New York: Oxford University Press, 1989.

Pearson, Lester B. *Democracy in World Politics*. Toronto: S.J. Reynolds Saunders, 1955.

– *Mike: The Memoirs of the Right Honourable Lester B. Pearson*. vol. 3, *1957–1968*. Toronto: Universtity of Toronto Press, 1975.

Perras, Galen Roger. *Franklin Roosevelt and the Origins of the Canadian-American Security Alliance, 1933–1945: Necessary, But Not Necessary Enough*. Westport, Conn.: Praeger, 1998.

Perry, Ross. *The Future of Canada's Auto Industry: The Big Three and the Japanese Challenge*. Toronto: Lorimer, 1982.

Pickersgill, J.W., and D. Forster, eds. *The Mackenzie King Record*. Toronto: University of Toronto Press, 1960–70.

Powell, James. *A History of the Canadian Dollar*. Ottawa: Bank of Canada, 1999.

Price, David, and Michael Lupfer. 'On the Merits of Face-to-Face Campaigning.' *Social Science Quarterly* 53, 1 (1972), 534–43.

– 'Volunteers for Gore: The Impact of a Precinct Level Canvass in Three Tennessee Cities.' *Journal of Politics* 35 (1973), 410–38.

Rae, John B. *The American Automobile Industry*. Boston: Twayne. 1984.

Regenstrief, Peter. *The Diefenbaker Interlude: Parties and Voting in Canada: An Interpretation*. Toronto: Longmans, 1965.

Reisman, Simon S. 'The Issue of Free Trade.' In Edward R. Fried and Philip H. Trezise, eds., *U.S.–Canadian Relations: Next Steps?* Washington, DC: Brookings Institution, 1984.

– 'The Relevance of the Auto Pact to Other Sectoral Arrangements.' *Canada-United States Law Journal* 10 (1985), 75–84.

Reuber, Grant L. *The Growth and Changing Composition of Trade between Canada and the United States*. Montreal: Canadian–American Committee, 1960.

Ritchie, Charles. *Storm Signals: More Undiplomatic Diaries, 1962–1971*. Toronto: Macmillan, 1983.

Ritchie, Gordon. *Wrestling with the Elephant: The Inside Story of the Canada–US Trade Wars*. Toronto: Macfarlane Walter and Ross, 1997.

Robertson, Heather. *Driving Force: The McLaughlin Family and the Age of the Car*. Toronto: McClelland and Stewart, 1995.

Robinson, H. Basil. *Diefenbaker's World: A Populist in World Affairs*. Toronto: University of Toronto Press, 1989.

Rossignol, Michel. *NORAD: Its History and New Challenges*. Ottawa: Library of Parliament, 1991.

Safarian, A.E. *Foreign Ownership of Canadian Industry*. Toronto: McGraw-Hill, 1966.

Saywell, J.T., ed. *The Canadian Annual Review*. Toronto: University of Toronto Press, various years.

Schwartz, Mildred A. *Public Opinion and Canadian Identity*. Scarborough: Fitzhenry and Whiteside, 1967.

Sekaly, Raymond R. *Transnationalization of the Automotive Industry*. Ottawa: University of Ottawa Press, 1981.

Shapiro, Helen. *Engines of Growth: The State and Transnational Auto Companies in Brazil*. Cambridge: Cambridge University Press, 1994.

Sharp, Mitchell. 'Canada's Independence and U.S. Domination.' In Edward R. Fried and Philip H. Trezise, eds., *U.S.-Canadian Economic Relations: Next Steps?* Washington, DC: Brookings Institution, 1984.

– *'Which Reminds Me ... A Memoir.'* Toronto: University of Toronto Press, 1994.

Smith, Denis. *Gentle Patriot: A Political Biography of Walter Gordon*. Edmonton: Hurtig, 1973.

Speigel, Steven L., and Kenneth N. Waltz. *Conflict in World Politics*. Cambridge, Mass.: Winthrop Publishers, 1971.

Spencer, Robert, John Kirton, and Kim Richard Nossal, eds. *The IJC Seventy Years On*. Toronto: Centre for International Studies, 1981.

State of the Ark: The Economic Decline of the North American Auto Industry. Toronto: Association, 1982.

Stevenson, Heon. *Selling the Dream: Advertising the American Automobile 1930–1980*. London: Academy, 1995.

Stone, Frank. *Canada, the GATT and the International Trade System*. Montreal: Institute for Research on Public Policy, 1992.

Studer-Noguez, Isabel. *Ford and the Global Strategies of Multinationals: The North American Auto Industry*. New York: Routledge, 2002.

Stursberg, Peter. *Diefenbaker: Leadership Lost, 1962–1967*. Toronto: University of Toronto Press, 1976.

– *Lester Pearson and the American Dilemma*. Toronto: Doubleday Canada, 1980.

– *Lester Pearson and the Dream of Unity*. Toronto: Doubleday Canada, 1978.

Sugiman, Pamela H. *Labour's Dilemma: The Gender Politics of Auto Workers in Canada, 1937–1979*. Toronto: University of Toronto Press, 1994.

Swacker, Frank, Kennth Redden, and Larry Wenger. *World Trade without Barriers: The World Trade Organiaztion and Dispute Resolution*. Charlottesville, VA: Michie Butterworth, 1995.

Swanson, Roger Frank. 'The United States Canadiana Constellation I: Washington, DC.' *International Journal* 27, 2 (1972), 185–218.

– ed. *Canadian-American Summit Diplomacy, 1923–1973: Selected Speeches and Documents*. Toronto: McClelland and Stewart, 1975.

Tignor, Robert L. 'In the Grip of Politics: The Ford Motor Company of Egypt, 1945–1960.' *Middle East Journal* 44, 3 (1990), 383–98.

Thomas, Kenneth P. *Capital Beyond Borders: States and Firms in the Auto Industry, 1960–1994.* New York: St Martin's Press, 1996.

Thompson, Dale C. 'Continental Co-Existence: The American Approach as Seen by a Canadian.' *Canadian Review of American Studies* 1, 2, (1970), 75–88.

– *Louis St Laurent: Canadian.* Toronto: Macmillan, 1967.

Thompson, John Herd, and Stephen J. Randall. *Canada and the United States: Ambivalent Allies.* Montreal and Kingston: McGill-Queen's University Press, 1994.

Thordarson, Bruce. *Lester Pearson: Diplomat and Politician.* Toronto: Oxford University Press, 1974.

Traves, Tom. 'The Development of the Ontario Automobile Industry to 1939.' In Ian Drummond, ed., *Progress without Planning: The Economic History of Ontario from Confederation to the Second World War.* Toronto: University of Toronto Press, 1987, 208–23.

– *The State and Enterprise: Canadian Manufacturers and the Federal Government, 1917–1931.* Toronto: University of Toronto Press, 1979.

Trezise, Philip H. 'The Relevance of the Auto Pact to Other Sectoral Arrangements.' *Canada–United States Law Journal* 10 (1985), 63–74.

United Automobile Workers, Canadian Region. *The UAW in Canada.* Windsor, Ontario: UAW Publishing, 1960.

Upgren, Arthur R., and William J. Waines. *The Midcontinent and the Peace: The Interests of Western Canada and Central Northwest United States in the Peace Settlements.* Minneapolis: University of Minnesota Press, 1943.

Van Ameringen, M. 'The Restructuring of the Canadian Auto Industry.' In D. Cameron and F. Houle, eds., *Canada and the New International Division of Labour.* Ottawa: University of Ottawa Press, 1985.

Vernon, Raymond. *Sovereignty at Bay: The Spread of Multinational Enterprises.* New York: Basic Books, 1971.

– *Storm Over the Multinationals: The Real Issues.* Cambridge: Harvard University Press, 1977.

Wagenberg, R.H., ed. *Canadian–American Interdependence: How Much? Proceedings of the 10th Annual Seminar on Canadian–American Relations, 1968.* Windsor: University of Windsor, 1968.

Waverman, Leonard, and Melvyn Fuss. *The Canada–U.S. Auto Pact of 1965: An Experiment in Selective Trade Liberalization.* Toronto: Institute for Policy Analysis, 1986.

Wearing, Joseph. *The L-Shaped Party: The Liberal Party of Canada, 1958–1980.* Toronto: McGraw-Hill Ryerson, 1981.

Weintrub, Sidney. 'Canadian Anxieties and U.S. Responses: Introductory Thoughts.' In Peter Karl Kresl, ed., *Seen From the South*. Provo, Utah: Brigham Young University, 1989.

– *The U.S.–Canadian Automotive Products Agreement of 1965: An Evaluation for Its Twentieth Year*. Austin: University of Texas at Austin, 1985.

– and Christopher Sands, eds. *The North American Auto Industry under NAFTA*. Washington, DC: CSIS Press, 1998.

Wells, Don. 'The Impact of the Postwar Compromise on Canadian Unionism: The Formation of an Auto Worker Local in the 1950s.' *Labour / Le Travail*. 36 (Fall, 1995), 147–73.

Whitaker, Reg. *The Government Party: Organizing and Financing the Liberal Party of Ontario, 1930–1958*. Toronto: University of Toronto Press, 1977.

White, Lawrence J. *The Automobile Industry since 1945*. Cambridge: Publishers, 1971.

Wilkins, Mira. *The Maturing of Multinational Enterprise: American Business Abroad from 1914 to 1970*. Cambridge, MA: Harvard University Press, 1974.

Wilkins, Mira, and Frank Ernest Hill. *American Business Abroad: Ford on Six Continents*. Detroit: Wayne State University Press, 1964.

Willoughby, W.R. *The Joint Organizations of Canada and the United States*. Toronto: University of Toronto Press, 1979.

Wilton, David A. *An Econometric Analysis of the Canada–United States Automotive Agreement: The First Seven Years*. Ottawa: Minister of Supply and Services, 1976.

Wonnacott, Paul. 'Canadian Automotive Protection: Content Provisions, the Bladen Plan, and Recent Tariff Changes.' *Canadian Journal of Economics and Political Science* 31, 1 (1965), 98–116.

– *U.S. and Canadian Auto Policies in a Changing World Environment*. Toronto: C.D. Howe Institute, 1987.

Wonnacott, Paul, and R.J. Wonnacott. 'The Automotive Agreement of 1965.' *Canadian Journal of Economics and Political Science* 33, 2 (1967), 269–84.

Wonnacott, R.J. 'The Canada–U.S. Free Trade Agreement and the Auto Pact.' *Trade Monitor*, no 2 (March, 1988), 1–12.

Wright, Gerald, and Maureen Appel Molot. 'Capital Movements and Government Control.' *International Organization* 28 (1976), 671–88.

Yates, Charlotte. *From Plant to Politics: The Autoworkers Union in Postwar Canada*. Philadelphia: Temple University Press, 1993.

– 'Public Policy and Canadian and American Autoworkers: Divergent Fortunes.' In Maureen Appel Molot, ed., *Driving Continentally: National Policies and the North American Auto Policy*. Ottawa: Carleton University Press, 1993.

Zalucky, Zenon D. 'Public Policy and the Economics of the Canadian Automotive Industry with Particular Reference to the Canada–United States Automotive Products Trade Agreement.' Master's thesis, University of Manitoba, 1987.

Zeiler, Thomas. *Free Trade, Free World: The Advent of GATT.* Chapel Hill and London: University of North Carolina Press, 1999.

Internet Sources

Bell, Nancy E. 'Negotiating on Precedent: Any Analysis of the Nexus Between Auto Pact Success and FTA Implementation.' Accessed 17 June 1999. http://csf.colorado.edu/isa/isn/21-2/108403bell.htm

DesRosiers, Dennis. 'CAJAD Observations #21: Auto Pact Performance – Apples to Apples.' Accessed 2 Nov. 2000. Http://www.cajad.com/news/observations/obser21.htm

Molot, Maureen Appel. 'Parliamentary Breakfast Talk on Canadian Auto Tariff Policy: Why Japan and the European Union Took Canada to the WTO Over the Auto Pact.' Accessed 13 Aug. 2000. http://www.hssfc.ca/Prog/Molot/html

World Trade Organization. *Report of the Panel: Canada – Certain Measures Affecting the Automotive Industry.* WTO home page, 11 Feb. 2000. Accessed 2 July 2000. http://www.uto.org/english/tratop_e/dispw_e/distab_e.htm#car

Illustration Credits

Personal collection of Dimitry Anastakis: Simon Reisman

Ford Motor Company of Canada, Ltd.: Henry Ford II inspects Oakville assembly line, 1960; Henry Ford II at the opening of Ford's St. Thomas Assembly Plant, 1967; St Thomas Assembly Plant, 1984.

Library and Archives Canada: Lester B. Pearson and John F. Kennedy, 1963 (LAC C90482); Walter Gordon at the 1966 Liberal conference (LAC PA201544); Paul Martin, Sr, and Douglas Dillon, 29 April 1964 (LAC PA113495); Mitchell Sharp, 1966 (LAC PA 110221); Walter Reuther, 1963 (LAC PA182834); UAW meeting, 29 April 1965 (LAC E002852797); Lester B. Pearson and Lyndon B. Johnson prior to signing the auto pact (LAC PA117602); Lester B. Pearson and Lyndon B. Johnson on a tour of Johnson's ranch, 1965 (LAC PA110818); Signing of the auto pact, 16 January 1965 (LAC PA139787); cement signing at the Johnson ranch, Texas, 1965 (LAC PA139805); Signed photo of Paul Martin, Sr. and Lyndon B. Johnson, 1965 (LAC PA186937).

Toronto Star
'Siamese twins' (reprinted with permission – Torstar Syndication Services).

Index